Fourth
Edition

THE STRATEGY
AND TACTICS
OF PRICING:

A Guide to Growing More Profitably

Thomas T. Nagle

Monitor Company Group, L. P.

John E. Hogan

Monitor Company Group, L. P.

PEARSON
Prentice
Hall

Upper Saddle River, NJ 07458

Library of Congress Cataloging-in-Publication Data

Nagle, Thomas T.
   The strategy and tactics of pricing : a guide to growing more profitably / Thomas
T. Nagle, John E. Hogan.—4th ed.
      p.   cm.
   Includes bibliographical references and index.
   ISBN 0-13-185677-4
   1. Pricing. 2. Marketing—Decision making.   I. Hogan, John E., ph.D.   II. Title.
   HF5416. 5. N34 2006
   658.8'16—dc22

                                                                        2005028572

Acquisitions Editor: Katie Stevens
VP/Editorial Director: Jeff Shelstad
Product Development Manager: Ashley Santora
Editorial Assistant: Christine Ietto
Marketing Manager: Ashaki Charles
Managing Editor (Production): Renata Butera
Production Editor: Marcela Boos
Permissions Coordinator: Charles Morris
Associate Director, Manufacturing: Vincent Scelta
Production Manager: Arnold Vila
Manufacturing Buyer: Diane Peirano
Design Manager: Christy Mahon
Art Director: Jayne Conte
Cover Design: Bruce Kenselaar
Composition: TechBooks
Full-Service Project Management: Shelley Creager, TechBooks
Printer/Binder: R.R. Donnelley-Harrisonburg

Credits and acknowledgments borrowed from other sources and reproduced, with
permission, in this textbook appear on appropriate page within text.

Pearson Education LTD.   Pearson Education North Asia Ltd
Pearson Education Singapore, Pte. Ltd   Pearson Educación de Mexico, S.A. de C.V.
Pearson Education, Canada, Ltd   Pearson Education Malaysia, Pte. Ltd
Pearson Education—Japan   Pearson Education Upper Saddle River,
Pearson Education Australia PTY, Limited   New Jersey

ISBN 0-13-185677-4

To my mother
Whose quiet and steadfast support
encouraged me to explore less-traveled paths

—J.E.H.

Brief Contents

Contents

Preface

Pricing has moved to the top of many executive agendas driven by monumental and permanent shifts in the business environment. Business customers—from hospitals to retailers to automobile manufacturers—have built sophisticated supply chain management capabilities to extract more quality and service from suppliers while paying ever-lower prices. Intense global competition, which has long been on the horizon, has become a reality with the emergence of China and India as formidable business powers capable of competing on both quality and price. Product life cycles continue to shorten as competitors have perfected the twin arts of innovation and imitation, making it more difficult to recoup development costs through price premiums. In light of these powerful forces, it is not surprising that companies suffer from increased price erosion, loss of sales volume, and declining profitability. Never has the need for clear and effective pricing strategies been greater.

In previous editions of this book, the objective was to develop a practical and readable manager's guide for making pricing decisions. Although we have retained that worthy objective in this edition, we believe that in today's market, it is no longer sufficient to improve pricing practices in a piecemeal fashion. Executives in general, but marketing executives in particular, are being forced by competition to develop more systemic processes for creating, communicating, and capturing value. Profitable pricing in such a system cannot be merely an individual business decision; it must become a unifying business objective. Successful companies must build a robust pricing capability that can not only withstand the buffeting of powerful customers and competitors, but must also proactively shape those forces to their own benefit. We have designed this fourth edition to provide practical advice to help marketers build such capabilities in their firms.

Creating such a capability involves tremendous change. Marketers must change the way they think about the value of their products and services. They must change internal processes for price setting, discounting, and negotiation. They must develop systems to track competitive pricing information, customer purchase patterns, and price management. They must raise the skill level of marketing, sales, and finance personnel who are responsible for making pricing decisions. Ultimately, they must evolve the pricing culture from one in which pricing is viewed as a tactical lever to achieve sales goals to one in which pricing serves as a strategic lever to drive profitable growth.

As with any major endeavor, the change involved in developing an effective pricing capability is neither easy nor quick. That is why we have substantially revised this edition of *The Strategy and Tactics of Pricing* to more clearly define the elements of effective pricing strategy, provide deeper insight into how to create effective pricing processes, and identify the key hurdles to effective implementation. There has never been a more exciting time to work in pricing because the opportunities to make meaningful improvements have never been greater. It is our sincere hope that this book will help marketers make those improvements in their companies. Our references are not necessarily to the seminal articles on the subject, but to those that are most managerially relevant and accessible. Professors will be happy to learn that an expanded Instructor's Manual for this edition includes new classroom exercises, cases, and slides. We expect that the combination of clear writing and current, relevant examples will continue to make this the most popular reference on pricing for managers as well as the most popular text in the classroom.

Acknowledgments

We cannot practically enumerate all those people to whom we owe a debt of gratitude but collectively they have contributed substantially to the content of this work. We wish to renew our thanks to all who contributed to the first three editions whose specific contributions were acknowledged there. The success of those earlier works gave us access to client companies and managers from whom we have learned much more about pricing strategy and implementation than would have been possible from purely academic research. Many thanks to our students and seminar participants whose probing questions and challenging problems continue to keep our work interesting and relevant.

We gratefully acknowledge the advice of numerous experts in marketing, pricing, and business management whose published and unpublished insights we have incorporated into this text. While we could never enumerate them all, we wish to acknowledge our special debt to George Cressman, Kent Monroe, Dan Nimer, and Mike Marn. Richard Harmer has contributed immensely to our thinking about pricing over the past 15 years. His work in defining "value segments" and his concepts of "segmentation fences" and "price metrics" are now widely adopted by pricing practitioners. He also contributed to our thinking about the role of income and affordability in pricing. Gerald (Jerry) Smith of Boston College contributed substantially to this edition with insightful perspectives on value communications, channels, and value assessment. He also added numerous examples and scholarly references to this edition. Bob Donath edited several of the chapters which are substantially more readable thanks to his efforts. Eugene Zelek, an antitrust attorney and believer in creatively managing within rather than reacting to legal constraints, wrote the section in Chapter 14 on the law. Finally, we would like to thank our colleagues at Monitor Group who were understanding and supportive of our need for "writing time" and who accepted additional management and project responsibilities to give us that time.

CHAPTER

1

TACTICAL PRICING

Changing the Pricing Game to Drive Profitable Growth

Few managers, even those specializing in marketing, think strategically about pricing. Consider your experiences and observations. Were your company's pricing decisions made in reaction to a pricing problem, or were they carefully planned to exploit an opportunity? Did management arrive at those decisions by considering the immediate impact on profitability, or did it analyze how reactions of customers and competitors might change the picture down the road? Did the decisions focus purely on price, or did they involve alignment of a marketing program to support the pricing decision? When done correctly, pricing becomes a powerful lever to drive profitable growth and achieve strategic business goals. Unfortunately, few companies use the pricing lever to manage their markets effectively. The result is more rapid price erosion, lower volumes across segments, and most importantly, lower profits.

WHY PRICING IS OFTEN INEFFECTIVE

The difference between conventional pricing and strategic pricing is the difference between reacting to market conditions and proactively managing them.[1] It is the reason why companies with similar market shares and technologies often earn such different rewards for their efforts. With conventional pricing approaches, each functional area imposes constraints on pricing strategy that are individually consistent with their view of the market but that also limit the company's ability to get paid for the value it creates for customers. Finance mandates that products achieve minimum contribution margins causing the company to pass up low-margin/high-volume opportunities that can increase revenues or reduce costs through more efficient capacity utilization. Marketing fails to design and enforce effective pricing policies resulting in high price variability across customers that reward the most aggressive negotiators. Sales lacks the training and incentives to negotiate effectively with powerful customers, undercutting pricing performance.

1

Given these self-imposed constraints, it is not surprising that so few firms make the most of their pricing opportunities.

In contrast, strategic pricing entails the coordination of interrelated marketing, competitive, and financial decisions to set prices profitably. Strategic pricing requires more than a change in attitude; it requires a change in when, how, and who makes pricing decisions. For example, strategic pricing requires anticipating price levels early in the product development process to better understand which concepts can create and capture adequate value to justify their cost. It requires management to take responsibility for establishing a coherent set of pricing policies and procedures that will create the pricing discipline necessary for long-term profitability. Most importantly, strategic pricing requires a new relationship between functional areas of the firm such as marketing, sales, and finance. This cross-functional focus requires a balance between the customer's need to obtain good value for the price and the firm's need to cover costs and earn a suitable profit. Unfortunately, pricing at most companies involves more conflict than balance between these objectives.

If a key objective of pricing is to capture the value created for customers, then specific prices must be set by those best able to anticipate that value—marketing managers. But their efforts will not be effective unless they gather the right customer and competitor data to assess value. Pricing can only capture the value of an offering when the value has been communicated to the customer—a responsibility of sales. But sales cannot communicate value without the appropriate tools and training to manage negotiations with increasingly powerful customers. Finally, the efforts of marketing and sales will not generate sustainable profits unless constrained by appropriate financial objectives that require a new financial philosophy. Rather than attempting to "cover costs," finance must strategically focus on incremental profitability, learn how costs change with changes in sales, and use that knowledge to develop appropriate incentives and guidelines for marketing and sales to achieve their objectives profitably.

With their respective roles appropriately defined, marketing and finance can work together toward a common goal—to achieve profitability through strategic pricing. Before this goal can be achieved, however, managers in all functional areas must discard the flawed thinking about pricing that leads them into conflict and drives them to make unprofitable decisions. Let's look at these flawed paradigms and destroy them once and for all.

THE COST-PLUS DELUSION

Cost-plus pricing is, historically, the most common pricing procedure because it carries an aura of financial prudence. Financial prudence, according to this view, is achieved by pricing every product or service to yield a fair return over all costs, fully and fairly allocated. In theory, it is a simple guide to profitability; in practice, it is a blueprint for mediocre financial performance.

The problem with cost-driven pricing is fundamental: In most industries it is impossible to determine a product's unit cost before determining its price. Why? Because unit costs change with volume. This cost change occurs because a significant portion of costs are "fixed" and must somehow be "allocated" to determine the full unit cost. Unfortunately, because these allocations depend on volume, which changes with changes in price, unit cost is a moving target.

To "solve" the problem of determining unit cost, cost-based pricers are forced to make the absurd assumption that they can set price without affecting volume. The failure to account for the effects of price on volume, and of volume on costs, leads managers directly into pricing decisions that undermine profits. The historical landscape of company failures is littered with examples of companies that followed a cost-plus approach to pricing to their ultimate demise. One particularly tragic example, for the company and its customers, was Wang Laboratory's experience in pricing the world's first word processor. Following its introduction, Wang became an instant success, growing rapidly and dominating the market. However, as competition increased and growth slowed, the company's cost-driven pricing philosophy began killing its market advantage. As sales volume declined, unit costs were repeatedly recalculated and prices raised to reflect the rising overhead allocation. As a result, sales declined even further. Before long, even Wang's most loyal customers began making the switch to cheaper alternatives.

A price increase to "cover" higher fixed costs reduces sales further and causes unit cost to rise even higher. The result is often that price increases actually reduce profits. This leads to the "death spiral" of cost-based pricing in which fixed costs are spread over continuously declining unit volume as prices escalate ever higher. On the other hand, if a price cut causes sales to increase, fixed costs are spread over more units, making unit costs decline. The result is often increased profit. Instead of pricing reactively to cover costs and profit objectives, managers need to price proactively. They need to acknowledge that pricing affects sales volume, and that volume affects costs.

The dangers of cost-based pricing are not limited to products facing increasing competition and declining volume. In fact, cost-based pricing is even more insidious when applied to strong products because there are no signals (such as declining market share) to warn of the potential damage. For example, an international telecommunications company with many leading technologies uses cost-based pricing as a "starting point" for pricing. Product and sales managers review the cost-based "target prices" for consistency with market conditions and then argue for adjustments to reflect market conditions. Everyone in the organization finds this system fair and reasonable.

But does the system foster profitability? During the time this system has been in place, marketing has frequently requested and received permission to charge prices less than the cost-based "target" to reflect market conditions. How often do you think marketing argued that a target price should be raised to reflect market conditions? Never, despite the fact that the company often has a backlog of orders on some of its most popular products. At this company, as at many others, cost-based target prices have become cost-based "caps" on profitability for the most valuable products.

Cost-plus pricing leads to overpricing in weak markets and underpricing in strong ones—exactly the opposite direction of a prudent strategy. How, then,

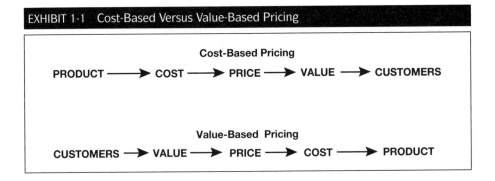

EXHIBIT 1-1   Cost-Based Versus Value-Based Pricing

should managers deal with the problem of pricing to cover costs and achieve profit objectives? They shouldn't. The question itself reflects an erroneous perception of the role of pricing, a perception based on the belief that one can first determine sales levels, then calculate unit cost and profit objectives, and then set a price. When managers realize that sales volume (the beginning assumption) depends on the price (the end of the process), the flawed circularity of cost-based pricing is obvious. The only way to ensure profitable pricing is to let anticipated pricing determine the costs incurred rather than the other way around. Value-based pricing must begin before investments are made.

Exhibit 1-1 illustrates the flawed progression of cost-based pricing and the necessary progression for value-based pricing. Cost-based pricing is product driven. Engineering and manufacturing departments design and make what they consider a "good" product. In the process, they make investments and incur costs to add features and related services. Finance then totals these costs to determine "target" prices for the various versions of the product that they might offer. Only at this stage does marketing enter the process, charged with the task of demonstrating enough value in these products to justify the prices to customers.

If cost-based prices prove unjustifiable, managers may try to fix the process by allowing "flexibility" in the markups. Although this tactic may minimize the damage, it is not, fundamentally, a solution because the financial return on the product remains inadequate. Finance blames marketing for cutting the price, and marketing blames finance for excessive costs. The problem keeps reoccurring as the features and costs of new products continue to mismatch the needs and values of customers. Moreover, when customers are rewarded with discounts for their price resistance, this resistance becomes more frequent even when the product is valuable to them. Solving the problems of cost-based pricing requires more than a quick fix. It requires a complete reversal of the process—starting with customers. The target price is based on estimates of value and the portion that the firm can expect to capture given the competitive alternatives. The job of financial management is not to insist that prices recover costs. It is to insist that costs are incurred only to make products that can be priced profitably given their value to customers.

Designing products that can be sold profitably at a target price has gone in the past two decades from being unusual to being the goal at most successful companies.[2] From Marriott to Boeing, from medical technology to automobiles, profit-leading companies now think about what market segment they want a new product to serve, determine the benefits those potential customers seek, and establish a price those customers can be convinced to pay. Then companies challenge their engineers to develop products and services that can be produced at a cost low enough to make serving that market segment profitable. The automobile industry has long been at the forefront of using price to drive the development process. The first companies to adopt such a strategy gained a huge market advantage. The laggards now have to learn value-based pricing for new products just to survive.

CUSTOMER-DRIVEN PRICING

Many companies now recognize the fallacy of cost-based pricing and its adverse effect on profit. They realize the need for pricing to reflect market conditions. As a result, some have taken pricing authority away from financial managers and given it to sales or product managers. In theory, this trend is consistent with value-based pricing, since marketing and sales are that part of the organization best positioned to understand value to the customer. In practice, however, the misuse of pricing to achieve short-term sales objectives often undermines perceived value and depresses profits even further.

The purpose of strategic pricing is not simply to create satisfied customers. Customer satisfaction can usually be bought by a combination of overdelivering on value and underpricing products. But marketers delude themselves if they believe that the resulting sales represent marketing successes. The purpose of strategic pricing is to price more profitably by capturing more value, not necessarily by making more sales. When marketers confuse the first objective with the second, they fall into the trap of pricing at whatever buyers are willing to pay, rather than at what the product is really worth. Although that decision enables marketers to meet their sales objectives, it invariably undermines long-term profitability.

Two problems arise when prices reflect the amount buyers seem willing to pay. First, sophisticated buyers are rarely honest about how much they are actually willing to pay for a product. Professional purchasing agents are adept at concealing the true value of a product to their organizations. Once buyers learn that sellers' prices are flexible, the buyers have a financial incentive to conceal information from, and even actively mislead sellers. Obviously, this tactic undermines the salesperson's ability to establish close relationships with customers and to understand their needs.

Second, there is an even more fundamental problem with pricing to reflect customers' willingness to pay. The job of sales and marketing is not simply to process orders at whatever price customers are currently willing to pay, but rather to raise customers' willingness to pay to a level that better reflects the product's true value. Many companies underprice truly innovative products because they ask potential customers, who are ignorant of the product's value, what they would be willing to pay. But we know from studies of innovations that the "regular" price has little impact on customers' willingness to try them. For example, most customers initially perceived that photocopiers, mainframe computers, and food processors lacked adequate value to justify their prices. Only after extensive marketing to communicate and guarantee value did these products achieve market acceptance. Forget what customers who have never used your product are initially willing to pay! Instead, understand the value of the product to satisfied customers and communicate that value to others. Low pricing is never a substitute for an adequate marketing and sales effort.

COMPETITION-DRIVEN PRICING

Finally, consider the policy of letting pricing be dictated by competitive conditions. In this view, pricing is a tool to achieve sales objectives. In the minds of some managers, this method is "pricing strategically." Actually, it is more analogous to "letting the tail wag the dog." Why should an organization want to achieve market-share goals? Because managers believe that more market share usually produces greater profit.[3] Priorities are confused, however, when managers reduce the profitability of each sale simply to achieve the market-share goal. Prices should be lowered only when they are no longer justified by the value offered in comparison to the value offered by the competition.

Although price-cutting is probably the quickest, most effective way to achieve sales objectives, it is usually a poor decision financially. Because a price cut can be so easily matched, it offers only a short-term market advantage at the expense of permanently lower margins. Consequently, unless a company has good reason to believe that its competitors cannot match a price cut, the long-term cost of using price as a competitive weapon usually exceeds any short-term benefit. Although product differentiation, advertising, and improved distribution do not increase sales as quickly as price cuts, their benefit is more sustainable and thus is usually more cost-effective.

The goal of pricing should be to find the combination of margin and market share that maximizes profitability over the long term. Often, the most profitable price is one that substantially restricts market share relative to the competition. Godiva chocolates, BMW cars, Peterbilt trucks, and Snap-on tools would no doubt all gain substantial market share if priced closer to the competition. It is doubtful, however, that the added share would be worth forgoing their profitable and successful positioning as high-priced brands.

Although the fallacy of competition-driven pricing is most obvious for high-priced products, the principle can be applied more generally. When companies struggling in competitive markets are recapitalized, they often learn that they can substantially increase cash flow simply by scaling back their market-share objectives. One low-margin, industrial company increased price by 9 percent and suffered a 20 percent loss of market share—proof, some might argue, that its market was price sensitive. On the other hand, this company retained four out of five sales. Apparently, most customers valued the product by at least 9 percent more than they had been paying! The company had been prevented from capturing that value by its market-share goal. Although some capacity was idled, the company's contribution to profit increased by more than 70 percent.

ASKING THE RIGHT QUESTIONS

Strategic pricing involves recognizing that not all pricing problems involve changing price as the best solution. The reason why pricing is ineffective is frequently not that the pricers have done a poor job. It is that decisions were made about costs, customers, and competitive strategy without correctly thinking through their broader financial implications. Because the fallacy in those decisions is frequently not revealed until the product is launched and the pricing proves unprofitable, it is the pricer's job to work back from the price to understand the problem. Is the price unprofitable because there is a better price to charge, or because the value has been ineffectively communicated? Is the market share goal too high, or is the market inadequately segmented? Is the product and service offering overbuilt (and therefore too expensive) for the value it delivers, or has the seller simply enabled customers to avoid paying for the value they get?

Often, the pricer's job is less focused on setting prices than on creating systems, policies, and an organization that can diagnose the true cause of pricing problems and implement the appropriate solution. Sometimes that solution will involve changing prices. More frequently, the solution will involve actions such as gaining a deeper understanding of the value created for customers, designing a price structure to fence off segments with different price sensitivities, or developing sales tools to communicate value more effectively. Recall the tactical questions about costs, customers, and competition that we argued often lead to poor pricing decisions because they treat price as a tactical lever to achieve business goals. When these questions come up, it is the pricer's job to reframe the discussion to consider overall financial profitability. Exhibit 1-2 lists the reactive, tactical questions commonly asked, and the questions that the pricing manager should be guiding the organization to ask instead.

Note that a key difference between the two types of questions is the ambiguity of the answers. The tactical answers to pricing problems are clear. To increase the margin, raise the price. To make the sale, cut the price. As with most marketing decisions, the answers to strategic questions about pricing are more open-ended. Pricing is both an art and a science. It depends as much on good judgment as on precise calculation. But the fact that pricing depends on judgment is no justification for pricing decisions based on hunches or intuition. Good judgment requires that one ask the right questions and comprehend the factors that make some pricing strategies succeed and others fail.

Good judgment also requires integrating information. The danger in the tactical approach to pricing is the narrow focus of the decisions. Profitable prices cannot be driven by a cost number with little or no understanding of how customers might respond, or by a customer's demands with little or no information about how competitors might respond, or by a market-share goal with little or no understanding of the company's ability to win a price war. The value in asking strategic questions is that they force one to integrate information across functional lines.

EXHIBIT 1-2 Strategic Pricing: Asking the Right Questions	
Tactical Questions Commonly Asked	**Strategic Questions That Should Be Asked**
What price do we need to cover our cost and profit objectives?	What sales changes would be necessary or tolerable for us to profit from a price change? Can we deploy a marketing strategy that will keep those sales changes within acceptable ranges? What costs can we afford to incur, given the prices we can achieve in the marketplace, and still earn a profit?
What price is the customer willing to pay?	Is our price justifiable given the objective value of our product or service to the customer? How can we better communicate that value, thus justifying the price?
What prices do we need to meet our sales and market share objectives?	What level of sales or market share can we most profitably achieve? What marketing tools should we use to win market share most cost-effectively?

THE DISCIPLINE OF STRATEGIC PRICING

Broadening the scope of your pricing efforts by asking strategic rather than tactical questions is only the first step toward pricing effectiveness. The next step involves setting clear objectives for your pricing strategy. Pricing objectives will vary depending on the industry characteristics and the firm's position within the industry.[4] However, regardless of the firm's size or position, its pricing strategy should be guided by the three fundamental principles. Strategic pricing is: (1) value-based, (2) proactive, and (3) profit-driven. Each principle represents one piece of the puzzle that, when combined correctly, leads to a fundamentally more powerful approach to pricing. Let's discuss these principles in more detail (see Exhibit 1-3).

Few would argue with the notion that prices ought to be based in some way on the value of the product to the customer. But let us step back and consider the implications of this statement by asking the question "What actions must we take in order to create alignment between value and price?" The most obvious activity is to collect the data necessary to estimate value to the customer. But simply understanding the value to the customer is insufficient for setting prices, much

EXHIBIT 1-3   The Guiding Principles of Strategic Pricing

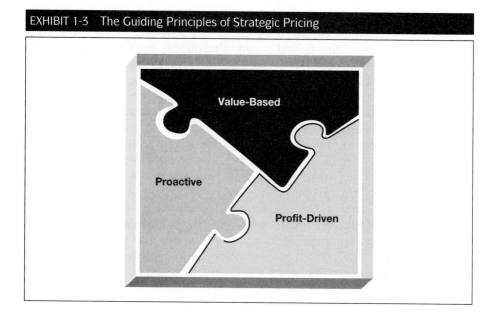

less developing a complete pricing strategy. Companies must also understand how value differs across market segments in order to set unique prices based on value received. Even if you understand the value delivered by your products, often your customers will not. Thus, value communications are a key element of a value-based pricing strategy. Value communication covers a wide spectrum of activities ranging from point-of-sale communication tools used by a direct sales force to carefully crafted ads and promotions, each designed to communicate a message that influences value perceptions and raises willingness-to-pay. Even when customers understand the value of your offering, they have a powerful financial incentive to negotiate lower prices. Thus, it is essential to establish clear and consistent pricing and discounting policies that enforce discipline in the face of customer negotiation tactics.

These actions around value assessment, value communications, and pricing policy represent a few of the elements of a value-based pricing strategy that will be discussed in more detail in subsequent chapters. When companies begin to tackle these issues it requires a hard look at the fundamental business processes that support the go-to-market approach. That initial look into pricing often leads to rethinking processes such as product development, account management, and business planning. Consider the software company that began transitioning to a value-based organization when it developed a value-based pricing strategy for a new product launch. The strategy involved researching the ways that their software created value for customers, selecting new pricing metrics by which to price the product, developing value communication tools to assist the sales force in selling the product, and creating a price menu that sets prices for each product variation. The key insight that emerged from this effort was that pricing would have been much easier and effective had they considered the value-based pricing elements earlier in the product development process. Following the successful launch of the product, the management enhanced their stage-gate product development process by adding "value-gates" that helped design value directly and facilitated "versioning" to meet the needs of different customer segments at different price points. Clearly, being a world-class pricing organization requires incorporating value into more than just the pricing process. It requires that value become a central focus of all of the business processes driving the go-to-market strategy.

It would be an understatement to say that today's marketplace provides a challenging environment for making pricing decisions proactively. Business customers have invested millions to turn their procurement groups into profit centers. Buyers are armed with focused strategies, well-designed incentives, and global information systems that create price transparency across vendors and borders. Consumers now rely on the Internet to access suppliers and prices from the world, become educated about the margins of auto dealers, and join buying clubs to get leverage in purchasing everything from travel to electronics. In contrast, vendors trying to sell to these price-savvy customers are often constrained by conflicting sales and margin goals, a lack of systems, and poorly conceived tactical pricing strategies based on costs or market-share goals. It is no surprise, therefore, when a majority of vendors find themselves perpetually locked into a passive stance in which they are reacting to the tactics of customers and competitors, rather than proactively managing them. In this kind of environment, strategic pricing requires more than just incorporating value into the pricing process. It requires that management change expectations and break ingrained behaviors—among customers, competitors, and its own employees. Instead of being buffeted by the forces of powerful customers and aggressive competitors, strategic pricing involves communicating information, forcing trade-offs, and establishing consistent policies that change how the market reacts to the company's pricing.

Consider the example of the industrial distributor whose margins suffered from the aggressive pricing tactics of a low-service competitor. Customers continually demanded prices comparable to those offered by the competitor despite the fact that the distributor provided industry leading technical and sales support to all customers. For many customers, technical support enabled them to sell integrated solutions to their end-users. In contrast, other customers didn't need technical support because their end-users did not require systems integration. Unfortunately, the distributor provided all customers with an "all you can eat buffet" of technical support included in the price of the product. Even those customers that could figure out things for themselves found themselves going back to the service buffet repeatedly because there was no price incentive to dissuade them. An interesting change occurred when the distributor proactively changed its price structure to charge for most technical support. Those customers that received a lot of value from it were willing to pay for it, while those that got little value from support reduced their usage. As a result, the company increased its margins both by reducing service costs to some customers and by getting paid for services provided to customers who valued them. The cost reductions enabled the distributor to compete more effectively on price for its commodity distribution business while preserving its ability to get paid for its differentiated services. Even in the most competitive markets, it is possible to improve profits by proactively aligning your pricing with the value customers perceive in your offer. In addition, you come one step closer to being able to use price as a strategic lever for driving profitable growth.

The final element of strategic pricing is that it be profit-driven. The ultimate goal of any pricing strategy is to increase profitability. But all too frequently, some managers are unwilling to make hard decisions about price because the decision could result in a loss of market share. Other managers, usually in finance, are unwilling to lower margins even in the face of severe competition and declining market share. Neither approach is rationally profit-driven—since profit is driven by percent margin and volume. The discipline of strategic pricing requires making informed trade-offs between price and volume in order to maximize profits.

These trade-offs come in two forms. The first trade-off involves the willingness to lower price to exploit a market opportunity to drive volume. Cost-plus pricers are often reluctant to exploit these opportunities because they reduce the average contribution margin across the product line, giving the appearance that it is underperforming relative to other products. But if the opportunity for incremental volume is large and well managed, a lower contribution margin can actually drive a higher total profit! The second trade-off involves the willingness to give up volume by raising prices. Competitor- and customer-oriented pricers find it very difficult to hold the line on price increases in the face of a lost deal or reduced volume. Yet the economics of a price increase can be compelling. For example, a product with a 30 percent contribution margin could lose up to 25 percent of its volume following a 10 percent price increase before it resulted in lower profitability. Effective pricers regularly evaluate the balance between profitability and market share and are willing to make hard decisions when the balance tips too far in one direction.

Consider the situation faced by a marketing manager for a test equipment manufacturer that was evaluating a price increase for a recently released innovative product. After reviewing the economics of the price–volume trade-off, the manager estimated that a 25 percent price increase would result in $3 million in additional profits as long as the company would hold firm on the price and be willing to give up about 10 percent of its volume among small, price-sensitive customers. As it turned out, it was harder to sell the increase to the general manager of the division than to the customers that were asked to pay the higher price. In this instance, however, holding to that belief would have precluded a substantial profit improvement.

Transforming your company from tactical to strategic pricing is challenging. Interestingly, though, the hardest part is not learning how to apply pricing tools to assess and communicate value. The real challenge comes from changing ingrained behaviors and beliefs that limit the company's ability to proactively manage customers and competitors in a way that maximizes profitability. In recognition of this challenge, we have revised this latest edition of *The Strategy and Tactics of Pricing* to include new tools and applications that experience has shown to be helpful in making the transition.

OUTLINE OF THE BOOK

This book provides a roadmap to pricing strategically in which pricing becomes a lever to drive profitable and sustainable growth. The road is challenging and is filled with potholes along the way. However, our experience with hundreds of firms has shown that it is possible to make a successful transition from tactical to strategic pricing. The book is organized as follows: Chapters 1 through 7 are devoted to the building blocks of pricing strategy. They are organized around the pricing pyramid, introduced in Chapter 2, that details the five key elements of a pricing strategy. Chapter 8, on costs, explains how to analyze cost structures in order to understand the true profitability of a product or service. In an ideal world, this might not be part of a marketer's job. In the real world, marketers who do not understand costs unwittingly make bad decisions for their companies because they unknowingly work with misleading cost allocations. Chapter 9 focuses on the types of financial analyses needed to make profit-driven pricing decisions.

Chapter 10 explains the process of price competition and how to manage it dispassionately and proactively to minimize the damage that it can cause. Chapters 11 through 14 deal with key issues involved in implementing pricing decisions and addresses issues such as pricing through channels, pricing over the product life cycle, conducting pricing research, and legal issues in pricing.

Summary

Progressive companies have begun doing more than just worrying about pricing. To increase profitability, many are abandoning traditional reactive pricing procedures in favor of proactive strategies. More than ever before, successful companies are building products and marketing strategies to support pricing objectives, rather than the other way around. Traditional industry leaders in marketing and sales, such as Procter & Gamble and General Electric, made explicit corporate decisions to change their focus from growth in top-line sales to growth in profitability. In many industries the current profit leader is a company with a very explicit pricing strategy supported by its product and promotional strategies. Southwest in airlines, Intel in semiconductors, Dell in computers, Wal-Mart in retailing, Quad in printing, and *The New York Times* in publishing have all adopted pricing models that drive which customers they will serve and how they will serve them.

It is not surprising that pricing has taken its place as a major element in marketing strategy in the last two decades. After all, marketing itself has been in the midst of a revolution. The meaning of marketing has been transformed from "selling what the company produces" to "producing what the customer wants to buy." Marketing has become the means by which firms identify unmet needs in the marketplace, develop products to satisfy those needs, promote them honestly, and follow with postpurchase support to ensure customer satisfaction. As selfless as all this may sound, though, the ultimate goal of marketing is not to convert the firm into a charitable organization for the sole benefit of consumers. The ultimate goals are profits for the stockholders, jobs for the employees, and growth for the organization.

Perhaps it is reasonable that marketers have only recently begun to focus seriously on effective pricing. Only after managers have mastered the techniques of creating value do the techniques of capturing value become important. When companies were totally financially driven and internally focused, it was marketing's sole job to become an advocate for the customer's perspective. Today, however, marketeering management has won the power to make business decisions, not just advocate perspectives. With that responsibility, they must understand not only customer needs but also how and when to profitably satisfy those needs. The true test of a successful marketing strategy is its ability to create value profitably. As one marketing expert aptly stated, "For marketing strategists, pricing is the moment of truth—all of marketing comes to focus in the pricing decision."[5] The purpose of this book is to make sure that when you reach that moment, you know what to do.

Notes

1. The bias toward a reactive concept of "market orientation" has been described by Bernard Jaworski, Ajay Kohli, and Arvind Sahay, in "Market-Driven Versus Driving Markets," *Journal of the Academy of Marketing Science*, 28(1) (Winter 2000), pp. 45–54.
2. Peter F. Drucker, "The Information Executives Truly Need," *Harvard Business Review* (January–February 1995), p. 58.
3. In the past two decades, serious theoretical work has replaced simplistic, anecdotal guidelines for how to create a sustainably successful business. See Michael E. Porter, *Competitive Advantage* (New York: The Free Press, 1985); Gary Hamel and C. K. Parhalad, *Competing for the Future* (Cambridge, MA: Harvard Business School Press, 1994); Adrian Slywotzky and David Morrison, *The Profit Zone* (New York: Random House, 1997); Robert Kaplan and David Norton, *The Strategy-Focused Organization* (Cambridge, MA: Harvard Business School, 2001).
4. Most likely, pricing objectives will be subsidiary to general corporate objectives. Thus if the corporate objective is to establish a market presence in Brazil leading to eventual manufacturing there, the corporate objective may not be to maximize profitability. It may be, rather, to build volume or name recognition quickly. For purposes of this book and the analysis of pricing strategies, we will usually assume that sustainable profitability is the pricing objective, although we will see how there are often reasons to trade off near-term on one product's profitability to maximize the longer-term return from an entire product line.
5. Raymond Corey, *Industrial Marketing: Cases and Concepts*, 3rd ed. (Upper Saddle River, NJ: Prentice Hall, 1983), p. 311.

2

PRICING STRATEGY

An Integrated Approach

Pricing is a critical issue for management because it represents the key to unlocking profitable growth opportunities.[1] Although companies invest considerable time and capital to improve pricing performance, transitioning from tactical to strategic pricing in markets characterized by global competition, sophisticated procurement groups, and shortened product lifecycles is difficult to say the least. That difficulty is magnified because most companies have an incomplete understanding of the interlocking components of pricing strategy and how they must work in concert to achieve sustainable results. When managers in these companies formulate pricing strategies, too often the unfortunate outcome is a patchwork of ad hoc tactical decisions masquerading as strategy.

Pricing strategy is about proactively managing customer behavior rather than simply adapting to it. Strategic pricers don't ask "How should I change the price;" they ask "What has changed to make the price unacceptable and how can I fix that?" When faced with a pricing challenge such as pushback from long-term customers or increased price competition from competitors, price is just the tip of the iceberg that defines a complete pricing strategy. When customers complain about high prices it is possible that the price is, in fact, too high relative to the competition. It is also possible, however, that the problem is not with the price but with other elements of the pricing strategy. For example, a new customer unfamiliar with the differential value of a product might, quite naturally, think the price is too high. In this instance, however, the appropriate action is not to drop price, but to educate the customer on the value created by unique features of the product in order to justify the higher price. Another reason that customers complain about high prices is that the product does not meet their needs effectively. The solution to this problem is not necessarily to cut price, but to reposition the product to target customers that value the product more, or to unbundle attributes that are not valued. Simply resorting to price cutting for these customers would eventually destroy price integrity as high-value customers got wind of the discounts and demanded similar treatment.

As these examples illustrate, a company can experience price resistance from customers for many reasons. In most cases, however, the price alone is seldom the only cause of problem, and is often not the real cause at all. More often, it is the symptom signaling a problem with other elements of the pricing strategy. Just as a doctor is trained to look beyond a patient's symptoms to diagnose the underlying disease, companies must look beyond the pricing symptoms to diagnose flaws in their broader pricing strategy. Failing to diagnose the true cause of the pricing problem and treating only the symptom (i.e., cutting prices) can do long-term damage to profitability.

This is what happens when managers prematurely invest in price optimization systems to address price and margin erosion. Although the systems often deliver short-term improvements in price realization by aligning prices with the customer's willingness-to-pay, optimization software cannot address underlying problems such as product offerings that don't create value for customers, the inability of the sales force to communicate value, or pricing policies that incent customers to engage in high cost behaviors to avoid paying for the value they perceive. Defining pricing strategy in terms of "getting the right price" creates a false sense of security, delaying critical decisions about how to create value for customers and capture that value through a complete pricing strategy.

THE STRATEGIC PRICING PYRAMID

A comprehensive pricing strategy is comprised of multiple layers creating a foundation for price setting that minimizes erosion and maximizes profits over time. These layers combine to form the strategic pricing pyramid in Exhibit 2-1. In keeping with the value-based perspective, value creation forms the foundation of the pyramid. A deep understanding of how products and services create value for customers is the key input to the development of a price structure that determines how offerings will be priced. Once the price structure is determined, marketing can develop messaging and tools to communicate value to customers. The final step before setting the price is to ensure that the pricing processes in the company are able to maintain the integrity of the price structure in the face of aggressive customers and competitors.

It can be tempting to take a shortcut by skipping one or more elements of pricing strategy when setting prices. But shortcuts often lead you astray from the goal of higher profits. Consider Techco,[2] a leading computing and software company with a broad product line. Although Techco was a recognized market leader in technical support and breadth of selection, the company was experiencing price erosion and lost market share due to a smaller competitor that competed primarily on price. While customers turned to Techco for their complex purchases that required extensive technical support, they negotiated steep discounts on other products by threatening to take their business to the low-end competitor. Management initially viewed this situation as a pricing problem and prepared to change their operating model to compete as a low-cost provider. Once the management evaluated their pricing strategy more

EXHIBIT 2-1   The Strategic Pricing Pyramid

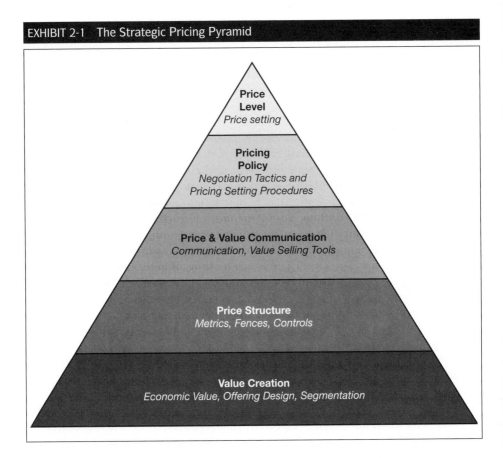

completely, however, it became clear that the underlying cause of lost sales and lower margins was a price structure that forced all customers to engage with Techco in identical ways even though they had a wide variety of service needs. Customers that received very little value from Techco's services were asked to pay the same price as customers who received tremendous value. As a result, Techco underpriced to its high-value customers and overpriced to its low-value customers.

The profit maximizing solution to this pricing challenge was not a wholesale reduction in prices. Instead, the solution was to redesign the price structure in a way that allowed customers to choose how they engaged with Techco. Customers that got little value from Techco's services were not asked to pay for them, nor were they allowed free access to service and support—an important change from past practice. Eliminating support to some customers enabled Techco to increase support to high-value customers to justify higher prices. By adopting a comprehensive approach to pricing strategy, Techco was able to increase volume in the low-end segments while improving margins in the high-end segments. As this example illustrates, strategic pricing involves more than just setting prices—it requires a systematic evaluation of the five elements of pricing strategy contained in the strategic pricing pyramid. In the next section we introduce each element in more detail.

VALUE CREATION

Product managers face an interesting challenge when it comes to pricing. They are expected to set prices that capture the value offered by their products and that also maximize profits. What makes the challenge interesting is that very few companies actually understand how much value their products create for customers. Typically, the product manager turns to marketing to provide insight into customer value. Marketing then conducts research into customer needs, importance weights for features, and overall satisfaction with the product. But how does one put a price on importance or satisfaction? Does the fact that your product scores 10 percent higher on satisfaction than the competitor's product mean that customers will be willing to pay a 10 percent higher price? Generally, the answer is no.

Recognizing the limitations of conventional research techniques, some product managers turn to more sophisticated approaches such as choice modeling and conjoint studies.[3] When used properly, these techniques provide estimates of a customer's willingness to pay for a feature or product. But does knowing willingness-to-pay lead to better prices? Once again, the answer is generally no. Willingness-to-pay can be an important input to the price setting process as long as customers understand how much value they derive from your product relative to the competitor's product and believe that your pricing policies require them to pay for the value they receive. But as we noted in Chapter 1, even long-time users may be highly uncertain about the value of a product because the vendor has never bothered to communicate value. The lack of understanding about the value is even more prevalent for new products with unfamiliar features and functionality. Reliance on conjoint techniques in these instances results in low prices that leave money on the table for many customers.

How, then, can a company measure the value created by its product? We provide a detailed treatment of value assessment in Chapter 3. For now, it is sufficient to say that estimating the value created by a product requires intimate knowledge of the customer's needs. This deep understanding of needs can then be used to translate a product's features into customer benefits which are then translated into a value estimate. In business markets, the value estimate centers on the economic impact a product or service has on the customer's costs and revenues.

Consider, for example, the introduction of the Intel Pentium chip. One of the differentiating features of the Pentium chip was a built-in math coprocessor that enabled computer manufacturers to eliminate other chips on the circuit board and thereby reduce manufacturing costs relative to competing chips by

Advanced Micro Devices (AMD). For a time, this differentiated feature enabled Intel to charge a significant premium for the Pentium chip. But AMD had invested heavily in its development program and soon matched the Pentium technology, eliminating Intel's pricing advantage. Recognizing that AMD could quickly match future technological advances made by Intel, management turned their attention from features that drove customer costs and were easy to copy to features that drove customer revenues and were harder to copy. Intel management recognized that their brand was well-known and respected by many of the computer manufacturer's own customers. Their research showed that end-customers were more likely to purchase a computer when they knew that the processor was made by Intel. In addition, customers were willing to pay more for a computer with an Intel chip. Once Intel understood how much its brand was worth to computer makers, it launched the "Intel Inside" campaign in order to command a price premium for its chips. To this day, every Dell computer with an Intel processor carries a sticker telling end-users that they have an Intel chip inside.

The Intel example illustrates that understanding how a product delivers value to customers creates a foundation for more profitable prices. But understanding how value is created for a single customer provides an insufficient basis for pricing because the value derived from a product typically will vary from one customer segment to the next. Just as marketers have advocated for the importance of segmentation to marketing success, we argue that price segmentation is critical to pricing success. By understanding how customer value varies across segments, companies can develop strategies to align price and value and thereby improve profits.

Let's revisit the Intel example to illustrate this point. Intel can charge a premium for its chips to premium computer makers like Dell because most of Dell's customers value the Intel brand. But what about makers whose business model involves serving price-sensitive customers that value basic functionality and are indifferent to the brand that delivers it? Understanding how the value of their product differs across the customer base enabled Intel to craft a pricing approach to serve both segments. In this case, the approach involved the creation of a "fighter" brand called Celeron, which was simply a Pentium chip with the math coprocessor turned off. Celeron price levels are set at a discount to Pentium chips and enable Intel to compete for both segments.

Although understanding the different values that existing products provide customers is a critical input to a pricing strategy, the ultimate objective is design for value in the first place. Companies often design products to satisfy needs and create customer delight. Customers love to be delighted—as long as they don't have to pay extra for the experience. When price is factored into the decision, however, many customers are willing to give up some delight in exchange for lower prices. The pricing challenge, therefore, is to understand what creates meaningful value for different customers in order to set prices that reflect the actual value received. Instead of creating products to satisfy customers, companies should create meaningful values that customers will pay for.

PRICE STRUCTURE

Once you understand how value is created for different customer segments, the next step in building a pricing strategy is to create a price structure that aligns price with the value delivered and that minimizes the cost-to-serve. A common mistake made by pricing managers is to assume that their objective is to set a price for the product rather than the customer segment. As the Intel example illustrated, however, the same product can deliver different value depending on the customer. In these instances, setting one price for the product ensures that at least one group of customers will be getting the wrong price. If you price high for high-value customers, then you risk overpricing to low-value customers and reducing profits. Conversely, pricing low to serve low-value customers leaves money on the table at the high end and also reduces profits. Many companies try to solve this dilemma by setting prices for the "average" customer. But this approach also fails to address the problem because the price will still be too high for low-value customers while still leaving some money on the table for high-value customers.

The solution to this dilemma is to create a price structure aligned with the value received instead of the products delivered. There are two techniques to creating a price structure: price metrics and fences. Price metrics are simply the unit by which price is applied to the product or service. Barbers serving primarily male clientele typically charged by the haircut—a metric that seems fair to customers and is profitable for the barber because each haircut takes approximately the same amount of time. But pricing by the haircut is less profitable in hair salons serving both men and women because women's hair is often longer and takes more time to cut. Pricing by the haircut would mean that haircuts of people with longer hair would be less profitable than those for people with shorter hair. To address this issue, salons frequently augment the "per haircut" metric with an additional "per length" metric in which customers with longer hair pay a higher price.

An interesting aspect of this example is that the metric was changed to align price with cost-to-serve and not value. Strategic pricing requires using the price structure to drive profitability by capturing value created across segments as well as getting paid for cost differences between segments. This last point is frequently overlooked by marketers with a strong customer orientation because they fail to appreciate how price can be used as an incentive to change customer behaviors in a way that reduces costs. Although it is unlikely that customers would adopt shorter hairstyles simply to reduce the cost of a haircut, in many instances price can be used to shape customer behaviors. In business markets, for example, customers that have a pressing need for rush orders will gladly pay more for a guarantee of quick delivery. We frequently counsel companies to augment their "per unit" pricing metric with a "delivery time" metric that forces customers that value quick delivery to pay for it. Although this price structure ensures that the company gets paid for value delivered, it also creates an incentive for customers that would prefer quick delivery but are not willing to pay for it to reduce their usage of a high-cost service.

Fences are another way to create a price structure to align price with value and cost-to-serve. Every airline traveler is familiar with price fences and their effect on the price paid. Why do airlines put policy restrictions on discount tickets such as requiring a Saturday night stay and 14-day advance purchase? The airlines recognize they are serving two segments that value an airline seat very differently. Business travelers require flexibility in their travel plans and may have to travel with very short notice to serve a customer or to address a pressing company issue. Leisure travelers that plan vacations months in advance do not value flexibility as highly and are willing to commit to their travel far in advance in exchange for better prices. By using the policy fences, the airlines have created a price structure that captures the value of travel flexibility from only those customers for whom it is important.

PRICE AND VALUE COMMUNICATION

Understanding the value your products create for customers and translating that understanding into an effective price structure provides an incomplete foundation for effective pricing. A complete pricing strategy requires justifying your prices based on the value created for different customers. Failure to communicate value results in higher price sensitivity and more intense price negotiations. Customers might not understand the value of your product because they may be unaware of new features, lack knowledge about how use them, or do not understand how a particular feature might satisfy an unmet need. It is the marketer's responsibility to address these issues through effective price and value communications.

Consider the iPod music player by Apple, for example. The iPod enables customers to purchase and consume music in entirely new ways. But some consumers thought the $299 launch price was too high because they believed the investment in their existing CD collection would be lost in the new format even though the iPod enabled them to upload their entire CD collection into memory. Others objected to the initial price because they didn't understand that the iPod would enable them to purchase individual songs they heard on the radio without having to buy an entire CD. The lack of knowledge about the value created by the iPod lowered willingness-to-pay and slowed initial sales. Interestingly, Apple chose a two-prong approach to communicate the value of the iPod. Apple targeted its advertising to cultural trend leaders by featuring cutting-edge songs and creative graphics in order to communicate to a broader audience that the iPod was both functional and trendy. Apple then invested heavily in a public relations campaign to give the new technology credibility with less informed potential customers. The communications strategy worked brilliantly—over 10 million iPods have been sold in the 3½ years since its introduction at a price far above that of traditional music players.[4]

Value communications are equally important in business markets. Business purchases are driven largely by the economic value delivered by the product. Thus, sending a salesperson in to negotiate price with a business customer without the right value communication tools is like sending a football player into the game without pads and a helmet—he would be forced to give up a lot of ground or get hurt. The tools and messaging will vary depending on whether the value is more economic or psychological in nature. Value communications for products delivering primarily economic benefits will be delivered using tools ranging from basic selling sheets to web-based applications capable of customizing value estimates, designing offerings, and supporting negotiations depending on the complexity of the product. Value communications for products delivering primarily social-psychological benefits such as status, security, or pleasure will rely on other types of tools such as testimonials and pictorial illustrations. The challenge for marketers is to determine which approaches are most appropriate and develop the messaging and tools to help customers understand the value offered by their products.

PRICING POLICY

Academic pricing research has increased the scientific and analytical quality of pricing strategy significantly over the last decade. But no amount of scientific research changes the fact that pricing involves the art of managing expectations of customers and employees to encourage more profitable behaviors. These expectations are set by the company's commitment to enforce its pricing policies in the face of aggressive customers. For example, a policy of never walking away from business sends a clear message to customers encouraging them to be extremely aggressive on price in order to test just how low you will go.

The financial impact of poor pricing policies can be tremendous. Consider the self-inflicted problem faced by Gillette in the late 1990s. Senior management at Gillette was under pressure to generate revenue growth each quarter in order to sustain its lofty stock price. Not surprisingly, the management team tracked sales closely to ensure the company hit its revenue targets each quarter. If the sales forecasts indicated a shortfall in the final month of the quarter, management would offer "one-time" price discounts to any customer that would accept delivery before quarter end. This unstated policy of quarter-end discounts had a powerful effect on the expectations and behaviors of both customers and salespeople. Customers quickly learned not to purchase in the first half of the quarter because the expected "one-time" discounts never failed to materialize at the end of the quarter. Salespeople learned not to work too hard to sell to customers during the first half because their efforts would not be rewarded. One salesperson we know said he couldn't go into accounts and say there would be no more quarter-end discounts because they would just laugh him out of their office. Ultimately, management's lack of price discipline caught up with them and was a major contributor to the more than 50 percent decline in the stock price that occurred between 1999 and 2001.

Strategic pricing recognizes the link between formal and informal price policies and the expectations and behaviors they encourage with customers and employees. Unfortunately, many companies set prices in reaction to customer expectation instead of using price proactively to influence them. As the Gillette example demonstrates, the consequences of mismanaging pricing policies can be significant.

PRICE LEVEL

There can be only one ultimate objective for setting prices—to maximize profitability. The problem is that everyone in the firm has a different, and limited, view of what is needed to achieve the goal. Consequently, sales believes that lower prices will be rewarded by higher close rates and more volume resulting in higher profits. Finance believes that rigorous enforcement of minimum contribution margins ensures price integrity leading to more profit. Marketing believes that price should be used selectively to sustain market share leading to higher long-term profits in exchange for short-term discounts. The critical questions for the pricing manager are "Who is right?" and "How do I get support for whatever price I set when no one can agree on a common perspective?"

One reason that companies find pricing challenging is because they lack a systematic process to translate diverse inputs such as customer value, costs, competitor prices, and broad strategic objectives into the right price. What is required is a decision model that leverages all relevant data while leaving room for managerial judgment about how the market might respond to price changes.

Such a model would enable different functional areas to debate the appropriate price while explicitly identifying the profit impact of each price move. We recently coached a maker of electronic test equipment through such a process for a new product it had recently launched at a low introductory price. The product team performed in-depth-interviews with a variety of customers and used the findings to estimate the value of the product to key segments. For each segment, the team evaluated 10 factors contributing to higher or lower price sensitivity to estimate how much of the value could be captured through a price increase. The price was adjusted downward in one segment in order to dissuade a competitor from entering the market. Finally, financial analyses were performed to understand how much volume the company could afford to lose for various levels of a price increase. The analysis indicated that if the company increased price by 25 percent it could afford to lose nearly 30 percent of its volume and still improve profits.

A careful analysis of the customer base convinced the team that it would lose few, if any, of its relationship accounts at the higher price, although it might lose some price buyers. Despite the loss of price-buyers, the team was convinced that it would lose no more than 10 percent of its total volume and would increase profits by $3 million in the first 6 months following implementation. The team gained an interesting insight into the nature of pricing when it presented their recommendation to the division general manager. Although he was convinced that the price change would increase profits as predicted, he was still reluctant to lose sales because of a sales-oriented culture. Overcoming that reluctance is just one example of the inherent challenges in transitioning to strategic pricing.

EMBEDDING THE STRATEGY

As any experienced marketer knows, developing strategy is one thing—managing the change process to embed that strategy in the organization is quite another. Ultimately, implementing pricing strategy involves changing the expectations and behaviors of all of the actors involved in the sales process. Customers must learn that they will be treated fairly and that abusive purchase tactics will not be rewarded with ad hoc discounts. Sales must learn that they will be rewarded for closing deals that increase firm profitability rather than using price as a tactical lever to increase sales volume. Finance must learn to look beyond costs as a determinant of price to better understand the trade-offs between price, costs, and market response. Successful implementation of pricing strategies requires targeting specific undesirable behaviors and devising a detailed plan to change them. Our experience has shown that there are three main ways to effect these behavioral changes.

PROVIDE INCENTIVES FOR CHANGE

When playwright Noel Coward said, "If you must have motivation, think of your paycheck on Friday," he might well have been talking about how to motivate salespeople to move to a value-based selling approach. Financial incentives are, without question, one of the most powerful levers for behavioral change among salespeople. Today, most salespeople are rewarded for top-line sales instead of profitability. When faced with a choice between working harder to sell value in order to gain additional price or closing an additional deal at a lower price—most opt to close the additional deal because they receive far more commission for the additional albeit, less profitable, volume. As we explain in Chapter 6 on pricing policy, it is nearly impossible to get salespeople to work harder to get higher prices without changing their commission structure so that total compensation is more closely tied to profitability. Making those changes, although often difficult, is a crucial first step toward more effective price negotiations.

Just as salespeople need appropriate incentives, so too do customers. Strategic pricing requires convincing customers to change deeply ingrained behaviors that have been reinforced by years of ad hoc discounting, poor pricing discipline, and poorly communicated value messages. Some customers will be asked to start paying for value received or accepting a lower-value alternative. Other customers must be convinced to limit usage of high cost services or else begin to pay for them. Still others may be asked to change purchase timing, volumes, or meet other conditions in order to qualify for continued discounts. Convincing customers to change behaviors like these requires discipline and thoughtful design of appropriate incentives.

Fortunately, pricers have many tools available to get the job done. For example, value-based metrics can be used to encourage service "abusers" to reduce their usage of high-cost services or to begin to pay for them by aligning price paid with value received. Marketers in distribution, manufacturing, and retail frequently use this technique to control delivery and logistics costs by offering a free minimum delivery option and then adding a metric that increases price for additional delivery guarantees. We discuss how to design appropriate incentives for customers through the use of price metrics, fences, tiered offerings, segmented pricing, and pricing policies in Chapters 4, 5, and 6.

Another tool that pricers can use to incent more profitable behaviors on the part of customers is discount levels. Consider the telecommunications manufacturer that had been giving costly support services away in order to match a major competitor's offering. The practice was highly unprofitable because the company could not price for the services for fear the competition would not follow and, like most services, they were costly to deliver. Because the company could not change customer usage by increasing prices, it looked to discounting instead. A simple financial analysis showed that the company would improve profitability by offering a 5 percent product discount for every customer that opted to accept a restricted service package in which they had to use online support to solve technical problems. Price-sensitive customers found the package appealing, in part, due to the lower price point, but also because they could purchase personal support for an additional fee if needed. As these examples illustrate, there are numerous opportunities to create incentives for more profitable behaviors on the part of customers and company personnel.

SET APPROPRIATE EXPECTATIONS

It's a basic truism that individuals will change only to the extent that change is expected of them. Unfortunately, in many companies, precisely what those expectations are is unclear. Pricing managers often receive mixed messages from senior management about the types of behaviors they ought to pursue. We recently attended a meeting of global pricing managers for a computer manufacturer at which the CEO spoke about the business goals for the coming year. On one slide of the presentation, the stated goal was to increase price realization by 6 percent. The very next slide described another goal of increasing market share by several points. When the CEO asked if there were any questions, one brave manager raised her hand to ask which of these seemingly conflicting goals should they focus on: price or market share? Caught off-guard by such a penetrating question, the embarrassed CEO stammered "uuhhh, both I suppose." Not surprisingly, the question-and-answer period ended a little earlier than planned. Although it is possible to increase price and volume simultaneously through a value-based price structure and tighter discounting policies, setting such conflicting expectations for managerial performance usually leads to poor performance and conflicting messages to the market.

Pricing discipline cannot be viewed as an oxymoron in your organization. That means that senior management must specify clear, consistent business objectives and provide the necessary resources for managers to achieve them. This can be one of the most challenging aspects of strategic pricing because it forces managers to explicitly consider the long-term costs of pricing actions. It can be incredibly tempting for a sales or pricing manager to approve a pricing exception to close a deal with a new account that has been negotiating aggressively. But doing so can have significant long-term costs. First, it teaches that account that you are not serious about getting paid for your value and that they can win concessions by being aggressive. Second, and often more importantly, it can place your relationships with long-time customers at risk if they find out that they are paying a higher price than a first-time purchaser. Finally, competitors are likely to copy this approach if it wins market share in the short term with the result that overall industry price levels start to decline and profits shrink for everyone.

Failing to have a consistent message to customers that they will have to pay for value received sets the expectations that they can "win" by negotiating aggressively or simply waiting you out to until the price comes down. Instead of setting prices based on short-term needs, companies need to set polices designed to enforce price discipline and send a clear message to customers that they cannot win special treatment through clever tactics. Ideally, policies are transparent and consistent. With transparent policies, customers need not engage in threats and misinformation to learn the trade-offs you are willing to make. Consistent policies communicate that it is impossible to "game the system" by shopping within the company for the best deal.

Provide the Knowledge and Skills to Change

Creating incentives and setting appropriate expectations are necessary, but not sufficient, conditions to change individual behaviors. Even when customers and company personnel are willing to change, the key question is whether they have the knowledge and skills that make them *able* to change. In negotiated environments, all of the work to create a proactive, profit-driven, and value-based pricing strategy comes to fruition when the deal is signed and the final price is set. Too much is riding on the outcome to simply admonish sales to "sell value" and defend price. Harvesting the fruit of your pricing labors requires teaching salespeople how to change from a fixed offering–variable price approach to the more profitable, fixed price–variable offering approach to negotiation. As we explain in Chapter 5 on value communications, training alone is often not enough—success requires developing tools to help customize and communicate the value message in a way that makes it relevant for customers.

Salespeople aren't the only ones in the company that need new skills to implement strategic pricing in the organization. Product managers must learn how to collect the data necessary to estimate economic value (Chapter 3), analyze relevant costs (Chapter 8), and set profit-maximizing prices (Chapters 6 and 9). The first step to developing these skills is education. However, true skills development requires putting the concepts to work on real products on multiple occasions. As we have already noted, strategic pricing is challenging, and many companies do not have the level of commitment necessary to make the transition. That's good news for those companies that persevere to developing the skills needed to change, because it means that pricing can become a source of competitive advantage that delivers incremental profits over time.

Communicating the rationale and benefits of a value-based pricing is one of the most critical steps in convincing customers to change how they set prices.

Customers must understand that the prices they are paying are fair and that other customers are not getting better deals through the use of aggressive price tactics. This communication happens through the use of transparent pricing policies that clearly define the ways in which customers can earn lower prices. Companies must also explain to customers that they will benefit from more choices about the types of offerings and ways that they engage with you. When customers receive high value or increase service usage, they will be expected to pay more. But strategic pricing does not equate to higher prices for all customers—low-value customers, or those that are willing to purchase in a way that reduces costs, may receive lower prices. Understanding these options is essential to setting the stage for a new pricing approach.

Summary

To say that pricing strategy is challenging would be an understatement. It requires analyzing data on costs, customers, and the competition, and integrating that analysis into prices that lead to long-term profitability. Moreover, the impact of pricing is felt throughout the organization, leading to contentious decisions driven by conflicting performance metrics and biased views of the market. Managing this conflict requires that companies adopt a common view of pricing strategy and its objective.

In this chapter, we have introduced the strategic pricing pyramid containing the five key elements of strategic pricing. Experience has taught us that achieving sustainable improvements to pricing performance requires adjustments to multiple elements of the pyramid. Companies operating with a narrow view of what constitutes a pricing strategy miss this crucial point leading to incomplete solutions and lower profits. Building a strategic pricing capability requires more than a common understanding of the elements of an effective strategy. It requires careful development of organizational structure, systems, individual skills, and ultimately culture. These things represent the foundation upon which the strategic pricing pyramid rests and must be developed in concert with the pricing strategy. But the first step toward strategic pricing is to understand each level of the pyramid and how it supports those above it.

Notes

1. McKinsey Global Survey of Business Executives (November 2004).
2. The name of the actual company has been disguised.
3. See Chapter 13 for a detailed treatment of pricing research techniques.
4. "Apple Emerges from the Pod," BBC News Online, December 16, 2003; Brian Wheeler; "iPod Invasion," *The BG News,* March 25, 2005, Dan Myers.

CHAPTER
3
VALUE CREATION

The Source of Pricing Advantage

Pricing harvests the fruit of a company's investment in product development and marketing by capturing the payoff for all the time, effort, and resources devoted to a business enterprise. Each stage of the Strategic Pricing Pyramid, introduced in Chapter 2, plays a critical role in maximizing profitable and sustainable revenue. At the foundation of the pyramid, in what should be the first task in marketing and offering design, is gaining a deep understanding of how products and services create value for customers—the essential initial input to pricing strategy.

For many firms, however, the pricing harvest is less than bountiful because they shortchange or ignore the value creation process. They erroneously assume that merely ladling performance features into an offering will justify charging a price premium. But that will not happen unless those features translate to actual, competitively superior economic and psychological value to the customer. Complicating the pricing process, the value derived from a product is likely to vary among different customers. By understanding how customer value differs across market segments, companies can better align price and value to win more customer loyalty and greater profit simultaneously.

Marketers have long admonished companies to set prices that reflect "value." Unfortunately, because value is often poorly defined and difficult to discern, managers frequently reject value-based pricing as impractical. Consequently, let's begin discussing value creation by explaining what we mean by value. Then we'll illustrate the process of Economic Value Estimation®, illustrating its application with business marketing examples. Finally, we will discuss value-based segmentation, an essential step for strategically setting prices that maximize profitable sales.

THE ROLE OF VALUE IN PRICING

The term *value* commonly refers to the total savings, monetary gains, or satisfaction that the customer receives from using the product/service *offering*. Economists call this *use value*—the utility gained from the product. On a hot

27

summer day at the beach, for example, the use value of a cold drink is quite high for most people—perhaps as high as $10 for 12 ounces of cold cola or a favorite brand of beer. But because few people would actually pay that price, knowing use value is of little help to, say, a mobile drink vendor walking the beach and pricing his or her wares.

Potential customers know that except in rare situations, they don't have to pay a seller all that a product is really worth to them. They know that competing sellers will come along with a better deal at prices closer to what they expect from past experience—say $1.50 for a soda. (Economists refer to the difference between the real value of a product and its market price as *consumer surplus*.) Or they might know that a half mile up the beach is a snack shop where beverages cost just $1, and that a convenience store selling an entire six-pack for only $3.49 is a short drive away. Consequently, thirsty sun worshipers probably will reject a very high price even when the product is worth much more to them.

The value at the heart of effective pricing strategy is not use value, but is what economists call *exchange value* and what marketers term *economic value* to the customer. This value depends primarily on customers' alternatives. Few people will pay even $2 for a cola, even if its use value is $10, if they think the market offers alternatives at substantially lower prices.

On the other hand, only a small segment of customers insists on buying the lowest-priced alternative. It is likely that many people would pay $1.50 for a cola from the mobile vendor strolling nearby despite the availability of the same product for less at a snack shop or convenience store. The seller is providing a *differentiated product offering* worth more than the alternatives to some segments of the market. How much more depends on the economic value customers place on not having to walk up the beach to the snack shop or not having to drive to the convenience store. For some, the economic value of not having to exert themselves is high; they are willing to pay for convenience. For others who wouldn't mind a jog along the beach, the premium they will pay for convenience will be much less. To appeal to that jogger segment, the mobile vendor would need to differentiate the offering in some other way that the segment values highly.

A product's *total economic value*, then, is the price of the customer's best alternative (the *reference value*) plus the economic value of whatever differentiates the offering from the alternative (the *differentiation value*). Differentiation value may have both positive and negative elements. Exhibit 3-1 illustrates these relationships. Total economic value is the maximum price that a "smart shopper," fully informed about the market and seeking the best value, would pay. In fact, sophisticated business buyers often demand proof, such as an Economic Value Estimation® (EVE), that quantifies the benefits of high-priced brands or that shows how low-priced brands can save more than the value of the benefits given up.[1]

Not every buyer is a smart shopper, however. Often product and service users, and particularly purchasing agents buying on the users' behalf, do not recognize the actual economic value they receive from an offering. That is, the offering's *perceived value* to a buyer might fall short of true economic value if the buyer is ill-informed. Therefore, it's critical that a company's sales presentations

EXHIBIT 3-1   Economic Value Estimation

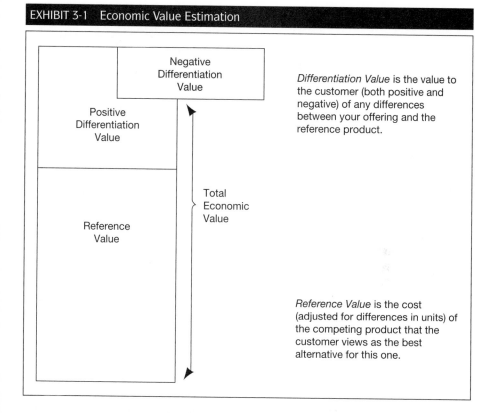

Differentiation Value is the value to the customer (both positive and negative) of any differences between your offering and the reference product.

Reference Value is the cost (adjusted for differences in units) of the competing product that the customer views as the best alternative for this one.

and marketing communications ensure that offering features likely to be important to the buyer—particularly competitively superior features—come to the buyer's attention. An Economic Value Estimation® can be especially useful in such situations by documenting the benefits a buyer is likely to receive from a product or service. EVE demonstrates how, in the case of a business customer, for example, an offering can reduce the customer's costs or increase customer revenue well in excess of what buyers might otherwise expect just from the features of the product.

A common problem in the marketing communications arena illustrates the importance of documenting economic value. A magazine publisher consistently encountered price resistance from media buyers drawn to the lower cost-per-subscriber prices of competitors. Despite the magazine's better writing, more interesting articles, snappier photography, and a more loyal and wealthier readership, advertisers still judged media quality mainly on the basis of total circulation. Because the magazine had 11 percent more circulation than its nearest competitor, media buyers figured that they should pay no more than an 11 percent premium to run an ad in the magazine.

Those objections seemed quite reasonable on their face when presented outside the context of the economic value delivered. But circulation hardly explains all the value an advertising medium delivers. The time readers devote to an issue,

	Competing Magazine	Our Magazine	Advantage
Circulation	1,400,00	1,550,000	11%
Readers per copy	1.8	2.1	
Readership	2,520,000	3,255,000	29%
% See ad	9.20%	14.50%	
% Motivated/ad seen	1.60%	2.20%	
% Sold/motivated	20%	20%	
# Readers sold	742	2077	180%
Sales per customer	$180	$200	
Gross margin	30%	30%	
Value of ad	$40,062	$124,601	211%
Cost of ad	$29,000	$67,400	
Return on ad	$11,062	$57,201	

EXHIBIT 3-2   Economic Value Estimation® for Advertising

the number of copies passed along to non-subscriber readers, the number of readers who see the average ad in the magazine, and the demographics, lifestyles, and purchasing patterns of readers, along with other factors, can give a magazine substantial differentiated value. Exhibit 3-2 shows the greater value delivered by many of those factors to the magazine's advertisers. The publisher had to quantify that additional value in order to change advertisers' perceptions and justify a price premium larger than 11 percent. That required the publisher to learn more about advertisers' businesses than they ever thought would be necessary.

Unfortunately, similar problems arise in virtually all industries. Companies often try to sell only the features of their products. Tending to be product-oriented rather than customer-oriented, they mistakenly assume that attribute superiorities are always important to customers and that customers recognize that. They fail to understand customers well enough to quantify the benefits as customers see them, even hypothetically. When, however, companies credibly estimate the economic value of their offerings through research and other techniques, the results can be astounding. In the magazine's case, what at first looked like only an 11 percent advantage over competition ballooned to a 211 percent advantage in true economic value! That difference easily justified a price per ad page more than twice that of the competition.

Sometimes, when an offering has significant intangible value, such as brand strength, received value can exceed true economic value. That's frequently the case with many consumer products when deft advertising and merchandising invests a product with strong emotional values such as prestige, safety, hope, or reassurance. Perceptions rather than physical characteristics provide the differentiated value a product holds for the buyer. Packaged goods with more or less the same physical attributes as the competition nonetheless command price premiums because their credible superiority claims create the perception of differentiated value, such as a sexier smile or a healthier body. An expensive Swiss timepiece attesting to wealth will sell to a prestige-minded market segment even if it's less accurate and possesses fewer timing features than a $25 digital watch. It is difficult if not impossible to quantify such perceptions objectively, forcing the pricer to measure the subjective value of those unquantifiable benefits.[2]

A similar perceptual phenomenon can occur in business markets as well when the strength of a brand name adds to differentiated value by reassuring buyers and quelling the fear of making a career-killing wrong decision. Usually, however, a business customer's total economic value can be expressed as revenues gained or costs avoided by purchasing the product. Those are objective benefit estimates the marketer can show to the customer and perhaps even guarantee. For that reason, the examples we use in this book are mostly business examples. Not only do they deal with quantifiable value elements, business negotiations over variable prices paid for varying product attribute bundles make business markets the ideal arena for value-based pricing. The EVE helps to identify the best appeals for promoting and selling an existing offering and it suggests what should be designed into an innovation still on the drawing board.

ECONOMIC VALUE ESTIMATION®: AN ILLUSTRATION

To determine the benefit that a product or service can offer to a business customer, a marketer should first determine the product's economic value. In the following example, GenetiCorp (a disguised name) created innovative products that accelerate the process of genetic testing. EVE determined what value those breakthroughs actually delivered to different types of institutional customers.

One GenetiCorp product, Dyna-Test, synthesizes a complementary DNA strand from an existing DNA sample, significantly reducing DNA molecule degradation and enhancing the precision of a DNA analysis. Dyna-Test preserves sample integrity much longer than does its primary competitor, EnSyn, improving DNA test yields and accuracy in a variety of applications. For example, criminal investigators use DNA to match hair, blood, or other human samples. Hospitals and medical professionals use DNA to diagnose diseases. Pharmaceutical manufacturers use DNA analyses to target genes susceptible to new drug treatments. In all applications, test failures can be costly. Getting a "fuzzy picture" in a criminal investigation may produce a false-negative result, requiring a retest that might take several weeks. But, tissue sample sizes in criminal cases are very limited, often precluding repeated tests. Similarly, for a pharmaceutical company, getting a fuzzy picture when analyzing a DNA strand may cause drug researchers to miss their true target, the genetic portion of the DNA suspected of triggering a disease.

Unfortunately, when it first marketed Dyna-Test, GenetiCorp did not have a clue about its product's economic value. It set prices based on a high markup over costs and then discounted those prices under pressure from purchasing organizations that could buy large volumes. To improve its profits, GenetiCorp decided to learn what its product is really worth to customers: Dyna-Test's reference value (the price of what the customer considers the best alternative product) plus its positive and negative differentiated values (the customer use value of the attributes that distinguish Dyna-Test from the best alternative). Buyers will pay no more than the reference value for features and benefits that are the same as the competing product's. When multiple competitors offer customers the same benefits, those benefits are commoditized; a customer need not pay anything close to a product's worth because it can get the product elsewhere. A product earns a price premium over the reference value for the extra performance—the differentiated value—it alone delivers. The total of reference and differentiated values is the economic value estimate.

Dyna-Test has more than one economic value because different types of users have different reference alternatives and receive different use value from Dyna-Test's distinguishing features. Let's examine the value estimation components in two different market segments.

Commercial researchers in pharmaceutical and biotech firms most often consider EnSyn the best alternative to Dyna-Test. EnSyn sells for $30 per test kit; that's the product category's reference value for such users. To determine Dyna-Test's differentiation value, GenetiCorp studied the five primary drivers of Dyna-Test's positive differentiation value among commercial researchers.

Driver 1—Yield Opportunity Costs: Dyna-Test provides a greater yield of full-length cDNA, the compound DNA structures used for analysis, which is extremely valuable. With more full-length cDNA to work with, researchers can reduce the number of experiments needed to find the relevant portions of DNA, saving an average of a week's valuable research time, according to GenetiCorp's customer interviews.

The annual revenue from a successful commercial drug ranges from $250 million to $1 billion. GenetiCorp used a conservative estimate of $400 million revenue, which, with a 75 percent contribution margin, generated $300 million in annual profit contribution. The cost of developing a typical drug was approximately $590 million. These contribution and cost estimates yield an average net present value of $41 million a year profit for a successful drug over a 17-year patent life. But it takes 500 target tests on average to finally identify the gene sequence leading to a successful new drug, so each target test eventually is worth $82,000. With a 260-day work-year (approximately 2,100 hours), the value of a target test is $39 per hour. If using Dyna-Test saves the researcher an additional week that can be devoted to another new drug, the value of those additional 40 hours is $1,560.

Driver 2—Yield Labor Savings: Dyna-Test's cDNA yield superiority over EnSyn also produces more efficient laboratory staff work. Customer interviews indicated that using Dyna-Test saved 16 hours of processing labor compared to using EnSyn. Because laboratory personnel receive an average of $24 per hour, labor savings from Dyna-Test are about $384.

Driver 3—Quality Control Labor Savings: Prior to Dyna-Test, researchers frequently checked test-chemical batches for quality, sterility, and reproducibility, adding two hours to a test. However, Dyna-Test maintained uniform quality and performance over several years, assuring researchers that they could eliminate quality-control checks. In interviews, customers said "I am confident with Dyna-Test because it is a quality and tested product" or "Dyna-Test has been around long enough; you know it works. If someone says they ran the experiment with Dyna-Test it must be right." High quality produced 2 hours of customer cost savings totaling $48.

Driver 4—Sample Size Opportunity Costs: Using traditional methods, analyzing a DNA sample usually requires using some "starter" sample material at the outset. Often, the amount of original sample material is very small; gathering more on an emergency basis might take about 3 weeks of lost research time. But the Dyna-Test kit has a two-step system that reduces the need for starter samples, making available more testable original sample material and freeing researchers from the search for more. Using the value per week of Dyna-Test usage, GenetiCorp estimated the opportunity cost of searching for new material at $4,680 (3 × $1,560) per project. But because such emergency searches happened only about 10 percent of the time, the likely opportunity cost averages to $468.

Driver 5—Sample Size Labor Savings: Similar to Driver 4, gathering additional emergency starter material requires researchers to repeat the entire analytical test—an extra 16 hours of research labor time about 10 percent of the time. But with the Dyna-Test kit yielding more usable material and with labor costing $24 per hour, the value of using Dyna-Test on this dimension is $38 ($24 × 16 × 0.1).

In sum, for pharmaceutical and commercial biotechnology firms, the estimated total economic value of Dyna-Test is calculated by adding together the reference value of $30, plus the estimates of differentiated value associated with each value driver, yielding a total estimated economic value of $2,528. In other words, purchasing the new Dyna-Test kit instead of the EnSyn kit would produce $2,528 in cost reductions and new product profit gains for a commercial researcher. Exhibit 3-3 illustrates the EVE for that industrial buying segment.

Nonindustrial markets such as academic institutions and government laboratories estimate economic value in a similar fashion. Their reference value is also the $30 price of the EnSyn test kit, however, the most price-sensitive among them simply have lab assistants—essentially free student labor—make DNA test products from scratch. Their differentiating value drivers are similar to those of industrial customers, but modified to reflect a different research environment and economic reward structure.

EXHIBIT 3-3   Economic Value Estimation® for Dyna-Test Industrial Buyers

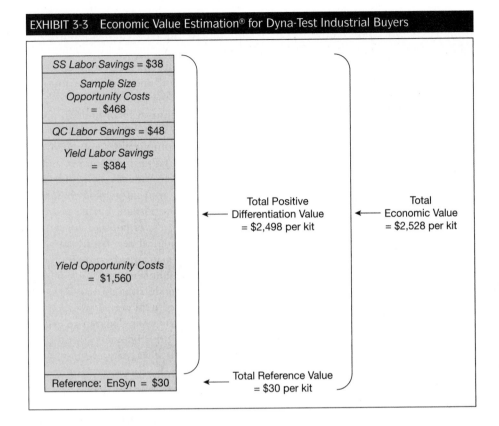

Driver 1—Yield Opportunity Costs: The yield opportunity cost avoided by using Dyna-Test is $1,055, somewhat less than for commercial researchers because of the lower economic rewards from breakthroughs in primary research.

Drivers 2, 3, 4, and 5:   The yield labor savings of $231, quality control savings of $29, sample size opportunity cost avoided of $468, and sample size labor savings are also less because of the reduced cost of labor within university systems.

Thus, the estimated total economic value of Dyna-Test for academic laboratories is calculated by adding the reference value of $30 plus the estimates of value associated with each value driver, yielding a total EVE of $1,685. Exhibit 3-4 illustrates the relationships.

Remember that the economic value derived from EVE is not necessarily the perceived value that a buyer might actually place on the product. A customer might not know about a reference product and won't be influenced by its price. A buyer might be unsure of a product's differentiating attributes and may be unwilling to invest the time and expense to learn about them. If the product's price is small, the buyer may make an impulse purchase without really thinking about its economic value. Similarly, other effects such as brand image and equally unquantifiable factors can influence price sensitivity, reducing the impact of economic value on the

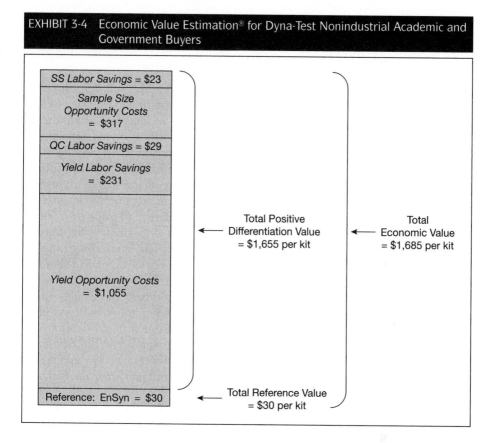

EXHIBIT 3-4   Economic Value Estimation® for Dyna-Test Nonindustrial Academic and Government Buyers

purchase decision. Ultimately, a product's market value is determined not only by the product's economic value, but also by the accuracy with which buyers perceive that value and by the importance they place on getting the most for their money.

This limitation of Economic Value Estimation® is both a weakness and a strength. It is a weakness because economic value cannot indicate the appropriate price to charge. It only estimates the maximum price a segment of buyers would pay if they fully recognized the product's value to them and were motivated to purchase. That is a strength, however, by indicating whether a poorly selling product is overpriced relative to its true value or is underpromoted and unappreciated by the market. The only solution to the overpricing problem is to cut price. A better solution to the perception problem often is maintaining or even increasing price while aggressively educating the market. That is what GenetiCorp did with Dyna-Test. After previously cutting price to meet the demands of its apparently price-sensitive buyers, GenetiCorp raised prices two- to fivefold, at the same time launching an aggressive marketing campaign. While customer purchasing agents expressed dismay, sales continued growing because even the new prices represented but a small fraction of the value delivered. Profits increased significantly in the following year as purchasers learned about

EXHIBIT 3-5 Economic Value Profile for Dyna-Test

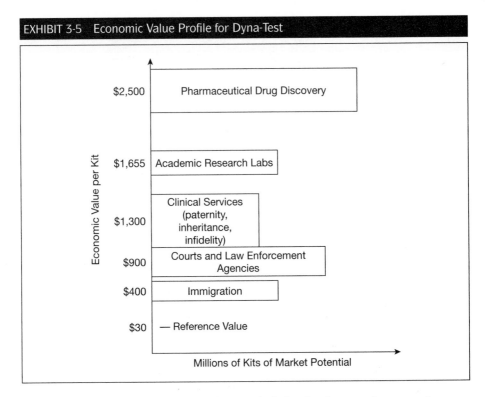

Dyna-Test's superior economic value to their institutions and accepted, sometimes grudgingly, the need to pay for that value.

GenetiCorp's experience also shows how value can vary among market segments. To determine a pricing strategy and policy for a product, you must determine the economic value delivered to all segments and the market size of each. With that information, you can develop an *economic value profile* of the entire market and determine which segments you can serve most profitably at which prices. Exhibit 3-5 profiles the economic value and market potential for each Dyna-Tech market segment.

EVE is an especially effective sales tool when buyers facing extreme cost pressures are very price sensitive. For example, since healthcare reimbursement systems began giving hospitals and doctors financial incentives to practice cost-effective medicine, pharmaceutical companies have been forced to add cost and performance evidence to their traditional claims about a drug's clinical effectiveness. Some now offer purchasers elaborate tests to show that greater effectiveness is worth a higher price. Johnson & Johnson's invention of the medicated arterial stent, for instance, initially appeared expensive at $1,300 each. J&J successfully countered customer resistance by demonstrating that dramatically reducing the probability of an artery reclogging was worth at least $3,500 per treatment in avoided surgery and hospital costs.

THE HIGH COST OF SHORTCUTS

When setting prices, there are no shortcuts for understanding the economic value received by the customer. Many companies nonetheless shortchange themselves by assuming that if their differentiated product is "x" percent more effective than the competition, then the product will be worth only "x" percent more in price. While that relationship makes sense superficially, closer examination reveals how wrong it is. If you had cancer and knew of a drug that was 50 percent more effective than the competition's in curing your disease, would you refuse to pay more than a 50 percent higher price? Of course not. Suppose you were planning to paint your house and discovered a paint sprayer that lets you finish the job in half the usual time—a doubling of your productivity. Would you pay no more than twice the price of a brush? Obviously not, unless you're some rare individual who can paint twice as fast with two brushes simultaneously. Otherwise, the value to a busy person of the painting time saved by the sprayer is much greater than the price of a second brush.

As these examples show, the value-based price premium one can charge is often much greater than the percentage increase in an offering's technical efficiency. The total economic value of a differentiated product is proportional to its technical efficiency *only* when a buyer can receive the benefits associated with a superior product simply by buying more of the reference product. In our example, that would be the case only if using 50 percent more of the competitive cancer drug or painting with two brushes at the same time would produce the same increase in efficiency as using the superior products. Because of this misunderstanding, many companies committed to value-based pricing have been misled into believing that they cannot price to capture their value if their ratio of price-to-use value would exceed that of their competitors.

At the center of this misconception is the popular concept of customer value modeling (CVM), which emerged from the total quality management movement when companies tried to measure and deliver superior quality at a competitive price. Marketers and a variety of value consultants have applied CVM in many contexts, including early criteria of the Malcolm Baldrige National Quality Award, largely because it is easy to implement. CVM relies on customers' subjective judgments about price and product attribute performances. It assumes that customers seek to purchase the products that give them the greatest perceived benefit—which might be quantified in monetary terms, but need not be—per unit price. Avoiding the translation of relative attribute performance into hard-dollar estimates, CVM is analytically simpler than EVE, particularly for pricing consumer products with their heavily psychological values.

The fact is, however, that CVM underestimates the value of the more differentiated products in a market and overestimates the value of the less differentiated products. CVM methods define value differently than does EVE. CVM rates each competitive supplier's relative strength on each product attribute, weighing each attribute by customer estimates of importance, according to customer and prospect surveys. Then CVM calculates the average relationship between perceived quality and price, creating what is variously called a "fair-value line," a "value equivalence line," "indifference line," or other term for the presumed linear relationship between price and perceived quality. A point on the line putatively indicates a "fair" balance of price for quality. For a given price, a product with less than fair perceived quality is disadvantaged and stands to lose market share, say CVM theorists, while a product offering more than fair quality will gain share.

There are flaws in that thinking, however. First, customers don't pay for average differential benefit estimates; they pay for the *worth* of the benefits they receive. That is, they mentally convert benefits into monetary terms so that they can judge how much more they should pay for the extra value received from a more expensive product. If it's worth more than the price premium charged, they buy it.

Second, CVM fails to distinguish between the value of common benefits that are priced as commodities and the value of the unique benefits associated with a differentiated offering. Total economic value—what the customer *really* gets from the offering—does not have a single linear relationship to price. One of the two components of economic value, the reference value, usually is much less than the use value of the benefits delivered by the reference product. The reference value is the *price* a customer pays for the next best alternative offering—like the price of the second paintbrush, the price of the EnSyn DNA test kit, or the price of a soda at the refreshment stand. Benefits offered by more than one supplier become commodity benefits; customers can get them from more than one source. Competition among suppliers drives the price for those benefits below their use value, making the price-to-use value ratio of the reference product low, less than one-to-one.

In contrast, differentiation value, the second component of total economic value, is the *extra* use value a product delivers compared to the reference product. The differentiation value, expressed in monetary terms, is equivalent to the price premium the differentiated supplier could charge as a fair price. It's fair because the customer gets just what she's paying for in additional value, no more and no less. The price premium-to-differentiation value ratio is one-to-one. In other words, the relationship between price and economic value is a function of two different price-to-quality ratios, not the single average ratio hypothesized in a CVM model.

The difference is significant because the larger the proportion of differentiation value in a product's total economic value delivered, the more the truly fair price to the customer—the EVE price—can exceed the CVM-hypothesized "fair-value line" price.[3] Pricing your highly differentiated product at the supposed "fair-value line" level will be hazardous to your bottom line!

The simple example in Exhibit 3-6 illustrates the EVE versus CVM difference. For simplicity, let's assume that all widget customers have complete information about the respective benefits they can receive from suppliers A, B, C and D. Perceived quality therefore equals economic value in this example. The overall "fair-value line" (FVL) represents the CVM-determined average relationship of price to economic value delivered, in this case a ratio of 0.61. The reference value

EXHIBIT 3-6   EVE versus CVM Pricing

P	Reference Value	Differentiation Value	Total Economic Value	EVE "Fair" Price	CVM "Fair" Price	Price Difference EVE less FVL
						(avg price value = .61)
Widget A	$40	$0	$80	$40	$49	($9)
Widget B	$40	$20	$100	$60	$61	$1
Widget C	$40	$30	$110	$70	$67	$3
Widget D	$40	$40	$120	$80	$73	$7

* This example assumes that "perceived quality" equals economic value.

is $40, the most that any supplier can charge for commoditized everybody-offers-them benefits, even though the use value of reference product A is $80. (The low reference price forces the average price-to-value relationship designated by a single CVM FVL into a slope that's less than 1.0, implying that a dollar's worth of price produces only 61 cents additional value! More accurate might be a curvilinear FVL, or a linear FVL representing only differentiation values. Even better would be curves showing accelerating and decelerating marginal value at different price levels. But to figure all that out requires the harder work of EVE in the first place. Sadly, there are no shortcuts for profitable strategic pricing.

Note how the fair EVE price exceeds the fair CVM price as the differentiation value of the product grows. Were widget D priced at the fair-value CVM price of $73, its manufacturer would be leaving $7 per unit, nearly 9 percent of the value widget D creates, on the table. (As we shall see in later chapters, how much of widget D's $40 differentiation value the manufacturer actually receives is a matter of price negotiation.)

HOW TO ESTIMATE ECONOMIC VALUE

In theory, estimating economic value should not be difficult. In practice, however, understanding how customers gain value from a product can be complex, requiring detailed knowledge about product users. Often, such as in most business product sales and in some consumer product purchases, product and service benefits are quantified and measurable, such as profit margin increases and cost reductions. Where, however, product benefits are less tangible, quantifying value is more difficult. The pricer frequently must rely on inferences such as those drawn from the prices of products offering similar differential benefits or on choice-based research techniques—trade-off analysis or simulated test markets, for example—that assess proxies for value rather than true economic value itself.

Notwithstanding that problem with intangible benefits, let's examine in detail the steps involved in an Economic Value Estimation® that reveal quantifiable information such as in our Dyna-Test example. EVE involves the three steps

EXHIBIT 3-7   Process for Economic Value Estimation®

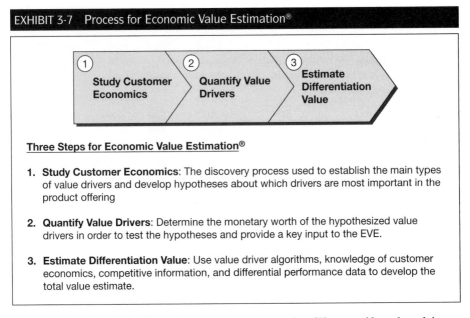

Three Steps for Economic Value Estimation®

1. **Study Customer Economics**: The discovery process used to establish the main types of value drivers and develop hypotheses about which drivers are most important in the product offering

2. **Quantify Value Drivers**: Determine the monetary worth of the hypothesized value drivers in order to test the hypotheses and provide a key input to the EVE.

3. **Estimate Differentiation Value**: Use value driver algorithms, knowledge of customer economics, competitive information, and differential performance data to develop the total value estimate.

shown in Exhibit 3-7: (1) study customer economics, (2) quantify value drivers, and (3) estimate differentiation value.

STEP 1: STUDY CUSTOMER ECONOMICS

Two things drive customer purchases: customer objectives and the alternative supply sources available, the "next best competitive alternative" (NBCA). Value estimation begins by determining both. The *price* the competitor charges (not necessarily the NBCA's use value) for the reference product is the EVE *reference value*. For example, the reference value of a hotel room on a business trip is the price charged for the next-best hotel choice in town, representing the traveler's idea of the minimum lodging service level he or she will accept. In the Dyna-Test example, the next-best choice in testing kits is the EnSyn product, the $30 price of which is the reference value for the product category. As we said, because the values delivered by the NBCA are also delivered by at least one other competitor, competition drives the price of such commodity values below their actual value.

In some cases, the reference product or service is not necessarily a specific competitive offering, but a class of processes or self-designed solutions that buyers have used to achieve their objectives. For example, most accounting software suppliers for years assumed that buyers would compare their wares to traditional double-entry bookkeeping methods. Software vendors designed products to automate double-entry accounting and its rigorous debit and credit data entry requirements. Intuit, however, learned that double-entry methods were the wrong reference process for the two-thirds of small-business bookkeepers who used their own simpler cash-based accounting solutions. Working closely with those customers to learn their needs for simplicity, Intuit created Quickbooks, which quickly outsold competitors in the small-business market because it automated those simpler approaches.

Value drivers are customer needs upon which our product or service could have an impact. As we noted earlier, business purchases tend to be dominated by objective value drivers such as productivity improvement, fuel economy, or durability—factors critical to the customer's business model and cash flow. Subjective perceptions tend to drive consumer purchases. Of course, there are exceptions. Individual investors seek objective information about mutual fund fees and returns, for instance, while a business meeting planner subjectively judges the quality of a hotel's food, room appearance, golf course, and other services. In our Dyna-Test example, pricing researchers quantified five significant profit-improvement and cost-reduction value drivers.

Differentiation value is the extra benefit that your product or service delivers to customers over and above that provided by the competitive reference product. Our soft drink vendor strolling right up to the customer's beach blanket provides convenience compared to a distant refreshment stand. The traveler's hotel of choice provides a free breakfast and free cocktail hour not available at the next-best hotel. Dyna-Test allows researchers to create more new drugs a year and save researcher labor costs relative to EnSyn. Competing products in a category likely provide many potential differentiation value drivers. It's important, however, that an EVE concentrate on those drivers having the most differentiation bang-for-the-buck for a customer and a customer market segment. The degree to which a supplier differentiates its offer in terms of those needs will have the greatest impact on the price the marketer can successfully charge above the reference value.

In business markets, customers' business models and strategies determine just about all value drivers. (Whether they can articulate them in a way that reveals value drivers could be another story.) We have found that a proper value-based market segmentation will distinguish between the business models, generally one or two, that dominate an industry. For example, a flooring supplier learned that two segments pursuing two distinct business models characterized the bulk of its distribution channels. Volume-driven retailers heavily advertised budget and mid-range product to generate mass market awareness and new customer trial. In the second segment, higher-end brands, wide selection, service excellence, and tailored solutions drove sales.

Typically, in-depth analysis of just a few business models, perhaps as few as one or two depending on the industry, is usually sufficient when followed by validation interviews or surveys confirming your hypothesis that some other customers operate with similar models. In most business markets, an adept salesperson aware of a potential customer's likely business model has a head start in probing for a specific buyer's critical needs and concerns, and how the supplier's product can help. As we will see in subsequent chapters, salespeople lacking such knowledge are more likely to let a selling situation degrade quickly into squabbles over price rather than win-win demonstrations of value.

Value hypothesis development usually begins with a list of your offering's potential value drivers: superior performance, greater reliability, additional features, reduced maintenance costs, smaller startup costs, faster service, etc. Some are *cost drivers,* which save the customer time, money, or effort if they use your product instead of the competitive reference product. They can range from immediate savings to longer term cost reductions such as in capital and inventory investments or replacement costs. For example, one set of potentially important value driver hypotheses focuses on capacity constraints and bottlenecks in the buyer's business operations and the costly expedients the buyer uses to alleviate them such as labor overtime, temporary workers, and independent contractors.

Revenue drivers deliver value to business customers by improving the revenue and profit they earn from their customers. Perhaps your product allows your customers to increase the differentiated value of their offerings, enabling them to boost their prices and profit margins. Intel, for example, recognized that design speed is critical to original equipment manufacturer (OEM) computer manufacturers, so it achieved a competitive advantage with microprocessors that customers could design into their products faster, allowing customers to get to market ahead of their rivals. The profit contribution in that industry between a first-to-market share of, say, 50 percent and a follower share of 20 to 30 percent, is significant.

Psychological value drivers focus on the psychological dimensions of the purchase, and are often difficult to estimate or quantify. Academic researchers consider these "higher-order values" to be natural extensions of buyers' goals. Michelin's long-time positioning strategy, for example, targets consumers who are particularly motivated by high-level values such as peace of mind or personal security. Or, to cite an old business marketing adage from "Big Blue's" mainframe computing heyday, "Nobody got fired for specifying IBM." But, as we've noted earlier, psychological value drivers can be difficult or impossible to measure directly, and the proxy metrics researchers use—conjoint analysis, focus groups, expressed willingness to buy, for instance—can be misleading about the actual value the customer receives.

STEP 2: QUANTIFY VALUE DRIVERS

In the next step of estimating economic value, you gather the data needed to assign monetary amounts to each important value driver. Customer depth interviews are the best source of information. (See Chapter 13 for a discussion of pricing research methods.) Very different from survey or even focus group methods, depth interviews probe the underlying economics of the customer's business model and your product's prospective role in it. You are particularly interested in devising *value driver algorithms,* the formulas and calculations that estimate the differentiated monetary worth of each unit of product performance. In the Dyna-Test example, customer interviews indicated that using Dyna-Test saved 16 hours of processing labor compared to using EnSyn. Because laboratory personnel receive an average of $24 per hour, labor savings from Dyna-Test were about $384.

This kind of depth interview requires a different skill set than many qualitative research methods. Rather than striving for statistical precision, validity, reliability, and significance, the price researcher seeks approximations about complex customer processes that might defy accurate, to-the-decimal point calculations.

Note the assumptions behind GenetiCorp's estimation of the 17-year patent-period value of a new drug, for instance. It's critical, as a wise adage goes, to be approximately right rather than be precisely wrong. Depth interviews usually yield useful information about product and service needs, types of features to consider, attractive services to augment the product, and new ways to bundle product and service offerings.

STEP 3: ESTIMATE DIFFERENTIATION VALUE

The third step produces a clear understanding of the impact your product has in the competitive marketplace by estimating the monetary value it gives the customer beyond the value the customer can receive from buying the reference product. The answer depends on competitive offering prices and capabilities measured in terms familiar to customers in the segment (e.g., price per pound, price per hour). Be sure to state the reference value as the price for the quantity of competitive product a customer would buy to substitute for your product. If one unit of your product replaces two of theirs, then the reference value for your product is the price of two units of the NBCA.

Next, you build the economic value model using inputs from Step 2: the differentiated value drivers, value algorithms, and the financial and market data calculations. Remember to include both positive and negative drivers of differentiated value. Negative differentiation could include extra costs or reduced revenue associated with using your product compared to the NBCA, inferior performance on some attribute, or other negative consequences. For example, a more user-friendly software program might process information slower than the NBCA. Of course, your product's net differentiated value must be positive if you are to sell at prices at least as high as the NBCA's price.

As a final step, sum the reference value and the differentiation value to determine the *total economic value,* the value that someone would pay who was fully informed and economically rational when making the purchase decision.

To avoid several common errors when conducting an Economic Value Estimation®:

- Consider only the value of the *difference* between your product and the NBCA product. The value of any benefits that are the same as those delivered by the NBCA is already determined by competition. You can charge no more for them than the price of the NBCA product, regardless of their use value to the customer.
- Measure the differentiation value either as costs saved to achieve a particular level of benefit *or* as extra benefits achieved for an identical cost. Don't add both; that's double counting.
- Do not assume that the percentage increase in value is simply proportional to the percentage increase in the effectiveness of your product. Many additional factors might be affected. Although your part might last twice as long, your medicine might be effective in twice as many patients and your computer chip might be twice as fast, it does not follow that your value is

only twice as large. Not having to replace the part as often has greater value than the price of the part itself; downtime, labor costs, and other expenses avoided add to the more reliable product's value. Using a medicine that is twice as successful is worth much more than the doubled price; consider other medical costs and patient suffering saved. A faster computer chip may well enable computations to be completed that were impossible with two of the slower ones.

Having estimated value delivered, you can apply pricing strategies and policies to set selling prices, processes discussed at length in upcoming chapters. The point to consider here is that the relationship between prices and economic value delivered can differ depending on circumstances. For example, new products usually must be priced below economic value to motivate purchase. The prices of established products that already have the customer's business can include a "reputation premium," analogous to the inducement that the untested newcomer must offer. When buyers have little ability or interest to determine economic value, or when the cost of switching suppliers is high, the factors affecting the "inducement" or "premium" might be more important for pricing than the economic value.

THE STRATEGIC IMPORTANCE OF EVE®

Economic Value Estimation® is more than just an effective pricing tool. The feature-benefit-value chains EVE identifies should be the foundation of marketing strategy, guiding critical marketing and sales decisions. For example, identifying key value drivers for different customer segments provides a strategy blueprint for your offering options and account planning. Salespeople can proffer different product/service bundles to customers in different value-based market segments, trading individual customers up or down as needed depending on their price sensitivities. Armed with options, salespeople can counter price resistance in a sales negotiation by presenting lower-cost, lesser-feature offerings, keeping the discussion focused on customer value received rather than price paid.

Even before you set actual prices for existing products, EVE provides critical marketing strategy inputs. Your value-based market segmentation will identify different customer value models, with segment-specific reference products and value drivers most important. (We discuss value-based market segmentation in detail, beginning on p. 45.) Then you design value propositions—the reasons customers should buy—for each segment, making the best total value package and its price to a segment the anchor for your marketing communications and sales presentations to that segment. Make your claims credible and persuasive by using EVE information to document projected differential savings and revenue estimates.

Your differential value drivers also should weigh heavily in product and service development, and customer support strategies. Positive value drivers become the basis for product and service configurations that appeal to value-based segments. Negative value drivers should inspire corrective action such as customer support programs that help customers minimize switching and training costs.

Finally, your EVE should influence your distribution channel strategies. Which channels will best serve different value-based segments? Often value received or perceived is a more effective discriminator than top-line business firmographics for predicting who is more likely to buy. Different types of channels give you flexibility in how you deliver value to each segment. Brokers and wholesalers, while perhaps appropriate for routine purchases, might not provide adequate support for customers perceiving high risk in buying your product, for example.

VALUE-BASED MARKET SEGMENTATION

Market segmentation is one of the most important tasks in marketing. Identifying and describing market subgroups in a way that guides marketing and sales decision-making makes the marketing and pricing process much more efficient and effective. For example, customers who are relatively price insensitive, costly to serve, and poorly served by competitors can be charged more than customers who are price sensitive, less costly to serve, and are served well by competitors. At many companies, however, segmentation strategy focuses on customer attributes that are not useful for pricing decisions, creating customer groupings that do not adequately describe differences in purchase motivations among customers and prospects, or classify them in a way that's meaningful for making pricing decisions.

Consultants and market researchers abound who peddle various segmentation modeling schemes. Often those plans emphasize the obvious, such as statistical differences in personal demographics or company *firmographics* (customer size, standard industrial classification, etc.). While the results seem clear and sometimes coincidentally differentiate buying motivations, those segmentations seldom assist pricing decisions, especially for setting different prices that maximize profit from different segments. More useful are value-based segmentation models that facilitate pricing commensurate with actual value perceived and delivered to customers. Only then can a marketer ensure that each different customer subgroup is paying the most profitable price that the marketer can charge. Charging the entire market a single price risks undercharging some segments, causing foregone profit to you, and overcharging others, costing you additional foregone profit as those customers buy from other suppliers.

Significant differences between value-based segmentation and other methods are especially critical for pricing. First, most segmentation criteria correlate poorly with different buyers' motivations to pay higher or lower prices. Both plumbers and personal-injury lawyers consider yellow pages advertising to be very important, for example. They advertise to attract customers who have an immediate, unexpected, and high-value need. Directory publishers charge both groups the same advertising rates, but the lawyer can afford to pay more than the plumber because of the greater value of each legal client. Raising ad prices across the board would eventually price plumbers out of the yellow pages and into less expensive media, costing the publisher the plumbers' business. Value-based segmentation would illustrate each segment's different value received and the publisher could adjust prices by class of trade accordingly.

Second, even needs-based segmentations give priority only to those differences that are important to the customer. They miss the other half of the story, those customer needs that have the greatest operational impact on the seller's costs to serve those needs. The seller's costs and constraints are, however, important to pricing decisions, as we will see below.

Third, needs-based segmentations do not estimate the monetary value of satisfying high-priority customer needs. Value-based segmentations do.

Finally, the customer depth interviews required for value-based segmentations also uncover *why* customers find certain product benefits appealing—or would find them appealing were they sufficiently informed. Such knowledge reveals opportunities to develop new products and services and can reveal flawed strategies based on less comprehensive research. That is a lesson International Harvester Company (IH), in a classic example, learned the hard way.

For years, IH classified farmers according to surveys of farmer "benefit perceptions," particularly IH's equipment reliability compared to that of archrival John Deere. Farmers consistently rated Deere equipment as "more reliable," so IH invested heavily to ensure that a Deere tractor could not be more reliable than an IH tractor. Still, Deere kept leading the ranking. IH learned the true situation only when it conducted depth interviews. Asking farmers about repair problems revealed that IH breakdowns were no more frequent than with Deere equipment. The difference was the downtime caused by each breakdown. IH customers viewed them as a "big deal" to be avoided because of one to two days' lost productivity. But, Deere customers viewed Deere's equivalent reliability as much less of a problem because Deere's extensive, service-oriented dealer network stocked spare parts and offered loaner tractors, getting a farmer working again in less than a day. IH's benefit segmentation had missed the mark. A value segmentation would have revealed that Deere served a different segment of farmers—those driven by the value of a total-service solution, which perfectly fit Deere's strengths.

To conduct a value-based segmentation, we recommend a six-step process.

STEP 1: DETERMINE BASIC SEGMENTATION CRITERIA

The goal of any market segmentation is dividing a market into sub-groups whose members have common *criteria that differentiate their buying behaviors.* A simple example illustrates the concept. A business marketer of, say, an industrial grinding machine could segment customers in terms of their industries, their applications for which they use the marketers' product, or the total value they receive from the product. A segmentation by industry using industrial classification criteria would not indicate, however, whether customers use the grinders in similar ways. A segmentation based on application criteria would account for different ways of using the grinders, but would not indicate if the grinder is more important to one segment's business model than to another's. Only a segmentation based on value delivered by the grinder would reveal, for instance, that customers in one segment consider grinder use a small part of assembly line costs, while in another segment the grinder delivers much more value by performing a finishing step that allows the grinder buyer to earn a price premium from its customers. In our tractor marketing example, had IH chosen rapid service needs as its segmentation criterion, it would have seen that it could not match Deere's field service capabilities. Had IH done its homework, it would have realized that it needed to try and outweigh its service shortcomings with other offering attributes—which would be tough with farmers for whom downtime is very costly—or concentrate on other segments that put relatively more emphasis on attributes where IH excels.

Choosing appropriate segmentation criteria starts with a descriptive profile of the total market to identify obvious segments and differences among them. In consumer markets, basic demographics of age, gender, and income provide obvious discriminators. Enterprise firmographics such as revenue, industry, and number of employees clearly separate firms into nominally homogenous groups. Inputs for this basic analysis can include existing segmentation studies, industry databases, government statistics, and other secondary sources. Outputs include buying patterns, customer descriptions, a preliminary set of current customer needs, and a provisional list of unmet customer needs. You should be able to design first-pass segmentation maps based on those outputs. Along the way, check if those preliminary maps look sensible to salespeople and sales managers. Though your eventual pricing strategy will rely on value-based segmentation, communications and sales strategies are likely to be heavily dependent on those obvious customer characteristics on which media choices and sales territory assignments are based.

STEP 2: IDENTIFY DISCRIMINATING VALUE DRIVERS

Having preliminary segmentations in hand, you identify those value drivers— the purchase motivators—that vary the most among segments but which have more or less homogenous levels within segments. The GenetiCorp example earlier in this chapter determined that segments classified by obvious firmographics—commercial and nonindustrial research institutions—also differed on several cost-reduction and profit-enhancement value drivers. Never assume for pricing purposes, however, that preliminary segmentations based on obvious criteria will coincidentally yield effective discrimination on value criteria. Commercial and nonindustrial medical laboratories probably have similar needs, for instance, and derive similar value from an undifferentiated product such as laboratory glassware.

Depth interviews probing how and why buyers choose among competitive suppliers provide the input. Industry experts, distributors, and salespeople can provide supplemental information for double checking the value perception patterns revealed by the depth interviews. The outputs of this step include a number of useful building blocks for value-based market segmentation, including a list of value drivers ranked by their ability to discriminate among customers (statistical cluster analysis of quantitative data is a useful tool here), an explanation of why each driver adds value, and whether customers in each segment recognize that value. The list should also include the value the customer will receive if your product/service offering satisfies unmet needs.

STEP 3: DETERMINE YOUR OPERATIONAL CONSTRAINTS AND ADVANTAGES

In this step you examine where you have operational advantages. Which value drivers can you deliver more efficiently and at lower cost than others? Also, which drivers are constrained by your resources and operations? Experience, capital spending plans, personnel capabilities and overall company strategy are among the inputs to this step. Use the discipline of activity-based costing (a fascinating diagnosis of your own business, but a topic beyond the scope of this book) to build a *customer behavior spectrum* mapping your true costs serving different customers. Will some require more on-site service than others? Which have shorter decision-making cycles? Those factors contribute to customer profitability, value delivery, and the price you can charge for bundled and unbundled offering features. You should also examine competitive strengths and weaknesses on key drivers as closely as you can.

With these data, you can cross-reference and compare lists of customer needs served and unserved, the seller's advantages and resource limitations, and competitors' abilities. Where do you have sustainable competitive advantages, and where do rivals hold the upper hand? Which customers can you therefore better serve than can competitors, and which are likely to be beyond your reach, assuming that prospective customers are well-informed?

STEP 4: CREATE PRIMARY AND SECONDARY SEGMENTS

This step combines what you've learned so far about how customer values differ and about your costs and constraints in serving different customers. Unless you're comfortable with multivariate statistical analyses accounting for several value drivers simultaneously, you'll find it most convenient to segment your marketplace in multiple stages, value driver by value driver. The number of stages depending on the number of critical drivers that create substantial differences in value delivery among customer groups. In theory, your primary segmentation is based on the most important criterion differentiating your customers. Your secondary segmentation divides primary segments into distinct subgroups according to your second most important criterion. Your tertiary segmentation divides second segments based on the third most important criterion, and so on.

In practice, however, the deeper your successive segmentations, the more unmanageable the number of segments you identify. It doesn't make sense to split hairs by segmenting according to drivers with less than critical discriminating power. Minor differences among such subsegments will have little impact on pricing policies.

Also, your primary segmentation should account for your company's capabilities and constraints as well as customer needs. A primary value segmentation

EXHIBIT 3-8   Primary and Secondary Segmentation: Catalog Printing Industry

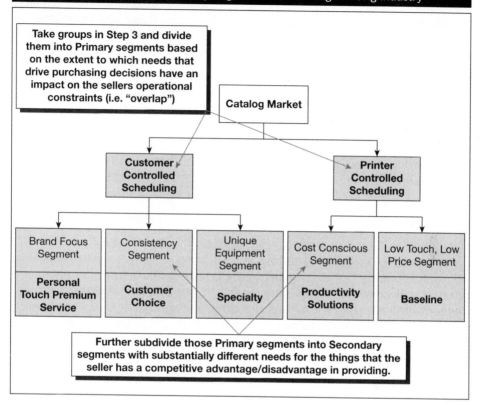

Take groups in Step 3 and divide them into Primary segments based on the extent to which needs that drive purchasing decisions have an impact on the sellers operational constraints (i.e. "overlap")

Further subdivide those Primary segments into Secondary segments with substantially different needs for the things that the seller has a competitive advantage/disadvantage in providing.

that recognizes such a "strategic overlap" discriminates on what is likely to be the most important differentiator among customers: the needs that have the most impact on the seller's operational constraints and whether those needs can be satisfied profitably, if at all. Your secondary segmentation therefore will use the value driver that varies the most among the subsegments within each primary segment.

The example in Exhibit 3-8 illustrates the process for an industry-leading commercial printing company serving catalog marketers. Catalog companies have a variety of printing needs. Some are primarily concerned with brand image and ensuring that their direct marketing integrates well with their other sales channels such as retail stores. Others have unique needs, such as publishers tailoring catalogs to particular segments of their markets by varying the "signatures" (groups of printed pages) bound into different parts of the print run. However, printing timing appears to be the major value differentiator. Some catalog companies insist on firm printing dates demanded by their business models, while others are more willing to let the printer determine when their jobs run. The strategic overlap is the implications that the constraints of a finite number of presses and so many hours in the day have for the costs of serving each timing-defined segment.

Exhibit 3-8 shows a primary segmentation based on the strategic overlap of customer scheduling needs and printer operational capabilities. Two primary segments emerge: buyers needing precise timing and those who are willing to relinquish timing control for a break on price. Within the "customer controlled scheduling" primary segment, three secondary segments have different needs for special service:

- A "brand focus" segment requires custom services and tailored solutions. (Using processes we describe in Chapter 4, we recommended that the printer offer these customers a personal-touch premium service at a premium price.)
- "Consistency" segment customers, more value-driven and concerned with their own margins, insist on getting what they pay for in standard services such as printing, binding, and trimming.
- A "unique equipment" segment has special needs such as odd trim sizes, small print orders, and customer-tailored binding, yet still wants control of the print scheduling process.

The printer originally treated the other primary segment, "printer-controlled scheduling," like all other customers, giving those customers priority treatment even as they demanded and negotiated lower prices. Value-based segmentation revealed, however, that these buyers would be willing to trade on-demand printing for reduced prices. The printer could schedule their jobs for off-peak demand periods when capacity otherwise would be idle. Secondary segments differed by the services they would trade for a lower price.

- A "cost conscious" segment responded to certain service options, which the printer called "productivity solutions."
- The "low-touch, low-price" segment accepted bare-bones service, even a requirement for Internet-only transactions, in return for even lower prices.

STEP 5: CREATE DETAILED SEGMENT DESCRIPTIONS
Value-based segmentation variables can look fine to the price strategist, but segments should be described in everyday business terms so that salespeople and marketing communications planners know what kinds of customers each segment represents. Exhibit 3-9 lists the needs and typical firmographics of the customer-controlled scheduling segment's three subsegments. It also lists specific catalog publishers within each segment.

STEP 6: DEVELOP SEGMENT METRICS AND FENCES
This is the next logical step in pricing strategy and management, a step we cover in greater detail in Chapter 4. Here, it's important to recognize that a segmentation isn't truly useful until you develop the metrics of value delivery to market segments and devise *fences* that encourage customers to accept price policies for their segments.

Metrics are the basis for tracking the value customers receive and how they pay for it. For example, car rental companies once used a distance-based value

EXHIBIT 3-9	Associate More Detailed Descriptions for Easier Identification		

	CUSTOMER CONTROLLED		
Segment	**Brand Focus**	**Consistency**	**Unique Capability**
Needs	• Maintain brand image across channels • Custom services tailored to customer needs • Proactive problem resolution development • High Maintenance • Full service bundled solutions	• Margin Management • Expects big 3 standard services, managed by the customer's staff • Precision Printer Performance • Moderate Maintenance • Needs Print/Bind, Dist—will provide won PMT • Paper supply options	• Products that are distinct to the end-user • Advanced targeting techniques to drive demand • Product longevity requires longer catalog shelf life
Representative Catalogs	• Coldwater Creek • Spiegel • Eddie Bauer • William Sonoma	• J Crew • Brylane • Fingerhut • Brooks Brothers	• Viking • Bon Marche • Quill • Industrial Catalogs
Key Demographics	• Large Print Order Quantities • Mid-size Catalogs • Prints 1-4 or > 12 times per year • Uses high quality paper grades • Mostly Saddle Stitched	• Small to Medium Print Order Quantities • Mostly Short Cut-off/ Standard Trim Sizes • Medium Sized Catalogs • Mostly Saddle Stitched	• Small Print Order Quantities • Smaller sized catalogs • Must have Supplied Component Parts • Catalogs carry numerous store brands • Higher percentage of B2B catalogs

metric and charged customers for the mileage traveled, in addition to the time used. Over time, competition forced rental companies to drop mileage charges. Time alone has become the market-recognized value metric. Sellers define discounts such as weekly and monthly rental rates on time bundles.

Fences are those policies, rules, programs, and structures that customers must follow to qualify for price discounts or rewards. For example, minimum volume requirements, time-based membership requirements, bundled purchase requirements, and so on keep prices paid and the value delivered to customers in line. Some fences can also force customers to pay higher prices regardless of the seller's costs; the notorious Saturday night stay requirements for reduced airline fares are a good example. Until competition forced airlines to drop the requirement, Saturday night stays effectively separated business travelers, who, presumably, could afford higher fares, from price-sensitive pleasure travelers.

You choose metrics and fences that establish and enforce premium prices for high value segments, and allow feature repackaging and unbundling to appeal to low-value and low-cost-to-serve segments. As we shall see later in this book, the result is a menu of prices, products, services, and bundles that reflect different value received for different prices paid.

Identifying value-based segments, the metrics of pricing offerings, and the fences that maintain a price structure allow a marketer to expand its profit margins by aligning its prices, service bundles, and capacity utilization with the different value levels demanded by different customers. That's a win-win balance for sellers and buyers; everyone gets something. But, as we will see in later chapters, just how much either side wins depends on how much each side captures the differential value created in a transaction. That's when meaningful price negotiations begin.

Summary

Although price is often more important to the seller than to the buyer, the buyer can reject any price higher than he is willing to pay. Firms that fail to recognize this fact and base price solely on their internal needs generally fail to attain their full profit potential. An effective pricing strategy requires a good understanding of the economic value the product delivers to buyers and the extent to which they recognize the value received. That is why Economic Value Estimation® can fail to capture the actual impact of price in individual decision making. Most consumers do not fit the fully informed "economic buyer" model who always seeks the best value in the market regardless of the effort required. Human factors similarly confound business transactions, such as when a purchasing agent receives a bonus for hammering prices down no matter what, or an engineer fears the risk of specifying a lesser-known supplier.

The analysis must go beyond economic value to the other factors driving the purchase decision. In addition, an effective segmentation must recognize the strategic overlap between seller capabilities and customer needs. Then, the value-based, perception-adjusted, and capacity-constrained segmentation model must be translated into the metrics that tell buyers what they get for their money, and into the fences that keep value delivered in line with price paid. Finally, segments must be described in ways that allow marketing communications people to deliver the right messages to the right audiences, and that allow salespeople to qualify prospects accurately.

Were the value creation process easy, everyone would be doing it. But, many companies still take the lazy route of simplistic segmentation and pricing that's clueless about value. If you're lucky enough to have such competitors, read on to learn how to expand your marketing advantage. If your competitors already know the strategy and tactics of value-based pricing, read on, and quickly!

Notes

1. In previous editions, we referred to this concept as "economic value analysis." Unfortunately that term was subsequently trademarked for an entirely different concept. See, for example, *The EVA Challenge: Implementing Value-added Change in an Organization,* by Joel M. Stern and John S.

Shiely (Toronto: John Wiley and Sons, 2001) and *EVA and Value-based Management: A Practical Guide to Implementation,* by S. David Young and Stephen F. O'Byrne (New York: McGraw-Hill, 2001).

Our firm, Strategic Pricing Group, Inc., has trademarked Economic Value Estimation® to preserve its meaning. We hereby grant anyone the right to use the term in this way so long as our trademark registration is acknowledged.

2. Decision makers frequently misperceive concisely stated estimates of demand elasticity, customer value, or competitive response as precise measures of stable underlying processes. In fact, such estimates are often inaccurate and give the decision maker a false sense of certainty. Instead, decision makers must recognize the probabilities and risks tied to estimates. A method of quantifying decisions without losing sight of the underlying uncertainty in the data is Bayesian analysis—definitely is the best approach for managers who are comfortable dealing with statistical possibilities—which predicts the likelihood of events based on past experiences.

3. For additional related discussion of this "proportional value-proportional price" argument see Gerald E. Smith and Thomas T. Nagle, "The Problem with Customer Value Modeling: For Pricing It Makes a Difference," *Marketing Management,* in press; and Gerald E. Smith and Thomas T. Nagle, "The Answer is Economic Value Modeling: For Pricing It Makes The Difference," *Marketing Management,* in press.

CHAPTER

4

PRICE STRUCTURE

Segmentation Pricing Tactics for Separating Markets

After developing products or services that create value for customers, a marketer must then determine how to capture a share of that value in the prices charged. Achieving that goal involves more than merely setting a price. Even well-informed customers value products differently, and for different reasons. Moreover, their demands for services, the timing of their needs, their procurement process, and the speed of their payments drive significant differences across customers in the cost to serve them. Often these differences reflect the different uses to which the product is put, the urgency of the need, or the availability of alternatives in the local market. Others reflect the motivations of the buyers themselves. Some customers are concerned with maximizing the benefits they receive and so are willing to pay premium prices for the best product or service, regardless of the alternatives. Others who also enjoy high value will nevertheless search the market for all alternatives to ensure that they pay no more than they have to. Still others can afford no more than the minimum necessary to meet their basic needs, and are willing to trade off services and to suffer a variety of inconveniences to achieve that end.

The failure to deal with this variety causes many companies to under perform in both profitability and market share. Unless a company has a price structure that operationally segments customers who receive different levels of economic value or cause different costs to serve them, management will struggle with one of two dilemmas. If it tries to serve all customers with one price, or a standard markup in the case of distributors and retailers, it will find itself squeezed between accepting low margins or low market share. If it attempts to negotiate different prices in an ad hoc, non-systematic way, customers will adopt procurement tactics to minimize the supplier's understanding of and ability to set prices aligned with the value delivered. Either way, much of the economic value that should be captured in profit will be lost.

To illustrate the huge benefits of a segmented price structure, suppose that a supplier faced five different segments, all willing to pay a different price to get the benefits they sought from a product (see Exhibit 4-1). Segment 1 with sales

54

EXHIBIT 4-1	The Benefits of Price Segmentation					
	A	*B*	*C*	*D*	*E*	*Total*
Viable prices	$20	$15	$10	$8	$6	
Segment's sales potential (000)	50	150	350	250	200	1,000
Percent of market	5	15	35	25	20	100
Contribution (,000) with:						
1 Price $10	$250	$750	$1,750	0	0	**$2,750**
2 Prices $15, $8	$500	$1,500	$1,050	$750	0	**$3,800**
5 Prices $20, $15, $10, $8, $6	$750	$1,000	$1,750	$750	$200	**$4,950**

Source: Richard Harmer. "Strategies for Segmented Pricing," The Pricing Institute 6th Annual Conference (Chicago, March 22–25, 1993).

potential of 50,000 units is willing to pay $20 for the firm's product. Segment 2 with sales potential of 150,000 units is willing to pay $15, and so on. What price should the firm set? The right answer in principle is whatever price maximizes profit contribution. If you calculate the profit contribution at each of the five prices assuming a variable cost of $5 per unit, the single price that produces the maximum contribution ($2,750) is $10.

However, a single price strategy clearly leaves excess money on the table for many buyers who are willing to pay more: those willing to pay $20 and $15. These high-end buyers perceive significantly greater value from purchasing this product, relative to other buyers. At the price of $10, they are enjoying a lot of what economists call "consumer surplus." The firm would be better off if it could capture some of this surplus by charging higher prices to these buyers.

The second problem is that the supplier leaves nearly half of the market unsatisfied, even though it could serve those customers at prices above the $5 per unit variable cost. In industries with high fixed costs, serving those additional customers is very tempting, and possibly very profitable. Moreover, by ignoring these buyers, the firm leaves an opportunity wide open for low-cost competitors to enter the market and establish a competitive presence. Xerox's dominance of the photocopier market was undermined when Japanese competitors entered with low-end copiers to serve markets that Xerox considered too marginal to be bothered pursuing. When those competitors won a large enough installed base at the low end to establish a reliable service network, they were then able to attack Xerox's higher-margin markets.

How many segments with associated price points should the supplier serve? To return to our illustration, Exhibit 4-1 shows that if the firm were to set two price points serving two general price segments—high-end buyers willing to pay $15 or more, and mid-level buyers willing to pay $8 or more—it could increase profit contribution by 40 percent. But if the supplier could charge separate prices to each of the five market segments, it could increase profit contribution by 80 percent relative to the single price strategy. In principle, more segmentation is always better. In practice, however, the extent of price segmentation is limited by the creativity of the pricer and the cost to enforce the segments.

If charging different customers different prices were easy, everyone would do it. In fact, customers who received higher prices have every incentive to undermine segmented pricing—and often do. Customers whom management would like to charge a higher price will not identify themselves as members of a relatively price-insensitive segment simply to help the seller charge them a higher price. Rather, they will learn how to disguise themselves as customers who qualify for a lower price. Or, if they need the sellers' technical advice or sales support, customers will buy the minimum they need to qualify for it, but then buy the balance of their needs from cheaper suppliers who don't offer those services. Distributors too can undermine a segmented-pricing strategy. If they can figure out how to buy the product cheaply and resell it to segments that will pay more, they can capture the profit from segmented pricing for themselves.

How can the firm charge different prices to different customers? The answer is by creating a profit-driven price structure that varies not just the price, but also the offer or the criteria to qualify for it. A profit-driven price structure is one that causes revenues to vary with differences in the two key elements that drive potential profitability: the economic value that customers receive and the incremental cost to serve them. Achieving that objective requires finding, or creating, appropriate measurable criteria for price variation. The criteria come in two types: continuous, which we refer to as *price metrics,* and discontinuous, which we refer to as *price fences.*

PRICE METRICS

Price metrics are the units to which the price is applied. They define the terms of exchange—what exactly will the buyer receive per unit of price paid. For example, a health club could set its prices per hour, per visit, per "membership" providing unlimited access for a period of time, or per unit of performance (inches lost at the hips or gained at the chest). It could also vary prices by time of day (low for a mid-day membership, higher for peak-time membership) or by season of the year. In addition, it could bundle towels, bottles of spring water, and personal trainer advice into the fees, or charge for them separately. Although seemingly minor choices, how the health club sets its fees will determine the nature and breadth of its clientele, its costs per member, and its ability to price competitively.

PERFORMANCE-BASED METRICS

An ideal price metric would tie what the customer pays directly to the economic value received and the incremental cost to serve. In a few cases, called "performance-based" pricing, price structures can actually work that way.[1] Attorneys often litigate cases for which they are paid their out-of-pocket expenses plus a share of the award that is won, rather than for hours worked. Internet ads are usually priced based on the number of "click-thrus" rather the traditional metric of cost "per exposure." Systems that control the lights, heating, and cooling within office buildings are sometimes installed in return for contracts that share the energy cost saving, rather than charges for the equipment installed. In each case, the price metric naturally charges customers differently for the same product or service based on differences in the value they receive.

Performance-based pricing has the added effect of shifting the performance risk from the buyer to the seller. General Electric (GE) used bundling to reduce risk when it launched a new series of highly efficient aircraft engines, its GE90 series. These engines promised greater fuel efficiency and power that could make them much more profitable to operate. The catch was a high degree of uncertainty about the cost of maintenance. Some airlines feared that these high-powered engines might need to be overhauled more frequently, thus easily wiping out the financial benefits from operating them. This undermined GE's ability to win buyers at the price premium that power and fuel efficiency would otherwise justify.

Rather than accept a lower price to account for a buyer's perceived risk, GE absorbed the risk by changing the price metric. Instead of selling or leasing an engine alone, GE offered to sell "power by the hour." For the first time, customers could lease a GE aircraft engine for a fee per hour flown that included all costs of scheduled and unscheduled maintenance. Without the uncertainty of maintenance cost, GE90 engines quickly became popular despite a price premium. In fact, the program was so popular that GE extended it by offering a "Maintenance Cost per Hour" program on its older engines with established maintenance track records.

In most cases, however, "performance-based pricing" is simply impractical. It requires too much information and too much trust that the buyer will actually report the information accurately. It also leaves the buyer uncertain regarding the cost of a purchase until after it is used. In practice, therefore, marketers must design profit-driven price structures by finding measures that only roughly predict the value a customer will receive and the costs to serve. Often the difference between a good and a great pricing strategy lies in finding, or creating, such measures.

CREATING GOOD METRICS

The problem with most price structures is that they are adopted by default or tradition, rather than to achieve the strategic goals of value capture and cost control. For example, initially software companies charged a price per copy installed on one "server" machine. In most cases, that led to a poor alignment with value. A few creative vendors recognized that when more users accessed the software, the buyer was getting more value. Consequently, they changed the price metric from a price "per server" to a price "per seat," resulting in customers paying more who had more users accessing the software. When this "per seat" metric proved much more profitable for the computer-aided design and financial analysis companies that adopted it, other software companies copied it. For many of their applications, however, the number of users still aligned poorly with value, leaving many customers underpriced while pricing others out of the market. The most thoughtful among them created still better price metrics. Leaders in manufacturing software replaced "price per seat" with "price per production unit." Storage management software suppliers replaced "price per server" with a "price per gigabit of data moved." Each time a company discovers a better metric than its competitors, it gains margin from existing customers and/or incremental revenue from customers formerly priced out of its markets.

The key to improving your metrics is first to understand the extent to which existing metrics align with value and cost to serve. What portion of your market gets economic value (relative to their alternatives) substantially in excess of what they pay? What portion involves differential costs to serve that are so substantial that their business is marginally profitable at best? How much volume are you missing that you could serve profitably on an incremental basis but for the price charged? The answers to these questions comprise your business case for change.

If there is a lot of margin and/or sales lost due to a poorly chosen price metric, then you need to identify an improved alternative. First, after identifying what causes different customers to have different economic value received or different cost to serve, begin brainstorming all the possible metrics that could be viable alternatives. Which track with value and/or cost differences? If one works even partly, it could be part of a bundle of metrics used to capture value from the market. Is the metric measurable and enforceable? If you can't get the data, or you can't get it until after the customer already has used the product, you may not be able to enforce what could otherwise be an ideal choice. Can pricing be structured according to the metric within the constraints of your channels? If the channels can profit by manipulating the customer orders to achieve discounts that they then pocket for themselves, they almost certainly will.

Another very important consideration is how the metric makes your pricing appear in comparison with competitors' pricing, and the impact of that on the perceived attractiveness of your offer. Consider, for example, the software company that introduced new hosted voice-recognition software that enabled a call center to meet the needs of more callers without their speaking with a live operator. The value of processing calls faster and without human intervention was huge. Unfortunately, the traditional metric for hosted call center software was a price per minute. Since voice-recognition software processes callers faster, a value-based price using that metric would be at least three times the price per minute for traditional software—inviting resistance from purchasers. To overcome that, the company adopted a new metric based on "cost per call processed." That metric naturally required conversion of the competitors' cost-per-minute metric into a

	Traditional Caller-Response Software	Natural Voice-Recognition Software	Percent Difference
EXHIBIT 4-2 Hosted Call Center Software			
Call Length	7.2 minutes	4.4 minutes	−39%
"Price" of software per minute	0.90	$1.55	+72%
"Price" of software per call	$6.48	$6.82	+5%
% of calls requiring human intervention	47%	12%	
Cost of Operator Intervention	$3.50	$3.50	
Total cost per minute	$1.13	$1.65	+46%
Total cost per call	$8.14	$7.26	−11%

cost-per-call metric. While the new software was still more expensive, its percent price premium was much smaller when framed in terms of cost per call than in terms of a cost per minute (see Exhibit 4-2). Moreover, the differentiation value of the avoided operator intervention was much larger on a per-call basis than on a per-minute basis. Thus the total cost per call was less with the new software, despite being higher on a per minute basis. While the favorable economics of the new software was exactly the same using either metric, the per-call basis of comparison made the attractiveness of the economics much more apparent.

MANAGING COSTS WITH METRICS

When customers' behavior influences the incremental cost to serve them and those costs are significant, profit-maximizing price metrics need to reflect that as well. A service cost is significant if the cost of measuring, monitoring, and charging for differences in its usage exceeds the cost to deliver it. Marketers are often reluctant to charge for services due to fear that, if others offer similar services, they will become uncompetitive. In fact, the opposite is the case. Giving services for "free" attracts those customers who are higher users of them. For example, customers who want to minimize their inventories will gravitate to suppliers who offer free rush orders. Customers with a lot of employee turnover and poor equipment maintenance will gravitate to equipment suppliers who offer unlimited and quick on-site service. Customers who are minimum service users will, in similar fashion, gravitate to competitors offering little or no service but lower prices. As a result, the differentiated high-service supplier in many markets is the least profitable because of its high "overheads."

By adding charges for services, or at least for those customers who are excessively costly to serve, companies are able to keep their core product prices competitive and avoid attracting a mix of customers who are high cost to serve. As their markets have become more competitive, software suppliers have added charges for formerly "free" online telephone support. Banks have added charges for small account holders to use a teller, or to access a teller machine more than some minimum amount. United Parcel Service added a $1.75 charge for delivery to a residential address, a $5 charge for customers who don't put their account number on their delivery slip, and a $10 charge for a wrong address. These charges reflect the added cost of service for such packages, and the tendency for customers to cause those costs when they don't have to pay for them. Suppliers without such charges can price competitively for the core business (the software, the checking account, the package delivery) of those customers who are lower cost to serve, while still attracting higher cost customers if they are willing to pay for higher service levels that they demand.

As these examples illustrate, establishing new pricing metrics need not involve replacing the prior commodity-based metric entirely. They simply enable the supplier to lower prices on the commodity-based metric while adding new ones to the mix to create a better alignment of prices with differences in value and service costs across segments. A commodity chemical supplier traditionally priced its product based on "price per ton" for each product grade. We helped that company profitably cut its "price per ton," thus attracting new customers, while simultaneously increasing its plant efficiency by adding charges for "rush orders" and "special orders." We also encouraged longer-term, more easily scheduled business by adding a discount for standing orders that were unchanged within 10 days of shipment. The company attracted more standing order customers, drove its worst "rush order" customer to the competition, and got higher margins from its special order accounts. More importantly, the new mix of customers substantially improved plant productivity as well as company profitability.

PRICE FENCES TO OPERATIONALLY SEGMENT MARKETS

Because metrics are based on the type and quantity of features and service that customers buy, they work well when buyer needs define the customer segments. Often, however, value and/or cost to serve differs across customers for reasons that have nothing to do with what they want or need. To make the price structure reflect those differences requires the use of price "fences" in addition to metrics.[2] Price fences are criteria that customers must meet to qualify for a lower price. At theaters, museums, and similar venues, price fences are usually based on age (with discounts for children under 12 years of age and for seniors) but are sometimes also based on educational status (full-time students get discounts), or possession of a coupon from a local paper (which benefit "locals"). All three types of customers have the same needs and cost to serve them, but perceive a different value from the purchase.

Price fences are the least complicated way to charge different prices to reflect different levels of value. Unfortunately, while simple to administer, the obvious price fences are often too easy for customers to get over whenever there is an economic incentive to do so. Americans looking for discounts on

VALUE-BASED PRICING FINANCES HAMLET'S CASTLE

The seeds of value-based pricing were planted centuries ago with the first documented use of value-based pricing metrics to improve profitability. The use occurred in *the* 15th century when Erik of Pomerania, King of the United Kingdom of Scandinavia, summoned to Copenhagen a group of merchants from the powerful German Hanseatic League, which at the time dominated nearly all trade in northern Europe. He informed them that henceforth he intended to levy a new toll: Every ship wishing to sail past Elsinore, whether on its way out of or into the Baltic, would have to dip its flag, strike its topsails, and cast anchor so that the captain might go ashore to pay the customs officer in the town a toll of 'one English noble'.

Nobody challenged the right of the King of all Scandinavia to impose a toll of this kind. After all, mere barons who owned castles on the banks of the Rhine, the Danube, and other major European waterways had for centuries forced all passing ships to pay a similar toll. However, its relative heaviness, combined with the obligation to cast anchor at Elsinore in order to hand over the money, made it highly unpopular. Erik foresaw that if he also established a proper town at Elsinore, sea-captains, after paying their toll and then waiting for a favourable wind, would welcome an opportunity to replenish stocks of water, wine, meat, vegetables, and whatever else they needed. In other words, even if they had to pay toll, calling in at Elsinore could have its attractions—all he had to do was provide them.

Elsinore's fortunes changed in 1559 with the accession to the throne of Frederik II, aged 25. He was young, ambitious, and entertained imperialistic ideas about reconquering Sweden and restoring the Nordic Union. [Consequently,] he declared war, and it dragged on for seven years. Like all wars, it was a severe drain on Denmark's finances. By 1566 the situation was so serious that Frederik II and his councillors decided as a last resort to enlist the help of a man with special talents named Peder Oxe. Oxe was acknowledged to be a financial wizard, which was just what Frederick needed.

Erik of Pomerania's toll fee of one English noble per ship had long been regarded by skippers and shipowners as grossly unfair. After all, ships were of so many different sizes, carried so many different cargoes, and according to nationality, had various interests and affiliations. But the system had also been proving increasingly disadvantageous from the Danish king's point of view. The first four or five kings after Erik of Pomerania had therefore continually tried to introduce amendments of one kind or another, and these in turn made it necessary to introduce

(Continued)

various special concessions. Some nationalities were exempted completely and others enjoyed preferential treatment in certain respects.

By this time, the basic toll had been raised from one to three nobles per ship, but it was still far from being a satisfactory system. Peder Oxe realized that the only answer lay in a radical reform of the whole basis upon which the [tolls] were calculated. Henceforth, instead of a simple toll per ship, payment must be made, he suggested, on the basis of the cargo carried: to start with, two rix-dollars 'per last' [a 'last' being approximately two tons of cargo]. Soon this was changed to an even subtler and more flexible system: a percentage of the *value* of each last of cargo.

The King held the right of pre-emption, that is to say an option to buy, if he so chose, all cargoes declared. This royal prerogative encouraged the captain of a ship to make a correct declaration. Naturally, if he thought the King might be interested in buying his cargo, he was tempted to put a high value on it. However, in doing so he ran the risk that His Majesty might be totally disinterested, in which case he would have to pay a duty calculated on this high valuation. Conversely, if he played safe and declared a low value in the hope of getting away with paying a low duty, the King might decide to buy the whole consignment which could leave the captain seriously out of pocket.

Summoning Peder Oxe to reorganize the levying of the Sound Dues proved to be a masterful stroke: Within a few years the King's income from this source practically tripled. At the age of thirty-eight, Frederik II married his fifteen-year-old cousin, Sophie of Mecklenburg, and in 1574 embarked on what was to become the major architectural project of his life: the building of a new castle at Elsinore.

Abridged from *Hamlet's Castle and Shakespeare's Elsinore* by David Hohnen (Copenhagen: Christian Ejlers, 2000)

---

pharmaceuticals travel to Canada to buy the same brands at lower prices, thwarting the geographic fence. Purchasers join together into "buying groups" to overcome a price fence meant to favor volume buyers. People get the student in their family or retired relatives to make purchases for them, undermining discounts intended for those price-sensitive groups. The art of price fencing involves not only finding a natural separation of buyers by price sensitivity, but also a means to enforce the separation.

We will describe seven generic approaches to segment using price fences and identify the criteria necessary for their success. We will also illustrate the creative ways that each has been used. Your success with segmented pricing will depend on picking a generic approach that reflects differences in value and cost-to-serve within your market, and then creating metrics and fences that are enforceable within your industry.

SEGMENTING BY BUYER IDENTIFICATION

Occasionally pricing differently among segments is easy because buyers in the different segments have obvious characteristics that distinguish them. Barbers charge different prices for short and long hair because long hair is usually more difficult to cut. During nonpeak hours, barbers cut children's hair at a substantial discount because many parents view home haircuts as acceptable alternatives to costly barber cuts for their children. For barbers, simple observation of the customers is the key to segmented pricing. Banks and Internet mortgage lenders are increasingly using quantitative models to evaluate a set of buyer characteristics to design a mortgage package that uniquely reflects each buyer's likely alternatives and the cost to serve her. These lenders combine computer-based data, such as the person's credit score, geographic location, neighboring property values, property taxes, primary versus secondary residence, whether the borrower is a potential repeat customer, occupation—teachers and doctors are considered good credit risks, for example. The person's profile can then be processed and approved within hours, with a mortgage rate and closing points that uniquely match the credit-worthiness and potential risk-adjusted profitability of the buyer. Many companies offer discounts for nonprofit organizations and governmental departments, which are more price sensitive than for-profit businesses because the quality of their services rarely affects the revenues they take in. Thus they generally equate good value with low price.

Although observation is the most common method of segmentation—and is being aided by online technologies—it is often ineffective or counterproductive. Some sellers naively think they can segment simply by being responsive to those customers who complain about the price. For example, some mid-level and even upper-level hotel chains have tried offering customers the "regular" room rate first. If the customer indicates that the price is too high, they query the customer about possible ways they might qualify for a small discount [e.g., Automobile Association of America (AAA) membership]. If the customer still resists and the hotel anticipates excess capacity for that night, the reservation agent will create some excuse to offer a still better rate from a "special block" of discounted rooms.

Although some hotels still do this, most have learned their lesson. The customers who complain are rarely the most price sensitive. On the contrary, they are the frequent, seasoned business travelers who learn quickly about a hotel's segmentation scheme and love to negotiate. They also love to brag to the other business travelers they meet at the hotel's bar about how they paid a lower rate. In contrast, the people who don't complain are more likely to be pleasure travelers who are more price sensitive but don't know the game. Instead of negotiating the price, they will simply hang up and call an economy option like Motel 6.

Even less effective is the tactic of some business-to-business salespeople of discounting when customers complain about prices. Large business customers can afford professional actors—better known as purchasing agents—who have mastered the art of acting price sensitive even when they are not. When constrained by engineering or manufacturing to purchase from a particular supplier, they may still solicit other bids to extract discounts. Salespeople who don't understand this game end up giving away value unnecessarily to these large customers. Effective price segmentation requires basing discounts on more objective indicators of price sensitivity than mere complaining.

Rarely is identification of customers in different segments straightforward. Yet, management can sometimes structure a pricing policy that induces the most price-sensitive buyers to volunteer objective information necessary to segment them based on known demographic data that clearly identifies a price-sensitive segment. For example, teachers and educators in the public sector are more price sensitive than similar professionals within companies, yet they are highly desirable customers because of their influence on other potential buyers. Consequently, software companies will offer substantial discounts to teachers and educators provided they present documentation verifying their current status as educators. Theaters give discounts to college students who are more price sensitive because of their low incomes and their alternative sources of campus entertainment. Students readily volunteer their college identification cards to prove that they are members of the price-sensitive segment. Members of the less price-sensitive segment identify themselves by not producing such identification.

Even schools and colleges charge variable tuitions for the same education based on their estimates of their students' price sensitivities. Although the official school catalogs list just one tuition, it is not the one most students pay at private colleges. Most receive substantial discounts called "tuition remission scholarships" obtained by revealing personal information on financial-aid applications. By evaluating family income and assets, colleges can set tuition for each student that makes attendance attractive while still maximizing the school's income.

Deal proneness is another form of self-induced buyer identification—especially through the use of coupons and sales promotions, a frequent tool of consumer marketers. Coupons provided by the seller give deal-prone shoppers a way to identify themselves.[3] Supermarkets put coupons in their newspaper ads because people who read those ads are part of the segment that compares prices before deciding where to shop. Packaged-good and small appliance manufacturers print coupons and rebate instructions directly on the packages, expecting that only price-sensitive shoppers will make the effort to clip them out and use them for future purchases.[4]

Adept consumer marketers use coupons with differing discount levels to attract different price segments. For example, deep discount coupons are used to attract brand switchers or first-time users. More modest discount coupons are often included inside the product's package to encourage buyers to repurchase the brand; these repeat buyers are less price sensitive than brand switchers because they have experienced the benefits of the product. People who use the coupons are, however, assumed to be more price sensitive than people who cannot be bothered to use coupons at all.

Often a buyer's relative price sensitivity does not depend on anything immediately observable or on factors a customer freely reveals. It depends instead on how well informed about alternatives a customer is and on the personal values the customer places on the differentiating attributes of the seller's offer. In such cases, the classification of buyers by segment usually requires an expert salesperson trained in soliciting and evaluating the information necessary for segmented pricing.

The retail price of an automobile is typically set by the salesperson, who evaluates the buyer's willingness to pay. Notice how the salesperson takes a personal interest in the customer, asking what the customer does for a living (ability to pay), how long he has lived in the area (knowledge of the market), what kinds of cars she has bought before (loyalty to a particular brand), where she lives (value placed on the dealer's location), and whether she has looked at, or is planning to look at, other cars (awareness of alternatives). By the time a deal has been put together, the experienced salesperson has a fairly good idea how sensitive the buyer's purchase decision will be to the product's price.

SEGMENTING BY PURCHASE LOCATION

When customers who perceive different values buy at different locations, they can be segmented by purchase location. This is common practice for a wide range of products. Dentists, opticians, and other professionals sometimes have multiple offices in different parts of a city, each with a different price schedule reflecting differences in their clients' price sensitivity. Many grocery chains classify their stores by intensity of competition and apply lower markups in those localities where competition is most intense. Ski resorts near Denver use purchase location to segment sales of lift tickets. Tickets purchased slope side are priced the highest and are bought by the most affluent skiers who stay in the slope side hotels and condos. Tickets are cheaper (approximately 10 percent less) at hotels in the nearby town of Dillon, where less affluent skiers stay in cheaper, off-slope accommodations. In Denver, tickets can be bought at grocery stores and self-serve gas stations for larger discounts (approximately 20 percent less). These discounts attract locals, who know the market well, including the less advertised tourist spots, and who are generally more price sensitive.

Segmentation by location occurs quite often in international marketing. Deutsche Grammophon historically has sold its music CDs for up to 50 percent more in the European market than in the highly competitive U.S. market. After the dollar depreciated relative to other major currencies, many American electronics and equipment companies have maintained higher prices in Europe and Asia than in America. Typically, industrial manufacturers must charge less to the bargain-conscious Chinese than to the wealthy sheiks of the Mideast. Such geographic price segmentation works when high shipping costs or the need for after-sale service ensure that buyers in low-price countries will not order goods for resale in countries where prices are higher.

A clever segmented pricing tactic common for pricing bulky industrial products such as steel and coal is *freight absorption*. Freight absorption is the agreement by the seller to bear part of the shipping costs of the product, the amount of which depends upon the buyer's location. The purpose is to segment buyers according to the attractiveness of their alternatives. A steel mill in Pittsburgh, for example, might agree to charge buyers the cost of shipping from either Pittsburgh or from Chicago, where its major competitor is located. The seller in Pittsburgh receives only the price the buyer pays, less the absorbed portion of any excess cost to ship from Pittsburgh. This enables the Pittsburgh supplier to cut price to customers nearer the competitor without having to cut price to customers for whom his Chicago competitors have no location advantage. The Chicago competitor probably uses the same tactic to become more competitive for buyers nearer Pittsburgh.

Trade barriers between countries used to make segmentation by location viable even for products that are inexpensive to ship. As trade barriers have declined around the world, and especially within the European Union, the tactic has increasingly become less effective. For example, automobiles used to be sold throughout Europe at prices that varied widely across borders. German luxury cars sold in Britain were often 20 percent more expensive than when sold just across the channel in Belgium. Now, brokers in Britain will survey the continent for cars, which people can fly to and drive home—or have the broker bring it back for them. Fortunately, there are usually alternatives to segmenting by location that are equally effective, but more difficult to craft.

SEGMENTING BY TIME OF PURCHASE

When customers in different market segments purchase at different times, one can segment them for pricing by time of purchase. Theaters segment their markets by offering midday matinees at substantially reduced prices, attracting the price-sensitive retirees, students, and unemployed workers who can most easily attend at such times. Less price-sensitive evening patrons cannot so easily arrange dates or work schedules to take advantage of the cheaper midday ticket prices. Similarly, restaurants usually charge more to their evening patrons, even if they cater primarily to a lunch crowd. There are more numerous inexpensive substitutes for lunches than there are for dinners. A Big Mac or a brown bag, acceptable for lunch, is generally viewed as a poor substitute for a formal dinner as part of an evening's entertainment.

Priority pricing is one example of segmenting by time of purchase. New products in a retail store are offered at full price, or sometimes premium surcharges over full price in the case of extreme excess demand. Over time, as product appeal fades in comparison to other newer and better competitive alternatives, buyers discount the product's value until they are willing to pay only a fraction of its original price for leftover models. This is a frequent tactic in the retail fashion and automobile industries, where customers with high incomes and low price sensitivity pay premium prices for the latest lines and models and can choose from a full inventory of sizes and colors. Over time, as inventories age and the availability of sizes and colors declines, prices are reduced in successive rounds of promotions to appeal to more price-sensitive buyers who are willing to wait for the opportunity to buy high-quality, but less trendy, inventory and with less certainty of obtaining their preferred size or color.

Priority pricing also applies in business-to-business purchases. A favorite strategy of Intel is to introduce a leading-edge semiconductor at a premium price, and then discount its existing semiconductor product lines. Leading edge original equipment manufacturer (OEM) computer manufacturers who produce and sell the fastest and latest computers to innovative professional buyers with low price sensitivity pay the price premium for the latest chip technology. More price-sensitive buyers who are willing to accept slightly outdated technology are then offered older-model computers equipped with Intel's now older semiconductors at lower prices.

Similarly, most television and radio stations charge premium prices for their highly perishable inventory of advertising time by offering discounts for "pre-emptible" ads. Price-sensitive buyers of advertising inventory pay low prices for high levels of preemptibility. When other less price-sensitive buyers come along wanting a highly desirable prime-time advertising slot that has already been sold to a customer paying a lower preemptible rate, the original price-sensitive customer's ad can be displaced.

Periodic sales offering the same merchandise at discounted prices can also segment markets. This tactic is most successful in markets with a combination of occasional buyers who are relatively unfamiliar with the market, and with more regular buyers who know when the sales are and plan their purchases accordingly. Furniture manufacturers employ this tactic with sales every February and August, months when most people usually would not think about buying furniture. However, people who regularly buy home furnishings, and who are more price sensitive because of the reference price and total expenditure effects, know to plan their purchases to coincide with these sales.

Segmenting by time is also useful when demand varies significantly with the time of purchase but the product or service is not storable. Airlines, for example, face greater demand for seats on Mondays, Thursdays, and Fridays than on other days. Early morning and late afternoon departures are also more in demand than departures during the midday and evening. An airline, however, cannot store the excess seats it has on Tuesdays in order to meet exceptional demand on Fridays. Seats left unused on Tuesday flights are lost, whereas the ability to serve customers on Friday afternoon is limited by capacity at that time. The same general problem plagues hotels and restaurants, electric utilities, long-distance telephone companies, theaters, computer time-sharing companies, beauty salons, toll bridges, and parking garages. Unable to move supplies of their products from one time to another, their only option is to manage demand. One way of doing so is with peak-load pricing, the implementation of which we will discuss in Chapter 8 when we explain how to account for capacity costs in pricing.[5]

Pricing for travel through the Eurotunnel between England and France is an interesting application of segmented pricing for a product with fixed capacity. The channel tunnel allows transport of an automobile and its occupants for a flat price between Folkestone, England, and Calais, France (see Exhibit 4-3). Prices that allow travel at whatever time of day you choose are twice as high (£39 day round-trip) as during the off-peak evening and night period (£19 day round-trip). This reflects the opportunity cost of limited capacity. More interesting is the fact that rates increase with the time elapsed between the outbound and the return trips—from £39 for return within 1 day, to £89.00 for return within 2 to 5 days, to £124

EXHIBIT 4-3 Eurotunnel Price Structure

These offers may be withdrawn at any time

REGULAR FARES

Day Trip Return

A supplement of £6 applies on certain dates: click here for more details

Ticket name	Travel Validity (day/time)	Advanced Booking	Amendable	Refundable	Car Prices from[2]	Motorcycle Prices from[2]
Afternoon	Mon-Sun Outward after 12.00 Inward before midnight same day	1 day	Yes £10 fee[4]	No	£34	£34
Late Afternoon	Mon-Sat Outward after 15.00 Inward before 01.00 next day	1 day	Yes £10 fee[4]	No	£29	£29
Evening	Mon-Sat Outward after 18.00 Inward before 02.00 next day	1 day	Yes £10 fee[4]	No	£19	£19
Flexible	All	1 day	Yes	Yes	£39	£39
Standard	All	none[3]	Yes	Yes	£97	£97

Overnighter Return

A supplement of £6 applies on certain dates: click here for more details

Ticket name	Travel Validity (day/time)	Advanced Booking	Amendable	Refundable	Car Prices from[2]	Motorcycle Prices from[2]
Weekday	Mon-Thu Outward after 12.00 Inward between 06.00 and 15.00 next day	1 day	Yes £10 fee[4]	No	£39	£39
Weekend	Fri-Sun Outward after 12.00 Inward between 06.00 and 15.00 next day	1 day	Yes £10 fee[4]	No	£39	£39

Short Stay Return (from 2 to 5 calendar days)

Ticket name	Travel Validity (day/time)	Advanced Booking	Amendable	Refundable	Car Prices from[2]	Motorcycle Prices from[2]
Saver	All	7 days	Yes £30 fee[4]	Yes £40 fee	£153	£73.50
Weekend	Must include a Saturday night	1 day	Yes £30 fee[4]	Yes £40 fee	£163	£78.50
Flexible	All	3 days	Yes	Yes	£173	£83.50
Standard	All	None[3]	Yes	Yes	£183	£89.00

Long Stay Return (more than 5 day return)

Ticket name	Travel Validity (day/time)	Advanced Booking	Amendable	Refundable	Car Prices from[2]	Motorcycle Prices from[2]
Saver	Mon-Thu	14 days	Yes £30 fee[4]	Yes £60 fee	£223	£108.00
Flexible	All	3 days	Yes	Yes	£243	£118.00
Standard	All	None[3]	Yes	Yes	£253	£124.00

for return 5 or more days after departure. Clearly, this has nothing to do with cost, so what drives it? The answer is that the value of having your own car with you on the trip, versus having to rent one after traveling by plane or train, increases with the length of the stay.[6]

SEGMENTING BY PURCHASE QUANTITY

When customers in different segments buy different quantities, one can sometimes segment them for pricing with quantity discounts. Quantity discount tactics are of four types: volume discounts, order discounts, step discounts, and two-part prices. All are common when dealing with differences in price sensitivity, costs, and competition.[7] Customers who buy in large volume are usually more price sensitive. They have a larger financial incentive to learn about all alternatives and to negotiate the best possible deal. Moreover, the attractiveness of selling to them generally increases competition for their business. Large buyers are often less costly to serve. Costs of selling and servicing an account generally do not increase proportionately with the volume of purchases. In such cases, volume discounting is a useful tactic for segmented pricing.

Volume discounts are most common when selling products to business customers. Steel manufacturers grant auto companies substantially lower prices than they offer other industrial buyers. They do so because auto manufacturers use such large volumes they could easily operate their own mills or send negotiators around the world to secure better prices. Volume discounts are based on the customer's total purchases over a month or year rather than on the amount purchased at any one time. At some companies, the discount is calculated on the volume of all purchases; at others, it is calculated by product or product class. For example, Xerox gives volume discounts based on a buyer's total purchases of copiers, typewriters, and printers. Many companies give discounts for multiple purchases of a single model but, in addition, give discounts based on a buyer's total expenditure on all products from the company.

Although less common, some consumer products are volume discounted as well. Larger packages of most food, health, and cleaning products usually cost less per ounce, and canned beverages cost less in twelve-packs than in six-packs. These differences reflect both cost economies for suppliers and the greater price sensitivity for these products by large families. Warehouse food stores, such as Wal-Mart, Costco, Sam's, and BJ's often require consumers to buy in large-quantity packages to qualify for discounted prices.

Often sellers vary prices by the size of an order rather than by the size of a customer's total purchase volume. *Order discounts* are the most common of all quantity discounts. Almost all office supplies are sold with order discounts. Copier paper, for example, can be purchased for about $20 per case of about 10 reams, but purchased individually it costs several dollars per ream. The logic for this is that many of the costs of processing an order are unrelated to the size of it. Consequently, the per-unit cost of processing and shipping declines with the quantity ordered. For this reason, sellers generally prefer that buyers place large, infrequent orders, rather than small frequent ones. To encourage them to do so, sellers give discounts based on the order quantity. Order discounts may be offered in addition to volume discounts for total purchases in a year, because volume discounts and order discounts serve separate purposes. The volume discount is given to retain the business of large customers. The order discount is given to encourage customers to place large orders.

Step discounts differ from volume or order discounts in that they do not apply to the total quantity purchased, but only to the purchase beyond a specified amount. The rationale is to encourage individual buyers to purchase more of a product without having to cut the price on smaller quantities for which they would pay a higher price. Thus, in contrast to other segmentation tactics, step discounting may segment not only different customers, but also different purchases by the same customers. Such pricing is common for public utilities from which customers buy water and electricity for multiple uses and place a different value on it for each use.

Consider, for example, the dilemma that local electric companies face when pricing their product. Most people place a very high value on having some electricity for general use, such as lighting and running appliances. The substitutes (gaslights, oil lamps, and hand-cranked appliances) are not very acceptable. For heating, however, most people use alternative fuels (gas, oil, coal, and kerosene) because of their lower cost. Utilities would like to sell more power for heating and could do so at a price above the cost of generating it. They do not want to cut the price of electricity across the board, however, since that would involve unnecessary discounts on power for higher-valued uses.

One solution to this dilemma is a step-price schedule. Assume that the electric company could charge a typical consumer $0.06 per kilowatt-hour (KWH) for general electricity usage but that it must cut its price to $0.04 per KWH to make electricity competitive for heating. If the company charged the lower price to encourage electricity usage for heating, it would forgo a third of the revenue it could earn from supplying power for other uses. By replacing a single price with a block-price schedule, $0.06 per KWH for the first block of 100 KWH and $0.04 for usage thereafter, the company could encourage people to install electric heating without forgoing the higher income it can earn on power for other purposes. To encourage people to use electricity for still more uses, utilities often add another step discount for quantities in excess of those for general use and heating. Exhibit 4-4 illustrates a step-price schedule for an electric utility.

Another type of volume discount is *two-part pricing*. Two-part prices involve two separate charges to consume a single product. For example, amusement parks sometimes have an entry fee plus a ticket charge for each ride, car rental companies have a daily rate plus a mileage charge, and health clubs charge an annual membership fee plus additional fees for racquetball and tennis court time. In each of these cases, heavy users pay less than do light users for the same product, since the fixed fee is spread over more units. Sometimes the rationale for two-part pricing is obvious: there are two distinguishable benefits. Nightclubs, for example, offer patrons both entertainment and drinks. They could include the entertainment in the price of the drinks, but then heavy drinkers would pay disproportionately for it and light drinkers would pay little. The heavy drinkers might therefore go elsewhere, while entertainment revenue that could be earned

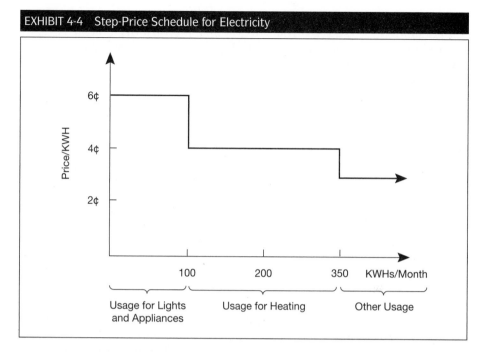

EXHIBIT 4-4   Step-Price Schedule for Electricity

from light drinkers would be lost. To overcome this problem, nightclubs have both a cover charge for the entertainment and a charge for drinks.[8]

The presence of two products is not, however, the reason for most two-part pricing. Car renters, for example, do not obtain value from merely having the car; they also want to go somewhere in it. The rationale for two-part pricing in this case is simply that there are significant differences in the incremental cost of serving different types of car renters. Since cars depreciate the more they are driven, it costs more to rent a car to someone who puts more mileage on it. Car rental companies sometimes charge a daily fee based on the average number of miles driven. But, as we discuss in Chapter 8, there is a danger in averaging costs for different types of buyers: Competitors undercut prices for the most low-cost customers. When costs are incurred in two parts, segmentation by two-part pricing enables a company to remain competitive in serving low-cost customers while still profitably serving the high-cost segment. By charging a mileage fee for more than 100 miles driven per day, the rental company can avoid attracting high cost customers unless they recover those costs.

Given the clear increase in profit using either step discounts or two-part pricing to segment the purchases of each individual customer, why do most companies still charge each individual customer a single price? The answer is that segmenting different purchases by each customer is possible only under limited conditions. It is profitable only when all of the following are true:

1. *Purchase volume by individual buyers is significantly price sensitive.* For many products, an individual buyer's demand is an all-or-nothing proposition.

Think of some common products (toilet paper, soap, salt, refrigerators, breakfast cereals, umbrellas), and ask yourself whether the quantity bought is really sensitive to even large price variations. Either individual customers buy the product or they do not, but price has very little effect on how much they buy. In this situation, step discounting and two-part pricing are futile.

2.   *The product cannot be easily resold or stored for later use.* If resale is easy, one buyer could purchase large quantities at a low price (bearing the high prices of initial steps or the fixed fee of a two-part price only once) and resell it to others who want only small amounts and would otherwise have to pay a higher price or a fixed fee to get them. If storage is easy, buyers could obtain discounts by purchasing large quantities at a time without significantly increasing their total use of the product.

3.   *Buyers' demands are similar, or it is possible to segment buyers for pricing into groups with similar demands.* The more diversity there is among buyers in the quantities that they are willing to purchase at various prices, the less possible it is to effectively segment purchases. The right step-price schedule or fixed fee for one buyer would be wrong for another.

Segmenting by Product Bundling

Product bundling is a widely used tactic for segmented pricing, although its rationale often goes unnoticed. Retailers bundle free parking with a purchase in their stores. Grocery stores and fast-food outlets bundle chances in games with purchase of their products. Newspapers with morning and evening editions bundle advertising space in both of them. Restaurants bundle foods into fixed-price dinners, generally a cheaper alternative to the same items served à la carte. Symphony orchestras bundle diverse concerts into season subscription tickets. These are but a small fraction of the goods sold in bundles, but they illustrate the breadth of the practice—from commodities to services, from necessities to entertainment. What makes bundling a successful segmented-pricing tactic? In each case the products bundled together have a particular relationship to one another in their value to different buyer segments.[9]

Residential satellite or cable television companies offer hundreds of television channels to their subscribers based on a menu of product-service packages at various prices. Subscribers may choose from among a limited series of bundled offerings, but cannot subscribe to an individual channel separate from its bundle. This structure enables the satellite or cable company to realize revenues from less popular channels that might rarely be purchased, by requiring buyers to buy a bundled package that includes more popular channels that are frequently purchased.

Consider how that relationship applies when bundling advertising space for the morning and evening editions in a newspaper. Advertising space in the morning edition is valued more by one segment of advertisers (for example, grocers, retailers) than by another segment (for example, theaters, restaurants), whereas the reverse is true for the evening edition. Exhibit 4-5 shows hypothetical valuations of advertising space by these two types of buyers. Both value advertising space in the

EXHIBIT 4-5 Value of Advertising Space by Two Different Segments		
Advertiser	**Morning Edition**	**Evening Edition**
Segment A (grocers, retailers)	$1,000	$400
Segment B (theaters, restaurants)	700	600

morning edition more than in the evening edition. What is important for a bundling strategy, however, is that segment A values space in the morning edition more than does segment B ($1,000 versus $700), whereas the reverse is true for the evening edition ($400 vs. $600).

Why would the newspaper want to bundle morning and evening advertising together, requiring buyers to purchase both in order to get either? Without bundling, the paper would have to charge no more than $700 for a morning ad and $400 for an evening ad to attract both segments for both editions. Thus it would collect $1,100 ($700 + $400) from each advertiser. But how much does each segment value the bundle? Segment A values it at $1,400 ($1,000 + $400), whereas segment B values it at $1,300 ($700 + $600). Thus the newspaper can sell a bundle of morning and evening advertising space to both segments for up to $1,300. That is $200 more per buyer than it could earn if it sold the same space separately.

Why is this segmented pricing? Because each segment pays the difference between the separate price of the advertising ($1,100) and the bundled price ($1,300) for a different product. Segment A pays the extra money because of the value it places on morning advertising; segment B pays because of the value it places on the evening edition.[10]

Generally, products are not sold only in indivisible bundles. Most firms follow the tactic of *optional bundling* where products can be bought separately, but the option is available to buy them in a bundle at prices below their cost if bought separately. Optional bundling is more profitable than indivisible bundling whenever some buyers value one of the items in the bundle very highly but value the other less than it costs to offer it. For such a customer, the extra revenue the firm earns from selling the bundle is less than the extra cost of producing it.

Residential telephone companies such as Qwest or Verizon sell basic telephone service for very little, but for perhaps $6 to $7 more per feature consumers can also obtain valuable features such as call waiting, caller identification, or three-way calling. Or they can buy the bundle of three or more services for perhaps an additional $10 to $12. The à la carte pricing of each feature enhances the perceived value of the three-feature package, resulting in many buyers trading up to the bundle from the basic telephone service. Residential cable companies offer bundles of cable internet, cable-based telephone, and cable television services for reduced prices off their à la carte price.

Supermarkets often use optional bundling in the form of special promotions. For example, a supermarket might offer anyone who buys $5 worth of groceries the opportunity to buy one stoneware dish at a very low price. The purpose of this optional bundle is to segment the market. Some customers are loyal shoppers at whatever store is most convenient. They are willing to pay a lot to shop at a particular store but do not value stoneware dishes. In contrast, lower-income customers and those with large families will shop around for the best prices. They are not willing to pay as much for the convenience of shopping at any particular store. Many of those shoppers, however, may value the opportunity to buy a nice set of dishes inexpensively. Thus the necessary condition for bundling (a reversal in the relative valuation of the products) is met. Supermarkets make the bundle optional because some shoppers may not want the stoneware dish even at the low price. To force them to purchase it would create unnecessary resentment that could drive them away.

Similarly, giving buyers the option to buy parts separately is common in most cases where bundles are offered. Although tickets to sporting and cultural events are available at a discount in a season ticket bundle, they can be purchased individually as well. Restaurants offer their customers dinner specials (appetizer, entrée, dessert, and beverage bundles), but customers can buy just some of the individual parts at higher à la carte prices. For purposes of segmentation, there is never any reason not to give buyers the option of purchasing separately at higher prices. There are, however, psychological reasons for bundling that may justify making the bundles indivisible. (We discuss these reasons in Chapter 5 in the section called Gain-Loss Framing.)

A subtle variation on mixed bundling is *value-added bundling*. Rather than cutting prices to price-sensitive customers, the value-added bundler offers them an additional value of a kind that less price-sensitive buyers do not want. With that strategy, a company can attract price-sensitive buyers without reducing prices to those who are relatively price insensitive. For only $1 extra, Qantas airlines of Australia offered travelers a choice of "land packages" for tourist-class hotels and sightseeing packages in Australia or for a camper-van for 5 days in New Zealand. These options would be unattractive to the typical business traveler but make traveling on Qantas attractive to pleasure travelers whose alternatives would be a charter flight to Australia or a less expensive vacation elsewhere. Alcoa used value-added strategy to encourage the use of aluminum-core electrical cable. For most buyers, aluminum's light weight gives it unique and highly valued advantages over competing materials, and Alcoa's prices reflected that value. At those high prices, however, aluminum could not compete with copper in making electrical cable. To overcome this problem, Alcoa began manufacturing aluminum-core electrical cable itself. It did not, however, pass on the full cost of converting aluminum into cable when pricing cable. In effect, it sold the aluminum in cable for less than it sold virgin aluminum. The combination of the raw aluminum and the processing into cable created an effective bundle since buyers who valued the processing more valued the raw aluminum less.

A good metric can also enable you to cut costs and attract a more profitable mix of customers than competitors can attract with the current metric. There are a number of guidelines for achieving that objective.

1.   Unbundle the pricing of any value-added service that is used at customers' discretion, rather than in some natural proportion to the core product or service. If the discretionary value-added service is differentiating, put a price on it. If it is industry standard, offer a discount for forgoing it.

2.   Unbundle differentiating product attributes, if possible, and price them separately if only some portion of the market is willing to pay a premium for them. However, you may profitably offer a discounted bundle of differentiating features or services if the value of them is inversely related across customers.

3.   Unbundle costs to serve (e.g., shipping costs) that vary across customers, unless the variation is inversely related for you and a competitor. In the latter case, consider bundling the costs to discount only to those customers for whom your competitor is more attractive.

SEGMENTING BY TIE-INS AND METERING

Segmentation by tie-ins or metering is often extremely important for pricing tangible and intangible assets. The reason is that buyers generally place greater value on an asset the more intensely they use it. Food processors canning fruit year-round in California value canning machines more than fish packers do in Alaska, who can salmon only a few months each year. A fast-food franchisee in a high-volume location values use of the franchise name and processes more than a franchisee in a lower-volume location. A software buyer who needs the software more frequently values it more than one who uses it only occasionally. In such cases, tactics that segment buyers by use intensity can substantially improve both sales volume and profitability.

Before the Clayton Antitrust Act of 1914, a common method of monitoring usage intensity was the *tie-in sale*. Along with the purchase or lease of a machine, a buyer contractually agreed to purchase a commodity used with the machine exclusively from the seller. Thus the Heaton Peninsular Company sold its shoe-making machines with the provision that buyers buy only Heaton Peninsular buttons.[11] The A. B. Dick Company sold its mimeograph equipment with the provision that buyers buy paper, stencils, and ink only from the A. B. Dick Company.[12] American Can leased its canning machines with the provision that they be used to close only American's cans.[13]

In each of these cases, the asset itself sold for a very low explicit price, close to the incremental cost of production. The tied commodity, however, was priced at a premium. Thus the true cost of the asset was its low explicit price, plus the sum of the price premiums paid for the tied-in commodity. Since buyers who used the asset more intensely bought more of the tied commodity, they effectively paid more for the asset.

Companies frequently use technological design to tie the consumable uniquely to the asset. For example, Hewlett-Packard led the industry in the development and manufacture of inkjet printers. HP strategically priced the printer—the asset—low to make the up-front cost competitive with lower-quality printers.

The replacement ink cartridge—the consumable—was designed with proprietary technology to fit uniquely with the asset and carried a wholesale margin of 60 percent. The key to HP's pricing success is that its pricing allows light users to get access to HP technology at low cost—the low price of the printer plus low total expenditures on printer cartridges since light users replace ink cartridges infrequently. But heavy users pay substantially more on printer cartridges since these users replace ink cartridges frequently. HP's inkjet division maintains a 50 percent market share and its profit per dollar sales is twice that of the company in general.

Gillette is legendary for the classic razor and blade strategy—with an innovative twist. Gillette has maintained a commanding market position in wet-shaving products (64 percent market share versus Shick's 13 percent), primarily due to its continual stream of innovative shaving systems. Gillette keeps its customers moving up to ever better, and proprietary, technologies by keeping the cost of each new razor very low while profiting handsomely from the replacement blades. The Gillette Mach III was introduced in June 1998 using heavy advertising, sampling, sales promotions, and low introductory prices for the asset. Gillette then charged prices for the replacement blades, the consumables, 50 percent higher than those of its predecessor. Customers whose facial hair is soft probably gain little from the new technology, but also pay little because they replace blades infrequently. However, customers with coarse beards benefit greatly from Gillette's innovations, and they pay substantially for them because they need to replace blades more frequently. By enabling Gillette to collect revenues proportionate to the value its new technologies deliver, the tie-in pricing strategy ensures both large market share and profitability. Gillette's razor division accounts for one third of corporate sales, but two thirds of total profits. Its razors—the asset—account for 5 percent of the razor division's earnings; blades—the consumable—account for 95 percent.

In service-based companies tie-in contracts are frequently used to reduce the cost for new buyers to try their services. Wireless phone providers offer a digital telephone for a nominal fee, and sometimes free, if the buyer agrees to purchase a long-term service contract to use the company's wireless network for 12 or 24 months. Satellite entertainment companies offer households a satellite dish and receiver unit for a much reduced price or for free, if the buyer agrees to subscribe to a higher-priced entertainment package of channels and outlets, for a minimum of 12 or 24 months. Buyers more than pay for the initial price of the dish and receiver by agreeing to purchase high-margin entertainment packages instead of lower-margin packages. These packages can be particularly effective for low-knowledge buyers, who perceive significant risk in investing in a new and little-known technology—and then developing them into loyal buyers who become accustomed to the firm's technology and programming.

Since passage of the Clayton Act, the courts have refused to enforce tying contracts that tie other purchases to the sale of a patented or unique product, except for service contracts where service is essential to maintain the performance and the reputation of the product.[14] Thus, if just one company had a patent on the technology for a particular digital PCS phone, it could not require customers to buy phone service from a particular supplier in order to buy a phone. Although tying contracts are often illegal when used for segmented pricing,[15] many opportunities to use this tactic without contracts still exist. No court has ever considered prohibiting theaters from requiring that food consumed on the premises be purchased only from the premium-priced, in-house concession; nor has any court considered prohibiting razor manufacturers from creating unique shaving technologies that tie blades to razors. Maintenance and repair services are natural tie-ins to the sale of equipment. Recently, the U.S. Supreme Court explicitly confirmed that such noncontractual tie-ins are an acceptable pricing tactic.[16]

The courts have, nevertheless, severely limited tie-in arrangements in precisely the cases where they are most dramatically effective. Rulings challenge sellers to monitor use without restricting competition. For example, Xerox was eventually prohibited from forcing buyers to purchase paper from the company. In modern times, that challenge has frequently been met by *metering* something that correlates with value other than use of a tied product. Internet sites charge advertisers based on the number of "click thrus." Syndicated newspaper columns are sold to local papers at prices based on use intensity. The metering device is simply the papers' circulation figures. Film distributors rent movies at prices based on the number of seats in the theater. Fast food franchisers lease their brand names and reputations to franchisees not for a fixed fee but for a percentage of sales. No matter how intangible the asset, metering use can be an important part of its pricing.

SEGMENTING BY PRODUCT DESIGN

Segmenting by product design involves making changes in the discount offer that make it unacceptable for use by customers who could otherwise be charged a higher price. For example, as the dollar depreciated relative to other currencies, electronics products sold in the United States for dollars became much cheaper than those sold for British pounds, Euros, and many other currencies. Electronics manufacturers have used product design to keep buyers outside the United States from buying in the United States for export. Apple replaced its universal transformers with ones specifically adapted to the local market. Plugging an Apple iMac designed for the 110 volt U.S. market into a 220-volt source abroad would cause the equipment to malfunction. Hewlett Packard was even more creative. To keep owners of its printers from buying their ink cartridges from online retailers in low priced countries, it added electronics to each printer that could identify where the cartridge was purchased. A U.S.-purchased cartridge would simply not be accepted by a printer purchased in the UK, or vice versa.

The important factor in segmenting by product design is not usually differences in production costs; there is frequently little or no cost difference in the different versions. It is differences in value driven by differences in alternatives, uses, or income. To make this tactic work, one must offer a lower-priced version that is in some way inadequate to meet the needs of price-insensitive buyers but still acceptable to price-sensitive buyers. Microsoft has a lower-priced version of its dominant Windows operating software, targeted at first-time computer users in developing countries. This Windows Starter Edition allows users to open only three applications at a time and restricts instant messaging. It also offers very limited word processing, no out-of-the-box Internet access, and a screen resolution that won't support the newest computer games. The cost to constrain or limit the capabilities of this new product are minimal, consisting mostly of "turning off" different elements of the software's code.

Often the key to enhanced profitability is unbundling costly differentiating features and services, enabling a company to provide them only to those customers who value them while pricing lower to customers who are unwilling to pay for some or all of those features. Contralto, a firm selling software and services for enhancing sales force effectiveness, improved its profitability by unbundling. Like many firms, Contralto offered one product with discounts. Its volume-based pricing program rewarded big customers who got the most value from its product, while alienating smaller ones. At the same time, medium and large customers were aggressive negotiators and expected frequent and significant discounts beyond the standard ones for volume. To win business from competitors Contralto provided many support services, but gave them away to the customer despite substantial cost to Contralto. Consequently, some customers used them so heavily that nearly all profit was squeezed from the sale.

Contralto decided to create new product variations that would make its pricing better reflect value and cost, expanding its market with smaller customers and capturing more profit from larger ones. These included a basic time and expense software product that met the needs of small customers. They could add a compensation module for an added charge. For its higher-end standard sales effectiveness package that included travel and entertainment compensation, Contralto included a "standard" level of customer support that was more than sufficient for a "typical" user, and then charged customers for additional use. This provided a new revenue stream, but also reduced costs to serve those customers willing to change their behavior to use less costly services. Finally, Contralto developed a Premium Sales Effectiveness Service that appealed to customers who needed lots of user support and more customized services. These customers were more costly to serve, but now paid higher prices to reflect the value they received and the cost to serve them. The result was both more volume and higher margins.

IMPORTANCE OF SEGMENTED PRICING

For industries with high fixed costs, a price structure that supports segmented pricing is often essential. The U.S. rail system, for example, could never have been built and could not currently be maintained were it not for a strategy of extensively segmented prices. Railroad tariffs are based on the value of the goods hauled. Coal and unprocessed grains, for example, are carried at much lower cost per carload than are manufactured goods. If railroads had to charge all shippers the same tariff charged for unprocessed grain, they would lack sufficient income per shipment to cover their fixed costs. Were they required to charge all shippers the tariff for manufactured goods, they would lose many shippers and would again lack sufficient revenue. Without segmented pricing, many rail lines could never cover their costs, whereas others would be forced either to raise tariffs above the highest currently charged or suffer the same fate. The railroads survive to serve all their customers at reasonable rates only because the customers can be effectively segmented for pricing.

Segmented pricing also spurs competitive innovation. Companies improve their products because improvement enables them to charge more profitable prices, but such improvements are often valued differently by different buyers. When only a subsegment of a firm's buyers value a potential improvement, the ability to segment them for pricing—to recover costs of development and to earn a profit—provides the sole incentive for such advances. Without segmented pricing, the unique demands of small market segments would more often go unsatisfied.

Worse still is when they are satisfied by a competitor. In his book *The Innovator's Dilemma,* Clayton Christensen cites numerous examples of companies that failed to meet the lower-performance, lower-margin end of a market that they dominated. Invariably, someone eventually addressed that need and used it as a base to begin driving into higher margin segments. He cites, for example, how Seagate ignored the data storage needs of the small, lower-performance laptop computer market, leaving it to new startups to market 3.5-inch disk drives even though Seagate had already developed similar technology. Ultimately, those low-end manufacturers (Conner and Quantum) used their accumulated experience and growing laptop volume to displace Seagate from its dominant role in all personal computers.[17]

Summary

Designing an optimal price structure that effectively segments your market and maximizes your profitable sales opportunities is clearly among the most difficult aspects of pricing strategy. While the types of segmentation tactics discussed can serve as a guide to separating markets, finding a basis for a segmentation (i.e., a particular buyer characteristic or a particular bundling combination) ultimately requires creative insight. Since each example of segmented pricing is unique in its method of implementation, there can be no simple formula. Finding a basis for segmentation is the key to maintaining a strong competitive position; in some cases, it is essential to remaining viable.

Notes

1. For a complete treatment of performance-based pricing see Benson P. Shapiro, "Performance-Based Pricing is More Than Pricing," Harvard Business School Note 9-999-007, February 25, 2002.
2. We have adopted the terms "metrics" and "fences" from Richard Harmer, "Strategies for Segmented Pricing," The Pricing Institute 6th Annual Conference (Chicago, March 22–25, 1993).
3. See Narasimhan Chakravarthi, "Coupons as Price Discrimination Devices—A Theoretical Perspective and Empirical Analysis," *Marketing Science,* 3 (Spring 1984), pp. 128–147; Naufel J. Vilcassim and Dick R. Wittink, "Supporting a Higher Shelf Price Through Coupon Distributions," *Journal of Consumer Marketing,* 4(2), (Spring 1987), pp. 29–39.
4. See discussion in Chapter 5 of the

framing effect to understand why rebates may influence purchases by customers who do not ultimately redeem them.

5. See Romarao Desiraju and Steven Shugan, "Strategic Service Pricing and Yield Management," *Journal of Marketing,* 63(1) (January 1999) pp. 44–56.

6. www.eurotunnel.com/ukcMain/ukcPassengers/ukcFaresandTimetables (accessed May 15, 2005).

7. For an in-depth discussion of the motivations for quantity discounting, see Robert J. Dolan, "Pricing Structures with Quantity Discounts: Managerial Issues and Research Opportunities," Harvard Business School working paper, 1985.

8. Sometimes charging a single price for a bundle of two separate products is necessary for segmented pricing. It is an effective strategy, however, only when preferences for the two products meet certain conditions. See Segmenting by Product Bundling later in this chapter.

9. This principle was first identified in George Stigler, "United States v. Loew's Inc.: A Note on Block Booking," *The Supreme Court Law Review* (1965), pp. 152–57; see also Gary D. Eppen, Ward A. Hanson, and R. Kipp Martin, "Bundling—New Products, New Markets, Low Risk," *Sloan Management Review,* 32, no. 4 (Summer 1991), pp. 7–14. The section entitled Framing Multiple Gains or Losses in Chapter 12 gives another rationale for bundling.

10. This is only one of the ways newspapers practice segmented pricing. They also charge higher prices for the same advertising space if the ad is from a national rather than a local advertiser. They charge different prices for different types of advertising, and they give volume discounts. Radio and television stations use similar tactics.

11. Heaton Peninsular v. Eureka Specialty Co., 77F288 (6th Circuit Court, 1896).

12. Henry v. A. B. Dick, 224 U.S. 1 (1912).

13. United States v. American Can Company (Northern District Court of California, 1949).

14. United States v. Jerrold Electronics Co., 187 F.Supp. 545 (E.D. Pa., 1960), affirmed 365 U.S. 567 (1961). Motion Picture Patents Co. v. Universal Film Mfg. Co. 243 U.S. 502 (1917). United Shoe Machinery Corporation v. United States (Supreme Court, 1922). International Business Machines Corporation v. United States (Supreme Court, 1936).

15. See Chapter 14 for situations when contractual tie-ins are legal for purposes other than pricing.

16. Pringle, David and Steve Stecklow, "Electronics with Borders: Some Work Only in the U.S.," *Wall Street Journal* (January 17, 2005), p. B1.

17. Clayton M. Christensen, *The Innovator's Dilemma* (Cambridge MA: Harvard Business School Press, 1997), pp. 44–46.

CHAPTER

5

PRICE AND VALUE COMMUNICATION

Strategies to Influence Willingness-to-Pay

Unless customers actually recognize the value that you create and ask them to pay for, value-based pricing will fail. Although this statement seems obvious for new, innovative products, marketers frequently disregard it for established offerings. When marketing surveys and sales representatives simply ask customers how much they are willing to pay for a product, they assume that customers know the value of what they buy. But, unless the product represents a large expenditure for a customer and provides benefits the customer can easily measure, the time and effort of estimating economic value probably exceeds the customer's gain.

The reality is that customers generally don't know the true value delivered by items they buy unless the seller informs them. That leaves the most differentiated and highest quality supplier vulnerable to competitors who offer a lower-price alternative possessing only those value components the customer recognizes, and who portrays additional value elements as merely "nice to have" but unessential attributes not worth the extra price. Ultimately, communicating value is designed to inform customers of all the value they receive, justifying the extra price the seller charges. Value communication—involving advertising, personal sales, trial offers, endorsements, guarantees and other tools supporting the seller's promises—raises the buyer's willingness to pay to the same level as that of better informed and experienced customers.

Communicating price is also critical to raising the customer's willingness to pay. The same monetary amount of price, paid in return for the same value, can produce a different effect depending upon how it is presented to and perceived by customers. In this chapter, we build on the discussions of value creation in Chapter 3 and price structure in Chapter 4 to discuss the art and science of marketing communication in a pricing context. When properly applied, the techniques we describe can ensure that the value created becomes value recognized at acceptable prices.

VALUE COMMUNICATION

Value communication works when your product or service creates value that is not otherwise obvious to potential buyers, but is important to them nevertheless. The less experience a customer has in a market, the more innovative a product's benefits and the more separated the purchaser is from the actual user, the more likely it is that customers will not recognize nor fully appreciate the value of product or service. For example, without an explicit message from the seller, a business buyer might not realize that a nearby distribution center offering shorter delivery times could reduce or eliminate the cost of carrying inventories. An unsophisticated buyer, for example, might not recognize how quickly inventoried items depreciate. Properly informed, the customer would see how much money faster delivery saves, justifying a price premium.

Still, the buyer must be motivated to listen to even a well-documented value proposition. Value communication is effective only when customers see the price as economically important[1] for getting "a good deal" or "the most for my money," rather than being price indifferent and simply making any purchase that meets their need. There are many factors that can influence the weight customers place on value in the purchase decision.

- *Size of expenditure.*   Some expenditures are just too small to justify serious thought or effort to find the economically best deal rather than simply buy any brand that meets the need. In business markets, small purchases might not justify a purchasing agent's time. Consumers make "impulse" purchases without prior consideration.

- *Shared costs.*   Some expenditures involve spending other people's money in whole or in part. Business travelers on an expense account have little incentive to look for the best deal, for example.

- *Switching costs.*   Some expenditures involve making additional supplier-specific investments before getting maximum value from a purchase. A business might have to train its employees to use a particular software package. A consumer might have to educate her lawyer, child care provider, and hairdresser on her needs and expectations before they can fully meet them. Unless these customers have reason to expect that a price difference between brands exceeds the cost of switching, they will stay with their current supplier.

- *Perceived Risk.*   Some expenditures involve products and services that are difficult to evaluate prior to purchase, creating risk that the actual value proposition may turn out to be much less than promised. When the potential cost associated with that risk is large relative to the expenditure, a buyer will simply ignore a supplier's promise of better value in favor of the merely adequate value proposition offered by a well-known or highly reputable supplier.

- *Importance of the end-benefit.*   Some expenditures are just a small part of a total package of costs necessary to achieve an end-benefit. Consumers often pay little attention to the price of accessories when buying a car, for example, because the cost seems small in the context of a larger expenditure. The effect is not simply economical but psychological as well for most people.[2] Getting a good deal is usually not an important consideration when picking the restaurant for an important date, or when purchasing flowers for one's daughter's wedding.

* ***Price-quality perceptions.***   When it is difficult to objectively assess value, customers will often use price as a proxy for quality—the higher the price, the higher the perceived quality. Technically unsophisticated customers that have difficulty judging quality will often use price as a proxy when shopping for high-end consumer electronics such as plasma TVs or home computers because they do not have the expertise to discern which ones really have the best technology and performance.

Still, in most product categories, "getting a good deal" relative to value is an important motivation in determining whether and what brand to buy. Consequently, it is usually possible and cost-effective to influence customers' willingness to pay with a systematic value communication strategy.

DEVELOPING A VALUE COMMUNICATION MESSAGE

The first step in developing a value communication strategy is determining which customer perceptions to influence. In some cases, the best opportunity may be to educate customers that they need a product or service enough to justify a purchase. Or, it might be most important to influence buyer perceptions of competitive alternatives. If you have significant market share and high repeat purchase rates but are fighting tough competition, the value communication strategy should attempt to raise the perceived switching costs of your customer moving to an unproven supplier. Understanding the customer's value drivers allows you to infer which alternatives the customer is likely to consider and how knowledgeable he or she is about your brand, product category and what differentiates you positively or negatively from those alternatives.

Two factors determine how you should try to influence buyer perceptions of your value and price: the target customer's *relative cost of search* for information about the differentiating attributes of your offering and the *type of benefits sought*—economic or psychological. *Relative cost of search* is the customer's financial and nonfinancial cost to determine alternative products' features and performance differences, *relative to that customer's expenditure in the category.* Several factors determine relative cost of search including search characteristics, customer expertise, and size of expenditure. The relative search cost is less, for example, when the customer can easily determine product differences before purchase. Such products, called *search goods,* allow buyers to find information and choose among them prior to purchase. Examples include commodity chemicals, desktop computers, home equity loans, cosmetics and digital cameras, as shown in Exhibit 5-1.

In contrast, *experience goods* have differentiating attributes that are more difficult to evaluate across brands, requiring the customer to make a substantial commitment to purchase and use such products before being able to evaluate their performance. Examples include most services such as management consulting,

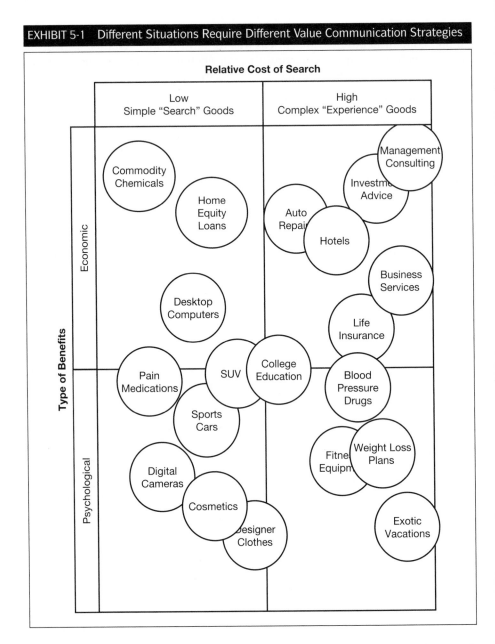

EXHIBIT 5-1   Different Situations Require Different Value Communication Strategies

auto repair, investment advice, and exotic vacations, as well as some products such as pharmaceuticals, batteries, and home appliances. Some products are complex hybrids with both search and experience attributes, such as automobiles.

The relative cost of search declines significantly for expert customers with extensive knowledge about the product category. A technophile can read the feature specifications for a personal computer and quickly infer how it will perform various tasks. A more typical buyer, however, would have to try different brands with the same software to make the same inferences. As a result, the less sophisticated buyer might avoid search costs by purchasing a brand name or relying on the advice of someone more expert.

The relative cost of search also diminishes as a customer's expenditure for the product increases. The relative cost of search is high for an individual buying an automobile because so much of the car's performance cannot be determined prior to purchase. However, for a fleet buyer planning to purchase 2,000 cars, the relative cost to evaluate different brands extensively, including buying one of each and trying it for a month, is not prohibitive.

Type of benefits sought also influences communication strategy. Measurable economic benefits such as profit, investment return rate, or productivity motivate many purchases and translate directly into quantified value differences among competing brands. But, for other purchases, especially consumer products, psychological benefits such as comfort, appearance, pleasure, status, health, or personal fulfillment play a critical role in customer choice. Psychological benefits do not translate objectively into economic value, but depend on each buyer's subjective assessment of value. One can describe the physical features of a wedding gown and even observe them before buying, but it's impossible to objectively determine what those features should be worth to an individual buyer—even if you knew all that buyer's relevant demographic information and the prices of alternatives being considered.

Exhibit 5-2 illustrates the four different generic value communication strategies determined by the relative cost of search for the market segment you want to influence and the type of differentiating benefits, economic or psychological, your offering delivers. Different communication approaches are most appropriate for favorably differentiating your product in each quadrant.

Strategy 1: Economic Value Communication

When it is relatively easy to judge differences in brands prior to purchase, and the benefits that buyers seek are primarily economic, the most effective value communication strategy is to promote differential economic value quantitatively. Economic Value Estimation® (EVE), discussed in Chapter 3, describes the process conceptually. The form of communication depends on the diversity among customers in benefits sought and value delivered.

When customers are fairly homogeneous, at least across a few broad market segments, the value communication can be standardized and delivered via media advertising and sales collateral materials. Marriott focuses its sales efforts for timeshare condominiums on customers who, already at a resort location and experiencing its benefits, have low relative search costs. Marriott's Web site and sales materials encourage prospects to compare the long-term costs of timesharing to inflation-prone year-by-year resort hotel room rates.

When customer benefits sought are more diverse, the quantitative value communication needs to be customized for each similar type of account. International Truck, a leading manufacturer, sells trucks to buyers for multiple applications,

EXHIBIT 5-2   Framework of Value Communication Strategies

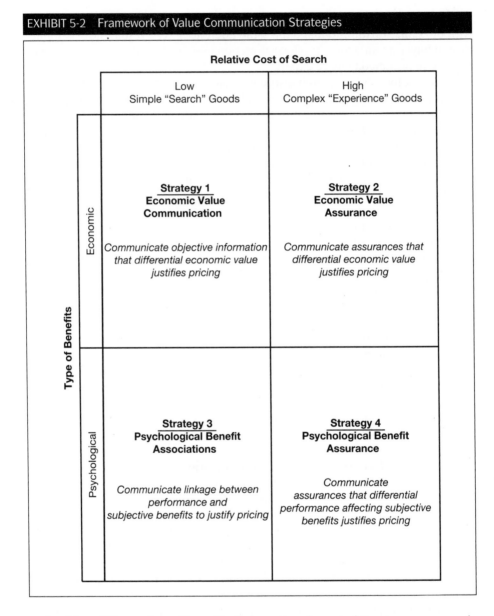

each with a different benefit profile. International created "customer economic value comparison" selling sheets for just about every competitive analysis its customers might make, resulting in a large book and computerized database of value-based differences. Exhibit 5-3 shows a value-selling sheet comparing an International model to that of a rival supplier for the "municipal dump/plow trucks" application. The sheet lists International's differential cost performance for each of four value drivers described in detail, and totals the specific potential savings. The presentation complements International's claims about other benefits

EXHIBIT 5-3   International Truck Value-Selling Sheets

CEV* (Customer Economic Value) Comparison

International Model: 4400 4x2 Competitor Model: Freightliner FL 70

Application: Municipal Dump/Plow – 10 years/15,000 miles/yr, 10,000 hours
(Applies in other applications with similar missions)

Expected Differential Savings for International Trucks and Tractors versus Competition

VALUE CATEGORY	31268	ISB 5.9L	MBE 900 6.4
Resale	$ 535 - 800	$ 570 - 860	$ 570 - 860
PM Savings	$ 605 - 910	$ 250 - 375	$ 80 - 570
Repairability	$2,553 - 2,553	$2,553 - 2,553	$2,553 - 2,553
Engine rebuild	$1,990 - 2,985	$1,485 - 2,230	
TOTAL (See Value Notes below for explanations)	$5,683 - 7,248	$4,858 - 6,018	$3,503 - 3,983

(Figures in table are net differences in expected dollar costs or value of International vs. competitor)

VALUE NOTES

RESALE Resale value figures are stated in today's dollars (NPV) and based on published resale values from NADA. Truck Blue Book or from International Used Truck Organization resale data. Resale values for new International or competitor models are estimated. Resale values are capped at 10 years.

PM SAVINGS PM savings are stated in today's dollars (NPV) and based on published OEM recommended service intervals and procedures for on/off highway usage (where available).

REPAIRABILITY Repairability value is derived from expected savings associated with International's breakway mirrors and three-piece hood based on published OEM repair procedures. The dollar value assumes a single incident for each feature during the vehicles lifecycle for the first owner.

ENGINE REBUILD If customer's application and usage requires an engine overhaul, rebuild values are labor and parts estimates. The figures are stated in today's dollars (NPV) and derived from the OEMs service publications.

not quantified such as greater windshield visibility, less wiring, a roomier cab, and greater maneuverability and handling.

In markets where the value drivers vary widely among customers but sales involve direct person-to-person communication, companies can arm their sales representatives with customizable value models. The sales rep can input basic data about the buying firm, how it uses the product or service, and the costs associated with alternatives to estimate the economic value delivered. Exhibit 5-4 shows an exemplary customizable value-selling spreadsheet from a computer network service company selling an automated help desk system. System benefits include greater quality and efficiency in detecting, managing, and solving network outages. By plugging in customer-specific data, the sales rep can estimate the incremental value the customer can expect to receive from a purchase.

Fortunately, such models can be very valuable even when the seller has only rough estimates about the actual customer numbers, so long as the model accurately

EXHIBIT 5-4 Spreadsheet Value-Based Selling Tool	

Variable	ENTER AMOUNTS HERE
ENTER these Inputs:	
Help Desk and/or Customer Service	
Total customers in impacted service area	4000
Average no. of trouble calls per day - normal	150
Avg. no. of trouble calls per day - outage incident	200
Duration of outage or network congestion - days	60
Average call duration in minutes	3.8
Help Desk wages & benefits - hourly	$ 11.50
Management Time	
No. Managers needed to resolve incident	1
Percent of Management time required	15%
Management loaded salary and benefits	$ 75,000
Other Costs	
Percent calls unresolved or receive bill credits	50%
Average billing credit (1 month)	$ 17.95
Percent impacted calls that are long distance	100%
Avg. cost per minute for 800 calls to help desk	$ 0.07
General	
Number of users per port	10
Calculation:	
Total ADDITIONAL man hours cust. service	190
Total cost for additional help desk & cust. service labor required	$ 2,185
Total cost for management time	$ 1,875
Total billing credits	$ 26,925
Total 800 call costs	$ 798
Avg. cost per call (less mgt. expense)	$ 9.97
TOTAL COST SAVINGS TO CUSTOMER (per outage incident)	$ 31,783
Estimated number PRI in impacted service area	17
COST SAVINGS PER PRI	$ 1,870

reflects the structure of the customer's economics. Buyers frequently question the sales rep's assumptions about their costs and revenues, but that can help the seller by focusing discussion on actual benefits the customer receives, by raising information that might not otherwise be addressed, and by shifting discussion away from price. In a business-to-business selling situation, for example, quantified value estimates bring information to the attention of a purchasing department that otherwise might have little interest in cost savings or revenue increases. Our clients have frequently reported that even after a purchasing agent initially ignored a sales rep's value analysis, someone else from operations or finance called to request a meeting to further review it. That is the best result a seller has a right to expect: a fair hearing from those who actually recognize and care about the value delivered.

Strategy 2: Economic Value Assurance

When the cost to ascertain the differences among brands exceeds the benefits for a target segment, communicating quantifiable economic value information alone is unlikely to be sufficient and may be impractical. It is great to tell buyers that a product that could halve usage costs would be worth a large price premium, but that may not motivate a purchase if customers cannot determine for themselves before purchase that your product or service will actually enable such a saving. Documenting a connection between features and long-term benefits, such as the effectiveness of a drug therapy or the durability of a car, might be prohibitive until the product has been on the market for years.

Studies have shown that when customers cannot directly evaluate a brand's performance, they will respond positively to narrative, experiential, or anecdotal information.[3] Such communications familiarize buyers with the benefits and then reassure them indirectly that a product or service probably delivers differential value that more than justifies its price premium. Such an *economic value assurance* strategy involves testimonials from credible experts, opinion leader endorsements from known and trusted sources, and claims of superior market share or repeat purchase frequency—coupled with frequent mentions and connections to your brand name.

For example, premium battery manufacturers for years have claimed that their batteries last longer, justifying their higher prices. However, most buyers find that claim difficult to verify. Instead, simple assurance strategies about longer battery life should be more effective. Duracell introduced an ad campaign designed to credibly communicate differential value rather than merely counter-attack its archrival's oft-repeated claim that "Eveready keeps going and going." Duracell ads (one version appears in Exhibit 5-5) emphasize that Duracell is the battery brand of choice when critical missions depend on long life and reliability. Even without any quantified performance data, the message that thoughtful users with big benefits at stake depend on Duracell reassures new buyers about the brand's superiority.

Even in business markets, an endorsement can be nearly as powerful as hard data. Opinion leaders are those whose lower search costs lead them to make what

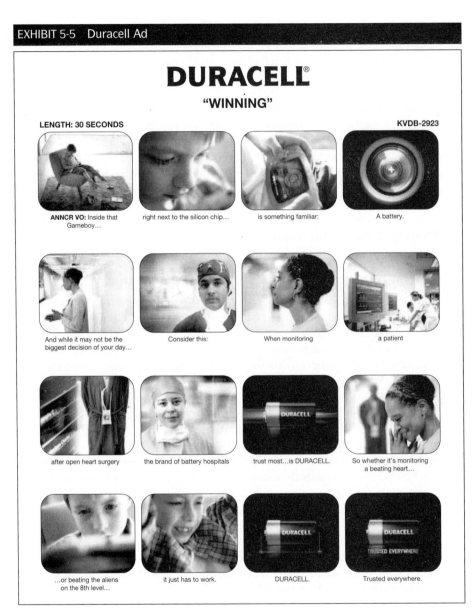

others consider to be more informed decisions. For example, Kaiser Permanente, a western U.S. health maintenance organization, has a reputation for being a well-informed buyer of the most cost-effective medical products. The company often tests drugs and devices itself and will not buy a more expensive product without economic justification. Consequently, many other hospitals and health maintenance organizations (HMOs) that learn that Kaiser Permanente has adopted a more expensive product or service assume that its price premium is cost-justified.

Multiple testimonials from satisfied customers, even when they are not opinion leaders, can also reassure those attempting to make a purchase decision involving objective economic benefits. To counter the threat from lower-cost Linux operating systems, Microsoft commissioned independent consultants to develop "customer case studies," each a video clip from a chief information officer or other systems professional. Each explained why, after considerable study, they decided to remain with the Microsoft Windows platform despite its higher price. Microsoft reinforced these testimonials with "white papers" showing how the total lifetime cost open-source operating systems could exceed the costs for a comparable Windows operating system despite their lower purchase price.

Strategy 3: Psychological Benefit Associations

When psychological benefits such as comfort, pleasure, safety, security, status, companionship, adventure, or fulfillment motivate customers, it is not possible to define economic value objectively. Even when a low relative cost of search enables customers to recognize differences in product or service features, the psychological value they associate with those features is subjective. The key to influencing perceived value for such products is to help buyers make connections between the differentiating features they recognize and the psychological benefits they could gain.

One of the most effective ways to do this is by reframing the way the customer views the product or service differentiation, not in terms of the product's immediate attribute performance ("this razor will give you a closer shave"), but in terms of a benefit ("the shave this razor gives you will make you more attractive on a date"). Hart Shaffner & Marx, for example, ran a campaign showing elegantly dressed business executives with the message: "The right suit might not help you achieve success, but the wrong suit could limit your chances."

The key to successfully creating performance-benefit communications is picking the most important benefit that can credibly be associated with the product for each target market segment. For decades, Michelin, the French tire company, had positioned its tires to appeal to men based on superior performance. Recognizing the demographic trend of baby boomers starting families with more joint decision making, Michelin adroitly leveraged its tire's reputation for performance by associating it with a new benefit: family safety captured by the tagline, "There's a lot riding on your tires" (see Exhibit 5-6). Moreover, Michelin's advertising gradually portrayed more women as tire decision makers, culminating in its 1998 "Baby Shower" commercial in which an expectant mother receives four Michelin tires as a baby shower gift. This value repositioning proved to be one of the most successful in history, winning Michelin a consistent price premium.[4]

Creating performance-benefit associations can influence the willingness-to-pay for differentiated product features. Unlike economic benefits, psychological benefits have no objective dollar value; what something "should" cost is often very fluid, particularly for an infrequent purchase where past expenditure is no guide. Thus, the seller of student study aids might point out that the cost is no more per day than a cup of coffee even though the study aids are so much more valuable.

EXHIBIT 5-6   Michelin Ad

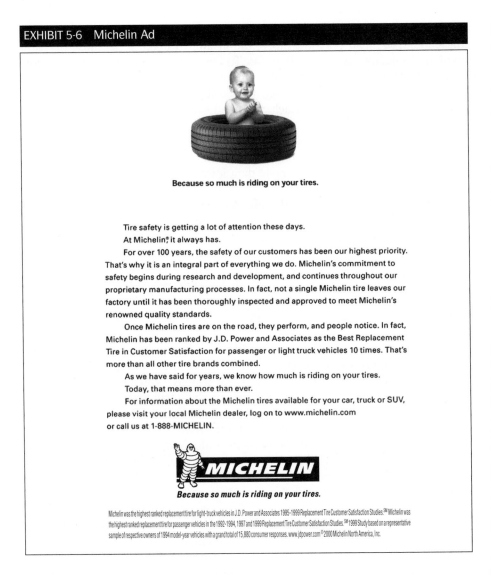

Because so much is riding on your tires.

Tire safety is getting a lot of attention these days.
At Michelin, it always has.
For over 100 years, the safety of our customers has been our highest priority.
That's why it is an integral part of everything we do. Michelin's commitment to
safety begins during research and development, and continues throughout our
proprietary manufacturing processes. In fact, not a single Michelin tire leaves our
factory until it has been thoroughly inspected and approved to meet Michelin's
renowned quality standards.
Once Michelin tires are on the road, they perform, and people notice. In fact,
Michelin has been ranked by J.D. Power and Associates as the Best Replacement
Tire in Customer Satisfaction for passenger or light truck vehicles 10 times. That's
more than all other tire brands combined.
As we have said for years, we know how much is riding on your tires.
Today, that means more than ever.
For information about the Michelin tires available for your car, truck or SUV,
please visit your local Michelin dealer, log on to www.michelin.com
or call us at 1-888-MICHELIN.

MICHELIN

Because so much is riding on your tires.

Michelin was the highest ranked replacement tire for light-truck vehicles in J.D. Power and Associates 1995-1999 Replacement Tire Customer Satisfaction Studies.℠ Michelin was the highest ranked replacement tire for passenger vehicles in the 1992-1994, 1997 and 1999 Replacement Tire Customer Satisfaction Studies. ℠ 1999 Study based on a representative sample of respective owners of 1994 model-year vehicles with a grand total of 15,880 consumer responses. www.jdpower.com ©2000 Michelin North America, Inc.

Woolite successfully argued that the price of its soap is reasonable because it does
the same job "for pennies" that a dry cleaner would do "for dollars."

While most communication strategies focused on creating performance-benefit
associations are designed to increase the perceived value of positive differentiation,
a negatively differentiated brand can use the same techniques in reverse to minimize the discount required to win sales. "Why pay more?" challenges the customer
and competitors to justify their higher prices. Red Roof Inn, a basic, no-frills hotel
chain, ran a simple advertisement that asked, "What's the value of all those amenities at the higher priced hotels? At 3 a.m. it's hard to tell." By framing the difference
between Red Roof Inn and its competitors in terms of features that lack much

benefit for those who just want a good night's sleep, Red Roof was able to position itself as a better value, not just as a lower-priced alternative.

Strategy 4: Psychological Benefit Assurances

The most difficult challenge in value communication occurs when the benefits are psychological and the differences among brands are difficult for customers to ascertain. Personal services (e.g., hair salons), personal experience products (vacations), and personal improvement products (weight loss programs) are in this quadrant. Because comparison is difficult, the risk for customers of making a disappointing purchase decision is high. Consequently, buyers tend to rely heavily on even small amounts of direct experience (trial), on endorsements from people with whom they can identify, and on their prior experience with a brand or brand name.

Whenever possible, the most effective way to influence value perceptions in this quadrant is to subsidize trial. Health clubs offer free trial memberships. Suppliers of baby products pay hospitals to give away samples of baby formula to new parents. New brands of food products often spend significantly to induce trial with coupons, trial sizes, and free samples in addition to advertising. Their messages strive to increase buyer confidence that the product, when tried, will deliver enough psychological value to justify the choice.

Endorsements are a proven way to communicate confidence in a value delivery that cannot be documented objectively. While endorsements related to objective economic benefits rely on authorities who should know, endorsements for psychological benefits are more effective when made by people with whom the consumer can personally identify. Product promotion in this quadrant shows satisfied real or dramatized users—"people like me" thinks the customer who imagines achieving the same result. Celebrity endorsers can communicate value, not as experts but as people with a defined image to which a target segment could relate—NASCAR drivers touting male potency supplements, for example.

Many successful self-improvement products and services—such as exercise equipment and diet products—use similar marketing techniques, bolstering extensive product demonstrations with large numbers of testimonials from satisfied users. They also offer guarantees that the product will not only perform as claimed, but will satisfy the customer as well.

The high cost of search for customers and the communication challenge facing sellers gives known brands a large competitive advantage in this quadrant. Upstart brands attack leaders with an economic argument, promising all the same features and benefits at a lower price. To respond in economic terms, brand leaders would have to acknowledge their rivals, giving them more publicity, and would have to quantify the value of their superiority, which would be difficult given uncertainty about the new competitors' performance. A brand leader's advantage lies in its reputation and customers' satisfactory prior experience with the brand. A new brand's claim to perform as well cannot be tested until it is purchased and tried. Consequently, established brands can recast the purchase in terms of the psychological value of avoiding a mistake. For example, Federal Express ads show hapless employees who fear losing their jobs because they didn't use Federal Express and were blamed when a package did not arrive.

MARKET SEGMENTS AND DIFFERENTIATED VALUES

To select from among the four generic value communication strategies, consider two additional factors: your target segments and the features that differentiate your product or service. When appealing to experienced buyers in a category who can easily judge performance, or to large buyers who will invest in trial purchases, the appropriate strategies are on the left side of Exhibit 5-2, low relative cost of search. The features to focus on are those that differentiate your brand from others. In the same market, however, you might want to convince novice buyers with little ability to discern brand performance to enter the category. For them, employ strategies in the right-hand column to assure them of use value, communicating motivating benefits even if you are not better than rivals in delivering them. Such a strategy definitely makes sense if there is some other reason for the buyer to pick your brand from a set of substitutes, such as an affinity group (e.g., Harley-Davidson motorcycle clubs, or recreational vehicle groups) or your large market share ("It's the leading brand so it must be good").

To illustrate using different tactics for different segments, think of international air travel advertising. Airlines appeal to experienced business travelers by describing their feature differences (fully reclining seats, showers at destination, gourmet meals) and the resulting benefits (arrive rested and ready for work). They appeal to pleasure travelers by comparing the psychological end-benefits of the destination with the price.

You may need to communicate both economic and psychological benefits for the same product to the same customers. Hybrid car buyers may want to feel good about protecting the environment, a psychological benefit a manufacturer could promote by reporting the car's reduced pollution ratings while showing it driving through unspoiled scenery. However, the price premium buyers will pay for a hybrid car also depends on how much money they expect to save from improved gas mileage, an economic benefit the company could communicate by citing gas mileage data. Finally, customers also might be wary of the new technology's possibly adverse impact on reliability (a negative economic benefit), making reassuring testimonials from existing owners or independent experts, like J.D. Power and Associates, a valuable part of the communication.

Often, a value communication strategy involves using different tactics to deal with different types of benefits and customer constituencies. Such complexity is common in the market for medical products. In mid-2003, for example, Johnson & Johnson had to justify a substantial price premium for its new and unique drug-coated coronary stent, used to keep clogged arteries open. J&J priced its stent at $3,500—250 percent higher than traditional uncoated stents and well in excess of the cost of the drug used to coat the stent. Such aggressive pricing aroused critics in the medical professions and in the public press, accusing the company of price gouging and challenging J&J to reconcile the value of the new product with its price. J&J did so by explaining the economic benefits to medical professionals. Stent implantation surgery costs more than $30,000, including the cost of the stent. But in 20 percent of cases, an uncoated stent reclogs in less than a year, requiring a repeated procedure at another $30,000 cost. With J&J's new drug-eluting stent reducing the likelihood of reclogging, the surgery repeat rate fell to around 5 percent. Thus, the objective differentiation value from the smaller reclogging rate was $4,500: the 15 percent rejection rate difference multiplied by the cost of a second surgical procedure. In addition, patients received substantial psychological value in avoiding the risk and discomfort of a repeat procedure, a benefit J&J emphasized to the public. The combination of economic and psychological justification enabled J&J to not only win a larger reimbursement from payers when surgeons used its drug-eluting stent but also to defuse the initial hostility and resistance to its price.

PRICE COMMUNICATION

Although it is easy to understand how value can be influenced, particularly the perceived value of psychological benefits, prices would seem to be hard data that are relatively easy to compare and communicate. But research over the years has repeatedly shown that people do not necessarily evaluate prices logically. Customers can perceive the same price paid in return for the same value differently depending on how it is communicated. Let's examine four aspects of price perception and their implications for price communication: proportional price evaluations, reference prices, perceived fairness, and gain-loss framing.

PROPORTIONAL PRICE EVALUATIONS

Buyers tend to evaluate price differences proportionally rather than in absolute terms. For example, one research study asked customers if they would leave a store and go to one nearby to save $5 on a purchase. Of respondents who were told that the price in the first store was $15, some 68 percent said they would go to the other store to buy the product for $10. Of respondents who were told that the price in the first store was $125, only 29 percent would switch stores to buy the product for $120. Similar studies have replicated this effect, including research with business manager respondents.[5] When the $5 difference was proportionally more—33 percent of the lower price—it was more motivating than when it was proportionally a small part, 4 percent of the higher price.

Psychologists call the tendency to evaluate price differences proportionately the Weber-Fechner effect. It has clear implications for price communication. For example, auto companies increased the motivational power of their rebate promotions when they offered the option of free financing instead of a fixed-dollar rebate only. Despite the fact that the present value of the interest saved was no more, and often less, than the value of the fixed-dollar rebate, free financing proved more popular. Why? Because eliminating 100 percent of the financing cost motivated consumers more than a 5 percent discount on a $20,000 car. Similarly, hotel chains have found it more effective to offer "free breakfast" or "free Internet access" with their rooms rather than offer a slightly lower price.

An important implication of Weber-Fechner is that price change perceptions depend on the percentage, not the absolute difference, and that there are thresholds above and below a product's price at which price changes are noticed or ignored.[6] A series of smaller price increases below the upper threshold is more successful than one large increase. Conversely, buyers respond more to one large price cut below the lower threshold than to a series of smaller, successive discounts. For example, one full-service brokerage house raised its commissions every 6 months over a 3-year period with little resistance from customers. Seeing this success, its competitor tried to match these increases in one large step and received intense criticism.

REFERENCE PRICES

Economists and market researchers generally focus on the trade-off that buyers make between the utility they get from the product or service and the price they pay. One key element in this research is called *transaction utility theory,* which suggests that buyers are motivated by more than just the utility associated with obtaining and using a product.[7] The *transaction utility* also motivates buyers. That is the difference between the price actually paid and what the buyer considers a reasonable or fair *reference price* for the product.

Chapter 3 explored the role of competitive prices in pegging what buyers consider the reference price. Other types of information also influence the reference price, information sellers can manage to their advantage.

A common approach relies on careful product line pricing, as illustrated in Exhibit 5-7. A controlled experiment asked subjects to choose among different models of microwave ovens. Researchers asked half the subjects to choose between two models (Emerson and Panasonic); the other half chose from among three models (Emerson, Panasonic I, and Panasonic II). Although 13 percent of the subjects were drawn to the top-end model, the Panasonic II, the largest impact

EXHIBIT 5-7 Reference Price Effects of a High-End Product		
	Choice (%)	
Microwave Oven Model	Group 1 (n = 60)	Group 2 (n = 60)
Panasonic II (1.1 cubic feet; regular price $199.99; sale price 10% off)	—	13
Panasonic I (0.8 cubic feet; regular price $179.99; sale price 35% off)	43	60
Emerson (0.5 cubic feet; regular price $109.99; sale price 35% off)	57	27

Source: Itamar Simonson, and Amos Tversky, "Choice in Context: Tradeoff Contrast and Extremeness Aversion," *Journal of Marketing Research,* 29 (August 1992), 281–95.

from adding that third-model choice was on the Panasonic I, which gained 17 additional share points when it became the mid-priced choice. The implications of product-line pricing are clear. Adding a premium product to the product line may not necessarily result in overwhelming sales of the premium product itself. It does, however, enhance buyers' perceptions of lower-priced products in the product line and encourage low-end buyers to trade up to higher-priced models.

Another way marketers can influence reference prices is by suggesting potential reference points. For example, buyers' reference prices can be raised by stating a manufacturer's suggested price, a higher price charged previously ("Was $999, Now $799!"), or a higher price charged by competitors ("Their price $999, Our price $799!"). Research indicates that advertisements suggesting reference prices are more effective in influencing consumer durable product purchases (video cameras) than ads that do not, particularly among less knowledgeable buyers who rely more on price to make buying decisions.[8] Other studies have found that providing buyers with a suggested reference point enhances perceptions of value and savings, even if the advertised reference point is exaggerated.[9] Although buyers may discount or question the credibility of such claims, the claims still favorably influence perceptions and behaviors.[10]

The order of presentation evidently influences customers' reference prices. In seminal research on this effect, two groups of experimental subjects saw the same sets of prices for a number of products in eight product classes. One group saw the prices in descending order (from highest to lowest); the other group saw them in ascending order (from lowest to highest). Researchers then asked each subject how much the same individual product in each product class was priced "high" or "low" relative to its value. From those judgments, the researchers calculated average reference prices for each product. The result: subjects who saw the prices in descending order formed higher reference prices than those who saw them in ascending order, even though both groups saw the same set of prices.[11] When forming their reference prices, buyers apparently give greater weight to the prices they see first.

These results clearly have important implications for price communication. In personal selling, this reference price effect implies that a salesperson should begin a presentation by first showing products above the customer's price range, even if the customer ultimately will choose from among cheaper products. This tactic, known as "top-down selling," is common for products as diverse as automobiles, luggage, and real estate. Direct-mail catalogs take advantage of this effect by displaying similar products in the order of most to least expensive. Within a retail store, the order effect has implications for product display. It implies, for example, that a grocery store might sell more low-priced (but high-margin) house brands by *not* putting them at eye level where they would be the first to catch the customer's attention. It may be preferable to have consumers see more expensive brands first and then look for the house brands.

Finally, promotional deals such as coupons, rebates, and special package sizes can influence reference prices strategically. Some marketers have argued that new products should be priced low to induce trial and thus build a market of repeat purchasers, after which price can be raised. But if the low initial price lowers buyers' reference prices, it may actually affect repeat sales adversely. This is the result that some researchers have found. In one well-controlled study,[12] five new brands were introduced to the market in two sets of stores. During an introductory period, one set of stores sold the new brands at a low price without any indication that this was a temporary promotional price; the control stores sold the new brands at the regular price. As expected, the brands sold better during the introductory period where they were priced lower. During the weeks following the introduction, however, both sets of stores charged the regular price. In all five cases, sales during the post-introductory period were lower in the stores with the low initial price than in the control stores. Moreover, total sales for the introductory and post-introductory periods combined were greater in the control stores than in the stores where the low price initially stimulated demand. This and other studies showing similar results demonstrate the importance of discounting tactics. The seller should clearly establish a product's regular price and then promote the discount as a temporary price cut. Otherwise, initially low promotional prices designed to build product trial can establish low reference prices that will undermine the product's perceived value at regular prices later on.

PERCEIVED FAIRNESS

The concept of a "fair price" has bedeviled marketers for centuries. In the Dark Ages, merchants were put to death for exceeding public norms regarding the "just price." Even in modern market economies, putative "price gougers" often face press criticism, regulatory hassles, and public boycotts. Consequently, marketers should understand and attempt to manage perceptions of fairness. But what is fair? The concept of fairness appears to be totally unrelated to issues of supply and demand.[13] Assumptions about the seller's profitability influence perceived fairness, but not entirely. Oil companies have often been accused of gouging, even when their profits are below average. When hurricane Katrina disrupted gasoline supplies in the American south, gas station owners who raised prices were soundly criticized as "price gougers" even though they had only enough supply to serve those who wanted the product at that price. In contrast to the situation faced by oil companies, popular forms of entertainment (Disney World, for example, or state lotteries) are very profitable and expensive, yet their pricing escapes widespread criticism.

Recent research seems to indicate that perceptions of fairness are more subjective, and therefore more manageable, than one might otherwise think.[14] Buyers apparently start by comparing what they think is the seller's likely margin now to what the seller earned in the past, or to what others earn in similar purchase contexts. In a famous experiment, people imagined that they were lying on a beach, thirsty for a favorite brand of beer, and that a friend was walking to a nearby location and would bring back beer if the price was not too high. Researchers asked them to specify the maximum amount that he or she would pay. Subjects did not know that half of them had been told that the friend would patronize a "fancy resort hotel" while the other half had been told that the friend would buy from "a small grocery store." Although these individuals would not themselves visit or enjoy the amenities of the purchase location, the median acceptable price of those who expected the beer to come from the hotel—$2.65—was dramatically higher than the median acceptable price given by those who expected it to come from the grocery store—$1.50.[15]

Presumptions about the seller's motive influence customers' perceived fairness judgments. A seller justifying a higher price with a "good" motive (e.g., funding employee health insurance, improving service levels) makes the price more acceptable than does a "bad" motive (e.g., exploiting a market shortage to increase stockholder profits). Research suggests that companies like Disney with good reputations are much more likely to get the benefit of the doubt about their motives. Those with unpopular reputations (e.g., oil companies) are likely to find their motives suspect.[16]

Finally, perceptions of fairness seem to be related to whether the price is paid to maintain a standard of living, or is paid to improve a standard of living. People consider products that maintain a standard to be "necessities," although humanity has probably survived without them for most of its history. Charging a high price for a necessity is generally considered unfair. For example, people object to prices for life-saving drugs because they feel that they shouldn't have to pay to be healthy. After all, they were healthy last year without having to buy prescriptions and medical advice. People react similarly to rent increases. Yet, the same individuals might buy a new car, jewelry, or a vacation without objecting to equally high prices or price increases.[17]

Fortunately, perceptions of fairness can be managed. Companies that frequently adjust prices to reflect supply and demand or to segment buyers with different price sensitivities are careful to set the "regular" price at the highest possible level, rather than at the average or most common price. This enables them to "discount" when necessary to move product at slow times (a "good" motive), rather than have to increase prices when demand is strong (a "bad" motive).[18] Similarly, because buyers believe that companies should not have to lose money, it's often best to blame price increases on rising costs to serve customers. Buyers believe that is fair, such as when petroleum prices increase. Landlords who raise rents should announce property improvements at the same time. Innovative companies raise prices more successfully when they are launching a new product and say they are recovering development costs.

GAIN–LOSS FRAMING

A final consideration in price communication is presenting the price to customers, who tend to evaluate prices in terms of gains or losses from an expected price point.[19] How they frame those judgments affects the attractiveness of the purchase. To illustrate this effect, grounded in *prospect theory,* ask yourself which of the following two gasoline stations you'd be more willing to patronize, assuming that you deem both brands to be equally good and you would always pay with a credit card.

- Station A sells gasoline for $2.20 per gallon, but gives a $0.20 per gallon discount if the buyer pays with cash.
- Station B sells gasoline for $2.00 per gallon, but charges a $0.20 per gallon surcharge if the buyer pays with a credit card.

Of course, the economic cost of buying gasoline from either station is identical. Yet, most people find the offer from station A more attractive than the one from station B. The reason is that people place more psychological importance on avoiding "losses" than on capturing equal size "gains." Also, both the gains and losses of an individual transaction are subject, independently, to diminishing returns, as one would expect from the Weber-Fechner effect we discussed earlier: A given change has less psychological impact the larger the base to which it is added or subtracted.

In our gas station example, cash buyers prefer A where they receive the psychological benefit of earning a discount, a "gain" to them. Paying the same $2.00 net price per gallon at station B, which offers no explicit discount, does not provide a psychological benefit.

Credit card buyers also prefer station A, mainly because station B's credit card surcharge creates a "loss," a negative psychological benefit to be avoided. Paying the same $2.20 net price per gallon at station A, which requires no explicit surcharge, does not provide a psychological benefit, positive or negative.

Buyers otherwise indifferent to paying by cash or credit will not be indifferent to stations A or B despite the sellers' economic value equivalence; such buyers would always pay cash to get the lowest price but would likely choose A to get the psychological satisfaction unavailable at B.

Prospect theory has many implications for price communication:

- To make prices less objectionable, make them opportunity costs (gains forgone) rather than out-of-pocket costs. Banks often waive fees for checking accounts in return for maintaining a minimum balance. Even when the interest forgone on the funds in the account exceeds the charge for checking, most people choose the minimum balance option. People find it less painful to pay for things like insurance or mutual funds with payroll deductions instead of buying them outright.

- When your product is priced differently to different customers and at different times, set the list price at the highest level and give most people discounts. This type of pricing is so common that we take it for granted. Colleges, for example, charge only a small portion of customers the list price and give everyone else discounts. To those who pay at or near the full price, the failure to receive more of a discount (a gain forgone) is much less objectionable than if they were asked to pay a premium because they are not star students, athletes, or good negotiators.

- *Unbundle gains and bundle losses.* Many companies sell offerings consisting of many individual products and services. For example, a printing company not only prints brochures but also helps design the job, matches colors, schedules the job to meet the buyer's time requirements, and so on. To maximize the perceived value, the seller should identify each of these as a separate product or service and promote the value of each one explicitly ("Look at all you get in our Deluxe Package!"), unbundling the gains. However, rather than asking the buyer to make individual expenditure decisions, the seller should identify the customer's needs and offer a package price to meet them ("One price brings it all to you"), bundling the loss. If the buyer objects to the price, the seller can take away a service, which will then make that service appear as a stand-alone "loss" that will be hard to give up.

Strategists who think only in terms of objective economic values might find these principles far-fetched. One might argue that buyers in these cases could easily think of the same choices as entirely different combinations of "gains" and "losses." That is precisely the point that prospect theorists make: Buyers can frame the same transactions in many different ways, each implying somewhat different behavior. Researchers have shown that changing how people think about their gains and losses in otherwise identical transactions consistently alters their behavior.

Summary

How customers respond to your pricing is determined by more than the value delivered by your product and the price you charge. It is also influenced by how they evaluate your product and your price. If you leave those judgments to chance, you are likely to be paid much less or sell much less than you could. Most customers lack the time or the incentive to fully inform themselves about their alternatives and to evaluate the information they do have. If you want them to recognize your value, you have to make the process easier for them by supplying them with information about your offer and what you think it should mean to them.

You also need to actively manage how you communicate the price to minimize adverse feelings about paying it. By controlling the visibility of price differences, the formulation of references, and the perceptions of fairness, you can reduce negative reactions to your pricing without reducing your overall margins.

Notes

1. Other elements of marketing, such as channel availability, and other issues in pricing, such as pricing policies, are still relevant even when the product is not economically important. Value communication, however, is not likely to have an impact in those cases.
2. Richard Thaylor, "Toward a Positive Theory of Consumer Choice," *Journal of Economic Behavior and Organization,* 1 (1980), pp. 39–40.
3. See Gerald E. Smith and Paul D. Berger, "The Impact of Direct Marketing Appeals on Charitable Marketing Effectiveness," *Journal of the Academy of Marketing Science,* 24(3) (Summer 1996), pp. 219–231; and R. M. Dawes, D. Faust, and P. E. Meehl, "Clinical Versus Actuarial Judgment." *Science,* 243 (1989), pp. 1668–1674.
4. Venkateshwar K. Reddy, Eric M. Olson, and Stanley F. Slater, "When Marketing Efforts Go Flat," American Marketing Association, www.marketingpower.com/content21161C5850S2; "Michelin Baby Hoops It Up in New Advertising," press release dated April 17, 2001, www.michelin.com; "Integrating Competition and Goal-Based Positioning: The Value Equation," Northwestern University, www.kellogg.nwu.edu/faculty/sterntha/htm/module3/5.
5. Daniel Kahneman and Amos Tversky, "Choices, Values, and Frames," *American Psychologist,* 39(4) (April 1984), pp. 341–350.

6. Kent B. Monroe and Susan M. Petroshius, "Buyers' Perceptions of Price: An Update of the Evidence," in *Perspectives in Consumer Behavior,* 3rd ed., ed. H. Kassarjian and T. S. Robertson, (Glenview, IL: Scott-Foresman, 1981), pp. 43–55.

7. Zarrel V. Lambert, "Perceived Prices as Related to Odd and Even Price Endings," *Journal of Retailing,* 51 (Fall 1975), pp. 13–22; Robert M. Schindler and Alan R. Wiman, "Consumer Recall of Odd and Even Prices," working paper, Northeastern University, 1983; Robert M. Schindler, "Consumer Recognition of Increase in Odd and Even Prices," in *Advances in Consumer Research,* 11, ed. T. C. Kinnear (Association for Consumer Research, 1983), pp. 459–462.

8. Gerald E. Smith, "Prior Knowledge and Effectiveness of Massage Frames in Advertising," unpublished dissertation, Boston University, 1992.

9. Joel E. Urbany, William O Bearden, and Dan C. Weilbaker, "The Effect of Plausible and Exaggerated Reference Prices on Consumer Perceptions and Price Search," *Journal of Consumer Research,* 15 (June 1988), pp. 95–110.

10. See Eric N. Berkowitz and John R. Walton, "Contextual Influences on Consumer Price Responses: An Experimental Analysis," *Journal of Marketing Research,* 17 (August 1980), pp. 349–358; Albert J. Della Betta, Kent B. Monroe, and John M. McGinnis, "Consumer Perceptions of Comparative Price Advertisements," *Journal of Marketing Research,* 18 (November 1981), pp. 415–427: Cynthia Fraser, Robert E. Hite, and Paul L. Sauer, "Increasing Contributions in Solicitation Campaigns: The Use of Large and Same Anchorpoints," *Journal of Consumer Research,* 15 (September 1988), pp. 284–287: Mary F Mobley, William O. Bearden, and Jesse E. Teel, "An Investigation of Individual Responses to Tensile Price Claims," *Journal of Consumer Research,* 15 (September 1988), pp. 273–279; James G. Barnes, " Factors Influencing Consumer Reaction to Retail Newspaper Sale Advertising," Proceedings, Fall Educators' Conference (Chicago: American Marketing Association, 1975), pp. 471–477; Edward A. Blair and E. Laird Landon, Jr., " The Effects of Reference Prices in Retail Advertisements," *Journal of Marketing,* 45(2) (Spring 1981), pp. 61–69; John Liefeld and Louise A. Heslop, "Reference Prices and Deception in Newspaper Advertising," *Journal of Consumer Research,* 11 (March 1985), pp. 868–876. See also Robert E. Wilkes, "Consumer Usage of Base Price Information," *Journal of Retailing,* 48 (Winter 1972), pp. 72–85; Sadrudin A. Ahmed and Gary M. Gulas, "Consumers' Perception of Manufacturers' Suggested List Price," *Psychological Reports,* 50 (1982), pp. 507–518; Murphy A. Sewall and Michael H. Goldstien, " The Comparative Advertising Controversy: Consumer Perception of Catalog Showroom Reference Prices," *Journal of Marketing,* 43 (Summer 1979), pp. 85–92.

11. Albert J. Della Betta and Kent Monroe, "The Influence of Adaptation Levels on Subjective Price Perceptions," in *Advances in Consumer Research,* 1973, Proceedings of the Association for Consumer Research, Vol.1, ed. Peter Wright and Scott Ward (Urbana, IL: ACR, 1974), pp. 359–369.

12. A. Door et al., "Effect of Initial Selling Price on Subsequent Sales," *Journal of Personality and Social Psychology,* 11 (1969), pp. 345–350.

13. Daniel Kahneman, Jack L. Knetsch, and Richard H. Thaylor, "Fairness As a Constraint on Profit Seeking: Entitlements In the Market," *American Economic Review,* 76(4) (September 1986), pp. 728–741.

14. Joel Urbany, Thomas Madden, and Peter Deckson, "All's Not Fair in Pricing: An Initial Look at the Dual Entitlement Principle," *Marketing Letters* I(1) (1989), pp. 15–25; Marielza Matins and Kent Monroe, "Perceived Price Fairness: A New Look at an Old Construct," *Advances in Consumer Research*, Vol. 21 (Provo, UT: Association for Consumer Research), pp.75–78.

15. Richard Thaler, "Mental Accounting and Consumer Choice," *Marketing Science*, 4 (Summer 1985), p. 206.

16. Margaret C. Campbell, "Perceptions of Price Unfairness: Antecedents and Consequences," *Journal of Marketing Research*, 36 (May 1999), pp. 187–199.

17. Daniel Kahneman, Jack L. Knetsch, and Richard H. Thayler, "The Endowment Effect, Kiss Aversion, and Status Quo Bias," *Journal of Economic Perspectives*, 5(1) (Winter 1991), pp. 203–204.

18. Campbell, *op. cit.*

19. Daniel Kahneman and Amos Tversky, "Prospect Theory: An Analysis of Decision Under Risk," *Econometrica*, 47 (March 1979), pp. 263–291; Daniel Kahneman and Amos Tversky, The Psychology of Preferences," *Scientific American*, 246 (January 1982), pp. 162–170; Daniel Kahneman and Amos Tversky, "Choices, Values, and Frames," *American Psychologist*, 39, 4 (April 1984), pp. 341–350; Amos Tversky and Daniel Kahneman, The Framing of Decisions and Psychology of Choice," in *New Directions for Methodology of Social and Behavioral Science: Question Framing and Response Consistency*, No. 11 (San Francisco: Jossey-Bass, March 1982); Amos Tversky and Daniel Kahneman, "Advances in Prospect Theory: Cumulative Representation of Uncertainty," *Journal of Risk and Uncertainty* (1992).

6

PRICING POLICY

Managing Customer Expectations and Behaviors

Companies that do not manage their pricing by policy will, in most markets, lose control of it. In the process, they risk alienating their best customers, slowing the sales process, and eroding profitability. It happens because customers' willingness to pay for a product or service depends not only on their perceived value of it, but also on the expectations customers form about the need to pay for the value they receive. Sound policies create expectations on the part of each customer that the price they are asked to pay is determined objectively and has some relationship to the value received and/or the cost to serve. Unsound or nonexistent policies lead buyers to expect that they can manipulate information or their own behavior to win discounts without giving anything of value in return.

But, when asked about their companies' pricing policies, most managers respond with a blank stare or a description of the discounting authority granted at every level of the organization. But discounting authority is not a policy; it's merely an attempt to keep the consequences of policy-free pricing from spinning out of control. Pricing policies specify the circumstances under which, and the amounts by which, the company will discount its prices in return for specific behaviors on the part of customers and the sales force.

When companies lack firm pricing policies, they fail to maintain price integrity and consequently lose credibility with customers. That becomes a major problem, particularly when selling to professional buyers who are trained to manipulate transaction terms to get the best deal. When they believe that price is negotiable by unspecified amounts for unspecified reasons, they devise purchasing strategies to create reasons—real or illusory—to extract those discounts.

In addition, many more business buyers have adopted "strategic sourcing" strategies over the past two decades than sellers who have employed "strategic pricing." As a result, many suppliers operate at a disadvantage, setting prices by reacting to the policies of buyers rather then proactively controlling the process. Sales reps for whom price negotiation is often a part-time job are outmatched by purchasing agents who make price negotiation a profession. While sales reps often lack a big picture view of market dynamics, their counterparts in procurement collect such information systematically. Worse, sales reps are usually rewarded entirely for closing deals and are left empty-handed if they do not. Companies increasingly reward their purchasing agents for implementing long-term strategies that may involve short-term costs.

Even suppliers that have pricing policies usually have developed them reactively without thinking through the long-term customer behaviors they want to encourage. Consider the common pricing policies cited in Exhibit 6-1 and their

EXHIBIT 6-1 Behavioral Implications of Pricing Policies

Policy	Behavioral Implication
Offer discounts only when a customer has a better price from a competitor	Customers who are loyal and give you all their business don't get anything for their loyalty. Customers who solicit offers from multiple suppliers, particularly those willing to offer lower prices, get rewarded for their disloyalty. Smart customers establish relationships with other competitors, diverting some business from you, their preferred supplier, in order to "keep you honest."
Offer higher than normal discounts only to meet sales goals	Because it is difficult to tell early in a quarter whether discounts will be needed to meet the quarterly goal, the discounts tend to come forth in the last few weeks. Customers see the pattern and begin to hold their orders until the last few weeks of a quarter and buy forward for the next quarter. You bear the cost of building up inventories to meet the end-of-quarter demand.
Give discounts for annual volume, regardless of order volume or share of customer's total need your sales represent	Customers are rewarded for centralizing purchasing, moving it away from users who understand the value that you deliver. They are also rewarded for joining with other companies into "buying groups" that can qualify for still larger discounts, expend more effort evaluating all the alternative suppliers, and add a costly additional step to the sales process.
Publish list prices, but avoid predictable patterns in discounting to keep competitors guessing	Competitors can't benchmark their pricing against yours and now have to guess what they are benchmarking against. They have to rely on the information from purchasing agents, leaving you with no power to influence your competitors' pricing, while your customers' purchasing departments can manipulate price "information" for their benefit.

likely impact on your customers' behavior. In many instances, seemingly prudent policies incent customer behaviors that increase price pressure and damage long-term profitability.

In contrast to dysfunctional practices, true pricing policies provide incentives and expectations that support greater customer loyalty and shorter, more efficient price negotiations. Functional policies require specifying detailed criteria for valid discounting indicating to customers that discounts reward good behavior and not intimidation. For example, policies that give customers lower prices for ordering larger quantities, for complete commitment to the supplier for their needs, for using on-site service more judiciously, for managing inventories to avoid rush orders, and for paying on time all encourage good behavior and reduce costs for the seller that justify price concessions.

This chapter is about creating pricing policies that minimize the opportunity and incentives for customers to use manipulative purchasing tactics. It explains how to organize for pricing by policy and how to set pricing policies that maintain control with flexibility. It also describes specific policies that have proven effective for managing common challenges.

ORGANIZING FOR POLICY-BASED PRICING

Figuring out who should control pricing is a decision fraught with conflicting objectives and constraints. On one hand, it is good to respond quickly to customer requests for quotes and meet customers' different needs with flexibility. It's also important to counter competitive threats quickly. Such objectives imply that pricing authority should reside with or be close to the sales reps in the field. Unfortunately, empowering so many people with pricing authority can lead to loss of control and reduce profitability for several reasons.

Inconsistency: With decentralized pricing, the company ends up with at least as many pricing strategies as it has sales reps. When one customer learns that another got a lower price for the same product or service, the rep who sold the product at the higher price loses that customer's trust and might lose future sales. The customer negotiates more aggressively and less honestly in the future to get a better deal. He or she may adopt multiple suppliers to gain more leverage in negotiations. Moreover, your company's weakest sales reps, who can at least sell on the basis of value, will discount more deeply and frequently to close deals. As other reps are forced to match those deals, your weakest sales reps become your pricers! These risks of ad hoc price negotiation can be minimized only when customers lack the incentive or ability to determine the prices that other customers pay.

Incentives: Sales reps in most companies receive commissions for driving revenue and, as a result, have a near-term time horizon. Although such incentives can motivate them to maximize their sales effort, short-term revenue goals are totally inappropriate for someone creating pricing strategy to drive long-term profitability. Managing customer expectations and preserving perceptions of price integrity are more important to the company than winning a bad deal. So, too, is avoiding the commitment of scarce resources like peak supply guarantees or your best technical service people to customers with low profitability. However, the individual sales rep that must walk from a bad deal bears all the cost but only a small share of any future benefit! Consequently, he or she has an incentive to make pricing decisions that are, in general, lower than those that would maximize profit for the firm.

Analytics: Particularly in business-to-business selling, companies increasingly face purchasing departments with long-term cost-reduction strategies based on performance data. Individual sales reps lack access to the win-loss ratios, competitive price trends, their company's capacity utilization, and often even to purchase and service histories that would be necessary to design margin improvement strategies and track the results.

Recognizing the downside to decentralized pricing, some companies attempt to swing the pendulum too far in the other direction by centralizing all pricing authority. That can work so long as the firm has few customers and infrequently negotiates contracts within each market. In these situations, the pricing department or top sales executive, in effect, manages price negotiations directly. When customers are many and price negotiations more frequent, however, centralizing all pricing authority slows responsiveness to market opportunities, lengthens price negotiations and reduces sales force productivity. In short, greater margins come at the expense of lost sales.

A better solution is to centralize pricing policy development and monitoring while simultaneously empowering sales reps to structure deals consistent with those policies. To achieve that, pricing policies must cover most situations and specify in detail preapproved trade-offs and criteria for discounting. This is a nearly complete reversal from the practice of most companies in business-to-business markets, where sales reps and customers often deal without any consistent guidance on what might be acceptable, and then go through varying levels of sales management seeking approvals. Rather than spending their time selling the customer on terms that will be approved by management, they spend their time selling management on a deal acceptable to the customer! And managers, not then having the time to analyze which trade-offs make sense strategically for the company overall, are forced to make ad hoc reactive decisions in the face of customer-imposed deadlines.

When companies fully define pricing policies, their sales reps can have full authority to offer even the deepest discounts—subject to rigid constraints based on the customer characteristics and behaviors allowing a customer to qualify for them. For example, when confronted by a customer demanding a lower price to meet competition from an Asian supplier, the policy-empowered sales rep would not need to appeal to a higher level of management to authorize a lower price, thus delaying the sales process and risking the deal. Instead, the rep would say, for example, that the company would grant a "must-take, advance order" discount of 20 percent if the customer committed to must-take volumes months in advance, just as the Asian supplier would require. In this scenario, the customer might still decide to fill most needs from Asia, but could want a contract with the company to cover just the amounts that might be required to meet short-term variations in demand. In that case, the sales rep should inform the customer of his company's policy to supply product in those situations only at spot prices, sympathizing with the customer but assuring him that price commitments require corresponding volume commitments.

The effects of pricing by policy are almost universally desirable. Customers learn that there is no reward for simply beating on the supplier and no need to fear that a competitor is getting a better deal. Consequently, customers lose the incentive to keep sellers in the dark about their true needs and the value of them. They also learn that there are trade-offs between the prices they pay and what they get. This process of "give–get negotiation" forces customers, even purchasing agents, to learn what their organizations really value. Finally, if policies are designed well, they drive changes in customer behavior that reduce your cost to serve them.

Of course, this new approach to pricing policy shifts a lot of responsibility for pricing strategy off the backs of sales reps and onto the plates of senior managers, where it belongs. But which managers? The answer to that question is multifaceted. First, successful pricing requires cross-functional information. Ultimate responsibility for pricing policies should belong to a group of managers, a pricing steering committee, with several functions represented. Obviously, committee members would include people from sales who know how direct customers (which may be distributors or centralized purchasing departments) make decisions, and representatives from finance likely to have at least some understanding of true costs. Marketers, who should know what customers value and how value perception differences define market segments, should also be included. If the product or service is not storable, making capacity management a key requirement of pricing, then someone from operations should also be involved. In all cases, pricing steering committee members should be responsible for and compensated on business unit profitability, not for meeting their respective departments' individual objectives. This last requirement ensures that they all channel their different viewpoints toward the same fundamental company objective.

Of course, most people on such a committee will have had no prior training in making pricing decisions. They should not be doing the analytics, but they should be able to rely on leadership from someone who will define pricing questions strategically and develop information to answer them. Sometimes, leadership comes from a committee member with prior pricing experience. More often, it comes from one or more people charged specifically with price management, perhaps a marketing manager or a specialist in pricing. The key to that person's success is not where he or she reports, but his or her credibility as an honest information broker who understands the challenges that pricing creates across the organization. That person might be a former sales manager who was successful in improving margins within a sales region, or may be a consultant with insights based on drawing on broad experience with other firms, or perhaps a successful pricing manager hired from another firm. The job of the committee is to make the decisions about policy that will comprise the business unit's pricing strategy, as we have broadly defined it in Chapter 2. The job of the pricing manager is to frame the right questions and guide the process that will lead to that result.

CREATING AND MANAGING PRICING POLICIES STRATEGICALLY

Building a pricing strategy is an incremental and ongoing process. You start with whatever you have now, and gain experience and profit as you improve it. A commitment to stick to a simple process ensures that you are, in fact, incrementally building a strategy rather than just "putting out fires." Creating and managing pricing policies strategically involves three steps: diagnosis, policy development, and implementation.

DIAGNOSIS

Busy managers on the pricing committee risk falling into the habit of reacting to individual pricing problems. The job of the pricing steering team is not to solve the individual problems reactively, but to develop general policies for dealing with them proactively. Rather than spending time thinking about how to respond to a specific customer's demand for a lower price, the pricing manager should find out why that customer is making that demand. Is it because this customer has learned that others have negotiated lower prices from you? Has a competitor offered a lower price without the services you offer because the purchasing department has taken over buying and does not recognize the unique value of your differentiation? Or is it because your logistics department frequently failed to deliver on time last year?

Each cause has a different policy-based solution. Before that solution can be designed and implemented, however, it is first necessary to clearly identify the problem and its source. Some standard diagnostic tools can help one understand pricing problems and opportunities. They include "price banding," "price waterfalls," and "customer (or segment) profitability analysis." Price banding and waterfall analysis reveal why you are capturing less value from some customers or products than others. Customer profitability analysis indicates whether your prices reflect differences in the cost to serve different customers or segments. These tools are not comprehensive; often the best approach is getting out and talking with customers about their needs at a time separate from a sales presentation. But these tools deserve some discussion here because of their unique applications in pricing.

EXHIBIT 6-2   Example of Discount Variability

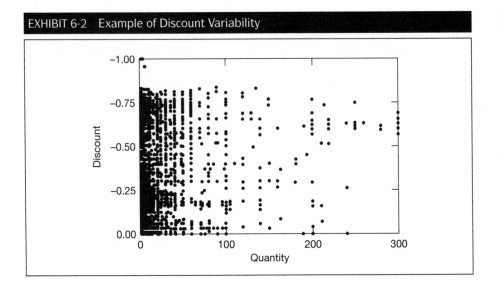

PRICE BANDING

Price banding is a statistical technique for identifying which customers are paying significantly more or significantly less than the band of "fair" prices for a given type of transaction. The technique provides actionable data to the pricing committee to develop policy by clearly identifying customers whose aggressive tactics enable them to earn unmerited discounts or by identifying customers that are paying more than average because they have not pushed hard enough for appropriate discounts. Exhibit 6-2 graphs the inconsistent, apparently random pattern of pricing that we often encounter at companies with flawed policies. However, the sales force or sales management responsible might argue that there's some sort of hidden logic to it, a method to the madness. To the extent that they are right, and sometimes they are, the pricing manager's job is to make that logic transparent to himself and the pricing steering committee. To the extent that the variation is truly random and therefore damaging the firm's profit and price integrity, the pricing committee's job is to create policies to eliminate it.

There are five steps in the price banding process:

1. Identify and get the steering team and sales reps to agree on the legitimate factors (service levels, size of orders, geographic region, customer's business type, etc.) that they believe justify price variations across accounts based on value.

2. Execute a statistical regression of price levels or discount percentages against measures of those legitimate variations:

   Percent discount = f(volume, services, region, etc) + ε

3. For each observation (an actual customer account or order), use the regression equation to estimate the price or discount that this customer would have gotten if given the average discount offered by all sales reps for each of the legitimate discount factors relevant to that customer. This is the

"fitted value" of the regression. Label these the "fair prices" or "fair discounts," with fairness defined as treating everyone by the same rules.[1]

4. Plot the actual prices customers pay and compare them to the fair prices or fair discounts along the regression line; examine the positive and negative differences, as illustrated in Exhibit 6-3. Plot a line one standard deviation above and one standard deviation below the "fair value" line to reveal the outliers. To the extent that price variation is actually caused by legitimate factors, the R^2 of the regression (called the *coefficient of determination,* it reports the degree to which the regression equation statistically "explains" the actual price distribution) will be high (near 1) and the band very narrow. To the extent that much discounting is truly random, or occurs for reasons that no one is willing to propose as legitimate, it will be low (close to zero) and the band around the fair price line will be wide.

5. Brainstorm possible causes of the random variation and identify correlations to test those hypotheses. For example, does a minority of sales reps account for most of the negative variation while a different group accounts for the positive? Is the negative-variation minority composed of the newest reps while the group accounting for the positive differences is more experienced? If so, the key to your problem is probably documenting what the savvy reps know about selling value that the new ones need to be taught, and applying tighter policy guidelines on the new ones. Other explanations for the random variation could relate to the customer's buying process (is it centralized?), indicating a need for different policies in dealing with different processes. Still others could relate to when contracts were signed during a past recession, indicating a need to revisit policies for contracting when sales and prices are depressed.

EXHIBIT 6-3 Price Banding Output

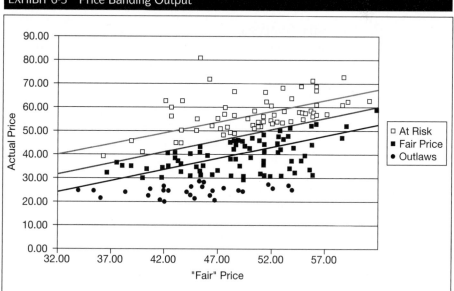

PRICE WATERFALLS

In some companies, the possible sources of lost revenue and profit are many and poorly tracked. In a classic and oft-quoted article, two McKinsey consultants showed how simply managing the plethora of discounts can vastly improve company profitability.[2] Exhibit 6-4 illustrates their *price waterfall* analysis. Although the company might estimate account profitability by the invoice price, there are often many other sources of profit leakage along the way. The "pocket price," revenue that is actually earned after all the discounts are netted out, is often much less. More importantly, the amount of that leakage could range from very small to absurdly high. In one case, a company that analyzed its pocket prices discovered that sales to some of its customers resulted in more leakages than the gross margin at list price! In addition to the salesperson's commission, there was a volume incentive for the retailer, a commission for the buying group to which the retailer belonged, a co-op advertising incentive, an incentive discount for the distributor to hold inventories, an early payment discount for the distributor, a coupon for the end customer, and various fees for processing the coupons.

Agreements to let the customer pay later, to let the customer place smaller orders, to give the customer an extra service at no cost, and so on all add up. The result can become a much wider variance in the pocket prices than in the invoice prices. Because companies often monitor such concessions less closely than explicit price discounts, the giveaways tend to grow. This does not mean that such discounts should be stopped; they often provide valuable incentives and can be effective in hiding discounts while still maintaining the important appearance of price integrity. The danger is simply in letting them go unmanaged, without applying rigid policies on their use. After discovering that sales reps waived shipping charges for customers much more often than necessary, a large distributor, for example, imposed policies to require more documentation before such orders were processed. That simple policy change resulted in tens of millions more dollars to the bottom line.

CUSTOMER PROFITABILITY ANALYSIS

Although cost should not drive the prices you charge, your prices can definitely affect the cost-to-serve customers and, therefore, your profitability. Many companies differentiate their offers with bundled services, even when demands on those services are subject to customer discretion and therefore are not proportional to the volume of sales. "Service abusers" can boost your average cost of sales while "service avoiders" drive up your average cost of sales by abandoning you in favor of cheaper, low-service competitors. Even when variations in service cost are outside the customers' control, it makes sense to pursue pricing policies that cause you to win low-cost, high-profit customers disproportionately.

Although a cost-to-serve analysis ideally reflects the measured cost to serve each customer or customer segment, in practice the cost of measuring frequently precludes such accuracy. Yet, the cost of ignoring differences in service expenses by allocating them equally is also high. In high-service industries like printing, equipment rentals, and building management, it's not uncommon to discover that 15 percent or more of volume is actually a drain on profit, while some low-price

EXHIBIT 6-4 Price Waterfall Analysis

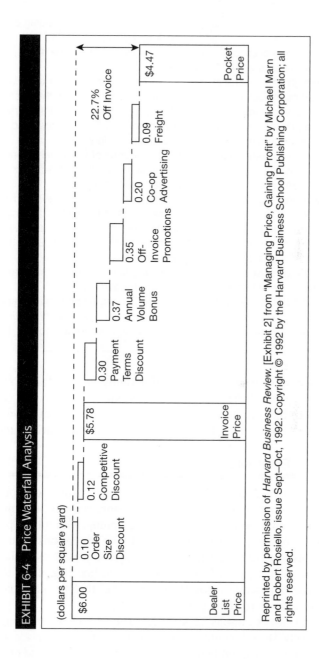

(dollars per square yard)

$6.00 — Dealer List Price
0.10 — Order Size Discount
0.12 — Competitive Discount
$5.78 — Invoice Price
0.30 — Payment Terms Discount
0.37 — Annual Volume Bonus
0.35 — Off-Invoice Promotions
0.20 — Co-op Advertising
0.09 — Freight
$4.47 — Pocket Price

22.7% Off Invoice

EXHIBIT 6-5   Creating a "Roughly Right" Cost Index

1. Identify buyer purchase behaviors (e.g., rush vs. spot vs. standing orders) or characteristics (e.g., has a loading dock for deliveries, no dock but drive up to door, no external access) that most likely drive cost-to-serve differences among customers. These are your "cost drivers."
2. Describe high-cost, average-cost, and low-cost behaviors for each value driver, creating as many distinct levels as necessary. For example, the description for high-cost delivery requirements might be "rush orders," that for average-cost delivery requirements might be "5 day or more advance orders," and that for low-cost delivery requirements might be "standing orders."
3. Classify each customer according to its incidence of those behaviors or characteristics. Classifications may be all-or-nothing (e.g., has a loading dock), or by degree (27 percent of orders fall into the "rush" category).
4. Determine which specific costs (e.g., labor, equipment utilization, inventories, billing expense) vary the most across each cost driver's classifications. Measure that variation using a sample of customers or orders in each group. For example, "rush orders" may involve 17 percent more labor cost and require 13 percent more equipment capacity than regular orders.
5. Let the average cost variation from the sample serve as the "standard cost variation" for that type of behavior or customer characteristic.
6. Estimate the cost to serve any particular customer by adding the service cost variations for characteristics, plus the cost variation of order types times the share of the customer's orders of each type, to the average cost to serve.

customers that were driven away could actually be profitable if cost-to-serve were measured properly. The solution is to create "roughly right" cost allocation indexes and use them to build a "roughly right" relative profit index by account or segment. Exhibit 6-5 describes the process for creating such an index.

POLICY DEVELOPMENT

The key to developing good policies is to treat each request for a price exception as a request to create or change a policy. The more requests, the more likely it is that the policy is in need of review. In the beginning, with lots of poorly defined and ineffective policies in place and lots of past exceptions granted, there are likely to be lots of requests. As new, well-thought-out policies replace poor ones, customers and sales reps need to learn that no ad hoc exceptions to policies will be granted. The only requests for "special pricing" that should be considered are for situations not covered by a policy.

Putting this "no exceptions" stake in the ground is a key to making pricing decisions strategically. Most discount proposals, whether to reduce price to win business or to increase price to exploit tight supply, have an immediate and obvious payback as well as a delayed and less obvious cost. Pricing by policy rather than by exception forces companies to consider longer-term costs when making final pricing decisions.

No longer should a pricing decision involve asking whether to grant a discount to win this customer's business or to meet this quarter's sales goal. It should involve asking whether it makes sense to establish a policy that says all customers like this one can be offered the same discount, or that quarterly sales shortfalls can be remedied with an end-of-quarter discount. Making the decision a policy question forces decision makers to think through the broader and longer-term implication of the precedents they are setting.

Establishing a policy involves specifying what pricing is acceptable under what circumstances for customers meeting which criteria. The goal of a good policy is to specify the circumstances and criteria in a way that maximizes the benefits you hope to gain while minimizing the costs. For example, a high-volume retailer through whom you would like to sell your product demands a better price than other retailers currently selling the same product. A simple price exception would open the door to discounting for other retailers and invite the current prospect to ask for more in the next contract. The key to doing the deal profitably is to design a policy that minimizes those adverse effects.

In this case, the pricing committee should ask why the value of the brand should be worth less to this retailer than to others, or why the cost to serve this retailer might be less. If neither question has a valid answer, it is hard to justify a pricing policy that treats this retailer differently than others. In the long term, you will end up having to offer all retailers the same lower price that you offer this one. Perhaps, however, the large retailer is a "destination store" where loyal buyers come to buy whatever brands that retailer offers. In that case, the value of your brand name to the retailer is less and the policy solution might be to offer a lower price for a house brand version of your product. Alternatively, perhaps this retailer requires a very low cost to serve because it takes no merchandizing credits, does not do co-op advertising and accurately forecasts minimal return rates. Then the manufacturer can set a policy of lower prices for retailers who also meet all those criteria. You can achieve your goal of increasing sales, but maintain pricing that has a value-based rationale and integrity across customers.

Ideally, policies are transparent, are consistent, and enable companies to address pricing challenges proactively. If policies are transparent, customers need not engage in threats and misinformation to learn the trade-offs you are willing to make. Airlines have transparent pricing rules that, while few of us like them, we accept because we know what they are and can make our choices about what, if anything, to give up (rebooking flexibility, Saturday night stay, priority upgrades) for a better price. Consistent policies communicate that it is impossible to "game the system" by contacting multiple points in the company to find the best deal. Communicating policies proactively by telling customers the options for how you will do business with them is much less contentious than telling them reactively what proposals of theirs your company has already prerejected.

POLICIES TO MANAGE PRICE EXPECTATIONS

Begin the process of creating a new policy by asking what expectations and resulting behaviors your current pricing creates. Then ask how a change in expectations could improve your ability to capture prices that reflect the value you deliver. Finally, begin crafting a transparent policy to change customer expectations and encourage preferred behavior on their part. There are four general areas for categorizing pricing decisions.

Promotional pricing: Promotional pricing is effective to the extent that it induces new product trial, or desirable behaviors by channel partners, without undermining the viability of the regular price. A lot of companies get addicted to promotional pricing, however, because they lack thoughtful policies that keep it from being misused to meet a short-term sales goal at the expense of long-term profitability. Some companies, for example, get hooked on end-of-quarter promotions because they have unwittingly trained customers to hold orders to the end of the quarter and to buy forward for their next quarter's needs, resulting in large amounts of volume sold at discount unnecessarily. Suppliers can change those expectations with a policy change: guarantee customers who buy at any time during a quarter that they will get a rebate if there is a lower price offered later in the quarter. Similarly, consumer package goods companies get addicted because customers and retailers learn to stock up on promotionally priced products. A policy that limits the form of trial discounting for established products to couponing solves that problem.

Negotiated pricing: A purchasing agent's worst nightmare is to discover, after negotiating what he or she thought was a good deal, that a competitor got a better one from the same supplier. By caving into threats and power plays, you educate your customers to believe that price is determined by the risk you perceive in losing their business. In reaction, smart buyers will adopt all types of dysfunctional buying behaviors to increase that risk and your perception of it. Transparent, but firm, policies reduce that dysfunctional perception and build the reputation that your pricing, and the sales rep communicating it, has integrity.

Initially, if your discounting has been inconsistent and unjustified in the past, you may need to guarantee your integrity with a "most-favored nation" clause assuring customers that no one else buying the same product and service package in the same quantities will get a lower price. Once customers believe that disinformation and intimidation will not get them better prices than would otherwise be offered, they become more forthcoming with information. A sales rep who reports that he or she has the authority to negotiate a better price, but only based on criteria specified by policy, communicates to the customer that there is a reward from working with him or her. The reward is in finding the best trade-off between price and value within the policies.

Quantity discounting: Most quantity discounting is designed purely to win the business of high-volume customers, and so it rewards customers for doing nothing but negotiating big deals. To achieve that end, large companies centralize purchasing and smaller companies join buying groups, thus separating the decision makers from the local users who understand the value you deliver. In most cases, neither centralized purchasing nor the buying groups guarantee any sales that still require a local sales effort. They simply create another sales hurdle and use their volume leverage to beat down the price before you even have the opportunity to sell the value. Moreover, not all volume is equally valuable. One high-quality supplier to the bottling industry actually negotiated discounts for annual volume at a fixed price despite the fact that demand for its product was highly seasonal. Thus, during the peak season, nearly all available volume was taken up by large companies buying under their fixed price contracts, while smaller vendors were selling at much higher spot prices. During off-peak times, the smaller vendors undercut the company's contract prices, reducing its volume.

To gain incremental volume from discounting without encouraging dysfunctional order aggregation, policies need to reward customers for loyalty, not just size. The solution for the supplier to the bottling industry was to establish a standard seasonal pattern for purchases. Anyone who wanted contract pricing for peak season purchases could have no more than 130 percent of the monthly average volume they purchased during off-peak months. Anyone who wanted more peak volume would pay a spot price, but with priority going to contract customers. Contract customers threatened to take their business elsewhere but, by sticking to a policy and exploiting the value customers placed on reliable peak supply, the company changed their expectations about who needed whom the most at peak times. As a result, the supplier gained a lot more off-peak volume at contract prices.

Bid-Loyalty Pricing: How you treat loyal customers versus those who repeatedly put the business out to bid has a strong effect on expectations. Companies that exploit their best customers with higher prices for less service, while giving their best prices and service to those who are always demanding a new concession to retain their business, deserve to be abused! After all, customers are only exploiting the company's own lack of price integrity. In the past decade, many companies have undermined their profitability and price integrity by agreeing to participate in unfair "reverse auction" bids. The goal and common result of these processes is usually not to find the lowest priced supplier in the market, but to cajole sellers into thinking of their products as commodities, driving them to accept hardball buying tactics and cut their prices.

Sellers that thwart this tactic adopt policies that change customers' expectations. Some simply refuse to bid. If you know that your customer has a strong preference to do at least some business with you, this can be the best way to go. An alternative is to think about all the ways that you would like the customer to do business with you to minimize your costs (e.g., must-take orders, no-rush orders, wide delivery windows, short payment terms, unbundled technical service). Bid at a price that would enable you to be equally profitable if the customer were to accept those terms, and tell the customers that you are bidding for a "commodity" offering, not what they have come to expect. When, as is likely, you win the bid, invite the customer to discuss the charges for any of those services they might like to have as an add-on. Let all customers know that you will not give away your regular product quality and service levels in bidding processes that commoditize the offer.

On the other side, think about how to build rewards for loyalty into your pricing policies. One way is to give customers a significant rebate for all purchases in excess of, say, 90 percent of their prior year's purchases. This substantially raises the cost to try a competitor's product, while rewarding customers who establish exclusive relationships. Another way is to give access to your most innovative products and services first to those customers with whom you have an exclusive or preferred relationship.

IMPLEMENTING POLICIES

A common fear for managers who are replacing ad hoc discounting with transparent and consistent pricing policies is that sales reps and customers will not accept the change. While a minority might not make the transition, most will accept the change if it is implemented well. Sales reps don't like being beaten up over price, don't like the long sales cycles that reactive price negotiations cause, and don't like having to spend their time making the case for discounts internally. The confidence that their management has the backbone to stand with them in resisting bad deals and is willing to empower them with the authority to cut good deals consistent with preapproved policies motivates good salespeople. Most customers do not enjoy manipulative, drawn-out price negotiations either. They do it to survive suppliers whom they believe will exploit open, loyal customers while rewarding disingenuous ones.

Even so, simply creating better policies isn't enough. You have to manage the implementation to make them effective. Managing the transition from ad hoc, reactive pricing to policy-driven, proactive pricing is a sequential process. Changing expectations takes time. What follows are steps and guidelines for the process.

MANAGEMENT RESPONSIBILITY

To be effective, the existence and rationale for policies must be appropriately positioned with customers. Remember, policies are not just consistent rules for the sales force; they are a means to manage customer expectations. If customers already expect that their sales rep is someone whose primary objective is to make the sale and with whom they negotiate deals that the rep's bosses must approve, a new, less flexible approach by the rep will not have much immediate credibility. And, if the sales rep is the source of the message, he or she will take the brunt of any hostility it generates.

To give the policies credibility, they need to come from management. For smaller customers, this can be in the form of a letter. For larger ones, particularly those who have negotiated inordinately large discounts, the communication needs to be direct from someone high in management. The message needs to be that this is about fairness in treating customers consistently, about establishing open and honest relationships and about empowering sales reps to offer a wider variety of trade-offs (the "give–get negotiation") to align what customers buy with their needs. With the message coming from management, the sales rep is not the cause of these constraints, but is instead someone to whom a customer can turn to ensure that they are getting a deal that best meets their needs within those constraints.

SALES FORCE BUY-IN

Good policies will make it easier for sales reps to resist pure price negotiation and to align price paid with value received. Sales reps, however, need to believe that those are necessary and valuable objectives for them, not just for their company. The first step in that direction, even before policies are in place, is to measure and reward salespeople for driving profitability, not just revenue. Many companies reward salespeople for making larger and more frequent sales, not for making more profitable sales. Unfortunately, giving salespeople revenue-based incentives and empowering them to negotiate prices is a toxic combination that poisons their motivation to sell value.

Consider the dilemma facing sales representatives, independent dealers, and manufacturers' representatives who are compensated as a percentage of sales. Say that the company's margin is 10 percent on high-volume deals. A sales rep who invests twice as much time with the account, selling value and/or getting the customer to change costly behaviors that drive up costs, might at best be able to increase the profit earned on the deal by an additional 10 percent of sales—doubling the profitability. Even if all that increase is in price, however, the sales rep's revenue-based commission increases by 10 percent at most. In contrast, instead of trying to sell value, one of her colleagues spends the same amount of time selling a second deal of equal size with only a 10 percent margin. As a result, the colleague's effort increases the company's profit contribution by the same amount, but he earns twice as much commission for doing so. Even if the colleague has to cut the price by 5 percent to win the deal, reducing the profit by half, he gets a bigger commission while the sales rep who spent time selling value rather than volume hears about her failure to keep pace!

Until you fix these perverse incentives associated with revenue-based measurement and compensation—driving revenue at the expense of profit—it will be difficult to get sales reps to do the right thing. The key to aligning sales incentives with those of the company is to link compensation with profitability. Exhibit 6-6 explains how to do that, using a contribution margin-based *profitability factor*. More than just theory, paying for profitability provides mutually beneficial sales incentives. And it encourages salespeople to pay more attention to value drivers beyond price such as innovative product features, quality defects, and delivery speed. Once the company aligns sales incentives, salespeople will begin clamoring for the other things they need to succeed. At one company, for example, sales reps traded in their company sedans for vehicles in which they could transport product to new customers with an urgent need.

Successful value-based pricing and sales requires an up-front investment to understand the value delivered to customers. It is unreasonable to expect each individual salesperson to make that investment; the effort should be centralized and the cost spread across the organization. The results then need to be translated into value-based sales tools that reflect the economics of the purchase decision. Salespeople have the right to expect product-specific sales training that focuses not only on the principles of value-based selling, but also on how to apply segment-specific tools to measure and demonstrate value to customers.

EXHIBIT 6-6   Creating a Sales Incentive to Drive Profit

The key to inducing the sales force to sell value is to measure their performance and compensate them not just for sales volume, but also for profit contribution. Although some companies have achieved this by adding Rube Goldberg—like complexity to their compensation scheme, there is a fairly simple, intuitive way to accomplish the same objective. Give salespeople sales goals as before, but tell them that the sales goals are set at "target" prices. If they sell at prices below or above the "target," the sales credit they earn will be adjusted by the profitability of the sale.

The key to determining the sales credit that someone would earn for making a sale is calculating the *profitability factor* for each class of product. To induce salespeople to maximize their contribution to the firm, actual sales revenue should be adjusted by that profitability factor (called the sales "kicker") to determine the sales credit. Here is the formula:

$$\text{Sales Credit} = [\text{Target Price} - k\,(\text{Target Price} - \text{Actual Price})] \times \text{Units Sold}$$

where k is the profitability factor (or "kicker").

The profitability factor should equal 1 divided by the product's percentage contribution margin at the target price, in order to calculate sales credits varying proportionally to the product's profitability. For example, when the contribution margin is 20 percent, the profitability factor equals 5 (1.0/0.20). When a salesperson grants a 15 percent price discount, the discount is multiplied by the profitability factor of 5, reducing the sales credit by 75 percent rather than by 15 percent had there been no profitability adjustment. Consequently, when $1,000 worth of product is sold for $850, it produces only $250 of sales credit. But when $500 worth of product is sold for $550 (a 10 percent price premium), the salesperson earns $750 of sales credit ($500 + 5 × $50).

Because salespeople are more likely to take a short-term view of profitability and can always move on to another company, the most motivating profitability factor for the firm is usually *higher* than the minimum kicker value based solely on the contribution margin. Obviously, the importance of this adjustment is directly related to the variable contribution margin. The larger the margin and, presumably, the greater the product's importance to the firm, the greater the profitability factor's ability to align what's good for the salesperson with what's good for the company.

This is not merely theory. As companies have moved toward more negotiated pricing, many have adopted this scheme in markets as diverse as office equipment, market research services, and door-to-door sales. Although a small percentage of salespeople cannot make the transition to value selling and profit-based compensation, most embrace it with enthusiasm. Managers should be prepared for the consequences, however, because salespeople's complaints about the company's competitiveness do not subside. Instead, salespeople who previously fretted about the company's high prices begin complaining about slow deliveries, quality defects, lack of innovative product features, the need for better sales support to demonstrate value, and so on. In short, sales force attention moves from reflexive gripes about price to legitimate concerns about value drivers the company does or does not provide to customers.

PRIORITIZE AND SEQUENCE CHALLENGES

Good policies can generate more business from customers who were disadvantaged in dealing with you in the past. We often find that companies who respond reflexively with lower price and more services for their biggest customers correspondingly neglect others. Some segment of mid-size customers may well need high levels of service, priority shipping, or other benefits routinely granted to large customers. But those mid-size customers might actually be willing to pay for it! Policies that force the lowest-priced customers to accept less service, even if they have high volumes, while enabling smaller customers to get the best service if they are willing to pay for it, can open profitable growth opportunities.

For example, a large commercial printer had nearly lost a profitable mid-volume client because it shipped the customer's catalog late to accommodate the needs of a high-volume customer. The cost of the delay to the mid-size company was huge relative to its size, so it explored taking its catalog job to a smaller printer—one with fewer capabilities that would treat the catalog account with respect. We advised the large printer to tighten its pricing policies, including making priority scheduling an unbundled "service" and stop simply giving it to the largest customers for free. When the large printer offered the mid-size cataloger the service at a premium price—coupled with a financial guarantee and a deep apology for failing to honor its needs in the past—the cataloger's management was delighted at finally being heard. They renewed the contract, with the higher service level, at a substantially higher price.

Remember that pricing policies also can empower sales reps to offer greater discounts. That is not a bad thing so long as the policy, built from an understanding of relative cost to serve, ensures that such business can be delivered cost effectively. One large trucking company has achieved a competitive advantage, and much of its profit, from selectively serving highly price-sensitive shippers. Whenever its sales reps encounter a price-sensitive customer, they can offer a lower price provided that the customer commits to various protocols allowing "backhaul" shipments with a 2-day window of time for pickup, advance scheduling, 24-hour pickup availability, and particular geographic shipping locations. The explicit protocols make serving those customers profitable even at low prices. Sales reps, paid on profitability rather than volume, love having the "backhaul option" available when needed.

NEGOTIATE TRANSITIONS, NOT CONCLUSIONS

When managers and sales reps see that the same policies that limit their ability to give away price and services to some customers empower them to win deals from others, they become more financially and psychologically prepared to face those customers who have most benefited in the past. They are easy to identify from the price banding analysis shown in Exhibit 6-3: they are the roughly 17 percent of customers whose prices fall one standard deviation below the "fair price" line, whom we call the "outlaws."

There are outlaws in every market. They are the ones in business markets who build their competitive advantages not on their own superior ability to create value, but on their superior ability to extract value from suppliers. In consumer markets, they are the ones who regularly return products after using them for months, buy only the products that are on sale, and have poor credit. One large retail electronics chain recently announced that it was targeting such customers in its database and developing new policies for dealing with them, including purging them from its mailings and adhering rigidly to its returns policy.

To handle outlaws, focus first on the ones you can best afford to confront. Tell them that they have done a great job in getting much for little in the past, but that their business no longer justifies continuing to serve them at current prices and service levels. Some will choose to take their business elsewhere. That is not necessarily bad because their business not only generates low profit but also risks the profitability of other business should other customers learn of lower pricing. Not all customers will leave, however. Some will simply get angry and have their more senior executives call your more senior executives to complain.

The complainers are the ones who can be redeemed if carefully managed. The more time and energy they invest in attempting to intimidate you into reversing the decision, the more you know that they realize they cannot get an equally good deal elsewhere. Ultimately, those buyers' egos will require that you give them some concession, including listening to their tirades, to retain their business. Still, never give them a concession on ultimately reaching a "fair price." Instead, give them some slack on how long they will have to reach the fair price, based on their commitment to you. For example, instead of insisting that they pay the full 18 percent increase that would be necessary to reach the fair-price line, they could sign a 1-year contract and pay 6 percent more in the first 4 months, 12 percent more in the second 4 months, and 18 percent more in the third 4 months. Their average increase is only 12 percent. But at the end, you have established and they have paid the fair price that is the basis for consistency across customers. It is also the basis from which they will be negotiating their next contract.

MONITOR AND MEASURE RESULTS

The value in pricing by policy is not only in the expectations they create among customers; it is also in the power a policy gives you to test, evaluate, and improve your pricing over time. The problem with pricing by exception rather than by policy is that you can never collect enough data from doing something once to determine whether or not it was a good decision. By having the entire sales force apply a policy to the same situation, you can see the effect of that policy on win-loss rates, price erosion, customer loyalty, and so on.

The challenges to policy-based pricing, particularly if it involves empowering sales reps to offer even larger discounts subject to restrictions, are ensuring that the policies are followed fully and capturing the data necessary to evaluate them. This is especially the case where elements of the product and service package are unbundled, where pricing is dependent on the demographics of the customer, and where many sales reps and deals are involved.

Fortunately, there are now many excellent software packages for price management and deal structuring.[3] They can be programmed to prevent orders at prices inconsistent with the policies, to propose alternative deal structures consistent with policy, and to capture data necessary to evaluate policies. They often also have features enabling pricing and sales managers to quickly generate analytics, such as price bands and price waterfalls, by product, by sales rep, and by customer. In cases where there are a lot of homogenous transactions, software vendors also offer packages to test and help "optimize" price setting—the topic that we will review in Chapter 7.

Summary

Strategic pricing is not a series of independent, on-off decisions. Every proposal you make creates expectations about the offers you will make in the future, not only for that customer but also for other customers who learn about the deal and for your sales force. Those expectations influence behavior, and many customers will change their behavior to reflect what they think will get them the best deal. As a result, it is extremely important in any market with repeat customers or with price visibility across customers to manage pricing by policy.

Policy-based pricing requires centralizing the policy development process even as it facilitates decentralization and empowerment in execution. Centralization leads to pricing based on broad diagnoses of the problem and the implications of a solution, rather than on analysis of each customer deal. It leads to creating price and service options proactively, rather than reacting to those proposed by customers. Ultimately, it changes customer expectations about the extent to which they can influence the prices they receive by manipulation and misinformation.

Successful implementation of pricing policies requires building support and consensus within your organization that the policies are good for the company. That may require changing incentives, taking on the easier challenges first, transitioning customers over time, and managing the price-quoting process using software and systems.

Notes

1. Note that the "fair-prices" line defined here is a different calculation than the "fair-value line" concept of Customer Value Modeling theorists who, following what we consider to be a flawed approach, plot average price-to-perceived quality ratios based on customer surveys of product attribute importance and brand performance. See our discussion in Chapter 3.

2. Michael Marn and Robert Rosiello, "Managing Price, Gaining Profit," *Harvard Business Review* (September–October 1992), pp. 84–93.

3. Leading companies selling price management software for markets in which deals are negotiated include Metreo, Rapt, Vendavo, and Zilliant.

7 | PRICE LEVEL

Setting the Right Price for Sustainable Profit

Setting prices is one of the most complex and challenging decisions facing marketers. Effective pricing requires gathering and integrating large volumes of information about the company's strategic goals and cost structure, the customer's preferences and actual needs, and the competition's pricing and strategic intent. Even the best marketers struggle to synthesize these data into coherent, profit-maximizing prices. The task is even more challenging because price setting often is a politically charged decision whose outcome affects all functional areas. Given the importance of pricing as a driver of profitable growth, the company must develop a pricing process that systematically incorporates all relevant information and wins the support of sales, marketing, finance, and operations.

Unfortunately, the complexity of pricing decisions leads many companies to take shortcuts that undercut their profits and increase the customer's ability to negotiate lower prices. For example, a biomedical device manufacturer we know has focused primarily on costs and to a lesser degree, value, when setting prices. The company knows that many of its products are differentiated, but it has not invested enough time and effort in value estimation to know how much that differentiation is worth to customers. As a result, its published prices tend to be quite high relative to the competition and the customer's willingness to pay. On the surface, theirs might seem like a prudent approach because it ensures the company never "leaves money on the table" when negotiating final prices. Over time, however, the differentiation value of many of its products has eroded as competitors introduced new, higher-performing products. The resulting price pressure has led to ad hoc discounting, which undercuts the company's reputation for price integrity. Customers have learned that published prices are only a starting point for negotiation and that the way to get better prices is to negotiate harder. Now, after several years of reduced price realization and lower profits, the company has correctly concluded that it must add discipline to its discounting process and set prices that are defensible to customers.

124

In this chapter, we present a three-stage process for setting prices that integrates the relevant customer, competitor, and cost data in a framework leading to more profitable prices. Our approach, based on our experience helping companies to improve their pricing capabilities, also builds organizational support by encouraging the active participation of each functional area at an appropriate point in the process.

The process is efficient and adaptable to most products, services, and market contexts. Key inputs include value estimation and segmentation, customer price sensitivity factors, costs, strategic objectives, and market response analysis. In many pricing decisions, however, it is unnecessary to dwell on each input. For example, there is little benefit in formally estimating value for an undifferentiated, low-priced product. Therefore, we will point out when it is worthwhile to gather and evaluate data for each of the key inputs such as value estimation. Finally, our framework suggests how to implement price changes by communicating the rationale for new prices to customers and the sales organization.

THE PRICE-SETTING PROCESS

We have developed a three-stage, price-setting process built on the fundamental premise that prices should be set for customer segments—not products. As we discussed in Chapter 3 on value creation, it's best to segment markets on the basis of value delivered and perceived. And, as Chapter 4 on price structure explained, companies forgo profit unnecessarily when they adopt price structures (e.g., "one size fits all") that do not adequately reflect differences in value delivered and cost-to-serve across segments. Thus, the three-stage process illustrated in Exhibit 7-1 starts with setting preliminary prices for each market segment.

Another underlying premise of our approach is that the price-setting process should be efficient. Managers have limited time and capital to invest in any single strategy decision, regardless of importance. We advise them to evaluate the return on their time invested at each stage of the process to determine whether each analysis provides enough actionable information to materially affect end prices. For example, a key question for setting preliminary segment prices is the amount of effort to invest in assessing the value of a product or service. For mature products with little differentiation and whose benefits are well understood by the customer, the pricer would not learn enough new actionable information to justify doing a precise value assessment, such as our Economic Value Estimation® (EVE) process, using external customer data.

Two additional questions must be answered in the first stage of setting preliminary, or baseline, prices for each segment. Given an understanding of how value accrues across each segment, how much of the differential value should the firm attempt to capture with price? The answer establishes a starting point for addressing the next question: How much should the firm adjust relative segment prices to account for different price sensitivities?

EXHIBIT 7-1 Price Setting Process

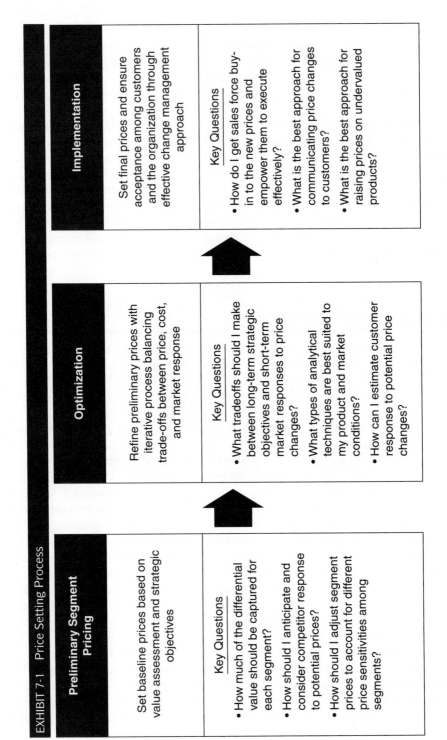

Preliminary Segment Pricing

Set baseline prices based on value assessment and strategic objectives

Key Questions

- How much of the differential value should be captured for each segment?
- How should I anticipate and consider competitor response to potential prices?
- How should I adjust segment prices to account for different price sensitivities among segments?

Optimization

Refine preliminary prices with iterative process balancing trade-offs between price, cost, and market response

Key Questions

- What tradeoffs should I make between long-term strategic objectives and short-term market responses to price changes?
- What types of analytical techniques are best suited to my product and market conditions?
- How can I estimate customer response to potential price changes?

Implementation

Set final prices and ensure acceptance among customers and the organization through effective change management approach

Key Questions

- How do I get sales force buy-in to the new prices and empower them to execute effectively?
- What is the best approach for communicating price changes to customers?
- What is the best approach for raising prices on undervalued products?

Once preliminary prices for each segment have been set, the next stage requires optimizing those prices based on potential customer response to new prices and the economics of price–volume trade-offs. This is the stage when the complexity of balancing competing factors often derails well-intentioned attempts to set profit-maximizing prices. To address this issue, we provide a simple yet effective approach to understanding the trade-offs between long-term strategic objectives and short-term market responses.

The final stage of the price-setting process requires identifying obstacles to successfully introducing new prices to the market and ensuring that they stick. Shifting to a segmented pricing approach is novel for many companies and often creates concern that the resulting price list will be complex and difficult to explain to customers. This is a valid concern that makes it imperative to communicate the rationale for the new prices to internal stakeholders such as the sales force as well as to external constituencies such as customers and competitors.

PRELIMINARY SEGMENT PRICING

When setting a baseline price for each segment, keep the analysis simple and do not become overly concerned about precision, which will come in the optimization stage. At the start, it's more important to make approximate judgments about the degree to which value influences customer price sensitivity and about how much of that value the firm should attempt to capture in the price versus leave as a motivation to purchase.

VALUE ASSESSMENT OPTIONS

A key to efficiency at this stage is to invest time and effort in the value assessment only when the results can be used to influence customer willingness-to-pay through value communications, as discussed in Chapter 5. It is neither necessary nor desirable to conduct a complete Economic Value Estimation® using external customer data for every product. Although we have presented EVE in earlier chapters as the ideal form of value estimation, it is important to identify when EVE benefits justify investing interview time, gathering competitive pricing information, and developing a full value model. In some cases, pricing decisions are best made with qualitative value estimates based on managerial judgment or on quantitative assessments of customers' current willingness-to-pay. There are even times when current market prices should be used.

When internal judgments of customer value are likely to be good enough, interdisciplinary teams of customer-facing employees—from sales, field engineering, and marketing—use their own knowledge of customer economics to identify value drivers and to estimate the dollar impact of a product or service on them. Typically, this can be accomplished in a single work session with minimal disruption of individual schedules. The resulting value model, while not as accurate as a full EVE, provides a worthwhile starting point for establishing preliminary segment prices. For more commodity-like products with relatively little differential value, and for products differentiated only by the degree to which they differ on well-understood product attributes, even the time required to estimate an EVE using internal judgments may not be justified. In these instances, it is sufficient to start the optimization process using current prices or managerial estimates of customer willingness-to-pay.

Given the four value assessment options—EVE with external customer data, EVE with internal judgment, estimates of willingness-to-pay, and current prices—choosing the best option depends on four factors: the stage of the product lifecycle, the degree to which customers already understand the value of product or service to them, the size of the market opportunity, and the time available for price setting.

Product lifecycle stage is important because products early in the lifecycle have some degree of differentiation that creates value that potential customers frequently do not understand fully. Consequently, when pricing products in relatively new product categories, developing an EVE using customer interview data is generally worthwhile. The insights gained from the value assessment can form the basis of value communications that educate customers and justify higher prices.

Sometimes, however, the rush to bring a new product to market might not leave enough time to schedule and conduct interviews and then build a value model. This is often the case for new products still in development that need preliminary prices for value creation, price structure, and value communication decisions. In these cases, the pricing manager might choose to assess value using managerial insights from market-facing personnel. Although the value estimation won't be as reliable as one built on data collected from customer interviews, it is generally sufficiently informative to improve the price setting process.

Estimating the economic value of products in later lifecycle stages can also be worthwhile when even users of the product have difficulty quantifying the value they are receiving. This is particularly true for what we described in Chapter 5 as "experience goods" that require a lot of use before a user can ascertain the value. Services such as advertising, pharmaceuticals that have long-term effects, and software often fit this description because the value can be difficult to assess prior to purchase. Consequently, many customers have only a vague idea of the value of these purchases even years after consuming them. In these instances, if the market opportunity is sizable and the product or service is differentiated, pricing managers should, at the least, estimate value using internal data to justify premium pricing to customers. Conversely, investing time in value estimates isn't warranted for small markets and for products with little differentiation.

THE PRELIMINARY PRICE RANGE

Once at least a rough estimate of economic value is determined, including identification of customer segments that would gain significantly different levels of value, the next step is to determine how aggressively to attempt to capture that value in the price. This decision should not be driven by altruism but rather by judgment about what will yield long-term, sustainable profitability. Leaving more of the economic value "on the table" will, other things equal, induce customers to migrate to a new product or service more quickly. They will not first need to fully understand the value if they can see that it is much greater but the price is only a little more. Moreover, the seller saves the cost of having to educate customers and the low price and quick market uptake discourages competitive entry. On the other hand, if the product's differentiation is likely to be sustainable for a long time, using price to drive sales requires forgoing a lot of potential margin in the long run. Unless value is initially established and paid by the early adopters, it is difficult if not impossible to raise prices to value-based levels later on.

There are four considerations that drive the decision of how much of the value to attempt to capture in the price:

1. How important is getting a "good value" as a purchase motivation for customers in the segment? People casually call this "price sensitivity," but it is really sensitivity to the price-value trade-off. If the expenditure is small for the segment of customers, if someone else is paying the bill, and if the expenditure represents a small piece of a large expenditure, then a new supplier can win sales and an established firm can defend them even while capturing a high share of the economic value to that segment. On the other hand, if customers feel that the price is unfair, even when justified by value, they will be highly sensitive to the price-value trade-off. We summarized the forces that drive price sensitivity in Chapter 5 because they also determine the importance of value communication. Those factors are summarized again in Exhibit 7-2. Appendix 7A suggests questions managers can ask about each factor as they establish a relative price range that will be fine-tuned in the optimization stage.

2. How costly and time consuming is it to quantify and communicate the differential value? The size of this challenge can vary by the segment (How technically sophisticated are the buyers?) and by specific sources of value. (It is usually easier to prove or guarantee the value of costs savings than revenue enhancements.) Again, we discussed these challenges in Chapter 5. If it is possible to objectively prove the value of differentiation in a way that creates high confidence, or if it is possible to quantify and guarantee the value received, a seller can successfully demand a high share of the value created.

3. How sustainable is a price differential relative to current or potential competitors? If the product lacks a patent, copyright, or lock on a unique resource, competitors will quickly attempt to penetrate a segment in which margins are high and there is much potential volume untapped. Would a price that induced more customers to make a purchase before competitive entry give the firm an advantage in holding them later, as is the case for example with software, or give it a cost advantage, as is often the case with electronics manufacturing? On the other hand, considering a price that would enable a firm to penetrate a market at the expense of competitors by giving away much of its differential value raises the question about whether the competitors would allow such a differential to remain. If they have costs that would enable them to protect share, or the ability

EXHIBIT 7-2   Price/Value Sensitivity Drivers

Driver	Description
Size of expenditure	Buyers are less sensitive to the prices of small expenditures which, in the case of households, is defined relative to income.
Shared costs	Buyers are less price sensitive when some or all of the purchase price is paid by others.
Switching costs	Buyers are less sensitive to the price of a product the greater the added cost (both monetary and non-monetary) of switching suppliers.
Perceived risk	Buyers are less price sensitive when it is difficult to compare suppliers and the cost of not getting the expected benefits of a purchase are high.
Importance of end-benefit	Buyers are less price sensitive when the product is a small part of the cost of a benefit with high economic or psychological importance.
Price–quality perceptions	Buyers are less sensitive to a product's price to the extent that price is a proxy for the likely quality of the purchase.
Reference prices	Buyers are more price sensitive the higher the product's price relative to the buyers price expectation.
Perceived fairness	Buyers are more sensitive to a product's price when it is outside the range that they perceive as "fair" or "reasonable".
Price framing	Buyers are more price sensitive when they perceive the price as a "loss" rather than as a forgone "gain." They are more price sensitive when the price is paid separately rather than as part of a bundle.

to launch discounted "fighter-brand" variations, the low price strategy is unlikely to pay off in volume.

4. How important is margin versus volume as a financial objective? Even when it is entirely possible to quantify and communicate value, the inability to establish fences between all value segments will force a supplier to make some major trade-offs between price and volume. The value of volume is determined primarily by a firm's cost structure. If a firm's costs are primarily variable (as in grocery retailing and personal service businesses), the amount of each sale that contributes to fixed costs and profit, the

percent contribution margin, will tend to be low. As a result, the leverage between incremental volume and incremental profitability will be low. In contrast, if costs are primarily fixed (as in software, pharmaceuticals, newspaper publishing), the portion of each sale that contributes to profitability, the percent contribution margin, will tend to be high. A high percent contribution margin creates high leverage between sales volume and profitability. These concepts, and the calculations to support them, are developed further in Chapters 8 and 9.

There are considerations other than cost structure that can drive the importance of volume over margin as well. If sales of the product draw customers to other profitable products in the firm's product line, then volume can be an important objective even if it does not drive incremental profit for the product itself. In some cases, driving incremental volume may help the firm gain experience or leverage with suppliers that gives it a competitive advantage. In that case, driving volume and improving margins are complementary.

The answers to these four questions enable a firm to determine the extent to which it should use price to capture value or to drive volume in each segment. That determination needs to be made before developing a marketing strategy since it will inform decisions about how much and with what rigor the value needs to be communicated, what types of distribution will be necessary to support that communication, how many different price segments the firm should attempt to maintain with its price structure, and even what policies the firm might need to make competitive entry more difficult.

PRICING STRATEGY OPTIONS

Obviously, answering the questions above does not produce an exact price point for each segment, but narrows the range of value capture. Deciding on a preliminary price range consistent with the strategy is, at this point, based on informed judgment. Managers, who have reviewed the value assessment and know what price sensitivity factors motivate the customers in each segment, propose prices that they believe would be consistent with a profit maximizing strategy. These pricing strategies are frequently described as falling into one of three categories: skim, penetration, and neutral pricing. Different pricing strategies often coexist in the same market segment, but an individual firm's selection of a strategy should not be arbitrary. Let's examine the conditions under which each strategy is appropriate. In some industries, particularly those with high fixed costs, profitable growth may require simultaneously pursuing multiple segments that require multiple strategies.

Skim pricing (or skimming) is designed to capture high margins at the expense of large sales volume. By definition, skim prices are high in relation to what most buyers in a segment can be convinced to pay. Consequently, this strategy optimizes immediate profitability only when the profit from selling to relatively price-insensitive customers exceeds that from selling to a larger market at a lower price. Under certain conditions, however, a brand relying heavily on providing intangible value might reap more profit in the long run by setting initial prices high and reducing them over time—the "sequential skimming" strategy we discuss below—even if those high initial prices reduce immediate profitability.

Buyers are often price insensitive because they belong to a market segment that places exceptionally high value on a product's differentiating attributes. For example, in many sports a segment of enthusiasts will often pay astronomical prices for the bike, club, or racquet that they think will give them an edge. You can buy a plain aluminum canoe paddle for $35. You can buy a Bending Branches Journey paddle (wood laminate, 44 ounces) for $129. Or you can buy the Werner Camano paddle (graphite, 26 ounces) for $349. The Werner Camano not only makes canoeing long distances easier but also signals that one belongs to a select group that has a very serious commitment to the sport.

Of course, simply targeting a segment of customers who are relatively price insensitive does not mean that they are fools who will buy at any price. It means that they can and will pay fully to get what they perceive to be an exceptionally high value product. Thus skim pricing generally requires a greater commitment either to communicate a value that justifies a high price, or to guarantee it. If neither is practical or cost-effective, then the firm must limit its pricing to reflect what it can communicate or to what potential customers are likely to believe simply from what they can observe.

Marketers often assume that skim pricing is impractical when production economies are large. Although that is sometimes true, it is not necessarily the case. If only 15 percent of a market is price insensitive, but many other firms are competing to serve the other 85 percent, the only firm that targets a niche market could become as large, and probably much more profitable, than the largest competitor focusing on the mass market. Skim pricing is also practical when the firm has a product line of lower-priced products that potential customers can purchase if deterred by the skim price of the premium product targeted at a less price-sensitive segment. Branded gasoline retailers set a skim price for their super premium, high-octane grade, knowing that anyone deterred by the price is more likely to purchase a lower grade than to drive to a competitive service station.

The competitive environment must be right for skimming. A firm must have some source of competitive protection to ensure long-term profitability by precluding competitors from providing lower-priced alternatives. Patents or copyrights are one source of protection against competitive threats. Pharmaceutical companies cite their huge expenditures on research to justify the skim prices they command until a drug's patent expires. Even then, they enjoy some premium because of the name recognition. Other forms of protection include a brand's reputation for quality, access to a scarce resource, and preemption of the best distribution channels.

A skim price isn't necessarily a poor strategy even when a firm lacks the ability to prevent competition in the future. If a company introduces a new product with a high price relative to its manufacturing cost, competitors will be attracted to the market even if the product is priced low relative to its economic value. Pricing low in the face of competition makes sense only when it serves to establish a competitive advantage or to sustain one that already exists. If a low price cannot do either, the best rule for pricing is to earn what you can while you can. When competitors enter by duplicating the product's differentiating attributes and thus undermine its competitive advantage, the firm can then reevaluate its strategy.

Sequential skimming can be a more appropriate strategy for products and services with low repurchase rates. The market for long-lived durable goods that a customer purchases infrequently, or products that most buyers would purchase only once, such as a ticket to a stage play, can be skimmed for only a limited time at each price. Skimming, in such cases, cannot be maintained indefinitely, but its dynamic variant, sequential skimming, may remain profitable for some time.

Sequential skimming, like the more sustainable variety of skimming, begins with a price that attracts the least price-sensitive buyers first. After the firm has "skimmed the cream" of buyers, however, that market is gone. Consequently, to maintain its sales, the firm reduces its price enough to sell to the next most lucrative segment. The firm continues this process until it has exhausted all opportunities for skimming, either because it has cut price low enough to attract even the most price-sensitive buyers or because it could not profitably lower the price further.

In theory, a firm could sequentially skim the market for a durable good or a one-time purchase by lowering its price in hundreds of small steps, thus charging every segment the maximum it would pay for the product. In practice, however, potential buyers catch on rather quickly and begin delaying their purchases, anticipating further price reductions. To minimize this problem, the firm can cut price less frequently, thus forcing potential buyers to bear a significant cost of waiting. It can also launch less attractive models as it cuts the price. This is the strategy Polaroid followed, introducing ever-cheaper models of its automatic-developing camera, to bring ever-larger segments into the market. The makers of digital cameras are now replicating that same strategy.

Sometimes, sequential skimming is a good strategy for introducing even nondurable, repeatedly purchased products. A firm gains in two ways by gradually lowering price to expand into new markets.

• First, if the product has a variety of potential uses, all of which require substantial effort in technical research and marketing from the seller, the company may more efficiently introduce the product by focusing all of its efforts on one use at a time. In fact, it may actually capture the most lucrative markets more quickly than if it spread its resources more thinly. Even if the product's initial growth is slowed, the firm may still benefit in the long run.

• Second, sequential skimming enables the firm to build production capacity gradually, learning improved manufacturing techniques as it expands. A company can finance expansion gradually with the cash flow that the product is already generating. Moreover, because the firm initially built less capacity, it bears less risk that demand will not be as great as expected. Having begun with a skim price, the firm can easily minimize the effect of overly optimistic fore-casts by scaling back its intended expansion and increasing the rate of its price reductions.

Penetration pricing involves setting a price low enough to attract and hold a large base of customers. Penetration prices are not necessarily cheap, but they are low relative to perceived value in the target segment. Lexus, for example, quickly penetrated the luxury car market, and induced many near-luxury buyers to trade up, because buyers perceived it as representing an exceptionally good value despite being a high-priced car. Similarly, Target and Trader Joe's stores position them-selves as offering the same or better value as their competitors at lower prices.

Penetration pricing will work only if a large share of the market is willing to change brands or suppliers in response to lower prices. A common misconception is that every market will respond to lower prices, which is one reason why unsuc-cessful penetration pricing schemes are so common. In some cases, penetration pricing can actually undermine a brand's long-term appeal. When Lacoste allowed its "alligator" shirts to be discounted by lower-priced mass merchants, high-image retailers refused to carry the product and traditional Lacoste cus-tomers migrated to more exclusive brands.

Of course, not all buyers need to be price sensitive for penetration pricing to succeed, but enough of the market must be adequately price sensitive to justify pricing low. Warehouse clubs (e.g., Sam's, Costco, B.J.'s) have used penetration pricing to target only buyers willing to purchase in large quantities. Charter vaca-tion operators sell heavily discounted travel to people who do not mind inflexible scheduling. Discount retail stores such as T.J.Maxx, Trader Joe's, and Buck-a-Book target those price-sensitive customers willing to shop frequently through limited and rapidly changing stocks to find a bargain. Some wholesalers of sheet steel use penetration prices to attract the high-volume buyers, who require no selling or service and who buy truckload quantities.

To determine how much volume one must gain to justify penetration pricing, a manager must also consider the cost environment. Costs are more favorable for penetration pricing when incremental costs (variable and incremental semifixed) represent a small share of the price, so that each additional sale provides a large contribution to profit. Because the contribution per sale is already high, a lower price does not represent a large cut in the contribution from each sale. For example, even if a company had to cut its prices 10 percent to attract a large segment of buy-ers, penetration pricing could still be profitable if the product had a high contribu-tion margin. In order for the strategy to pay with a 90 percent contribution margin, the sales gain would need to exceed only 12.5 percent. The lower the contribution per sale, the larger the sales gain required before penetration pricing is profitable.

Penetration pricing can succeed without a high contribution margin if the strategy creates sufficient variable cost economies, enabling the seller to offer penetration prices without suffering lower margins. The price sensitivity of tar-get customers enables penetration-priced retailers to vary the brands they offer depending on who gives them the best deal, thus increasing their leverage with suppliers. The penetration prices of Save-A-Lot grocers (a division of Supervalu Inc) enables them to maintain such high turnover, high sales per square foot, and high sales per employee that they can offer rock bottom prices and still earn higher profits than traditional grocers do.[1] To cite a manufacturing example, as personal computer users became more knowledgeable buyers, manufacturers such as Dell and Gateway leveraged the economies of mail-order distribution to sell high-quality products to knowledgeable buyers using penetration pricing. Competitors who distributed through retail stores could not match their prices.

For penetration pricing to succeed, competitors must allow a company to set a price that is attractive to a large segment of the market. Competitors always have the option of undercutting a penetration strategy by cutting their own prices, preventing the penetration pricer from offering a better value. Only when competitors lack the ability or incentive to do so is penetration pricing a practical strategy for gaining and holding market share. There are three common situations in which this is likely to occur:

1. When the firm has a significant cost advantage and/or a resource advantage so that its competitors believe they would lose if they began a price war
2. When the firm has a broader line of complementary products, enabling it to use one as a penetration-priced "loss leader" in order to drive sales of others
3. When the firm is currently so small that it can significantly increase its sales without affecting the sales of its competitors enough to prompt a response

As telecom markets have opened to competition in most developed countries, new suppliers have successfully used penetration pricing to capture market share. The low variable costs of carrying a call or message make such a strategy desirable. Regulatory constraints and the inability of large, established competitors to match the lower prices of new entrants on their large installed base of customers has made the strategy successful in many markets.

Occasionally, penetration pricing can be structured to attract new volume in a market without threatening competitors' current customer bases. For this strategy to work, the penetration pricer must somehow minimize interbrand price sensitivity at the same time that it attempts to encourage and exploit primary price sensitivity. Charter airline carriers can substantially undercut the prices of scheduled airlines without retaliation because their reduced service and inflexible schedules make them unattractive to many passengers of scheduled airlines. Warehouse clubs can undercut traditional supermarkets because their limited selection, large sizes, and spartan shopping environments will not attract most people from traditional grocery chains.

Neutral pricing involves a strategic decision not to use price to gain market share, while not allowing price alone to restrict it. Neutral pricing minimizes the role of price as a marketing tool in favor of other tactics that management believes are more powerful or cost-effective for a product's market. This does not mean that neutral pricing is easier. On the contrary, it is less difficult to choose a price that is sufficiently high to skim or sufficiently low to penetrate than to choose one that strikes a near perfect balance.

A firm generally adopts a neutral pricing strategy by default because market conditions are not sufficient to support either a skim or penetration strategy. For example, a marketer may be unable to adopt skim pricing when buyers consider the products in a particular market to be so substitutable that no significant segment will pay a premium. That same firm may be unable to adopt a penetration pricing strategy because, particularly if it's a newcomer to the market, customers would be unable to judge its quality before purchase and would infer low quality from low prices (the price–quality effect) or because competitors would respond vigorously to any price that undercut the established price structure. Neutral pricing is especially common in industries where customers are quite value sensitive, precluding skimming, but competitors are quite volume sensitive, precluding successful penetration.

Another reason to adopt a neutral pricing strategy is to promote a product line. Auto companies have traditionally-priced popular cars such as the Mazda Miata and the Chrysler PT Cruiser at a neutral level, even when they could not meet the demand for them. Auto companies want people across a broad range of potential car buyers to see their "hot" cars and associate the brand with them. Their experience has shown them that one very popular style draws people into showrooms who buy more of other car models as well. Similarly, performers often price their concert tickets at levels that leave many willing buyers unable to get a ticket because they know that people who attend concerts buy recordings and influence their friends to buy them. These effects would be seriously stifled if prices were set high enough that only high-income buyers or people who were already the most passionate fans were willing to buy.

Although neutral pricing is less proactive than skimming or penetration pricing, its proper execution is no less difficult or important to profitability. Neutral prices are not necessarily equal to those of competitors or near the middle of the range. A neutral price can, in principle, be the highest or lowest price in the market and still be neutral. Toshiba laptop computers and Sony TVs are consistently priced above competitors, yet they capture large market shares because of the high perceived value associated with their clear screens and reliable performance. Like a skim or penetration price, a neutral price is defined relative to the perceived economic value of the product.

PRICE OPTIMIZATION

Price optimization is an iterative process of adjusting price to maximize profits by analyzing the trade-off between price, volume, and cost. The term *optimization* is a bit of a misnomer because it implies that it is possible to analytically determine the single price that will maximize profits with a reasonable degree of confidence. But, as an experienced pricing manager will tell you, there is always uncertainty

EXHIBIT 7-3   Price Optimization

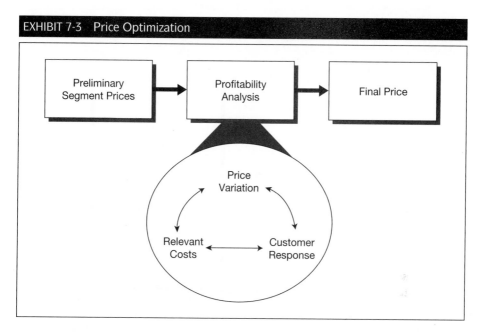

about whether a given price is "right." Still, approximating that price is the goal and, regardless of the analytical approach, there are three key steps to the optimization process:

1. Select price points within the preliminary price range to begin testing.
2. Start the iterative optimization process to evaluate the trade-off between customer response to new prices and the lost or gained margin.
3. Set final prices in order to begin implementation efforts with customers and the organization (see Exhibit 7-3).

PROFITABILITY ANALYSIS

Determining the profit-maximizing price requires a combination of analytical rigor and managerial judgment to understand the trade-offs between prices, costs, and customer response. The approach to profitability analysis will vary depending on the nature of the pricing environment, as illustrated in Exhibit 7-4. Regardless of the method, however, the goal is the same: finding the price point that balances costs and customer response in the most profitable way.

Incremental breakeven analysis, appropriate in markets where there are many transactions and prices change infrequently, can be implemented on a spreadsheet and easily combined with both data and managerial judgment to make price adjustments that improve profitability. Although similar in form to the breakeven analyses commonly used to evaluate investments, incremental breakeven analysis for pricing is quite different in practice. Rather than evaluating the price and volume required for the product to achieve overall profitability, incremental breakeven analysis focuses on the *change* in volume required for a price change to *improve* profitability.

EXHIBIT 7-4   Analytical Approaches to Profitability Analysis

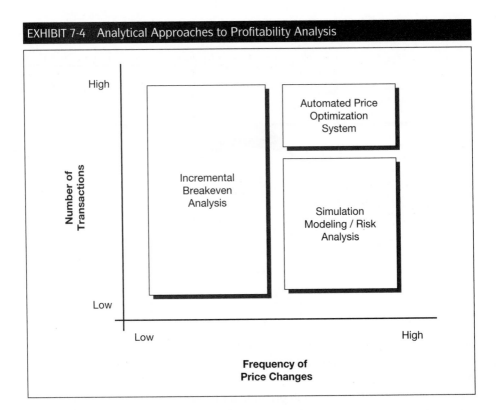

Depending on the strategic objective for the product, management might wish to consider the impact of a higher price to expand margin, or a lower price to build volume. To determine the likelihood that either change will generate incremental profitability, managers must first answer one of two questions: How much would sales volume have to increase to profit from a price reduction? or How much would the sales volume have to decline before a price increase became unprofitable? The answers to such "breakeven sales change" questions depend on both the size of the proposed price change and on the product's contribution margin, as Exhibit 7-5 illustrates. It shows how much unit volume must change for a given price change to produce an equivalent profit, depending on the product's contribution margin before the price change. (We will describe incremental breakeven analysis in detail in Chapter 9.)

One of the benefits of the breakeven sales change approach is practicality. Very few pricing decisions are made with the luxury of knowing in advance how competitors and customers are likely to respond to them. Even the most statistically rigorous research techniques (discussed in Chapter 13) rely either on making inferences from past data or from customer responses to surveys of their intentions, neither of which is highly reliable. Most managers must make decisions with less quantitative information than that. Incremental breakeven analysis enables managers to deal with the judgments they must make despite that

EXHIBIT 7-5   Incremental Percent Breakeven Sales Changes

		Contribution Margin									
		5%	10%	20%	30%	40%	50%	60%	70%	80%	90%
% Change in Price	35%	-88%	-78%	-64%	-54%	-47%	-41%	-37%	-33%	-30%	-28%
	25%	-83%	-71%	-56%	-45%	-38%	-33%	-29%	-26%	-24%	-22%
	15%	-75%	-60%	-43%	-33%	-27%	-23%	-20%	-18%	-16%	-14%
	5%	-50%	-33%	-20%	-14%	-11%	-9%	-8%	-7%	-6%	-5%
	0%	0%	0%	0%	0%	0%	0%	0%	0%	0%	0%
	-5%	NA	100%	33%	20%	14%	11%	9%	8%	7%	6%
	-15%	NA	NA	300%	100%	60%	43%	33%	27%	23%	20%
	-25%	NA	NA	NA	NA	167%	100%	71%	56%	45%	38%
	-35%	NA	NA	NA	NA	700%	233%	140%	100%	78%	64%

NA indicates "Not Achievable"

uncertainty. In our experience, managers who report that they have no idea what their customers' demand curve looks like, or even how much more customers would buy if prices were 10 percent lower, can and will estimate comfortably the probability that sales will change by more than the breakeven number. Fortunately, that is all the information they need to conclude whether or not the decision is directionally correct.

Simulations expand on a breakeven analysis by estimating the risks of customer and competitive response to a price change. Although the basic breakeven approach to profitability analysis has proven effective in many industries, some situations require more precise modeling of customer and competitor reactions to help the pricer better understand and manage risk. For example, the key issue in major account negotiations is not whether a price change will result in a small incremental change in volume, but whether demanding a higher price will risk losing the entire deal and a significant piece of business. Similarly, for high-profile products with prices customers and competitors watch closely, price changes are likely to invoke a competitive response. Modeling those dynamics improves pricing decisions. In such instances, companies should augment the basic breakeven analysis with a risk management approach using readily available simulation packages.[2]

Simulations combined with an appropriate decision framework provide a deeper understanding of the upside potential of a price change as well the potential downside risks. They also provide a powerful tool to compare different pricing strategies and develop action plans to manage identifiable risks. By performing thousands of simulated "runs" of the strategy, it is possible to estimate the distribution of potential outcomes for each strategy. To illustrate, Exhibit 7-6 is a risk profile comparing the outcomes from two different pricing strategies: a low-price discount strategy and a premium-price branding strategy. Although the premium branding strategy has a somewhat higher expected value, it also has more

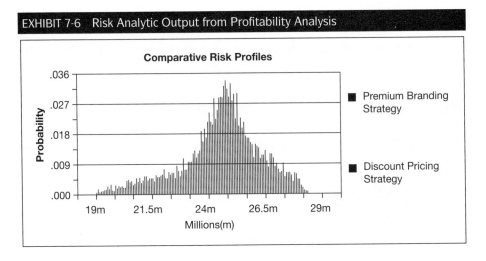

EXHIBIT 7-6   Risk Analytic Output from Profitability Analysis

downside risk. Using this analysis, managers can make informed, thoughtful deci-sions about the trade-offs between the risk and the potential gain of alternative strategies. Instead of assuming away uncertainty, the risk analytic approach accounts for it in a way that facilitates more effective decision making.

Automated price optimization is the best approach to profitability analysis when a market has a high transaction volume, standardized products, and nonnego-tiable pricing. Sophisticated software employing *real-time price optimization* tests price points, tracks sales volume changes, and iterates quickly toward optimal price levels. Using real-time sales data, retailers such as Dell, Home Depot, Sears, and Wal-Mart are increasingly turning to price optimization software to help manage pricing and inventory levels on a store-by-store basis. The high number of transac-tions in these environments enables even small price improvements to produce big financial returns while regional differences make pricing difficult to manage in any other fashion.[3] Using mathematical models to selectively test price changes and to pool data across products, locations, and customer segments, price optimization sys-tems generate reliable estimates of price elasticities that, along with relevant cost data, enable them to update prices and discount levels nearly in real time.

ESTIMATING CUSTOMER RESPONSE

The most difficult part of the profitability analysis involves estimating and man-aging the uncertainty of customer response to a price change. There are several approaches to deal with that challenge, ranging from the most sophisticated and costly to the least effective but easy to implement. The four main approaches are controlled price experiments, purchase intention surveys, structured inference from historical data, and incremental implementation. A thoughtful choice from among these options involves trade-offs between the cost to implement and the quality of data gained to make the pricing decision.

Price experimentation involves testing new prices on a controlled sample of customers before rolling the price change out to the entire market. After we helped a large business-to-business distributor restructure its pricing into three different service options, it had to reset price points for various products in its line. It did so by experimentally rolling out the new price structure to approximately 180 of its more than 1,000 value-added resellers (VARs). The rest of its value-added resellers served as a control group. After 3 weeks, a second round of price adjustments, some up and some down, were made based on the degree to which sales exceeded or fell short of the breakeven sales changes for each product category. After a final iteration a few weeks later, the profit improvement from the new structure and levels was clear and the new pricing was rolled out to the entire market.

Purchase intention surveys can be used when price experimentation is impractical, as it is for many products such as large, infrequent purchases (e.g., automobiles, enterprise software) that don't lend themselves to experimentation. In those cases, surveys of various types and sophistication ask customers to reveal their product preferences at various price points. By comparing differences in responses at different price points, and by adjusting for historical biases in responses, researchers infer how customers would respond if faced with those price differences in actual purchase situations. Chapter 13 describes the benefits and costs of alternative survey techniques.

Structured inference by managers is more popular with managers than surveys and experiments. Structured inferences about customer response can range from the highly formal and statistical to the purely judgmental. In all cases, the idea is to use results that managers have seen in the past to estimate the likelihood that they will achieve the necessary breakeven sales changes under new conditions. For example, in one case we built a model for a chain of newspapers that in the past had initiated multiple price changes at different locations. By pooling data and controlling statistically for differences in demographics and market conditions across geographies and time, we were able to create rough models that predicted the impact of future price changes accurately enough to justify additional profitable price changes. After each change, the publisher added the new data generated to the database, which management could use to make inferences about the effect of future price changes.

When companies lack historical data on their own products, as is common for new product launches, they often look for surrogate information about the impact of price differences in other geographic markets, or on similar products in the same market. For example, pharmaceuticals companies look for "analogs" when launching a new product to get some idea of how much of the value they might successfully capture. They look at what happened, both in their same category and ones they deem similar, when earlier drugs were launched with price premiums reflecting their value, and compare that to the market penetration gained by drugs priced closer to parity. Such analysis reveals that the ability to capture value varies widely depending on the category of disease being treated and the type of differentiation offered.

Incremental implementation can work when none of the other methods for estimating customer response are practical or reliable enough to produce confident inferences. This approach often works well for products for which price changes are not very costly to make, and to reverse. Pricing managers simply attempt to manage the risk by limiting price changes to a series of small steps, minimizing the risk of a pricing blunder that could have disastrous consequences. For example, a maker of distinctive pre-manufactured homes slowly repositioned its brand from being a cheaper alternative to being a premium-priced product with distinctive value in design and reliability. During that period, it raised prices a few percentage points more each year than the prices of similar traditional homes and tracked the effect on its sales relative to the industry. When the changes no longer improved profits, the manufacturer stopped making them.

As this example illustrates, managerial judgment is essential to evaluating potential price changes. When it is not possible or desirable to use sophisticated optimization techniques, marketing managers can still reach "optimal" prices by an iterative process, evaluating various prices in terms of customer response and profit impact. Although such a process does not have the statistical rigor of more sophisticated approaches and has the hidden cost of delaying the time to achieve price optimization, our experience indicates that it can lead to profit-maximizing pricing.

IMPLEMENTING NEW PRICES

This chapter introduced a process for price setting that is flexible enough to accommodate the demands of most markets and pricing organizations. But attempts to change business processes without also changing the motivation and behaviors of the individuals involved are doomed to fail. The new prices and pricing policies need to be introduced and effectively socialized both with individuals inside the organization such as salespeople and with customers. Salespeople need to be ready, willing, and able to sell at the new price points. They must understand the rationale for new prices, have appropriate incentives to enforce the new prices, and have the right tools to convince customers to pay the new prices. Similarly, customers must understand the reasoning behind price changes and be convinced that changes are fair and are being applied equitably across the customer base. All too often, we have seen well-conceived pricing strategies fail because the company did not address a few basic implementation considerations. Let's discuss how to avoid the most common mistakes.

COMMUNICATING NEW PRICES TO THE SALES FORCE

There is no surer way to derail a new pricing strategy than to hand it to the sales force with the admonition—borrowing Nike's slogan—"Just Do It." Implementing new prices forces salespeople to change the way they engage customers. In many cases they face difficult conversations explaining why prices are going up. It is no surprise when salespeople resist price increases, especially when change might affect their compensation.

Marketers should address three issues to help salespeople handle price changes. First, it is essential that each sales representative understand the rationale for new prices. Generally, this involves presenting the business case describing the problem (e.g., "three percent annual price erosion across key product lines is forcing change") and how the new pricing strategy will help to correct it. More important, salespeople must understand their role in making the strategy work through more effective communications and negotiation tactics. Pricing managers commonly place too little emphasis on communicating the "why" of pricing changes and then blame the sales department for not having the vision to see the big picture and failing to enforce the new prices rigorously. Our experience suggests that communicating the rationale for the new prices up-front improves price integrity down the road.

The second issue that must be addressed is knocking down hidden barriers that discourage behavioral change. The most obvious barrier is compensation. Sales force incentives focused on top-line revenues undercut the willingness to negotiate hard for higher prices. When faced with a choice of holding the line on price and risking the deal or giving a larger discount, any rational salesperson will opt for the discount. We discussed alternative compensation schemes in Chapter 6, so we won't repeat that discussion here. The key point is that a compensation plan that is not aligned with the pricing objective cripples the pricing strategy.

In addition to compensation, social norms and peer pressure can be a powerful, and often hidden, barrier to implementing new prices. Effective salespeople invariably have a competitive focus and a strong desire to win. That explains why sales contests are so effective; no one wants to come in second. In most cases, however, winning is defined in terms of revenues or unit sales, which does little to motivate pricing discipline. Recognizing this problem, creative marketers are redirecting sales reps' competitive energy to change pricing behaviors. For example, a building products distributor located in the northeast experienced steady increases in price discounts. Unable to come up with a set of enforceable policies to reverse the trend, the CEO decided to give each salesperson a quarterly discount "budget" which he or she could allocate any way the individual salesperson chose. Once the budget was used up, however, none of a rep's additional discounts would be approved until the following quarter. The results after the first quarter were stunning! Eight of the twelve salespeople didn't use their full budget. When the CEO asked how this was possible when discounts were so rampant in previous quarters, he learned that salespeople transferred their competitive focus from closing deals to managing the discount budget. Salespeople wanted to prove they were the best negotiators and did not want to lose out to their peers.

Once salespeople understand that the need for new prices and the barriers to change have been knocked down, the final step is to empower salespeople with appropriate training and sales tools. For major price changes, it is useful to organize a training session to introduce value-based selling tools—discussed in Chapter 5—and to practice handling objections through role-plays and coaching.

The training session also provides an opportunity to explore other barriers to effective implementation and enlist feedback for implementing price changes more effectively.

COMMUNICATING PRICE INCREASES TO CUSTOMERS

The most important consideration when communicating price changes to customers is that they understand the rationale for the change and believe it is fair. Perceived fairness is one of the most post powerful factors driving price sensitivity. Done correctly, communicating fairness can have dramatic effects. For example, a well-known medical device manufacturer successfully implemented a 40 percent price increase for one of its key products by carefully communicating why such a large increase was fair. The company recognized that it had made a tactical mistake by not raising prices annually along with industry practice, so it notified customers 3 months in advance of the increase to allow them to plan for the new prices. Not surprisingly, some customers "bought forward" at the lower prices, loading up before the price increase. But, giving them an option for dealing with the change made the company's decision seem fair and reasonable.

To further communicate fairness, the company's letter to customers noted it had not taken an increase in 8 years and the new price was still less than what it would have been had they increased prices in line with the medical device price index. Finally, the sales force met with each major account to explain that, prior to the price increase, the product was not generating sufficient returns to fund continued research and development. This was important to hospitals and doctors who relied on the company, a technology leader, to bring innovative solutions to market. Moreover, it communicated the inherent fairness of the price change by explaining that much of the additional profit would be invested in research and development (R&D) and returned to customers in the form of new products rather than end up in executive and shareholder pockets.

Just as there are different reasons for price changes, there are different approaches to communicating fairness. In some instances, rising raw material costs require a price increase. In such situations, customers are concerned about whether the vendor is being opportunistic by raising prices more than is justified and whether all customers are being treated equally. To communicate fairness in these situations, first send a letter, email, or press release to all customers simultaneously that explains why across-the-board price increases are necessary. Tie the increase clearly to the cost increase (e.g., "Energy prices have increased 24 percent; energy accounts for 10 percent of the price you pay, so prices must increase by 2.4 percent.") and be prepared to provide documented evidence. Where possible, index your prices to an objective measure of raw material costs such as a published commodity price index. Customers, and competitors, too, are more likely to accept a price increase if they know that prices will come back down when costs are lower. Indexed pricing is especially useful in times of significant price spikes because indices can be adjusted monthly or weekly depending on the frequency of raw material price changes.

Second, avoid being opportunistic by attempting to gain share by compromising on the increase. It can be tempting to waive a 5 percent increase for customers willing to give you 20 percent more volume, particularly in industries with excess capacity. But such an action is shortsighted because your competitors cannot afford to lose volume any more than you can. Although being opportunistic may lead to a short-term volume increase, it will surely invoke a competitive response and send a clear message to customers that the rationale for the price increase was not legitimate.

Finally, be prepared to play hardball with competitors who are opportunistic about the increase and cut deals like the one just described. Your ability to pass along cost increases will be undercut if even one credible supplier does not go along with it. Combined, these tactics send a clear message to customers that the price increase is fair and will be evenly enforced.

Another situation that requires communicating fairness occurs when a company increases prices after underpricing its products relative to the value delivered. This occurs frequently when companies begin to assess the economic value of their products for the first time and discover that they have an opportunity to increase price if they communicate value more effectively. The fairness issue stems from the fact that the company wasn't charging for value in the first place, so why start charging for it now? This is a legitimate question, the answer to which should be that over time all prices will be adjusted to align with value. In some cases, this will mean lower prices and in others, higher prices.

To ensure that customers do not think that price increases are being forced on them, offer them options on how they can adjust to the new prices. For example, when large customers resist the price change, offer them the ability to "earn" lower prices by increasing their share of spend with you. Alternatively, be prepared to unbundle the core offering from services and other value-adds in order to provide a lower value option at the old price. Whichever approach the company adopts, it is critical that customers pay for the value received. By providing choices for how that happens, you increase the perceptions of fairness and improve the odds that the price change will be successful.

Summary

Successful pricing strategy involves putting prices on products and making them stick. Setting the right price for the right customer requires integrating large amounts of data in a way that gains internal and external support, particularly from those most affected: the sales force and other channels, and customers. It is a challenging process, so difficult that many firms attempt to take shortcuts by following the competition or simply marking up costs. Other companies create false security by installing sophisticated price management systems that spit out "optimal" prices even when given inadequate data. The successful pricer must be committed to a discipline, investing to get the right customer, competitor, and cost information without wasting time and effort on unneeded data and analyses. Only then will companies begin to make real progress in driving profit growth through pricing.

Notes

1. "To Find Growth, No-Frills Grocer Goes Where Other Chains Won't", *Wall Street Journal* Vol. CCXLVI, No.42 (August 30, 2005) p. 1.
2. For example, Crystal Ball and @ Risk are both Excel add-ons for running Monte Carlo simulations that can be used to make decisions under uncertainty. The packages are available from Decisioneering Corporation (www.decisioneering.com) and Palisade software, Inc. (www.palisade.com), respectively.
3. See "Retailers Explore Price Optimization," *Computerworld*, January 20, 2003. Two companies currently leading the market in price optimization software are Zilliant for "online" and catalog companies, and Khimetrics for retailers.

Appendix 7A

BUILDING A MANAGERIAL PRICE SENSITIVITY ANALYSIS

A segment-by-segment evaluation of price sensitivity drivers is a useful way to make initial adjustments to segment prices. If several sensitivity drivers influence a particular segment, it may be prudent to reduce the value capture rate for that segment relative to other segments in which the sensitivity factors are less prevalent. This sensitivity analysis can often be performed by market-facing personnel judging the relative importance of each factor. The questions in this section can facilitate discussion and explore the importance of each factor systematically.

Sensitivity Drivers

1. **Reference prices:** Buyers are more price sensitive the higher the product's price relative to the prices of buyers' perceived alternatives.

   - What alternatives are buyers (or segments of buyers) typically aware of when making a purchase?
   - To what extent are buyers aware of the prices of those substitutes?
   - To what extent can buyers' price expectations be influenced by the positioning of one brand relative to particular alternatives, or by the alternatives offered them?
   - For a consumer product, finding out what alternatives buyers face usually requires little more than a visit or telephone inquiry to a few retailers or distributors. For an industrial product, identifying alternatives may be as easy as simply noting the products displayed at trade shows and asking about their availability in various locations and for various uses. One's sales force, sales agents, or manufacturer representatives are also particularly good sources for identifying buyer awareness of alternatives. For example, a brief form asking the salesperson to note each alternative mentioned by the buyer during a sales presentation can be a cheap, reliable source of

information. Finally, survey research that asks a question such as "How many brands of this product can you name?" can reveal awareness of alternatives.

- The second part of this effort involves gauging price awareness. Do buyers know the prices of alternatives? Are some segments of buyers much more, or less, informed than others? What do those who cannot recall specific prices believe is a typical price for this product? At what price level would they consider a brand in this market to be expensive or cheap?

2. **Perceived risk:**   Buyers are more price sensitive when they believe there is a significant probability they will not receive the full value of a product or service.

- How difficult is it for buyers to compare the offers of different suppliers?
- Can the attributes of a product be determined by observation, or must the product be purchased and consumed to learn what it offers?
- Is the product new or innovative to a segment of customers, meaning they may not understand the nature of its operation or how to use it effectively?
- Is this segment new to the product category or new to your firm as a supplier?
- Is the product highly complex, requiring costly specialists to evaluate its differentiating attributes?
- Are the prices of different suppliers easily comparable, or are they stated for different sizes and combinations that make comparisons difficult?

3. **Switching costs:**   Buyers are less sensitive to the price of a product the greater the added cost (both monetary and nonmonetary) of switching suppliers.

- To what extent have buyers already made investments (both monetary and psychological) in dealing with one supplier that they would need to incur again if they switched suppliers?
- For how long are buyers locked in by those expenditures?
- Have customers invested heavily in product-specific training that would have to be repeated if they chose to switch?
- Has the customer adapted its production, logistical, or marketing operations to accommodate your product?

4. **Price–quality perceptions:**   Buyers are less sensitive to a product's price to the extent that a higher price signals better quality.

- Is a prestige image an important attribute of the product?
- Is the product enhanced in value when its price excludes some consumers?
- Is the product of unknown quality with few reliable cues for ascertaining quality before purchase?

5. **Size of expenditure:**   Buyers are more price sensitive when the expenditure is larger, either in dollar terms or as a percentage of household income.

- How significant are buyers' expenditures for the product in absolute dollar terms (for business buyers) and as a portion of income (for consumers)?

6. **End-benefit:**   Buyers are less price sensitive when the product is part of a larger, overall purchase or benefit.

- What end-benefits do buyers seek from the product?
- How price sensitive are buyers to the cost of the end-benefit?
- What portion of the end-benefit does the price of the product account for?

- To what extent can the product be repositioned in customers' minds and associated with an end-benefit for which the buyer is less cost sensitive or which has a larger total cost?

7. **Shared costs:**   Buyers are less price sensitive when some or all of the purchase price is shared with others.

   - Does the buyer pay the full cost of the product?
   - If not, what portion of the cost does the buyer pay?

8. **Perceived fairness:**   Buyers are more sensitive to a product's price when it is outside the range that they perceive as "fair" or "reasonable" given the purchase context.

   - How does the product's current price compare with prices people have paid in the past for products in this category?
   - What do buyers expect to pay for similar products in similar purchase contexts?

- Is the product seen as necessary to maintain a previously enjoyed standard of living, or is it purchased to gain something more out of life?
- Is the price of the product high relative to its variable costs?
- Is the price of the product going to go up significantly and without obvious justification?

9. **Framing effects:**   Buyers are more price sensitive when they perceive the price as a "loss" rather than as a forgone "gain." They are more price sensitive when the price is paid separately rather than as part of a bundle.

   - Do customers see the price as something they pay to avoid a loss, or to achieve a gain?
   - Is the price paid as part of a larger cost or does it stand alone?
   - Is the price perceived as an out-of-pocket cost or as an opportunity cost?

8 | COSTS

How Should They Affect Pricing Decisions?

In most companies, there is ongoing conflict between managers in charge of covering costs (finance and accounting) and managers in charge of satisfying customers (marketing and sales). Accounting texts warn against prices that fail to cover full costs, while marketing texts argue that customer willingness-to-pay must be the sole driver of prices. The conflict between these views wastes company resources and leads to pricing decisions that are imperfect compromises. Profitable pricing involves an integration of costs and customer value. To achieve that integration, however, requires letting go of misleading ideas and forming common vision of what drives profitability.[1] In this chapter and in Chapter 9, we explain when costs are relevant for pricing, how marketers should use costs in pricing decisions, and the role that finance should play in defining the price-volume trade-offs that marketers should use in evaluating pricing decisions.

THE ROLE OF COSTS IN PRICING

Costs should never determine price, but costs do play a critical role in formulating a pricing strategy. Pricing decisions are inexorably tied to decisions about sales levels, and sales involve costs of production, marketing, and administration. It is true that how much buyers will pay is unrelated to the seller's cost, but it is also true that a seller's decisions about which products to produce and in what quantities depend critically on their cost of production.

The mistake that cost-plus pricers make is not that they consider costs in their pricing, but that they select the quantities they will sell and the buyers they will serve before identifying the prices they can charge. They then try to impose cost-based prices that may be either more or less than what buyers will pay. In contrast, effective pricers make their decisions in exactly the opposite order. They first evaluate what buyers can be convinced to pay and only then choose quantities to produce and markets to serve.

Firms that price effectively decide what to produce and to whom to sell it by comparing the prices they can charge with the costs they must incur. Consequently, costs affect the prices they charge. A low-cost producer can charge lower prices and sell more because it can profitably use low prices to attract more price-sensitive buyers. A higher-cost producer, on the other hand, cannot afford to underbid low-cost producers for the patronage of more price-sensitive buyers; it must target those buyers willing to pay a premium price. Similarly, changes in costs should cause producers to change their prices, not because that changes what buyers will pay, but because it changes the quantities that the firm can profitably supply and the buyers it can profitably serve. When the cost of jet fuel rises, most airlines are not naive enough to try passing on the fuel cost through a cost-plus formula while maintaining their previous schedules. But some airlines do raise their average revenue per mile. They do so by reducing the number of flights they offer in order to fill the remaining planes with more full-fare passengers. To make room for those passengers, they eliminate or reduce some discount fares. Thus the cost increase for jet fuel affects the mix of prices offered, increasing the average price charged. However, that is the result of a strategic decision to reduce the number of flights and change the mix of passengers served, not of an attempt to charge higher prices for the same service to the same people.

Such decisions about quantities to sell and buyers to serve are an important part of pricing strategy for all firms and the most important part for many. In this chapter, we discuss how a proper understanding of costs enables one to make those decisions correctly. First, however, a word of encouragement: understanding costs is probably the most challenging aspect of pricing. You will probably not master these concepts on first reading this chapter. Your goal should be simply to understand the issues involved and the techniques for dealing with them. Mastery of the techniques will come with practice.

DETERMINING RELEVANT COSTS

One cannot price effectively without understanding costs. To understand one's costs is not simply to know their amounts. Even the least effective pricers, those who mechanically apply cost-plus formulas, know how much they spend on labor, raw materials, and overhead. Managers who really understand their costs know more than cost levels; they know how their costs will change with the changes in sales that result from pricing decisions.

Not all costs are relevant for every pricing decision. A first step in pricing is to identify the relevant costs: those that actually determine the profit impact of the pricing decision. Our purpose in this section is to set forth the guidelines for identifying the relevant costs once they are measured. In principle, identifying the relevant costs for pricing decisions is actually fairly straightforward. They are the costs that are incremental (not average) and avoidable (not sunk). In practice, identifying costs that meet those criteria can be difficult. Consequently, we will explain each distinction in detail and illustrate it in the context of a practical pricing problem.

WHY INCREMENTAL COSTS?

Pricing decisions affect whether a company will sell less of the product at a higher price or more of the product at a lower price. In either scenario, some costs remain the same (in total). Consequently, those costs do not affect the relative profitability of one price versus another. Only costs that rise or fall (in total) when prices change affect the relative profitability of different pricing strategies. We call these costs incremental because they represent the increment to costs (positive or negative) that results from the pricing decision.

Incremental costs are the costs associated with changes in pricing and sales. The distinction between incremental and nonincremental costs parallels closely, but not exactly, the more familiar distinction between variable and fixed costs. Variable costs, such as the costs of raw materials in a manufacturing process, are costs of doing business. Because pricing decisions affect the amount of business that a company does, variable costs are always incremental for pricing. In contrast, fixed costs, such as those for product design, advertising, and overhead, are costs of being in business.[2] They are incremental when deciding whether a price will generate enough revenue to justify being in the business of selling a particular type of product or serving a particular type of customer. Because fixed costs are not affected by how much a company actually sells, most are not incremental when management must decide what price level to set for maximum profit.

Some fixed costs, however, are incremental for pricing decisions, and they must be appropriately identified. Incremental fixed costs are those that directly result from implementing a price change or from offering a version of the product at a different price level. For example, the fixed cost for a restaurant to print menus with new prices or for a public utility to gain regulatory approval of a rate increase would be incremental when deciding whether to make those changes. The fixed cost for an airline to advertise a new discount service or to upgrade its planes' interiors to offer a premium-priced service would be incremental when deciding whether to offer products at those price levels.

To further complicate matters, many costs are neither purely fixed nor purely variable. They are fixed over a range of sales but vary when sales go outside that range. The determination of whether such semifixed costs are incremental for a particular pricing decision is necessary to make that decision correctly. Consider, for example, the role of capital equipment costs when deciding whether to expand output. A manufacturer may be able to fill orders for up to 100 additional units each month without purchasing any new equipment simply by using the available equipment more extensively. Consequently, equipment costs are nonincremental when figuring the cost of producing up to 100 additional units. If the quantity of additional orders increased by 150 units each month, though, the factory would have to purchase additional equipment. The added cost of new equipment would then become incremental and relevant in deciding whether the company can profitably price low enough to attract that additional business.

To understand the importance of properly identifying incremental costs when making a pricing decision, consider the problem faced by the business manager of a symphony orchestra. The orchestra usually performs two Saturday evenings each month during the season with a new program for each performance. It incurs the following costs for each performance:

Fixed overhead costs	$1,500
Rehearsal costs	$4,500
Performance costs	$2,000
Variable costs (e.g., programs, tickets)	$1 per patron

The orchestra's business manager is concerned about her very thin profit margin. She has currently set ticket prices at $10. If she could sell out the entire 1,100-seat hall, total revenues would be $11,000 and total costs $9,100, leaving a healthy $1,900 profit per performance.[3] Unfortunately, the usual attendance is only 900 patrons, resulting in an average cost per ticket sold of $9.89, which is precariously close to the $10 admission price. With revenues of just $9,000 per performance and costs of $8,900, total profit per performance is a dismal $100.

The orchestra's business manager does not believe that a simple price increase would solve the problem. A higher price would simply reduce attendance more, leaving less revenue per performance than the orchestra earns now. Consequently, she is considering three proposals designed to increase profits by reaching out to new markets. Two of the proposals involve selling seats at discount prices. The three options are:

1.   A "student rush" ticket priced at $4 and sold to college students one-half hour before the performance on a first-come, first-served basis. The manager estimates she could sell 200 such tickets to people who otherwise would not attend. Clearly, however, the price of these tickets would not cover even half the average cost per ticket.

2.   A Sunday matinee repeat of the Saturday evening performance with tickets priced at $6. The manager expects she could sell 700 matinee tickets, but 150 of those would be to people who would otherwise have attended the higher-priced Saturday performance. Thus net patronage would increase by 550, but again the price of these tickets would not cover average cost per ticket.

3.   A new series of concerts to be performed on the alternate Saturdays. The tickets would be priced at $10, and the manager expects that she would sell 800 tickets but that 100 tickets would be sold to people who would attend the new series instead of the old one. Thus net patronage would increase by 700.

Which, if any, of these proposals should the orchestra adopt? An analysis of the alternatives is shown in Exhibit 8-1. The revenue gain is clearly smallest for the student rush, the lowest-priced alternative designed to attract a fringe market, while the revenue gain is greatest for the new series, which attracts many more full-price patrons. Still, profitability depends on the incremental costs as well as the revenues of each proposal. For the student rush, neither rehearsal costs nor performance costs are incremental. They are irrelevant to the profitability of that proposal since they do not change regardless of whether this proposal is implemented. Only the variable per-patron costs are incremental, and therefore relevant, for the student-rush proposal. For the Sunday matinee, however, the performance cost and the per-patron cost are incremental and affect the profitability of that option. For the totally new series, all costs except overhead are incremental.

To evaluate the profitability of each option, we subtract from revenues only those costs incremental to it. For the student rush, that means subtracting only the $200 of per-patron costs from the revenues, yielding a contribution to profit of $600. For the Sunday matinee, it means subtracting the performance cost and the variable per-patron costs for those additional patrons (550) who would not otherwise have attended any performance, yielding a profit contribution of $150. For the new series, it means subtracting the incremental rehearsal, performance, and per-patron costs, yielding a net loss of $200. Thus, the lowest priced option, which also happens to yield the least amount of additional revenue, is in fact the most profitable.

The setting out of alternatives, as in Exhibit 8-1, clearly highlights the best option. In practice, opportunities are often missed because managers do not look at incremental costs, focusing instead on the average costs that are more readily available from accounting data. Note again that the orchestra's current average cost (total cost divided by the number of tickets sold) is $9.89 per patron and would drop to $8.27 per patron if the student-rush proposal were adopted. The student-rush tickets, priced at $4 each, cover less than half the average cost per ticket. The manager who focuses on average cost would be misled into rejecting a

EXHIBIT 8-1   Analysis of Three Proposals for the Symphony Orchestra

	I Student Rush	II Sunday Matinee	III New Series
Price	$4	$6	$10
× Unit sales	$200	$700	$800
= Revenue	$800	$4,200	$8,000
− Other sales forgone	(0)	($1,500)	($1,000)
Revenue gain	$800	$2,700	$7,000
Incremental rehearsal cost	0	0	$4,500
Incremental performance cost	0	$2,000	$2,000
Variable costs	$200	$550	$700
Incremental costs	$200	$2,550	$7,200
Net profit contribution	$600	$150	($200)

profitable proposal in the mistaken belief that the price would be inadequate. Average cost includes costs that are not incremental and are therefore irrelevant to evaluating the proposed opportunity. The adequacy of any price can be ascertained only by looking at the incremental cost of sales and ignoring those costs that would be incurred anyway.

Although the orchestra example is hypothetical, the problem it illustrates is realistic. Scores of companies profit from products that they price below average cost when average cost includes fixed costs that are not true costs of sales.

- Packaged goods manufacturers often supply generic versions of their branded products at prices below average cost. They can do so profitably because they can produce them with little or no incremental costs of capital, shipping, and selling beyond those already incurred to produce their branded versions.
- A leading manufacturer of industrial cranes also does milling work for other companies whenever the firm's vertical turret lathes would not otherwise be used. The price for such work does not cover a proportionate share of the equipment cost. It is, however, profitable work since the equipment must be available to produce the firm's primary product. The equipment cost is therefore not incremental to the additional milling work.
- Airlines fly weekend flights that do not cover a proportionate share of capital costs for the plane and ground facilities. Those costs must be incurred to provide weekday service and so are irrelevant when judging whether weekend fares are adequate to justify this service. In fact, weekend fares often add incrementally more to profits precisely because they require no additional capital.

In each of these cases, the key to getting the business is having a low price. Yet one should never be deceived into thinking that low-price sales are necessarily low-profit sales. In some cases, they make a disproportionately large contribution to profit because they make a small incremental addition to costs.

WHY AVOIDABLE COSTS?

The hardest principle for many business decision makers to accept is that only avoidable costs are relevant for pricing. Avoidable costs are those that either have not yet been incurred or can be reversed. The costs of selling a product, delivering it to the customer, and replacing the sold item in inventory are avoidable, as is the rental cost of buildings and equipment that are not covered by a long-term lease. The opposite of avoidable costs are sunk costs—those costs that a company is irreversibly committed to bear. For example, a company's past expenditures on research and development are sunk costs since they cannot be changed regardless of any decisions made in the present. The rent on buildings and equipment within the term of a current lease is sunk, except to the extent that the firm can avoid the expense by subletting the property.[4]

The cost of assets that a firm owns may or may not be sunk. If an asset can be sold for an amount equal to its purchase price times the percentage of its remaining useful life, then none of its cost is sunk since the cost can be entirely recovered through resale. Popular models of commercial airplanes often retain their value in this way, making avoidable the entire cost of their continued use. If an asset has no resale value, then its cost is entirely sunk even though it may have much useful life remaining. A neon sign depicting a company's corporate logo may have much useful life remaining, but its cost is entirely sunk since no other company would care to buy it. Frequently, the cost of assets is partially avoidable and partially sunk. For example, a new truck could be resold for a substantial portion of its purchase price but would lose some market value immediately after purchase. The portion of the new price that could not be recaptured is sunk and should not be considered in pricing decisions. Only depreciation of the resale value of the truck is an avoidable cost of using it.

From a practical standpoint, the easiest way to identify the avoidable cost is to recognize that it is the future cost, not the historical cost, associated with making a sale. What, for example, is the cost for an oil company to sell a gallon of gasoline at one of its company-owned stations? One might be inclined to say that it is the cost of the oil used to make the gasoline plus the cost of refining and distribution. Unfortunately, that view could lead refiners to make some costly pricing mistakes. Most oil company managers realize that the relevant cost for pricing gasoline is not the historical cost of producing a gallon of gasoline, but rather the future cost of replacing the inventory when sales are made. Even LIFO (last-in, first-out) accounting can be misleading for companies that are drawing down large inventories. To account accurately for the effect of a sale on profitability, managers need to adopt NIFO (next-in, first-out) accounting for managerial decision making.[5]

The distinction between the historical cost of acquisition and the future cost of replacement is merely academic when supply costs are stable. It becomes very practical when costs rise or fall.[6] When the price of crude oil rises, companies quickly raise prices, long before any gasoline made from the more expensive crude reaches the pump. Politicians and consumer advocates label this practice "price gouging," since companies with large inventories of gasoline increase their reported profits by selling their gasoline at higher prices than they paid to produce it. So what is the real incremental cost to the company of selling a gallon of gasoline?

Each gallon of gasoline sold requires the purchase of crude oil at the new, higher price for the company to maintain its gasoline inventory. If that price is not covered by revenue from sales of gasoline, the company suffers reduced cash flow from every sale. Even though the sales appear profitable from a historical cost standpoint, the company must add to its working capital (by borrowing money or by retaining a larger portion of its earnings) to pay the new, higher cost of crude oil. Consequently the real "cash" cost of making a sale rises immediately by an amount equal to the increase in the replacement cost of crude oil.

What happens when crude oil prices decline? If a company with large inventories held its prices high until all inventories were sold, it would be undercut by any company with smaller inventories that could profitably take advantage of the lower cost of crude oil to gain market share. The company would see its sales, profits, and cash flow decline. Again, the intelligent company bases its prices on the replacement cost, not the historical cost, of its inventory. In historical terms, it reports a loss. However, that loss corresponds to an equal reduction in the cost of replacing its inventories with cheaper crude oil. Since the company simply reduces its operating capital by the amount of the reported loss, its cash flow remains unaffected.

Unfortunately, even level-headed businesspeople often let sunk costs sneak into their decision making, resulting in pricing mistakes that squander profits. The case of a small midwestern publisher of esoteric books illustrates this risk. The publisher customarily priced a book at $20 per copy, which included a $4 contribution to overhead and profit. The firm printed 2,000 copies of each book on the first run and normally sold less than half in the first year. The remaining copies were added to inventory. The company was moderately profitable until the year when, due to a substantial increase in interest rates, the $4 contribution per book could no longer fully cover the interest cost of its working capital.

Recognizing a problem, the managers called in a pricing consultant to show them how to improve the profitability of their prices in order to cover their increased costs. They were, however, quite resistant to the consultant's suggestion that they run a half-price sale on all their slow-moving titles. The publisher's business manager pointed out that half price would not even cover the cost of goods sold. He explained to the consultant, "Our problem is that our prices are not currently adequate to cover our overhead. I fail to see how cutting our prices even lower—eliminating the gross margin we now have so that we cannot even cover the cost of production—is a solution to our problem."

The business manager's logic was quite compelling, but his argument was based on the fallacy of looking at sunk costs of production as a guide to pricing rather than looking at the avoidable cost of holding inventory. No doubt, the firm regretted having printed many of the books in its warehouse, but since the production cost of those books was no longer avoidable regardless of the pricing strategy adopted, and since the firm did not plan to replace them, historical production costs were irrelevant to any pricing decision.[7] What was relevant was the avoidable cost of working capital required to hold the books in inventory.

If, by cutting prices and selling the books sooner instead of later, the publisher could save more in interest than it lost from a price cut, then price-cutting clearly would increase profit even while reducing revenue below the cost of goods sold. In this case, the publisher could ultimately sell all books for $20 if it held them long enough. By selling some books immediately for $10, however, the company could avoid the interest cost of holding them until it could get the higher price. Exhibit 8-2 shows the cumulative interest cost of holding a book in inventory, given that it could be sold immediately for $10 and that the cost of capital at the time was 18 percent. Since the interest cost of holding a book longer than 4 years exceeds the proposed $10 price cut, any book for which the firm held more than 4 years of inventory could be sold more profitably now at half price than later at full price.[8]

EXHIBIT 8-2	The Cumulative Interest Cost of Holding a Book in Inventory							
Years Inventory Held	**1**	**2**	**3**	**4**	**5**	**6**	**7**	**8**
Interest cost to hold inventory*	$1.80	$3.90	$6.43	$9.39	$12.88	$16.99	$21.85	$27.59

*Interest cost to year $n = \$10(1.18^n - 1)$.

The error made by the business manager was understandable. It is a common mistake among people who think about pricing problems in terms of a traditional income statement.

AVOIDING MISLEADING ACCOUNTING

Unfortunately, accounting statements can often be misleading. One must approach them with care when making pricing decisions. Let us further examine the publisher's error presented above, and others, to better understand the pitfalls of accounting data and how to deal with them. By accounting convention, an income statement follows this form:

Sales revenue
− Cost of goods sold
= Gross profit

− Selling expenses
− Depreciation
− Administrative overhead
= Operating profit

− Interest expense
= Pretax profit

− Taxes
= Net profit

This can lead managers to think about pricing sequentially, as a set of hurdles to be overcome in order. First managers try to get over the gross profit hurdle by maximizing their sales revenue and minimizing the cost of goods sold. Then they navigate the second hurdle by minimizing selling expenses, depreciation, and overhead to maximize the operating profit. Similarly, they minimize their interest expense to clear the pretax profit hurdle and minimize their taxes to reach their ultimate goal of a large, positive net profit. They imagine that by doing their best to maximize income at each step, they will surely then reach their goal of a maximum bottom line.

Unfortunately, the road to a profitable bottom line is not so straight. Profitable pricing often calls for sacrificing gross profit in order to reduce expenses further down the line. The publisher in our last example could report a much healthier gross profit by refusing to sell any book for less than $20, but only by bearing interest expenses that would exceed the extra gross profit, leaving an even smaller pretax profit. Moreover, interest is not the only cost that can be reduced profitably by trading off sales revenue. Discount sales through direct mail often save selling expenses that substantially exceed a reduction in sales revenue. While such discounts depress gross profit, the greater savings in selling expenses produce a net increase in operating profit. Discounting for a sale prior to the date of an inventory tax may also save more on tax payments than the revenue loss.

Effective pricing cannot be done in steps. It requires that one approach the problem holistically, looking for each trade-off between higher prices and higher costs, and cutting gross profit whenever necessary to cut expenses by even more. The best way to avoid being misled by a traditional income statement is to develop a managerial costing system independent of the system used for financial reporting,[9] as follows:

> Sales revenue
> − Incremental, avoidable variable costs
> = Total contribution (in dollars)
> − Incremental, avoidable fixed costs
> = Net contribution
> − Other fixed or sunk costs
> = Pretax profit
> − Income taxes
> = Net profit

The value of reorganization is that it first focuses attention on costs that are incremental and avoidable and only later looks at costs that are nonincremental and sunk for the pricing decision. In this analysis, maximizing the profit contribution of a pricing decision is the same as maximizing the net profit, since the fixed or sunk costs subtracted from the profit contribution are not influenced by the pricing decisions and since income taxes are determined by the pretax profit rather than by unit sales.

One could not do such a cost analysis simply by reorganizing the numbers on a traditional income statement. The traditional income statement reports quarterly or annual totals. For pricing, we are not concerned about the cost of all units produced in a period; we are concerned only with the cost of the units that will be affected by the decision to be made. Thus, the relevant cost to consider when evaluating a price reduction is the cost of the additional units that the firm expects to sell because of the price cut. The relevant cost to consider when evaluating a price increase is the avoided cost of units that the firm will not produce because sales will be reduced by the price rise. For any managerial decision, including pricing decisions, it is important to isolate and consider only the costs that affect the profitability of that decision.

ESTIMATING RELEVANT COSTS

The essence of incremental costing is to measure the cost incurred because a product is sold, or not incurred because it is not sold. We cannot delve into all the details of setting up a useful managerial accounting system here. For our purposes, it will suffice to caution that there are four common errors that managers frequently make when attempting to develop useful estimates of true costs.

1.   Beware of averaging total variable costs to estimate the cost of a single unit. The average of variable costs is often an adequate indicator of the incremental cost per unit, but it can be dangerously misleading in those cases where the incremental cost per unit is not constant. The relevant incremental cost for pricing is the actual incremental cost of the particular units affected by a pricing decision, which is not necessarily equal to average variable cost. Consider the following example:

A company is currently producing 1,100 units per day, incurring a total materials cost of $4,400 per day and labor costs of $9,200 per day. The labor costs consist of $8,000 in regular pay and $1,200 in overtime pay per day. Labor and materials are the only two costs that change when the firm makes small changes in output. What then is the relevant cost for pricing? One might be tempted to answer that the relevant cost is the sum of the labor and materials costs ($13,600) divided by total output (1,100 units), or approximately $12.36 per unit. Such a calculation would lead to serious underpricing when demand is strong, since the real incremental cost of producing the last units is much higher than the average cost. A price increase, for example, could eliminate only sales that are now produced on overtime at a cost substantially above the average.

What is the cost of producing the last units, those that might not be sold if the product's price was raised? It may be reasonable to assume that materials costs are approximately the same for all units, so that average materials cost is a good measure of the incremental materials cost for the last units. Thus a good estimate of the relevant materials cost is $4 per unit ($4,400/1,100). We know, however, that labor costs are not the same for all units. The company must pay time-and-a-half for overtime, which are the labor hours that could be eliminated if price is increased and if less of the product is sold. Even if workers are equally productive during overtime and regular hours, producing approximately 100 units per day during overtime hours, the labor cost is $12 per unit ($1,200/100), resulting in a labor and materials cost for the last 100 units of $16 each, substantially above the $12.36 average cost.[10]

2.   Beware of accounting depreciation formulas. The relevant depreciation expense that should be used for all managerial decision making is the change in the current value of assets. Depreciation of assets is usually calculated in a number of different ways depending on the intended use of the data. For reporting to the Internal Revenue Service, depreciation is accelerated to minimize tax liability. For standard financial reporting, rates of depreciation are estimated as accurately as possible but are applied to historical costs.[11] For pricing and any other managerial decision making, however, depreciation expenses should be based on forecasts of the actual decline in the current market value of assets as a result of their use.

Failure to accurately measure depreciation expenses can severely distort an analysis of pricing options. For example, the author of one marketing textbook wrote that a particular airline could price low on routes where its older planes were fully depreciated, but had to price high on routes where new planes were generating large depreciation charges. Such pricing would be quite senseless. Old planes obviously have a market value regardless of their book value. The decline in that market value should either be paid for by passengers who fly on those planes or the planes should be sold. Similarly, if the market value of new planes does not really depreciate as quickly as the financial statements indicate, excessive depreciation expenses could make revenues appear inadequate to justify what are actually profitable new investments. The relevant depreciation expense for pricing is the true decline in an asset's resale value.

3.   Beware of treating a single cost as either all relevant or all irrelevant for pricing. A single cost on the firm's books may have two separate components—one incremental and the other not, or one avoidable and the other sunk—that must be distinguished. Such a cost must be divided into the portion that is relevant for pricing and the portion that is not. Even incremental labor costs are often not entirely unavoidable (see Box 8-1).

BOX 8-1

PEAK PRICING: AN APPLICATION OF INCREMENTAL COSTING

The adverse financial impact of average costing is greatest for those companies, such as service providers, whose products are not storable. Such companies face the problem of having to build capacity to serve temporary but predictable "peaks" in demand. This creates the interesting situation where the cost of capacity goes from being incremental to sunk, and back to incremental again, over the period of a year, a month, a week, or even a day. Airlines face peaks at the beginning and ends of weeks but have excess capacity midweek and on weekends. Telecom companies face peaks in the middle of each weekday but have excess capacity in the evenings and on weekends. Restaurants, car rental companies, marketers of advertising space, commercial printers, health clubs, resorts, electric utilities, and landscape maintenance companies all face substantial peaks and valleys in demand for nonstorable products or services. One way to manage capacity in those cases, and to thus maximize profitability, is with price.

The key to using price to manage capacity profitably is to understand how to allocate the capacity costs over time. Most companies make the mistake of averaging the capacity cost over all of the units produced. If an electric utility sells 40 percent of its kilowatts during a few peak hours, and 60 percent during the other 21 hours in the day, then 40 percent of the capacity cost (the depreciation and maintenance cost for the power plants) would be allocated to the peak hours. This results in each kilowatt being assigned the same capacity charge. Although this is the usual approach (utilities have even been required to cost and price this way by regulation), it makes no sense in principle and undermines profitability in practice. Why? Because the need for the capacity is created entirely by the peak period demand. Off-peak demand can be satisfied without the additional capacity, so capacity costs are not incremental to decisions that affect the volume of off-peak sales. Consequently, the cost of capacity above what is necessary to meet off-peak demand should be allocated entirely to the peak period sales.

One effect of allocating those costs only to sales in the peak period is to raise the hurdle required to justify peak-period investment. The way to ensure that capacity costs are covered is to make no capacity investments that cannot be entirely justified by the revenue from peak demand. If additional capacity really is required only for a few hours a day, a few days a week, or a few months a year, then prices in those periods should be covering all the cost of the capacity, or the capacity should not be built. The other effect is to reveal the surprisingly high profitability of the lower-price, lower-margin sales in off-peak periods. Because the contribution from off-peak sales is not required to cover the cost of capacity, which will be there whether or not the capacity is used, that contribution falls directly to the bottom line. Companies that

fail to realize this overinvest for peak demand and then are forced either to cut their prices to fill their off-peak capacity or to suffer even greater losses during off-peak periods. On net, they invest themselves into unprofitability.

As a company moves toward pricing differently for the peaks and valleys, its average price decreases, but its profit and return on capital invested will increase. For companies with a peak capacity problem, it is usually far more important that they earn a high return per unit of capacity than it is for them to earn a high contribution margin per sale. For many years, hotels mismeasured their success by their ability to command and increase their "average daily rate." Of course, one way to increase average daily rate is simply to rent no rooms except at times of peak demand when the hotel can ask for and get its highest rates. That is unlikely, however, to yield a good return on assets. When hotels began being managed more rationally, the industry adopted a new measure, "revenue per available room," that changed the incentive to manage capacity. The bottom line became "Get all you can get at peak, but make sure you fill the room and earn something at off peak."

In past recessions, some steel producers found when they considered laying off high-seniority employees that the avoidable portion of their labor costs was only a small part of their total labor costs. Their union contracts committed them to paying senior employees much of their wages even when laid off. Consequently, those companies found that the prices they needed to cover their incremental, avoidable costs were actually quite low, justifying continued operations at some mills even though those operations produced substantial losses when all costs were considered.

4.   Beware of overlooking opportunity costs. *Opportunity cost* is the contribution that a firm forgoes when it uses assets for one purpose rather than another. Opportunity costs are relevant costs for pricing even though they do not appear on financial statements. They should be assigned hard numbers in any managerial accounting system, and pricers should incorporate them into their analyses as they would any other cost. In the earlier example of the book publisher, the cost of capital required to maintain the firm's inventory was the cost of borrowed funds (18 percent). It therefore generated an explicit interest expense on the firm's income statement. A proper analysis of the publisher's problem would have been no different had we assumed that the inventory was financed entirely with internally generated funds. Those internally generated funds do not create an interest expense on the publisher's income statement, but they do have alternative uses. Internally generated funds that are used to finance inventories could have been used to purchase an interest-bearing note or could have been invested in some profitable sideline business such as printing stationery. The interest income that could have been earned from the best of these alternatives is an incremental, avoidable cost of using internally generated funds, just as the interest paid explicitly is an incremental, avoidable cost of using borrowed funds.

The same argument would apply when costing the use of a manufacturing facility, a railroad right-of-way, or the seat capacity of an airline. The historical cost of those assets is entirely irrelevant and potentially a very misleading guide to pricing. There is often, however, a current cost of using those assets that is very relevant. That cost occurs whenever capacity used either could be used to make and sell some other product, or could be rented or sold to some other company. Even though the historical cost is sunk, the relevant cost of using those assets is positive whenever there are competing profitable uses. That opportunity cost is the contribution that must be forgone if the assets are not sold or used to produce the alternative product or service. It can easily exceed not only the historical cost but also even the replacement cost of the capacity.

Even if a company has current excess capacity but there is some probability that future business might have to be turned away, the capacity should be assigned an opportunity cost for pricing. Airlines, for example, stop selling discounted seats for a particular flight long before the flight is full. The opportunity cost of selling a discounted seat is near zero only if that seat would otherwise certainly be empty at flight time. As a plane's capacity fills, however, the probability increases that selling a discounted seat will require turning away a passenger who would have paid full fare on the day of the flight. The probability of such a passenger wanting the seat, times the contribution that would be earned at full price, is the opportunity cost of selling a discounted seat in advance (see Box 8-2).

Obviously, moving beyond these costing principles to estimating the true cost of a sale is not easy. Too often, however, managers shrink from the task because of the cost and complexity of measuring true costs on an ongoing basis. Usually, in our experience, it is possible to get much closer to true costs by doing even a

BOX 8-2

OPPORTUNITY COSTS: A PRACTICAL ILLUSTRATION

An airline's most important cost for pricing is the "opportunity cost" of its capacity. Incremental costs other than capacity costs (e.g., food, ticketing) are literally trivial in comparison. An airline that took the historical cost or even the replacement cost of buying planes would miss many opportunities for profitable pricing and, in a competitive market, would soon go bankrupt because most of the profitability of an airline comes from the "incremental" revenue that it generates selling some seats at prices below the average cost per seat. The key to making such a strategy profitable is to understand on an ongoing basis the expected opportunity cost of selling a seat at any particular time on any particular flight.

What is the opportunity cost of a seat? On Saturday afternoon to nonresort locations, it is probably zero since there is no way that the plane will ever be filled. At most times, however, a plane could easily be filled by offering a low discount price during the month before the flight. The opportunity cost of selling such a seat is the contribution that could be earned from a full-fare passenger, usually a business traveler, times the probability that such a price-insensitive passenger will in fact buy the seat before the plane departs. For example, if a plane currently has empty seats 1 month before the flight, the airline uses historical booking patterns to estimate that it has a 70 percent probability that the plane will depart with at least one empty seat. That means that there is a 30 percent probability that a seat would not be available to a last-minute passenger willing to pay full fare. If the contribution from a full-fare ticket for the flight is \$500, then the "opportunity cost" to sell a discount ticket in advance is $0.3 \times \$500 = \$150$, to which we add the cost of ticketing, food, and incremental fuel, to estimate the total cost of offering the ticket. This costing system explains why the price of a discount ticket on the same flight might go up or down many weeks before a flight departs, while there are still many seats available. Airlines have sophisticated "yield management" systems that use historical booking patterns to estimate the probability of an empty seat at departure. If a plane is not filling up as rapidly as historically expected, the probability of an empty seat goes up, the opportunity cost of selling more discounted seats goes down, so the airline's management system may offer some tickets at an exceptionally low price. If, however, a group of seven businesspeople suddenly books the flight, the probability of filling the flight jumps substantially, the opportunity cost goes up, and the airline's yield management system automatically blocks additional sales of the cheapest tickets.

simple point-in-time study of cost drivers. We have, for example, worked with a company that charged every item produced the same amount for paint, even though some items were produced in large lots and others in small lots. By doing a simple statistical regression, using prior year data, paint purchases by color as a function of production of that color product, and average lot size, we rationally reallocated paint costs to reflect the higher costs of small batches. In other cases, we have relied on cost drivers as subjective as a plant foreman's judgment about the relative difficulty of making different types of products. Are such judgments highly accurate? Probably not. That is not a reason to avoid making them if that is the best you can do with the time and money available. It is better to make pricing decisions based on rough approximations of the true costs of products or services than on precise accounting of costs that are sure to be, at best, irrelevant and, at worst, highly misleading.

ACTIVITY-BASED COSTING

Activity-based costing (ABC) provides more realistic estimates of how support costs change with increments in sales volume.[12] For example, traditional cost accounting systems use bases like direct labor and machine hours to allocate to products the expenses of support activities. Instead, ABC segregates support expenditures by activities, and then assigns those expenditures based on the drivers of the activities and how they are linked to product sales volume. Some applications of ABC have allowed firms to estimate not just manufacturing costs, but also costs to serve different customers. ABC enables managers to identify the characteristics or drivers that cause some customers to be more expensive or less expensive to serve. Robert Kaplan[13] identified the following differences in characteristics of high cost-to-serve versus low cost-to-serve customers:

High Cost-to-Serve Customers	Low Cost-to-Serve Customers
Order custom products	Order standard products
Small order quantities	High order quantities
Unpredictable order arrivals	Predictable order arrivals
Customized delivery	Standard delivery
Change delivery requirements	No changes in delivery requirements
Manual processing	Electronic processing (EDI)
Large amounts of presales support (marketing, technical, sales resources)	Little to no presales support (standard pricing and ordering)
Large amounts of postsales support (installation, training, warranty, field service)	No postsales support
Require company to hold inventory	Replenish inventory as produced
Pay slowly (high accounts receivable)	Pay on time

ABC extends incremental costing to cost categories that are neither fixed nor variable, but are semifixed costs. For example, these may be costs associated with order entry personnel, or shipping personnel, that are incurred in less frequent outlays or lumps, but nonetheless change with larger changes in volume. ABC allocates these semifixed costs according to activity drivers, usually related to transactions associated with the function—for example, the number of orders received by the order entry department, or the number of shipments shipped by the shipping department. ABC is especially valuable in refining the manager's estimate of the true cost to serve an incoming customer order.

PERCENT CONTRIBUTION MARGIN AND PRICING STRATEGY

There are three benefits to determining the true unit cost of a product or service for pricing. First, it is a necessary first step toward controlling costs. The best way to control variable costs is not necessarily appropriate for controlling fixed costs. Second, it enables management to determine the minimum price at which the firm can profitably accept incremental business that will not affect the pricing of its other sales. Third, and most important for our purposes, it enables management to determine the contribution margin for each product sold, which, as will be seen in Chapter 9 on financial analysis, is essential for making informed, profitable pricing decisions.

The percent contribution margin is the share of price that adds to profit or reduces losses. It is not the return on sales, which is used by financial analysts to compare the performance of different companies in the same industry. The return on sales indicates the average profit as a percentage of the price after accounting for all costs. Our concern, however, is not with the average, but with the added profit resulting from an additional sale. Even when variable costs are constant, the added profit from a sale exceeds the average profit because some costs are fixed or sunk. The share of the price that adds to profit, the contribution margin, is everything above the share required to cover the incremental, variable cost of the sale.

When variable cost is constant for all units affected by a particular pricing decision, it is proper to calculate the percent contribution margin from aggregate sales data. After calculating the sales revenue and total contribution margin resulting from a change in sales, one can calculate the percent contribution margin, or %CM, as follows:

$$\%CM = \frac{\text{Total contribution margin}}{\text{Sales revenue}} \times 100$$

When variable costs are not constant for all units (e.g., when the units affected by a price change are produced on overtime), it is important to calculate a dollar contribution margin per unit for just the units affected by the price change. The dollar contribution margin per unit, $CM, is simply

$$\$CM = \text{Price} - \text{Variable cost}$$

where variable cost is the cost per unit of only those units affected by the price change and includes only those costs that are avoidable. With the dollar contribution margin, one can calculate the percent contribution margin without being misled when variable costs are not constant. The formula for this calculation of the percent contribution margin is

$$\% CM = \frac{\$CM}{Price}$$

which gives the percent contribution margin in decimal form.

The size of the contribution as a percentage of the price has important strategic implications. First, the percent contribution margin is a measure of the leverage between a firm's sales volume and its profit. It indicates the importance of sales volume as a marketing objective. To illustrate, look at Exhibit 8-3. A company sells two products, each with the same net profit on sales, but with substantially different contribution margins. A company using full-cost pricing would, therefore, treat them the same. However, the actual effect of a price change for these two products would be radically different because of their varying cost structures (see Exhibit 8-3).

Product A has high variable costs equal to 80 percent of its price. Its percent contribution margin is therefore 20 percent. Product B has low variable costs equal to 20 percent of its product's price. Its percent contribution margin is therefore 80 percent. Although at current sales volumes each product earns the same net profit, the effect on each of a change in sales volume is dramatically different. For product A, only $0.20 of every additional sales dollar increases profit or reduces losses. For product B, that figure is $0.80.

The lower part of Exhibit 8-3 illustrates the impact of this difference on pricing decisions. In order for product A, with its relatively small percent contribution margin, to profit from a 5 percent price cut, its sales must increase by

EXHIBIT 8-3   Effect of Contribution Margin on Breakeven Sales Changes

	Product A	Product B
Percentage of setting price accounted for by:		
Variable costs	80.0	20.0
Fixed or sunk costs	10.0	70.0
Net profit margin	10.0	10.0
Contribution margin	20.0	80.0
Breakeven sales change (%) for a:		
5% Price reduction/advantage	+33.3	+6.7
10% Price reduction/advantage	+100.0	+14.3
20% Price reduction/advantage	∞	+33.3
5% Price increase/premium	−20.0	−5.9
10% Price increase/premium	−33.3	−11.1
20% Price increase/premium	−50.0	−20.0

more than 33 percent, compared with only 6.7 percent for product B with its larger percent contribution margin. To profit from a 10 percent price cut, product A's sales must increase by more than 100 percent, compared with only 14.3 percent for product B. Clearly, this company cannot justify a strategy of low pricing to build volume for product A nearly as easily as it can for product B. The opposite conclusion follows for price increases. Product A can afford to lose much more sales than product B and still profit from higher prices. Consequently, it is much easier to justify a premium price strategy for product A than for product B.

Second, the percent contribution margin is an indicator of the firm's ability to compete against competitors. If a competitor believes it has a substantially higher percent contribution margin than you do then it is likely that the competitor will engage in price discounting to drive sales volume because of the leverage between sales volume and profit. On the other hand, knowing that you have a comparable or higher percent contribution margins than your competitor provides some assurance that you have the ability to retaliate and counterattack opportunistic moves by competitors that attempt to steal customers with price discounting.

Third, the percent contribution margin is a measure of the extent to which you can use segmentation pricing to serve and penetrate multiple market segments. *Segmentation pricing* means setting different prices for different market segments, each of which has a different cost to serve and different level of price sensitivity. For a given product the greater your percent contribution margin, the more flexibility you have to set higher prices for some customer segments and lower prices for other segments. This enables you to serve not only customers who are willing to pay premium prices but also customers that are price sensitive and only willing to pay lower prices. Many companies strategically design their cost structure to ensure that their variable costs remain low so they can maintain a high percent contribution margin, which enables them to penetrate many market segments of varying price sensitivities. They support these penetration strategies with high fixed costs that enable them to drive product volume through investments in advertising, sales promotions, price discounting, and intensive distribution systems.

MANAGING COSTS IN TRANSFER PRICING

A frequently overlooked opportunity to use costs as a source of advantage in pricing occurs when the company can manage the structure of the prices of its upstream suppliers. These upstream suppliers might be independent companies or independent divisions of the same company that set the prices of products that pass between them. This situation, known as *transfer pricing,* represents one of the most common reasons why independent companies and divisions are sometimes less price competitive and profitable than their vertically integrated competitors.

Exhibit 8-4 illustrates this often-overlooked opportunity. Independent Manufacturing, Inc. sells its product for $2 per unit in a highly competitive market.

	Current Price, Costs, Sales	10% Price Cut, 30% Sales Increase	Change
EXHIBIT 8-4 Inefficiencies in Transfer Pricing			
Independent Manufacturing, Inc.			
Current unit sales	1,000,000	1,300,00	
Price	$2.00	$1.80	
Variable materials cost	$1.20	$1.20	
Variable labor cost	$0.20	$0.20	
Fixed cost	$0.40	$0.31	
Contribution margin	$0.60	$0.40	
% CM	30%	22%	
Annual pretax profit	$200,000	$120,000	($80,000)
Alpha Parts Inc.			
Current unit sales	1,000,000	1,300,000	
Price	$0.30	$0.30	
Variable cost	$0.05	$0.05	
Fixed cost	$0.20	$0.15	
Contribution margin	$0.25	$0.25	
Annual pretax profit	$50,000	$125,000	$75,000
Beta Parts Inc.			
Current unit sales	1,000,000	1,300,000	
Price	$0.90	$0.90	
Variable cost	$0.35	$0.35	
Fixed cost	$0.40	$0.31	
Contribution margin	$0.55	$0.55	
Annual pretax profit	$150,000	$315,000	$165,000

To manufacture the product, it buys different parts from two suppliers, Alpha and Beta, at a total cost per unit of $1.20. The parts purchased from Alpha cost $0.30 and those from Beta cost $0.90.

Independent Manufacturing conducts a pricing analysis to determine whether any changes in its pricing might be justified. It determines that its contribution margin (price minus variable cost) is $0.60, or 30 percent of its price.[14] It then calculates the effect of a 10 percent price change in either direction. For a 10 percent price cut to be profitable, Independent must gain at least 50 percent more sales (Chapter 9 presents the formulas for performing these calculations). For a 10 percent price increase to be profitable, Independent can afford to forgo no more than 25 percent of its sales.

Independent's managers conclude that there is no way that they can possibly gain from a price cut, since their sales will surely not increase by more than 50 percent. On the other hand, they are intrigued by the possibility of a price increase. They feel sure that the inevitable decline would be far less than 25 percent if they could get their major competitors to follow them in the increase.

As Independent's management considers how to communicate to the industry the desirability of a general price increase, one of its major competitors, Integrated Manufacturing, Inc. announces its own 10 percent price cut. Independent's management is stunned. How could Integrated possibly justify such a move? Integrated's product is technically identical to Independent's, involving all the same parts and production processes, and Integrated is a company with a market share equal to Independent's. The only difference between the two companies is that Integrated recently began manufacturing its own parts.

That difference, however, is crucial to this story (see Exhibit 8-5). Assume that Integrated currently has all the same costs of producing parts as Independent's suppliers, Alpha and Beta, and expects to earn a profit from those operations. It also has the same costs of assembling those parts ($0.20 incremental labor plus $0.40 fixed per unit). Moreover, Integrated enjoys no additional economies of logistical integration. Despite these similarities, the two companies have radically different cost structures, which respond quite differently to changes in volume and which cause the two companies to evaluate price changes quite differently. Integrated has no variable materials cost corresponding to Independent's variable materials cost of $1.20 per unit. Instead, it incurs additional fixed costs of $0.60 per unit ($0.20 plus $0.40) and incremental variable costs of only $0.40 per unit ($0.05 plus $0.35).

EXHIBIT 8-5   Efficiency from Cost Integration

	Current Price, Costs, Sales	10% Price Cut, 30% Sales Increase	Change
Integrated Manufacturing, Inc.			
Current unit sales	1,000,000	1,300,000	
Price	$2.00	$1.80	
Variable materials cost	None	None	
Variable labor cost ($0.20 + $0.05 + $0.35)	$0.60	$0.60	
Fixed cost ($0.40 + $0.20 + $0.40)	$1.00	$0.77	
Contribution margin	$1.40	$1.20	
%	70%	67%	
Annual pretax profit	$400,000	$560,000	$160,000

This difference in cost structure between Integrated (high fixed and low variable) and Independent (low fixed and high variable) gives Integrated a much higher contribution margin per unit than Independent's margin. For Integrated, $1.40, or 70 percent of each additional sale, contributes to bottom-line profits. For Independent, only $0.60, or 30 percent of each additional sale, falls to the bottom line. Integrated's breakeven calculations for a 10 percent price change are, therefore, quite different. For a 10 percent price cut to be profitable, Integrated has to gain only 16.7 percent more sales. But for a 10 percent price increase to pay off, Integrated could afford to forgo no more than 12.5 percent of its sales.

It is easy to see why Integrated is more attracted to price cuts and more averse to price increases than is Independent. For Integrated, sales must grow by only 16.7 percent to make a price cut profitable, compared with 50 percent for Independent. Similarly, Integrated could afford to lose no more than 12.5 percent of sales (compared with as much as 25 percent for Independent) and still profit from a price increase. How can it be that two identical sets of costs result in such extremely different calculations? The answer is that Independent, like most manufacturers, pays its suppliers on a price-per-unit basis. That price must include enough revenue to cover the suppliers' fixed costs and a reasonable profit if Independent expects those suppliers to remain viable in the long run. Consequently, fixed costs and profit of both Alpha and Beta become variable costs of sales for Independent. Such incrementalizing of nonincremental costs makes Independent much less cost competitive than Integrated, which earns more than twice as much additional profit on each unit it sells.

Independent's cost disadvantage is a disadvantage to its suppliers as well. Independent calculates that it requires a 50 percent sales increase to make a 10 percent price cut profitable. Independent, therefore, correctly rejects a 10 percent price cut that would increase sales by 30 percent. With current sales of 1 million units, such a price cut would cause Independent's profit to decline by $80,000. Note, however, that the additional sales volume would add $240,000 ($75,000 plus $165,000) to the profits of Independent's suppliers, provided that they produce the increased output with no more fixed costs. They would earn much more than Independent would lose by cutting price. It is clear why Integrated sees a 10 percent price cut as profitable when Independent does not. As its own supplier, Integrated captures the additional profits that accrue within the entire value chain (Alpha, $75,000; Beta, $165,000) as a result of increases in volume.[15]

Once Independent recognizes the problem, what alternatives does it have, short of taking the radical step of merging with its suppliers? One alternative is for Independent to pay its suppliers' fixed costs in a lump-sum payment, perhaps even retaining ownership of the assets while negotiating low supply prices that cover only incremental costs and a reasonable return. The lump-sum payment is then a fixed cost for Independent, and its contribution margin on added sales rises by the reduction in its incremental supply cost. General Motors does this with auto parts suppliers, bearing the fixed cost of a part's design and paying the supplier for all fixed costs of retooling and setup. In this case, the negotiated price per unit need cover only the supplier's variable costs and profit. As a result, General Motors earns more on each additional sale and so has a greater incentive to make marketing decisions, including pricing decisions that build volume.

A second alternative is to negotiate a high price for initial purchases that cover the fixed costs, with a lower price for all additional quantities that cover only incremental costs and profit. Sears sometimes uses this system with suppliers of its house-brand products. Since the lower supply price is the incremental cost of additional sales, Sears can profitably price its products lower to generate more volume. In Independent Manufacturing's case, it might negotiate an agreement with Alpha and Beta that guarantees enough purchases at $0.30 and $0.90, respectively, to cover their fixed costs, after which the price would fall to $0.10 and $0.50, respectively.

Both of these systems for paying suppliers avoid incrementalizing fixed costs, but they do not avoid the problem of incrementalizing the suppliers' profits. They work well only when the suppliers' profits account for a small portion of the total price suppliers receive. Lump-sum payments could be paid to suppliers to cover negotiated profit as well as fixed costs. This is risky, however, since profit per unit remains the suppliers' incentive to maintain on-time delivery of acceptable quality merchandise. Consequently, when a supplier has low fixed costs but can still demand a high profit because of little competition, a third alternative is often used. The purchaser may agree to pay the supplier a small fee to cover incremental expenses and an additional negotiated percentage of whatever profit contribution is earned from final sales.

It is noteworthy that most companies do not use these methods to compensate suppliers or to establish prices for sales between independent divisions. Instead, they negotiate arm's-length contracts at fixed prices or let prevailing market prices determine transfer prices.[16] One reason is that it is unusual to find a significant portion of costs that remain truly fixed for large changes in sales. In most cases, the bulk of costs that accountants label fixed are actually semifixed; additional costs would have to be incurred for suppliers to substantially increase their sales, making those costs incremental. One notable case where costs are substantially fixed is in the semiconductor industry. The overwhelming cost of semiconductors is the fixed cost of product development, not the variable or semifixed costs of production. Consequently, integrated manufacturers of products using semiconductors have often had a significant cost advantage. Bowmar, the company that pioneered the handheld calculator, was ultimately driven from the market precisely because it was not cost competitive with more integrated suppliers and failed to negotiate contracts that avoided the incrementalization of their fixed costs of product development.

Companies that buy computer software to sell as part of their products should note that software, too, is a high fixed-cost product that often represents a substantial portion of the cost of computer-aided equipment. Independent software development houses that price on a per-unit basis should note this as well. By forcing their customers to incrementalize the fixed costs and profit of software development, they will ultimately find that their buyers are not cost competitive with companies that either write their own software or that have different pricing arrangements with their suppliers.

Summary

Costs are central considerations in pricing. Without understanding which costs are incremental and avoidable, a firm cannot accurately determine at what price, if any, a market can profitably be served. By erroneously looking at historical costs, a firm could sell its inventory too cheaply. By mistakenly looking at nonincremental fixed costs, a firm could overlook highly profitable opportunities where price is adequate to more than cover the incremental costs. By overlooking opportunity costs, successful companies frequently underprice their products. In short, when managers do not understand the true cost of a sale, their companies unnecessarily forgo significant profit opportunities. They tend to overprice when they have excess capacity, while underpricing and overinvesting when sales are strong relative to capacity.

Having identified the right costs, one must also understand how to use them. The most important reason to identify costs correctly is to be able to calculate an accurate contribution margin. The contribution margin is a measure of the leverage between a product's profitability and its sales volume. An accurate contribution margin enables management to determine the amount by which sales must increase following a price cut or by how little they must decline following a price increase to make the price change profitable. Understanding how changes in sales will affect a product's profitability is the first step in pricing the product effectively. It is, however, just the first step. Next, one must learn how to judge the likely impact of a price change on sales. That requires understanding how buyers are likely to perceive a price change and how competitors are likely to react to it.

The coordination of pricing with suppliers, although not actually economizing resources, can improve the efficiency of pricing by avoiding the incrementalization of a supplier's nonincremental fixed costs and profit. Any of these strategies can generate cost advantages that are, at least in the short run, sustainable. Even cost advantages that are not sustainable, however, can generate temporary savings that are often the key to building more sustainable cost or product advantages later.

Notes

1. Gerald Smith and Thomas Nagle, "Financial Analysis for Profit-Driven Pricing," *Sloan Management Review,* 35(3) (Spring 1994).
2. Beware of costs classified as "overhead." Often costs end up in that classification, even though they are clearly variable, simply because "overhead" is a convenient dumping ground for costs that one has not associated with the products that caused them to be incurred. A clue to the existence of such a misclassification is the incongruous term "variable overhead."
3. Revenue = 1,100 × $10. Cost = $1,500 + $4,500 + $2,000 + ($1 × 1,100).
4. Most economics and accounting texts equate avoidable costs with variable costs, and sunk costs with fixed costs, for theoretical convenience. Unfortunately, those texts usually fail to explain adequately that this is an assumption rather than a necessarily true statement. Consequently, many students come away from related courses with the idea that a firm should always continue producing if price at least covers variable costs. That rule is correct only when the variable costs are entirely avoidable and the fixed costs are entirely sunk. In many industries (e.g., airlines) the fixed costs are often avoidable since the assets can be readily resold. Whenever the fixed costs are avoidable if a decision is not made to

produce a product, or to produce it in as large a quantity, they should be considered when deciding whether a price is adequate to serve a market.

5. LIFO and NIFO costs are the same in any accounting period when a firm makes a net addition to its inventory. In periods during which a firm draws down its inventory, LIFO will understate costs after the firm uses up the portion of its inventory values at current prices and begins "dipping into old layers" of inventory valued at unrealistic past prices.

6. Neil Churchill, "Don't Let Inflation Get the Best of You," *Harvard Business Review* (March–April 1982).

7. The forward-looking production cost of replacing the book in inventory would have been relevant if the firm intended to maintain its current inventory levels.

8. We are assuming here that the half-price sale will not reduce the rate of sales after the sale is over. When it will, then one must add the discounted value of those lost sales to the price discount and compare that figure with the interest cost of holding the inventory. In other industries (e.g., hotels and theaters), the cost of capacity is variable (you can build a hotel with any number of rooms or a theater with any number of seats), but this cost becomes sunk after capacity is built.

9. Robert S. Kaplan, "One Cost System Isn't Enough," *Harvard Business Review,* 66 (January–February 1988), pp. 61–66.

10. The calculation of the portion of output produced on overtime (assuming equal productivity) is as follows: $1,200 overtime is the equivalent in hours of $800 regular time ($1,200/1.5) and is 9.1 percent of the total hours worked ($800/[$8,000 + $800]). Multiplying 9.1 percent times 1,100 units shows that 100 units are pro-

duced on overtime if production is at a constant rate.

11. Since 1979, however, the Financial Accounting Standards Board (FASB) has required that large, publicly held corporations also report supplemental information on increases or decreases in current costs of inventory, property, plant, and equipment, net of inflation. See FASB Statement of Financial Standards No. 33, "Financial Reporting and Changing Prices" (1979).

12. See Robert S. Kaplan, "Introduction to Activity Based Costing," Harvard Business School Note 9-197-076 (1997; revised July 5, 2001); Robert S. Kaplan, "Using Activity-Based Costing with Budgeted Expenses and Practical Capacity," Harvard Business School Note 9-197-083 (1999); Robin Cooper and Robert S. Kaplan, "The Promise— And Peril—of Integrate Cost Systems," *Harvard Business Review* (July-August 1998), pp. 109–119; Robert Kaplan and Robin Cooper, *Cost and Effect* (Cambridge, MA: Harvard Business School Press, 1997); Robert S. Kaplan, "Cost System Analysis," Harvard Business School Note 9-195-181 (1994); Robin Cooper and Robert S. Kaplan, "Profit Priorities from Activity-Based Costing," *Harvard Business Review* (May–June 1991), pp. 2–7; Robin Cooper and Robert S. Kaplan, "Activity-Based Systems: Measuring the Costs of Resource Usage," *Accounting Horizons* (September 1992), pp. 1–13; James P. Borden, "Review of Literature on Activity-Based Costing," *Cost Management,* 4 (Spring 1990), pp. 5–12; Peter B. B. Turney, "Ten Myths About Implementing an Activity-Based Cost System," *Cost Management,* 4 (Spring 1990), pp. 24–32; George J. Beaujon and Vinod R. Singhal, "Understanding the Activity Costs in an Activity-Based Cost System," *Cost Management,* 4 (Spring 1990), pp. 51–72

13. Robert S. Kaplan, "Using ABC To Manage Customer Mix and Relationships," Harvard Business School Note 9-197-094 (1997).

14. $CM = $2.00 − $1.20 − $0.20 = $0.60
%CM = $0.60/$2.00 × 100 = 30%

15. An integrated company does not automatically gain this advantage. If separate divisions of a company operate as independent profit centers setting transfer prices equal to market prices, they will also price too high to maximize their joint profits. To overcome the problem while remaining independent, they need to adopt one of the solutions suggested for independent companies.

16. For a related recent perspective see Thomas W. Malone, "Bringing the Market Inside," *Harvard Business Review,* 82(4) (April 2004), pp. 106–115. For a succinct summary of tax-relevant transfer pricing methods, see "Transfer Pricing Clarified," *Finance Week,* (May 24, 2004), p. 66.

CHAPTER

9

FINANCIAL ANALYSIS

Pricing for Profit

Internal financial considerations and external market considerations are, at most companies, antagonistic forces in pricing decisions. Financial managers allocate costs to determine how high prices must be to achieve profit objectives. Marketing and sales staff analyze buyers to determine how low prices must be to achieve sales objectives. The pricing decisions that result are politically charged compromises, not thoughtful implementations of a coherent strategy. Although common, such pricing policies are neither necessary nor desirable. An effective pricing decision should involve an optimal blending of, not a compromise between, internal financial constraints and external market conditions.

Unfortunately, few managers have any idea how to facilitate such a cross-functional blending of these two legitimate concerns. From traditional cost accounting, they learn to take sales goals as "given" before allocating costs, thus precluding the ability to incorporate market forces into pricing decisions. From marketing, they are told that effective pricing should be entirely "customer driven," which ignores costs except as a minimum constraint below which the sale would become unprofitable. Perhaps along the way, these managers study economics and learn that, in theory, optimal pricing is a blending of cost and demand considerations. In practice, however, they find the economist's assumption of a known demand curve hopelessly unrealistic.

Consequently, pricing at most companies remains trapped between cost and customer-driven procedures that are inherently incompatible. This chapter suggests how managers can break this tactical pricing deadlock and infuse strategic balance into pricing decisions. Many marketers argue that costs should play no role in market-based pricing. This is clearly wrong. Without perfect segmentation (the ability to negotiate independently a unique price for every customer), pricers must make trade-offs between charging higher margins to fewer customers and lower margins to more customers. Once the true cost and contribution of a sale are understood, managers can appropriately integrate costs into what is otherwise a market-driven approach to pricing strategy.

This chapter describes a simple, logically intuitive procedure for quantitatively evaluating the potential profitability of a price change. First, managers develop a baseline, or standard of comparison, to measure the effects of a price change. For example, they might compare the effects of a pending price change with the product's current level of profitability, or with a budgeted level of profitability, or perhaps with a hypothetical scenario that management is particularly interested in exploring. Second, they calculate an incremental "breakeven" for the price change to determine under what market conditions the change will prove profitable. Marketing managers must then determine whether they can actually meet those conditions.

The key to integrating costs and quantitatively assessing the consequences of a price change is the incremental breakeven analysis. Although similar in form to the common breakevens that managers use to evaluate investments, incremental breakeven analysis for pricing is quite different in practice. Rather than evaluating the product's overall profitability, which depends on many factors other than price, incremental breakeven analysis focuses on the incremental profitability of price changes. Consequently, managers start from a baseline reflecting current or projected sales and profitability at the current price. Then they ask whether a change in price could improve the situation. More precisely, they ask:

- How much would the sales volume have to increase to profit from a price reduction?
- How much could the sales volume decline before a price increase becomes unprofitable?

Answers to these questions depend on the product's contribution margin.

The sample problems in this chapter introduce the four equations involved in performing such an analysis and illustrate how to use them. They are based on the experience of Westside Manufacturing, a small company manufacturing pillows for sale through specialty bedding and dry cleaning stores. Although the examples are, for simplicity, based on a small manufacturing business, the equations are equally applicable for analyzing any size or type of business that cannot negotiate a unique price for each customer.[1] If customers can be somewhat segmented for pricing, the formulas apply to pricing within a segment.

Following are Westside Manufacturing's income and costs for a typical month:

Sales	4,000 units
Wholesale price	$10.00 per unit
Revenue	$40,000
Variable costs	$5.50 per unit
Fixed costs	$15,000

Westside is considering a 5 percent price cut, which it believes would make it more competitive with alternative suppliers, enabling it to further increase its sales. Management believes that the company would need to incur no additional fixed costs as a result of this pricing decision. How much would sales have to increase for this company to profit from a 5 percent cut in price?

BREAKEVEN SALES ANALYSIS: THE BASIC CASE

To answer Westside's question, we calculate the breakeven sales change. This, for a price cut, is the minimum increase in sales volume necessary for the price cut to produce an increase in contribution relative to the baseline. Fortunately, making this calculation is simple, as will be shown shortly. First, however, it may be more intuitive to illustrate the analysis graphically (see Exhibit 9-1).

In this exhibit it is easy to visualize the financial trade-offs involved in the proposed price change. Before the price change, Westside receives a price of $10 per unit and sells 4,000 units, resulting in total revenues of $40,000 (the total area of boxes a and b). From this Westside pays variable costs of $5.50 per unit, for a total of $22,000 (box b). Therefore, before the price change, total contribution is $40,000 minus $22,000, or $18,000 (box a). In order for the proposed price cut to be profitable, contribution after the price cut must exceed $18,000.

After the 5 percent price reduction, Westside receives a price of only $9.50 per unit, or $0.50 less contribution per unit. Since it normally sells 4,000 units, Westside would expect to lose $2,000 in total contribution (box c) on sales that it could have made at a higher price. This is called the price effect. Fortunately, the price cut can be expected to increase sales volume.

The contribution earned from that increased volume, the volume effect (box e), is unknown. The price reduction will be profitable, however, when the volume effect (the area of box e) exceeds the price effect (the area of box c). That is, in order for the price change to be profitable, the gain in contribution resulting from

EXHIBIT 9-1   Finding the Breakeven Sales Change

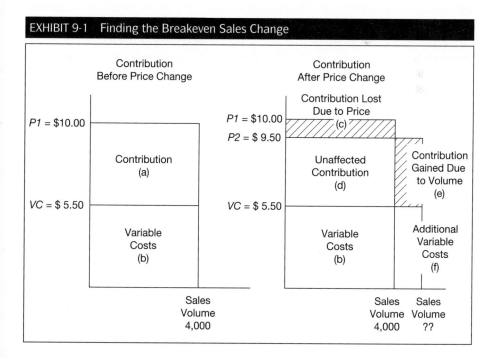

the change in sales volume must be greater than the loss in contribution resulting from the change in price. The purpose of breakeven analysis is to calculate the minimum sales volume necessary for the volume effect (box e) to balance the price effect (box c). When sales exceed that amount, the price cut is profitable.

So how do we determine the breakeven sales change? We know that the lost contribution due to the price effect (box c) is $2,000, which means that the gain in contribution due to the volume effect (box e) must be at least $2,000 for the price cut to be profitable. Since each new unit sold following the price cut results in $4 in contribution ($9.50 − $5.50 = $4), Westside must sell at least an additional 500 units ($2,000 divided by $4 per unit) to make the price cut profitable.

The minimum sales change necessary to maintain at least the same contribution can be directly calculated by using the following simple formula (see Appendix 9A for derivation):

$$= \frac{-\Delta P}{CM + \Delta P}$$

In this equation, the price change and contribution margin may be stated in dollars, percents, or decimals (as long as their use is consistent). The result of this equation is a decimal ratio that, when multiplied by 100, is the percent change in unit sales necessary to maintain the same level of contribution after the price change. The minus sign in the numerator indicates a trade-off between price and volume: Price cuts increase the volume and price increases reduce the volume necessary to achieve any particular level of profitability. The larger the price change—or the smaller the contribution margin—the greater the volume change necessary to generate at least as much contribution as before.

Assume for the moment that there are no incremental fixed costs in implementing Westside's proposed 5 percent price cut. For convenience we make our calculations in dollars (rather than in percents or decimals). Using the contribution margin equation (see Chapter 8), we derive the following:

$$\$CM = \$10 - \$5.50 = \$4.50$$

Given this, we can easily calculate the breakeven sales change as follows:

$$\% \text{ Breakeven sales change} = \frac{-(-\$0.50)}{\$4.50 + (-\$0.50)} = 0.125 \text{ or } 12.5\%$$

Thus, the price cut is profitable only if sales volume increases more than 12.5 percent. Relative to its current level of sales volume, Westside would have to sell at least 500 units more to maintain the same level of profitability it had prior to the price cut, as shown below:

$$\text{Unit breakeven sales change} = 0.125 \times 4,000 = 500 \text{ units}$$

If the actual increase in sales volume exceeds the breakeven sales change, the price cut will be profitable. If the actual increase in sales volume falls short of the breakeven sales change, the price change will be unprofitable. Assuming that

Westside's goal is to increase its current profits, management should initiate the price reduction only if it believes that sales will increase by more than 12.5 percent, or 500 units, as a result.

If Westside's sales increase as a result of the price change by more than the breakeven amount—say, by an additional 550 units—Westside will realize a gain in profit contribution. If, however, Westside sells only an additional 450 units as a result of the price cut, it will suffer a loss in contribution. Once we have the breakeven sales change and the profit contribution, calculating the precise change in contribution associated with any change in volume is quite simple: It is simply the difference between the actual sales volume and the breakeven sales volume, times the new contribution margin (calculated after the price change). For Westside's 550-unit and 450-unit volume changes, the change in contribution equals the following:

$$(550 - 500) \times \$4 = \$200$$
$$(450 - 500) \times \$4 = -\$200$$

The $4 in these equations is the new contribution margin ($9.50 - $5.50). Alternatively, you might have noticed that the denominator of the percent breakeven formula is also the new contribution margin.

We have illustrated breakeven analysis using Westside's proposed 5 percent price cut. The logic is exactly the same for a price increase. Since a price increase results in a gain in unit contribution, Westside can "absorb" some reduction in sales volume and still increase its profitability. How much of a reduction in sales volume can Westside tolerate before the price increase becomes unprofitable? The answer is this: until the loss in contribution due to reduced sales volume is exactly offset by the gain in contribution due to the price increase. As an exercise, calculate how much sales Westside could afford to lose before a 5 percent price increase becomes unprofitable.

It is important to note that the calculation resulting from the breakeven sales change formula is expressed as the percent change in *unit volume* required to break even, not the percent change in monetary sales (e.g., the percent change in dollar sales) required to break even. In the case of a price cut, the percent breakeven sales change in units necessary to justify the price cut is larger than the percent breakeven sales change in sales dollars because the price is now lower.

To convert from the percent breakeven sales change in units to the percent breakeven sales change in dollars you can apply the following simple conversion formula:

$$\%BE(\$) = \%BE(units) + \% \text{ Price change} [1 + \%BE(units)]$$

For example, for Westside's 5 percent proposed price cut above the percent breakeven sales change in unit volume terms was 12.5 percent. What is the corresponding percent breakeven sales change in *dollar sales* terms? The answer is calculated as follows:

$$\%BE (\$) = 0.125 + (-0.05)(1 + 0.125)$$
$$= 6.88\%$$

Thus, to break even on the proposed 5 percent price cut, Westside would have to increase its total dollar sales by 6.88 percent, which is exactly equivalent to a 12.5 percent increase in unit volume.

BREAKEVEN SALES INCORPORATING A CHANGE IN VARIABLE COST

Thus far we have dealt only with price changes that involve no changes in unit variable costs or in fixed costs. Often, however, price changes are made as part of a marketing plan involving cost changes as well. A price increase may be made along with product improvements that increase variable cost, or a price cut might be made to push the product with lower variable selling costs. Expenditures that represent fixed costs might also change along with a price change. We need to consider these two types of incremental costs when calculating the price–volume trade-off necessary for making pricing decisions profitable. We begin this section by integrating changes in variable cost into the financial analysis. In the next section, we do the same with changes in fixed costs.

Fortunately, dealing with a change in variable cost involves only a simple generalization of the breakeven sales change formula already introduced. To illustrate, we return to Westside Manufacturing's proposed 5 percent price cut. Suppose that Westside's price cut is accompanied by a reduction in variable cost of $0.22 per pillow, resulting from Westside's decision to use a new synthetic filler to replace the goose feathers it currently uses. Variable costs are $5.50 before the price change and $5.28 after the price change. By how much would sales volume have to increase to ensure that the proposed price cut is profitable?

When variable costs change along with the price change, managers simply need to subtract the cost change from the price change before doing the breakeven sales change calculation. Unlike the case of a simple price change, managers must state the terms on the right-hand side of the equation in currency units (dollars, pounds, French francs, and so forth) rather than in percentage changes:

$$\% \text{ Breakeven sales change} = \frac{-(\$\Delta P - \$\Delta C)}{\$CM + (\$\Delta P - \$\Delta C)}$$

where Δ indicates "change in," P = price, and C = cost. Note that when the change in variable cost ($\$\Delta C$) is zero, this equation is identical to the breakeven formula previously presented. Note also that the term ($\$\Delta P - \$\Delta C$) is the change in the contribution margin and that the denominator (the original contribution margin plus the change) is the new contribution margin. Thus, the general form of the breakeven pricing equation is simply written as follows:

$$\% \text{ Breakeven sales change} = \frac{-\$\Delta CM}{\text{New } \$CM}$$

For Westside, the next step in using this equation to evaluate the proposed price change is to calculate the change in contribution margin. Recall that the change in price is $9.50 − $10 or −$0.50. The change in variable costs is −$0.22. Thus, the change in contribution can be calculated as follows:

$$\$\Delta CM = (\$\Delta P - \$\Delta C) = -\$0.50 - (-\$0.22) = -\$0.28$$

Previous calculations illustrated that the contribution margin before the price change is $4.50. We can therefore calculate the breakeven sales change as follows:

$$\% \text{ Breakeven sales change} = \frac{-(-\$0.28)}{\$4.50 + (\$0.28)} = 0.066, \text{ or } + 6.6\%$$

In units, the breakeven sales change is 0.066 × 4,000 units, or 265.

Given management's projection of a $0.22 reduction in variable costs, the price cut can be profitable only if management believes that sales volume will increase by more than 6.6 percent, or 265 units. Note that this increase is substantially less than the required sales increase (12.5 percent) calculated before assuming a reduction in variable cost. Why does a variable cost reduction lower the necessary breakeven sales change? Because it increases the contribution margin earned on each sale, making it possible to recover the contribution lost due to the price effect with less additional volume. This relationship is illustrated graphically for Westside Manufacturing in Exhibit 9-2. Westside can realize a gain in contribution due to the change in variable costs (box f), in addition to a gain in contribution due to any increase in sales volume.

EXHIBIT 9-2   Finding the Breakeven Sales Change Given a Change in Variable Costs

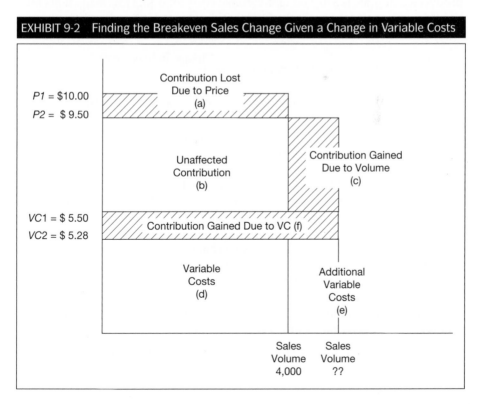

BREAKEVEN SALES WITH INCREMENTAL FIXED COSTS

Although most fixed costs do not impact the incremental profitability of a pricing decision (because they do not change), some pricing decisions necessarily involve changes in fixed costs, even though these costs do not otherwise change with small changes in volume. The management of a discount airline considering whether to reposition as a higher-priced business travelers' airline would probably choose to refurbish its lounges and planes. A regulated utility would need to cover the fixed cost of regulatory hearings to gain approval for a higher price. A fast-food restaurant would need to advertise its promotionally priced "special-value" meals to potential customers. These are incremental fixed costs, necessary for the success of a new pricing strategy but unrelated to the sales volume actually gained at those prices. Recall also that semifixed costs remain fixed only within certain ranges of sales. If a price change causes sales to move outside that range, the level of semifixed costs increases or decreases. Such changes in fixed and semifixed costs need to be covered for a price change to be justified, since without the price change these incremental costs can be avoided.

Fortunately, calculating the sales volume necessary to cover an incremental fixed cost is already a familiar exercise for many managers evaluating investments independent of price changes. For example, suppose a product manager is evaluating a $150,000 fixed expenditure to redesign a product's packaging. The product's unit price is $10, and unit variable costs total $5. How many units must be sold for the firm to recover the $150,000 incremental investment? The answer, as found in most managerial economics texts, is given by the following equation:

$$\text{Breakeven sales volume} = \frac{\$\text{ Change in fixed costs}}{\$\text{CM}}$$

Remembering that the $CM equals price − variable cost, the breakeven sales volume for this example is:

$$\text{Breakeven sales volume} = \frac{\$\,150{,}000}{\$10 - \$5} = 30{,}000\,\text{units}$$

How can the manager do breakeven analysis for a change in pricing strategy that involves both a price change and a change in fixed cost? She simply adds the calculations for (a) the breakeven sales change for a price change and (b) the breakeven sales volume for the related fixed investment.

The breakeven sales change for a price change with incremental fixed costs is the basic breakeven sales change plus the sales change necessary to cover the incremental fixed costs. Since we normally analyze the breakeven for a price change as a percent and the breakeven for an investment in units, we need to multiply or divide by initial unit sales to make them consistent. Consequently, the unit breakeven sales change with a change in fixed costs is as follows:

$$\begin{array}{c}\text{Unit breakeven}\\ \text{sales change}\end{array} = \frac{-\$\Delta\text{CM}}{\text{New }\$\text{CM}} \times \begin{array}{c}\text{Initial}\\ \text{unit sales}\end{array} + \frac{\$\text{ Change in fixed costs}}{\text{New }\$\text{CM}}$$

The calculation for the percent breakeven sales change is as follows:

$$\frac{\text{\% Breakeven}}{\text{sales change}} = \frac{-\,\$\Delta\text{CM}}{\text{New \$CM}} + \frac{\$\,\text{Change in fixed costs}}{\text{New \$CM} \times \text{Initial unit sales}}$$

In both cases, if the "$ change in fixed costs" is zero, we have the breakeven sales change equation for a simple price change.

To illustrate the equations for a price cut, return again to the pricing decision faced by Westside Manufacturing. Westside is considering a 5 percent price cut. We already calculated that it can profit if sales increase by more than 12.5 percent. Now suppose that Westside cannot increase its output without incurring additional semifixed costs. At the company's current rate of sales—4,000 units per month—it is fully utilizing the capacity of the equipment at its four workstations. To increase capacity enough to handle 12.5 percent more sales, the company must install equipment for another work station, at a monthly cost of $800. The new station raises plant capacity by 1,000 units beyond the current capacity of 4,000 units. What is the minimum sales increase required to justify a 5 percent price reduction, given that it involves an $800 increase in monthly fixed costs? The answer is determined as follows:

$$\frac{\text{Unit breakeven}}{\text{sales change}} = 0.125 \times 4{,}000 \text{ units} + \frac{\$800}{\$4} = 700 \text{ units}$$

$$\frac{\text{\% Breakeven}}{\text{sales change}} = 0.125 \times \frac{\$800}{\$4 \times 4{,}000 \text{ units}} = 0.175, \text{ or } 17.5\%$$

The company could profit from a 5 percent price reduction if sales increased by more than 700 units (17.5 percent), which is less than the 1,000 units of added capacity provided by the new workstation. Whether a prudent manager should actually implement such a price decrease depends on other factors as well: How likely is it that sales will increase substantially more than the breakeven minimum, thus adding to profit? How likely is it that sales will increase by less, thus reducing profit? How soon could the decision be reversed, if at all, if sales do not increase adequately?

Even if management considers it likely that orders will increase by more than the breakeven quantity, it should hesitate before making the decision. If orders increase by significantly less than the breakeven minimum, this company could lose substantially, especially if the cost of the new workstation is largely sunk once the expenditure has been made. On the other hand, if orders increase by significantly more, the most the company could increase its sales without bearing the semifixed cost for further expansion is 25 percent, or 1,000 units. Consequently, management must be quite confident of a large sales increase before implementing the 5 percent price reduction.

Consider, however, if the company has already invested in the additional capacity and if the semifixed costs are already sunk. The monthly cost of the fifth workstation is then entirely irrelevant to pricing, since that cost would have to be borne whether or not the capacity is used. Thus, the decision to cut price rests entirely on management's judgment of whether the price cut will stimulate unit sales by more than 12.5 percent. If the actual sales increase is more than 12.5 percent but less than 17.5 percent, management will regret having invested in the fifth workstation. Given that this cost can no longer be avoided, however, the most profitable course of action is to price low enough to use the station, even though that price will not fully cover its cost.

BREAKEVEN SALES ANALYSIS FOR REACTIVE PRICING

So far we have restricted our discussion to proactive price changes, where the firm contemplates initiating a price change ahead of its competitors. The goal of such a change is to enhance profitability. Often, however, a company initiates reactive price changes when it is confronted with a competitor's price change that will impact the former's sales unless it responds. The key uncertainty involved in analyzing a reactive price change is the sales loss the company will suffer if it fails to meet a competitor's price cut, or the sales gain the company will achieve if it fails to follow a competitor's price increase. Is the potential sales loss sufficient to justify cutting price to protect the sales volume? Or is the potential sales gain enough to justify forgoing the opportunity for a cooperative price increase? A slightly different form of the breakeven sales formula is used to analyze such situations.

To calculate the breakeven sales changes for a reactive price change, we need to address the following key questions: (1) What is the minimum potential sales loss that justifies meeting a lower competitive price? (2) What is the minimum potential sales gain that justifies not following a competitive price increase? The basic formula for these calculations is this:

$$\frac{\text{\% Breakeven sales change}}{\text{for reactive price change}} = \frac{\text{Change in price}}{\text{Contribution margin}} = \frac{\Delta P}{CM}$$

To illustrate, suppose that Westside's principal competitor, Eastside, has just reduced its prices by 15 percent. If Westside's customers are highly loyal, it probably would not pay for Westside to match this cut. If, on the other hand, customers are quite price sensitive, Westside may have to match this price cut to minimize the damage. What is the minimum potential loss in sales volume that justifies meeting Eastside's price cut? The answer (calculated in percentage terms) is as follows:[2]

$$\frac{\text{\% Breakeven sales change}}{\text{for reactive price change}} = \frac{-15\%}{45\%} = -0.333, \text{ or } 33.3\%$$

Thus, if Westside expects sales volume to fall by more than 33 percent as a result of Eastside's new price, it would be less damaging to Westside's profitability to match the price cut than to lose sales. On the other hand, if Westside expects that sales volume will fall by less than 33 percent, it would be less damaging to Westside's profitability to let Eastside take the sales than it would be to cut price to meet this challenge.

This analysis has focused on minimizing losses in the face of a competitor's proactive price reduction. However, the procedure for analysis is the same when a competitor suddenly raises its prices. Suppose, for example, that Eastside raises its price by 15 percent. Westside might be tempted to match Eastside's price increase. If, however, Westside does not respond to Eastside's new price, Westside will likely gain additional sales volume as Eastside's customers switch to Westside. How much of a gain in sales volume must be realized in order for no price reaction to be more profitable than a reactive price increase? The answer is similarly found using the breakeven sales change formula with a reactive price change. If Westside is confident that sales volume will increase by more than 33.3 percent if it does not react, a nonreactive price policy would be more profitable. If Westside's management does not expect sales volume to increase by 33.3 percent, a reactive price increase would be more profitable.

Of course, the competitive analysis we have done is, by itself, overly simplistic. Eastside might be tempted to attack Westside's other markets if Westside does not respond to Eastside's price cut. And Westside's not matching Eastside's price increase might force Eastside to roll back its prices. These long-run strategic concerns might outweigh the short-term profit implications of a decision to react. In order to make such a judgment, however, the company must first determine the short-term profit implications. Sometimes long-term competitive strategies are not worth the short-term cost.

CALCULATING POTENTIAL FINANCIAL IMPLICATIONS

To grasp fully the potential impact of a price change, especially when the decision involves incremental changes in fixed costs, it is useful to calculate the profit impact for a range of potential sales changes and to summarize them with a breakeven table and chart. Doing so is relatively simple after having calculated the basic breakeven sales change. Using this calculation, one can then simulate what-if scenarios that include different levels of actual sales volume following the price change.

The top half of Exhibit 9-3 is a summary of the basic breakeven sales change analysis for Westside's 5 percent price cut, with one column summarizing the level of contribution before the price change (the column labeled "Baseline") and one column summarizing the contribution after the price change (the column labeled "Proposed Price Change"). The bottom half of Exhibit 9-3 summarizes nine what-if scenarios showing the profitability associated with changes in sales volume ranging from 0 to 40 percent given incremental semifixed costs of $800 per 1,000 units. Columns 1 and 2 show the actual change in volume for each scenario. Columns 3 through 5 calculate the change in profit that results from each change in sales.

To illustrate how these breakeven sales-change scenarios are calculated, let us focus for a moment on scenario 6, where actual sales volume is projected to increase 20 percent. A 20 percent change in actual sales volume is equivalent to an 800-unit change in actual sales volume, since 800 units is 20 percent of the

EXHIBIT 9-3   Breakeven Sales Analysis and Breakeven Sales Simulated Scenarios: Westside Manufacturing Proposed 5% Price Reduction

Breakeven Sales Change Summary	Baseline	Proposed Price Change
Price/unit	$10.00	$9.50
% Price change		−5%
$ Contribution/unit	$4.50	$4.00
% Contribution	45%	42%
Breakeven sales change (%)		12.5%
Breakeven sales change (units)		500
Total sales volume (units)	4,000	4,500
Total contribution	$18,000	$18,000

Breakeven Sales Change Simulated Scenarios

		% Change in Actual Sales Volume	Unit Change in Actual Sales Volume	Change in Contribution After Price Change	Incremental Fixed Costs	Total Change in Profit After Price Change
Simulated Scenarios	1	0.0	0	−2,000	800	−2,800
	2	5.0	200	−1,200	800	−2,000
	3	10.0	400	−400	800	−1,200
	4	12.5	500	0	800	−800
	5	17.5	700	800	800	0
	6	20.0	800	1,200	800	400
	7	25.0	1,000	2,000	800	1,200
	8	30.0	1,200	2,800	1,600	1,200
	9	40.0	1,600	4,400	1,600	2,800

baseline sales volume of 4,000 units. How does this increase in sales translate into changes in profitability? Column 3 shows that a 20 percent (or an 800-unit) increase in sales volume results in a change in contribution after the price change of $1,200. This is calculated by taking the difference between the actual unit sales change (800 units) and the breakeven sales change shown in the top half of Exhibit 9-3 (500 units) and multiplying by the new contribution margin after the price change ($4). However, the calculations made in column 3 do not take into

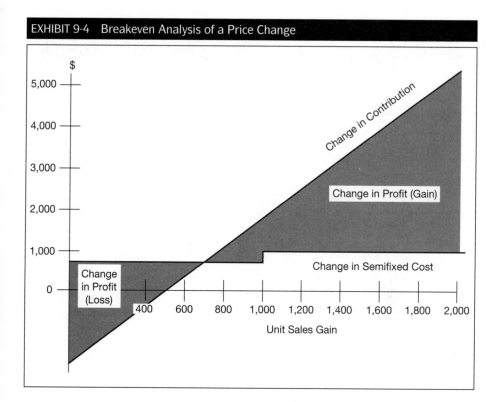

EXHIBIT 9-4   Breakeven Analysis of a Price Change

account the incremental fixed costs required to implement the price change (shown in column 4). Column 5 shows the change in profit after subtracting the change in fixed costs from the incremental contribution generated. Where there is inadequate incremental contribution to cover the incremental fixed costs, as in scenarios 1 through 4, the change in profit is negative. Scenario 5 illustrates the breakeven sales change. Scenarios 6 through 9 are all profitable scenarios since they result in greater profit after the price change than before.

The interrelationships among contribution, incremental fixed costs, and the sales change that results from a price change are often easier to comprehend with a graph. Exhibit 9-4 illustrates the relationships among the data in Exhibit 9-3. Appendix 9B (at the end of this chapter) explains how to produce breakeven graphs, which are especially useful in comprehending the implications of price changes when many fixed costs become incremental at different sales volumes.

BREAKEVEN SALES CURVES

So far we have discussed breakeven sales analysis in terms of a single change in price and its resultant breakeven sales change. In the example above, Westside Manufacturing considered a 5 percent price reduction, which we calculated would require a 17.5 percent increase in sales volume to achieve enough incremental contribution to cover the incremental fixed cost. However, what if the

EXHIBIT 9-5   Breakeven Sales Curve Calculations (with Incremental Fixed Costs)

Price Change	Price	Breakeven Sales Change	Unit Breakeven Sales Change	Unit Breakeven Sales Volume	Incremental Fixed Costs	Breakeven Sales Change with IFC
25%	$12.50	−35.7%	−1,429	2,571	0	−35.7%
20%	$12.00	−30.8%	−1,231	2,769	0	−30.8%
15%	$11.50	−25.0%	−1,000	3,000	0	−25.0%
10%	$11.00	−18.2%	−727	3,273	0	−18.2%
5%	$10.50	−10.0%	−400	3,600	0	−10.0%
0%	$10.00	0.0%	0	4,000	0	0.0%
−5%	$9.50	12.5%	500	4,500	$800	17.5%
−10%	$9.00	28.6%	1,143	5,143	$1,600	40.0%
−15%	$8.50	50.0%	2,000	6,000	$2,400	70.0%
−20%	$8.00	80.0%	3,200	7,200	$4,000	120.0%

company wants to consider a range of potential price changes? How can we use breakeven sales analysis to consider alternative price changes simultaneously? The answer is by charting a breakeven sales curve, which summarizes the results of a series of breakeven sales analyses for different price changes.

Constructing breakeven sales curves requires doing a series of what-if analyses, similar to the simulated scenarios discussed in the last section. Exhibits 9-5 and 9-6 show numerically and graphically a breakeven sales curve for Westside Manufacturing, with simulated scenarios of price changes ranging from 125 to 220 percent. Note in Exhibit 9-6 that the vertical axis shows different price levels for the product, and the horizontal axis shows a volume level associated with each price level. Each point on the curve represents the sales volume necessary to achieve as much profit after the price change as would be earned at the baseline price. For example, Westside's baseline price is $10 per unit, and baseline sales volume is 4,000 units. If, however, Westside cuts the price by 15 percent to $8.50, its sales volume would have to increase 70 percent to 6,800 units to achieve the same profitability. Conversely, if Westside increases its price by 15 percent to $11.50, its sales volume could decrease 25 percent to 3,000 units and still allow equal profitability.

The breakeven sales curve is a simple, yet powerful tool for synthesizing and evaluating the dynamics behind the profitability of potential price changes. It presents succinctly and visually the dividing line that separates profitable price decisions from unprofitable ones. Profitable price decisions are those that result in sales volumes in the area to the right of the curve. Unprofitable price decisions

EXHIBIT 9-6   Breakeven Sales Curve Trade-off Between Price and Sales Volume Required for Constant Profitability

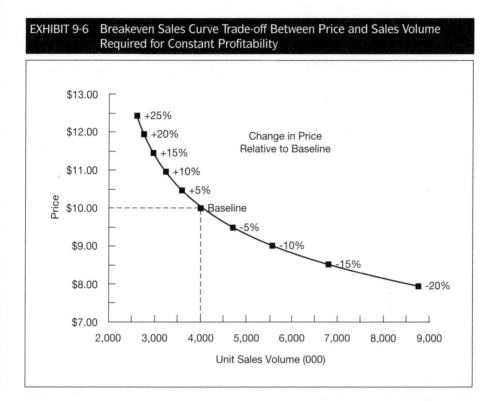

are those that result in sales volumes in the area to the left of the curve. What is the logic behind this? Recall the previous discussion of what happens before and after a price change. The breakeven sales curve represents those sales volume levels associated with their respective levels of price, where the company will make just as much net contribution after the price change as it made before the price change. If the company's sales volume after the price change is greater than the breakeven sales volume (i.e., actual sales volume is to the right of the curve), the price change will add to profitability. If the company's sales volume after the price change is less than the breakeven sales volume (that is, the area to the left of the curve), the price change will be unprofitable. For example, for Westside a price of $8.50 requires a sales volume of at least 6,800 units to achieve a net gain in profitability. If, after reducing its price to $8.50, management believes it will sell more than 6,800 units (a point to the right of the curve), then a decision to implement a price of $8.50 per unit would be profitable.

The breakeven sales curve also clearly illustrates the relationship between the breakeven approach to pricing and the economic concept of price elasticity. Note that the breakeven sales curve looks suspiciously like the traditional downward-sloping demand curve in economic theory, in which different levels of price (on the vertical axis) are associated with different levels of quantity demanded (on the horizontal axis). On a traditional demand curve, the slope between any two points on the curve determines the elasticity of demand, a measure of price sensitivity expressed as the percent change in quantity demanded for a given percent change in price. An economist who knew the shape of such a curve could calculate the profit-maximizing price.

Unfortunately, few firms use economic theory to set price because of the unrealistic expectation that they first have to know their demand curve, or at least the demand elasticity around the current price level. To overcome this shortcoming, we have addressed the problem in reverse order. Rather than asking "What is the firm's demand elasticity?" we ask, instead, "What is the minimum demand elasticity required?" to justify a particular pricing decision. Breakeven sales analysis calculates the minimum or maximum demand elasticity required to profit from a particular pricing decision. The breakeven sales curve illustrates a set of minimum elasticities necessary to make a price cut profitable, or the maximum elasticity tolerable to make a price increase profitable. One is then led to ask whether the level of price sensitivity in the market is greater or less than the level of price sensitivity required by the firm's cost and margin structure.

This relationship between the breakeven sales curve and the demand curve is illustrated in Exhibits 9-7 and 9-8, where hypothetical demand curves are shown with Westside's breakeven sales curve. If demand is more elastic, as in Exhibit 9-7, price reductions relative to the baseline price result in gains in profitability, and price increases result in losses in profitability. If demand is less elastic, as in

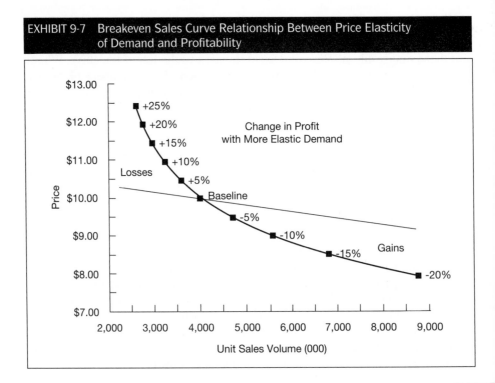

EXHIBIT 9-7   Breakeven Sales Curve Relationship Between Price Elasticity of Demand and Profitability

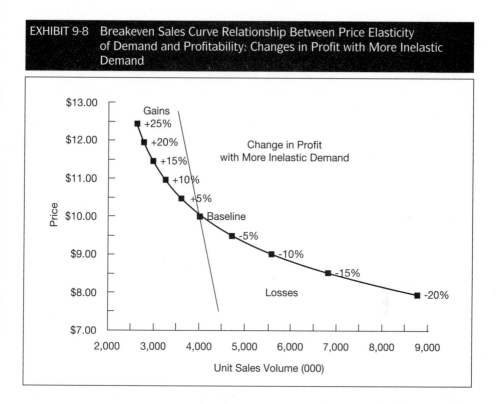

EXHIBIT 9-8   Breakeven Sales Curve Relationship Between Price Elasticity of Demand and Profitability: Changes in Profit with More Inelastic Demand

Exhibit 9-8, price increases relative to the baseline price result in gains in profitability, and price reductions result in losses in profitability. Although few, if any, managers actually know the demand curve for their product, we have encountered many who can comfortably make judgments about whether it is more or less elastic than is required by the breakeven sales curve. Moreover, although we have not found any market research technique that can estimate a demand curve with great precision, we have seen many (described in Chapter 13) that could enable management to confidently accept or reject a particular breakeven sales level as achievable.

WATCHING YOUR BASELINE

In the preceding examples, the level of baseline sales from which we calculated breakeven sales changes was assumed to be the current level. For simplicity, we assume a static market. In many cases, however, sales grow or decline even if price remains constant. As a result, the baseline for calculating breakeven sales changes is not necessarily the current level of sales. Rather, it is the level that would occur if no price change were made.

Consider, for example, a company in a high-growth industry with current sales of 2,000 units on which it earns a contribution margin of 55 percent. If the company does not change its price, management expects that sales will increase by 20 percent (the projected growth of total industry sales) to 2,400 units. However, management is considering a 5 percent price cut in an attempt to increase the company's market share. The price cut would be accompanied by an advertising campaign intended to heighten consumer awareness of the change. The campaign would take time to design, delaying implementation of the price change until next year. The initial sales level for the constant contribution analysis, therefore, would be the projected sales in the future, or 2,400 units. Consequently, the breakeven sales change would be calculated as follows:

$$\% \text{ Breakeven sales change } = \frac{-(-5\%)}{55\% + (-5\%)} = 0.10, \text{ or } 10\%$$

or

$$0.10 \times 2,400 = 240 \text{ units}$$

If the current sales level is used in the calculation, the unit breakeven sales change is calculated as 200 units, understating the change required by 40 units.

COVERING NONINCREMENTAL FIXED AND SUNK COSTS

By this point, one might be wondering about the nonincremental fixed and sunk costs that have been ignored when analyzing pricing decisions. A company's goal must surely be to cover all of its costs, including all fixed and sunk costs, or it will soon go bankrupt. This concern is justified and is central to pricing for profit, but it is misguided when applied to justify higher prices.

Note that the goal in calculating a contribution margin and in using it to evaluate price changes and differentials is to set prices to maximize a product's profit contribution. Profit contribution, you will recall, is the income remaining after all incremental, avoidable costs have been covered. It is money available to cover nonincremental fixed and sunk costs and to contribute to profit. When managers consider only the incremental, avoidable costs in making pricing decisions, they are not saying that other costs are unimportant. They simply realize that the level of those costs is irrelevant to decisions about which price will generate the most money to cover them. Since nonincremental fixed and sunk costs do not change with a pricing decision, they do not affect the relative profitability of one price versus an alternative. Consequently, consideration of them simply clouds the issue of which price level will generate the most profit to cover them.

All costs are important to profitability since they all, regardless of how they are classified, have to be covered before profits are earned. At some point, all costs must be considered. What distinguishes value-based pricing from cost-driven pricing is when they are considered. A major reason that this approach to pricing is more profitable than cost-driven pricing is that it encourages managers to think about costs when they can still do something about them. Every cost is incremental and avoidable at some time. For example, even the cost of product development and design, although it is fixed and sunk by the time the first unit is sold, is incremental and avoidable before the design process begins. The same is true for other costs. The key to profitable pricing is to recognize that customers in the marketplace, not costs, determine what a product can sell for. Consequently, before incurring any costs, managers need to estimate what customers can be convinced to pay for an intended product. Then they decide what costs they can profitably incur, given the expected revenue.

Of course, no one has perfect foresight. Managers must make decisions to incur costs without knowing for certain how the market will respond. When their expectations are accurate, the market rewards them with sales at the prices they expected, enabling them to cover all costs and to earn a profit. When they over-estimate a product's value, profit contribution may prove inadequate to cover all the costs incurred. In that case, a good manager seeks to minimize the loss. This can be done only by maximizing profit contribution (revenue minus incremental, avoidable costs). Shortsighted efforts to build nonincremental fixed and sunk costs into a price that will justify past mistakes will only reduce volume further, making the losses worse.

CASE STUDY: RITTER & SONS

The Westside Manufacturing example illustrates the principles of costing and financial analysis in the context of one product with easily defined costs. Applying these analysis tools in a more typical corporate setting is usually much more complex. The following case study illustrates how one company dealt with more complex incremental costing issues, and then used the financial analysis tools presented in this chapter to develop well-reasoned proposals for more profitable pricing. Note how, even in the absence of complete information, these tools enable managers to fully integrate the information they have, cross-functionally, to make better decisions.

Ritter & Sons is a wholesale producer of potted plants and cut flowers. Ritter's most popular product is potted chrysanthemums (mums), which are particularly in demand around certain holidays, especially Mother's Day, Easter, and Memorial Day, but they maintain a high level of sales throughout the year. Exhibit 9-9 shows Ritter's revenues, costs, and sales from mums for a recent fiscal year. After attending a seminar on pricing, the company's chief financial officer, Don Ritter, began to wonder whether this product might somehow be priced more profitably. A serious examination of the effect of raising and lowering the wholesale price of mums from the current price of $3.85 per unit was then begun.

Ritter's first step was to identify the relevant cost and contribution margin for mums. Looking only at the data in Exhibit 9-9, Don was somewhat uncertain how to proceed. He reasoned that the costs of the cuttings, shipping, packaging, and pottery were clearly incremental and avoidable and that the cost of administrative overhead was fixed. He was far less certain

EXHIBIT 9-9 Cost Projection for Proposed Crop of Mums		
Crop Preparer: DR	**6″ Mums Total**	**Per Unit**
Unit sales	86,250	1
Revenue	*$332,063*	*$ 3.85*
Cost of cuttings	34,500	0.40
Gross margin	*297,563*	*3.45*
Labor	51,850	0.60
Shipping	26,563	0.31
Package foil	9,056	0.10
Package sleeve	4,312	0.05
Package carton	4,399	0.05
Pottery	14,663	0.17
Capital cost allocation	66,686	0.77
Overhead allocation	73,320	0.85
Operating profit	$46,714	$ 0.54

about labor and the capital cost of the greenhouses. Some of Ritter's work force consisted of long-time employees whose knowledge of planting techniques was highly valuable. It would not be practical to lay them off, even if they were not needed during certain seasons. Most production employees, however, were transient laborers who were hired during peak seasons and who found work elsewhere when less labor was required.

After consulting with the production manager for potted plants, Don concluded that about $7,000 of the labor cost of mums was fixed. The remaining $44,850 (or $0.52 per unit) was variable and thus relevant to the pricing decision.

Don also wondered how he should treat the capital cost of the greenhouses. He was sure that the company policy of allocating capital cost (interest and depreciation) equally to every plant sold was not correct. However,

when Don suggested to his brother Paul, the company's president, that since these costs were sunk, they should be entirely ignored in pricing, Paul found the suggestion unsettling. He pointed out that Ritter used all of its greenhouse capacity in the peak season, that it had expanded its capacity in recent years, and that it planned further expansions in the coming year. Unless the price of mums reflected the capital cost of building additional greenhouses, how could Ritter justify such investments?

That argument made sense to Don. Surely the cost of greenhouses is incremental if they are all in use, since additional capacity would have to be built if Ritter were to sell more mums. But that same cost is clearly not incremental during seasons when there is excess capacity. Ritter's policy of making all mums grown in a year bear a $0.77 capital cost was simply misleading since additional mums could be grown without bearing any additional capital cost during seasons with excess capacity. Mums grown in peak seasons, however, actually cost much more than Ritter had been assuming, since those mums require capital additions. Thus, if the annual cost of an additional green-house (depreciation, interest, mainte-nance, heating) is $9,000, and if the greenhouse will hold 5,000 mums for three crops each year, the capital cost per mum would be $0.60 [$9,000/(3 × 5,000)] only if all greenhouses are fully utilized throughout the year. Since the greenhouses are filled to capacity for only one crop per year, the relevant capital cost for pricing that crop is $1.80 per mum ($9,000/5,000), while it is zero for pricing crops at other times.[3]

As a result of his discussions, Don calculated two costs for mums: one to apply when there is excess capacity in the greenhouses and one to apply when greenhouse capacity is fully utilized. His calculations are shown in Exhibit 9-10. These two alternatives do not exhaust the possibilities. For any prod-uct, different combinations of costs can be fixed or incremental in different situations. For example, if Ritter found itself with excess mums after they were grown, potted, and ready to sell, the only incremental cost would be the cost of shipping. If Ritter found itself with too little capacity and too little time to make additions before the next peak season, the only way to grow more mums would be to grow fewer types of other flowers. In that case, the cost of greenhouse space for mums would be the opportunity cost (measured by the lost contribution) from not growing and selling those other flowers. The relevant cost for a pricing decision depends on the circumstances. There-fore, one must begin each pricing prob-lem by first determining the relevant cost for that particular decision.

For Ritter, the decision at hand involved planning production quanti-ties and prices for the forthcoming year. There would be three crops of mums during the year, two during sea-sons when Ritter would have excess growing capacity and one during the peak season, when capacity would be a constraint. The relevant contribution margin would be $2.25, or 58.5 percent

EXHIBIT 9-10 Relevant Cost of Mums		
	With Excess Capacity	**At Full Capacity**
Price	$3.85	$3.85
− Cost of cuttings	0.40	0.40
− Incremental labor	0.52	0.52
− Other direct costs	0.68	0.68
= Dollar contribution margin	$2.25	$2.25
− Incremental capital cost	0	1.80
= Profit contribution	$2.25	$0.45

($2.25/3.85), for all plants. In the peak season, however, the net profit contribution would be considerably less because of the incremental capital cost of the greenhouses.

Don recognized immediately that there was a problem with Ritter's pricing of mums. Since the company had traditionally used cost-plus pricing based on fully allocated average cost, fixed costs were allocated equally to all plants. Consequently, Ritter charged the same price ($3.85) for mums throughout the year. Although mums grown in the off-peak season used the same amount of greenhouse space as those grown during the peak season, the relevant incremental cost of that space was not always the same. Consequently, the profit contribution for mums sold in an off-peak season was much greater than for those sold in the peak season. This difference was not reflected in Ritter's pricing.

Don suspected that Ritter should be charging lower prices during seasons when the contribution margin was large and higher prices when it was small. Using his new understanding of the relevant cost, Don calculated the breakeven sales quantities for a 5 percent price cut during the off-peak season, when excess capacity makes capital costs irrelevant, and for a 10 percent increase during the peak season, when capital costs are incremental to the pricing decision. These calculations are shown in Exhibit 9-11.

Don first calculated the percent breakeven quantity for the off-peak season, indicating that Ritter would need at least a 9.3 percent sales increase to justify a 5 percent price cut in the off-peak season. Then he calculated the basic breakeven percentage for a 10 percent price increase during the peak season. If sales declined by less than 14.6 percent as a result of the price increase (equal to 6,570 units, given Ritter's expected peak season sales of 45,000 mums), the price increase would be profitable. Don also recognized, however, that if sales declined that much, Ritter could avoid

---

EXHIBIT 9-11   Breakeven Sales Changes for Proposed Price Changes

5% Off-Peak Season Price Cut

$$\text{Breakeven sales change} = \frac{-(-5.0)}{58.5 - 5.0} = +9.3\%$$

10% Peak Season Price Increase

$$\text{Breakeven sales change} = \frac{-10.0}{58.5 + 10.0} = -14.6\%$$

$$\text{Breakeven sales with incremental fixed costs* } = -14.6\% + \frac{-\$9,000}{\$2.635 \times 45,000}$$

$$= -22.2\%$$

*The new dollar contribution margin is $2.635 after the 10% price increase.

constructing at least one new greenhouse. That capital cost savings could make the price increase profitable even if sales declined by more than the basic breakeven quantity. Assuming that one greenhouse involving a cost of $9,000 per year could be avoided, the breakeven decline rises to 22.2 percent (equal to 9,990 units). If a 10 percent price increase caused Ritter to lose less than 22.2 percent of its projected sales for the next peak season, the increase would be profitable.

Judging whether actual sales changes were likely to be greater or smaller than those quantities was beyond Don's expertise. He calculated a series of "what if" scenarios, called breakeven sales change simulated scenarios, and then presented his findings to Sue James, Ritter's sales manager (see Exhibit 9-12).

Sue felt certain that sales during the peak season would not decline by 22.2 percent following a 10 percent price increase. She pointed out that the ultimate purchasers in the peak season usually bought mums as gifts. Consequently, they were much more sensitive to quality than to price. Fortunately, most of Ritter's major competitors could not match Ritter's quality since they had to ship their plants from more distant greenhouses. Ritter's local competition, like Ritter, would not have the capacity to serve more customers during the peak season. The high-quality florists who comprised most of Ritter's customers were, therefore, unlikely to switch suppliers in response to a 10 percent peak-period price increase. If peak season sales remained steady, profit contribution would increase significantly, by about $50,000. If peak season sales declined modestly, the change in profit contribution would still be positive.

Sue also felt that retailers who currently bought mums from Ritter in the off-peak season could probably not sell in excess of 9.3 percent more, even if they cut their retail prices by the same 5 percent that Ritter contemplated cutting the wholesale price. Thus, the price cut would be profitable only if some retailers who normally bought mums from competitors were to switch and buy from Ritter. This possibility would depend on whether competitors chose to defend their market shares by matching Ritter's price cut. If they did, Ritter would probably gain no more retail accounts. If they did not, Ritter might capture sales to one or more grocery chains whose price-sensitive customers and whose large expenditures on flowers make them diligent in their search for the best price.

Don and Sue needed to identify their competitors and ask "How does their pricing influence our sales, and how are they likely to respond to any price changes we initiate?" They spent the next 2 weeks talking with customers and with Ritter employees who had worked for competitors, trying to formulate answers. They learned that they faced two essentially different types of competition. First, they competed with one other large local grower, Mathews Nursery, whose costs are similar to Ritter's. Because Mathews's sales area generally overlapped Ritter's, Mathews would probably be forced to meet any Ritter price cuts. Most of the competition for the largest accounts, however, came from high-volume suppliers that shipped plants into Ritter's sales area as well as into other areas. It would be difficult

EXHIBIT 9-12   Breakeven Sales Change Simulated Scenarios

With Excess Capacity
5% Off-Peak Season Price Cut

Scenario	% Change in Actual Sales Volume	Unit Change in Actual Sales Volume	Change in Contribution After Price Change
1	0%	—	$(16,504)
2	5%	4,313	$ (7,631)
3	10%	8,625	$ 1,242
4	15%	12,938	$ 10,115
5	20%	17,250	$ 18,988
6	25%	21,563	$ 27,861
7	30%	25,875	$ 36,734
Baseline price			$ 3.85
Baseline contribution margin			$ 2.25
New price			$ 3.66
New contribution margin			$ 2.06

At Full Capacity
10% Peak Season Price Increase

Scenario	% Change in Actual Sales Volume	Unit Change in Actual Sales Volume	Change in Contribution After Price Change
1	0%	0	$ 50,454
2	−5%	−4,313	$ 39,090
3	−10%	−8,625	$ 27,727
4	−15%	−12,938	$ 16,363
5	−20%	−17,250	$ 5,000
6	−25%	−21,563	$ (6,364)
7	−30%	−25,875	$(17,727)
Baseline price			$ 3.85
Baseline contribution margin			$ 2.25
New price			$ 4.24
New contribution margin			$ 2.64

for them to cut their prices only where they competed with Ritter. Moreover, they already operated on smaller margins because of their higher shipping costs. Consequently, they probably would not match a 5 percent price cut.

Still, Sue thought that even the business of one or two large buyers might not be enough to increase Ritter's total sales in the off-peak season by more than the breakeven quantity. Don recognized that the greater price sensitivity of large buyers might represent an opportunity for segmented pricing. If Ritter could cut prices to the large buyers only, the price cut would be profitable if the percentage increase in sales to that market segment alone exceeded the breakeven increase. Perhaps Ritter could offer a 5 percent quantity discount for which only the large, price-sensitive buyers could qualify.[4] Alternatively, Ritter might sort its mums into "florist quality" and "standard quality," if it could assume that its florists would generally be willing to pay a 5 percent premium to offer the best product to their clientele.

Don decided to make a presentation to the other members of Ritter's management committee, setting out the case for increasing price by 10 percent for the peak season and for reducing price to large buyers by 5 percent for the two off-peak seasons. To illustrate the potential effects of the proposed changes, he calculated the change in Ritter's profits for various possible changes in sales. To illustrate the profit impact for a wide range of sales changes, he presented the results of his calculations graphically. The graph he used to illustrate the effect of a 10 percent price increase at various

changes in sales volume is reproduced in Exhibit 9-13. After Don's presentation, Sue James explained why she believed that sales would decline by less than the breakeven quantity if price were raised in the peak season. She also felt sales might increase more than the breakeven percent if price were lowered in the off-peak seasons, especially if the cut could be limited to large buyers.

Since Ritter has traditionally set prices based on a full allocation of costs, some managers were initially skeptical of this new approach. They asked probing questions, which Don and Sue's analysis of the market enabled them to answer. The management committee recognized that the decision was not clear-cut. It would ultimately rest on uncertain judgments about sales changes that the proposed price changes would precipitate. If Ritter's regular customers proved to be more price-sensitive than Don and Sue now believed, the proposed 10 percent price increase for the peak season could cause sales to decline by more than the breakeven quantity. If competitors all matched Ritter's 5 percent price cut for large buyers in the off-peak season, sales might not increase by as much as the breakeven quantity.

The committee accepted the proposed price changes. In related decisions, they postponed construction of one new greenhouse and established a two-quality approach to pricing mums based on selecting the best for "florist quality" and selling the lower-priced "standard quality" mums only in lots of 1,000. Finally, they agreed that Don should give a speech at an industry trade show on how this pricing approach could improve capital utilization and

EXHIBIT 9-13   Profit Impact of a 10 Percent Increase

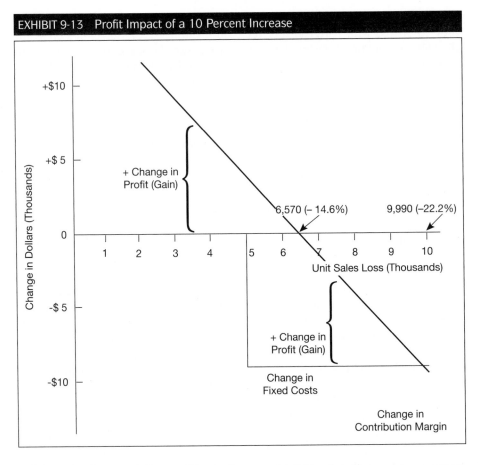

efficiency. In the speech, he would reveal Ritter's decision to raise its price in the peak season. (Perhaps Mathews' management might decide to take such information into account in independently formulating its own pricing decisions.) He would also let it be known that if Ritter were unable to sell more mums to large local buyers in the off-peak season, it would consider offering the mums at discount prices to florists outside of its local market. This plan, it was hoped, would discourage nonlocal competitors from fighting for local market share, lest the price-cutting spread to markets they found more lucrative.

At this point, there was no way to know if these decisions would prove profitable. Management could have requested more formal research into customer motivations or a more detailed analysis of nonlocal competitors' past responses to price-cutting. Since past behavior is never a perfect guide to the future, the decision would still have required weighing the risks involved with the benefits promised. Still, Don's analysis ensured that management identified the relevant information for this decision and weighed it appropriately. ■

Summary

The profitability of pricing decisions depends largely on the product's cost structure and contribution margin and on market sensitivity to changes in price. In Chapter 8 we discuss the importance of identifying the costs that are most relevant to the profitability of a pricing decision, namely, incremental and avoidable costs. Having identified the right costs, one must also understand how to use them. The most important reason to identify costs correctly is to be able to calculate an accurate contribution margin. An accurate contribution margin enables management to determine the amount by which sales must increase following a price cut, or by how little they may decline following a price increase, to make the price change profitable. Understanding how changes in sales will affect a product's profitability is the first step in pricing the product effectively.

It is, however, just the first step. Next one must learn how to judge the likely impact of a price change on sales, which requires understanding how buyers are likely to perceive a price change and how competitors are likely to react to it. We consider these subjects in the next two chapters.

Notes

1. The rule for analyzing the profitability of independently negotiated prices is simple: A price is profitable as long as it covers incremental costs. Unfortunately, many managers make the mistake of applying that rule when prices are not independent across customers. They assume, mistakenly, that because they negotiate prices individually, they are negotiating them independently. In fact, because customers talk to one another and learn the prices that others pay, prices are rarely independent. The low price you charge to one customer will eventually depress the prices that you can charge to others.

2. This equation can also accommodate a change in variable cost by simply replacing the "change in price" with the "change in price minus the change in variable cost." One can also add to it the breakeven necessary to cover a change in fixed costs.

3. We are assuming that a greenhouse depreciates no more rapidly when in use than when idle. If it did depreciate faster when used, the extra depreciation would be an incremental cost even for crops grown during seasons with excess capacity.

4. This option could expose Ritter to the risk of a legal challenge if Ritter's large buyers compete directly with its small buyers in the retailing of mums. Ritter could rebut the challenge if it could justify the 5 percent discount as a cost saving in preparing and shipping larger orders. If not, then Ritter may want to try more complicated methods to segment the market, such as offering somewhat different products to the two segments.

Appendix 9A

DERIVATION OF THE BREAKEVEN FORMULA

A price change can either increase or reduce a company's profits, depending on how it affects sales. The breakeven formula is a simple way to discover at what point the change in sales becomes large enough to make a price reduction profitable, or a price increase unprofitable.

Exhibit 9A-1 illustrates the breakeven problem. At the initial price P, a company can sell the quantity Q. Its total revenue is P times Q, which graphically is the area of the rectangle bordered by the lines 0P and 0Q. If C is the product's variable cost, then the total profit contribution earned at price P is

$(P - C)Q$. Total profit contribution is shown graphically as the rectangle bordered by the lines CF and 0Q.

If this company reduces its price from P to P', its profits will change. First, it will lose an amount equal to the change in price, ΔP, times the amount that it could sell without the price change, Q. Graphically, that loss is the rectangle labeled A. Somewhat offsetting that loss, however, the company will enjoy a gain from the additional sales it can make because of the lower price. The amount of the gain is the profit that the company will earn from each additional sale, $P' - C$, times

EXHIBIT 9A-1   Breakeven Sales Change Relationships

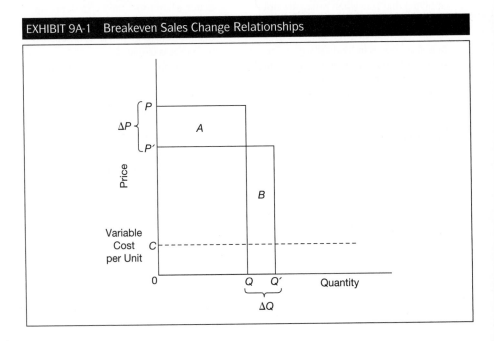

the change in sales, ΔQ. Graphically, that gain is the rectangle labeled B. Whether or not the price reduction is profitable depends on whether or not rectangle B is greater than rectangle A, and that depends on the size of ΔQ.

The logic of a price increase is similar. If P' were the initial price and Q' the initial quantity, then the profitability of a price increase to P would again depend on the size of ΔQ. If ΔQ were small, rectangle A, the gain on sales made at the higher price, would exceed rectangle B, the loss on sales that would not be made because of the higher price. However, ΔQ might be large enough to make B larger than A, in which case the price increase would be unprofitable.

To calculate the formula for the breakeven ΔQ (at which the gain from a price reduction just outweighs the loss or the loss from a price increase just outweighs the gain), we need to state the problem algebraically. Before the price change, the profit earned was $(P - C)Q$. After the change, the profit was $(P' - C)Q'$. Noting, however, that $P' = P + \Delta P$ (we write $+ \Delta P$ since ΔP is a negative number) and that $Q' = Q + \Delta Q$, we can write the profit after the price change as $(P + \Delta P - C)(Q + \Delta Q)$. Since our goal is to find the ΔQ at which profits would be just equal before and after the price change, we can begin by setting those profits equal algebraically:

$$(P - C)Q = (P + \Delta P - C)(Q + \Delta Q)$$

Multiplying this equation through yields

$$PQ - CQ = PQ + \Delta PQ - CQ + P\Delta Q + \Delta P\Delta Q - C\Delta Q$$

We can simplify this equation by subtracting PQ and adding CQ to both sides to obtain

$$0 = \Delta PQ + P\Delta Q + \Delta P\Delta Q - C\Delta Q$$

Note that all the remaining terms in the equation contain the "change sign" Δ. This is because only the changes are relevant for evaluating a price change. If we solve this equation for ΔQ, we obtain the new equation

$$\frac{\Delta Q}{Q} = \frac{-\Delta P}{P + \Delta P - C}$$

which, in words, is

% Breakeven sales change
$$= \frac{-\text{Price Change}}{\text{CM} + \text{Price change}}$$

To express the right side in percentages, multiply the right side by

$$\frac{\left(\dfrac{1}{P}\right)}{\left(\dfrac{1}{P}\right)}$$

Appendix 9B

BREAKEVEN ANALYSIS OF PRICE CHANGES

Breakeven analysis is a common tool in managerial accounting, particularly useful for evaluating potential investments. Unfortunately, the traditional forms of breakeven analysis appropriate for evaluating investment decisions are often misleading when applied to pricing decisions. Individual investments (should the company buy a new computer? should it develop a new product? should it field a sales force to enter a new market?) can often be evaluated apart from other investments. Consequently, it is appropriate to use traditional breakeven analysis, which compares the total revenue from the investment with its total cost.

Usually, however, one cannot set a price for each individual sale independent of other sales. To gain an additional sale by charging one customer a lower price normally requires charging other customers, at least others in that same market segment, the lower price as well. Consequently, it is usually misleading to evaluate the profitability of an additional sale by comparing only the price earned from that sale to the cost of that sale. To comprehend the profit implications of a price change, one must compare the change in revenue from all sales with the change in costs.

The need to focus attention on the changes in revenues and costs rather than on their totals requires a different kind of breakeven analysis for pricing decisions. Where traditional breakeven analysis of investments deals with total revenue and all costs, breakeven analysis of pricing decisions deals with the change in revenue in excess of variable cost (the dollar contribution margin) and with the change in incremental fixed costs. In the body of this chapter, you learned a number of formulas for breakeven analysis of pricing decisions and saw how to use them in the Westside Manufacturing example. In this appendix, you will learn how to use those equations to develop breakeven graphs and to analyze more complex pricing problems involving multiple sources of fixed costs that become incremental at different quantities.

Developing a Breakeven Chart

A breakeven chart, such as Exhibit 9-4, is useful in determining the possible effects of a price change. It plots both the change in the dollar contribution margin and the changes in relevant costs, enabling the pricing analyst to see the change in net profit that a change in sales volume would generate. To develop such a chart, it is useful to begin by preparing a table, such as Exhibit 9-5, organizing all relevant data in a concise form.

As an illustration, let us examine the case of PQR Industries. PQR manufactures and markets home video equipment. One of the most popular items in the company's product line is a video tape player with current sales of 4,000 units at $250 each. Sales have been growing rapidly and are expected to reach 4,800 units in the next year if the price remains unchanged. Variable costs are $112.50 per unit, resulting in the following percent contribution margin:

$$\% CM = \frac{\$250.00 - \$112.50}{\$250.00}$$
$$= 0.55 = 55\%$$

Despite its projected growth in sales at the current price, PQR is considering a 5 percent price cut to remain competitive and retain its share in this rapidly growing market. Since the cut would be implemented in the next year, the initial sales level, or baseline, is next year's projected sales (4,800 units). Calculation of the breakeven sales change is as follows:

$$\% \text{Breakeven sales change}$$
$$= \frac{-(-5.0)}{55.0 + (-5.0)} = \frac{5}{50}$$
$$= 0.10 = 10\%$$

Unit breakeven sales change
$$= 0.10 \times 4,800 \text{ units} = 480 \text{ units}$$

Production capacity is currently limited to 5,000 units but can be increased by purchasing equipment that costs $15,000 for each additional 1,000 units of capacity. The breakeven sales change, considering this change in fixed costs, is:

% Breakeven sales change
(with incremental fixed costs)
$$= 10 + \frac{\$15,000}{\$125.00 \times 4,800} = 12.5\%$$

Unit breakeven sales
$$= 0.125 \times 4,800 \text{ units} = 600 \text{ units}$$

Note that the price cut brings the price down to $237.50, resulting in a new dollar contribution margin of $125 per unit.

Since the actual sales change that would result from the price cut is unknown, a breakeven table and chart should be prepared to show the profitability of the price change at various possible sales changes.

Exhibit 9B-1 shows a breakeven table for PQR's proposed 5 percent price cut. The first two columns show the potential levels of sales changes. Column 3 shows the change in total contribution margin that would result at each level using the change in profit formula. In the case of a 5 percent change in sales, the result would be:

Change in profit = (240 units − 480 units) × $125/unit = −$30,000

Subtracting the change in fixed costs shown in column 4 from column 3 results in column 5, the change in profit contribution. Alternatively, we could have generated column 5 more directly by calculating the breakeven sales change including the change in fixed costs and substituting that number in the change in profit equation (see Exhibit 9B-1 and Exhibit 9B-2).

When plotted on a graph, the data from this table form a breakeven chart (Exhibit 9B-2). The horizontal axis represents the change in unit sales and the vertical axis represents dollars of change. The line labeled "change in fixed costs" shows the increase in costs due to added capacity, as taken from column 4 of the table. The data in column 3 were used to plot the "change in

EXHIBIT 9B-1   Breakeven Table for PQR Industries' Proposed 5% Price Cut

(1)	(2)	Change in (3)	(4)	(5)
Sales				
(%)	(Units)	Contribution Margin	Fixed Costs	Profit Contribution
0.0	0	-$60,000	0	-$60,000
5.0	240	-$30,000	$15,000	-$45,000
10.0	480	0	$15,000	-$15,000
12.5	600	$15,000	$15,000	0
15.0	720	$30,000	$15,000	$15,000
20.0	960	$60,000	$15,000	$45,000
25.0	1200	$90,000	$15,000	$75,000
30.0	1440	$120,000	$30,000	$90,000
40.0	1920	$180,000	$30,000	$150,000

Note: Proposed change ; nd5% or $12.50/unit; initial price = $250; %*CM* = 45%; semifixed cost = $15,000 per 1,000 units capacity over 5,000 units.

contribution margin" line. The distance between the two lines represents the change in profit contribution (column 5). At the points where the "change in contribution margin" line is above the "change in fixed costs" line, the change in profit contribution (and net profit) is positive. The price cut would be profitable if sales changed by those amounts.

Breakeven Analysis with More than One Incremental Fixed Cost

To this point, we have always assumed that a company has only one fixed cost that changes with a price change. Frequently, however, a company will have several semifixed costs that change at different levels of volume. This makes analysis of a price change more complicated and the use of

breakeven analysis more essential to the management of that complexity.

Let us return to PQR Industries. Because of the cost of adding a machine, management investigated alternative methods of increasing production. It was determined that the addition of one machine operator could delay purchase of a machine until sales exceeded 5,400 units (or 600 units more than the baseline initial sales). Although labor costs are normally variable with production, machine operators are skilled laborers who, according to union rules, can only be hired as full-time employees working only at their specialties. The result is that a machine operator's salary is a semifixed cost. It was also discovered that the union contract required one skilled worker to be added for each 1,000 units of increased production. Finally, the plant engineer informed

EXHIBIT 9B-2   Breakeven Analysis of PQR Industries' 5% Price Cut

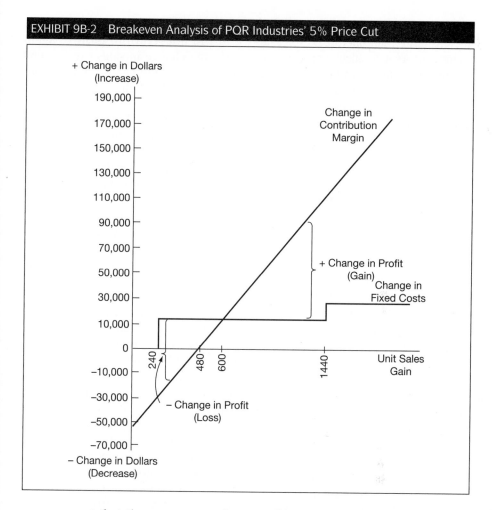

management that there was space for only one additional machine. If more equipment were purchased, more space would have to be rented, at a cost of $105,000 per year. The situation is summarized as follows:

Sales	4,800 units
Wholesale price	$250/unit
Variable cost	$112.50/unit
Semifixed costs:	
Machine operators	$7,500 per 1,000 units of added production
Equipment	$15,000 per 1,000 units of added production beyond a 600-unit gain
Space	$105,000 per year for rental if more than one machine is added

Due to the complexity of these costs, there is more than one breakeven sales change and a single calculation is not sufficient. For example, any increase in sales will require the hiring of a machine operator. The breakeven sales change for a 5 percent price cut becomes:

% Breakeven sales change
(with cost of machine operator)

$$= 10\% + \frac{\$7,500}{\$125 \times 4,800} = 11.25\%$$

Unit breakeven sales change
$$= 0.1125 \times 4,800 \text{ units} = 540 \text{ units}$$

If, however, the total sales exceed 5,400 units and equipment must be purchased, a new calculation is required as follows:

% Breakeven sales change
(with cost of equipment)

$$= 11.25\% + \frac{\$15,000}{\$125 \times 4,800} = 13.75\%$$

Unit breakeven sales change
$$= 0.1375 \times 4,800 \text{ units} = 660 \text{ units}$$

If more space would have to be rented, still another breakeven calculation would be required.

It seems obvious that when there are multiple sources of incremental fixed costs, analysis via calculation of breakeven sales changes could become both tedious and confusing. A breakeven table and chart are usually essential to the clear sorting out of these problems. Organizing the data into a table (Exhibit 9B-3) and plotting it on a graph (Exhibit 9B-4) make the options much clearer. At changes in sales of between 540 and 600 units, the price change is slightly profitable. Once the change in sales exceeds 600 units, however, fixed costs must rise again due to the need for more equip-

ment, and profits will become negative and will not return to positive again until the change in sales exceeds 660 units, causing the change in contribution to rise above the change in fixed costs.

Note that 12.5 percent, or 600 units, is the maximum sales change possible before additional costs must be incurred. To determine whether the investment in additional equipment is worthwhile, management must decide whether the possibility that sales will grow enough to achieve a profit contribution of more than $7,500 (i.e., by more than 15 percent) after the equipment is purchased would be enough to justify forgoing the more certain profit to be gained from reaching only a 12.5 percent increase in sales.

This type of situation arises whenever there is a change in fixed costs, most dramatically when the second machine is bought and space must be rented. It seems unlikely that sales growth due to the price change would be sufficient to justify renting more space. In fact, sales would have to increase by more than 53 percent before such an increase in fixed costs would produce a positive net profit. Moreover, the investment would not be justified if the profit that could be earned by not meeting the entire sales gain were higher.

Breakeven Graphs

The calculations for determining breakeven sales changes for a price increase are the same as those for a price cut. For price increases, however, sales volumes decline rather than increase. Consequently, the direction

EXHIBIT 9B-3   Revised Breakeven Table for PQR Industries' Proposed 5% Price Cut

Sales (%)	Sales (Units)	Contribution Margin ($)	Changes in				Profit Contribution ($)
			Cost of Operators ($)	Cost of Equipment ($)	Cost of Space ($)	Total Fixed Costs ($)	
0.00	0	−60,000	0	0	0	0	−60,000
5.00	240	−30,000	7,500	0	0	7,500	−37,500
10.00	480	0	7,500	0	0	7,500	−7,500
11.25	540	7,500	7,500	0	0	7,500	0
12.50	600	15,000	7,500	0	0	7,500	7,500
13.75	660	22,500	7,500	15,000	0	22,500	0
15.00	720	30,000	7,500	15,000	0	22,500	7,500
20.00	960	60,000	7,500	15,000	0	22,500	37,500
25.00	1,200	90,000	15,000	15,000	0	30,000	60,000
30.00	1,440	120,000	15,000	15,000	0	30,000	90,000
35.00	1,680	150,000	15,000	30,000	105,000	150,000	0
40.00	1,920	180,000	15,000	30,000	105,000	150,000	30,000

Note: Proposed change: −5%, or $12.50/unit; initial price = $250; %CM = 45%; semifixed costs = $7,500/1,000 units for machine operators $15,000/1,000 units over 5,400 units for equipment $90,000/year for space rental if more than one piece of equipment is added.

209

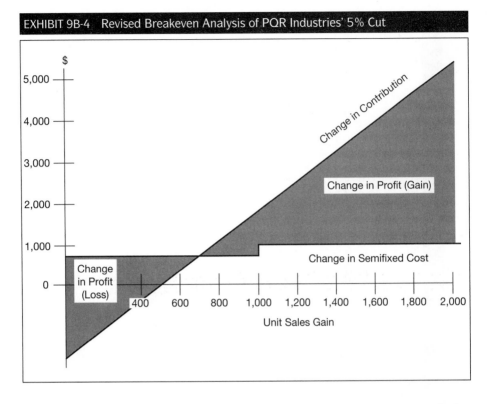

of the horizontal axis measures declines in sales volumes rather than increases.

To illustrate, let us consider again the case of PQR Industries. In addition to VCRs, PQR sells projection televisions for $3,000. Variable costs of $1,650 per unit leave the company with a contribution margin of $1,350 per unit, or 45 percent. The company is considering a price increase next year on this item. The initial sales level for evaluating the increase (next year's projected sales) is 4,000 units, which exceeds the company's current capacity of 3,600 units.

Concern about capacity constraints and the slowing growth of the market for this product have caused management to consider instituting a price increase in order to maximize profits. The breakeven sales change for the proposed 5 percent price increase is:

$$\frac{-(5)}{45 + 5} = -10\%$$

Unit breakeven sales change
$= -0.10 \times 4,000 \text{ units} = -400 \text{ units}$

As long as the price increase causes sales to decline by less than 10 percent or 400 units, the price increase will cause the total dollar contribution from this product to increase.

To increase production beyond the current 3,600 unit capacity, additional equipment must be bought at a cost of $150,000. If, however, as a result of the price increase, sales decrease to the point that current capacity is sufficient,

EXHIBIT 9B-5　Breakeven Table for PQR Industries Proposed' 5% Price Increase

		Change in		
(1)	(2)	(3)	(4)	(5)
Sales		Contribution	Fixed	Profit
(%)	(Units)	Margin ($)	Costs ($)	Contribution ($)
0.0	0	600,000	0	600,000
5.0	200	800,000	0	300,000
10.0	400	0	−150,000	150,000
12.5	500	−150,000	−150,000	0
15.0	600	−300,000	−150,000	−150,000
20.0	800	−600,000	−150,000	−450,000
25.0	1000	−900,000	−150,000	−750,000
30.0	1200	−1,200,000	−150,000	−1,050,000

Note: Proposed change −5% or $150/unit initial price = $3,000; % CM = 45%; semifixed cost = $150,000 for capacity over 3,600 units.

EXHIBIT 9-6　Breakeven Analysis for PQR Industries' 5% Price Increase

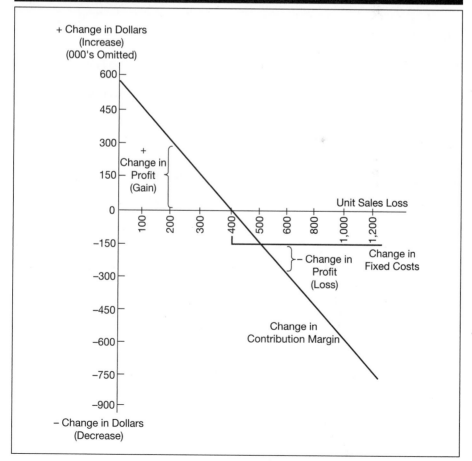

purchase of new equipment would not be necessary. The expenditure avoided is a negative change in fixed costs from the level required to achieve the 4,000 unit baseline sales level. A new breakeven sales change is calculated as follows:

% Breakeven sales change
(including change in fixed costs)

$$= -10\% + \frac{-\$150,000}{\$1,500 \times 4,000}$$

$$= -12.5\%$$

On the basis of the data in Exhibit 9B-5, we can produce a breakeven graph for this price change (Exhibit 9B-6). The lines representing changes in contribution margin and fixed costs run opposite to the directions we are accustomed to seeing for price cuts, but the change in profit contribution, as indicated by the relative positions of these lines, is still interpreted as in earlier examples.

To verify this, let us refer to the graph and examine the results of a 5 percent, or 200 unit, sales decrease. At this point, there has been no change in fixed costs. Therefore, the change in profitability should equal a positive $300,000, the distance between the line indicating change in contribution margin and the horizontal axis. Reference to the related table will show that this is indeed true.

Summary

Predicting the outcome of a price change is not an exact science as later chapters will show. A manager should, therefore, consider all possible outcomes of such a change in order to choose the wisest course of action. Tables and graphs of breakeven analyses are useful, easily produced tools for this purpose.

Acknowledgments

This chapter is coauthored by Professor Gerald E. Smith of Boston College.

CHAPTER

10 | COMPETITION

Managing Conflict Thoughtfully

Pricing against competition is more challenging and hazardous than pricing a unique product.[1] In the absence of competition, managers can anticipate the effect of a price change entirely by analyzing buyers' price sensitivity. When a product is just one among many, however, competitors can wreak havoc with such predictions. Price discounting in competitive markets—whether explicit or disguised with rebates, coupons, or generous payment terms—is almost a sure bet to enhance immediate sales and profits. It is easy to become seduced by these quick highs and fail to recognize the long-term consequences. The price cut that boosts your sales today will invariably change the industry you compete in tomorrow. Frequently, that change is for the worse.

The experience of a large building-products manufacturer illustrates just such a problem. This company had been consistently profitable as a market-share leader. Despite the commodity like nature of its product, the company enjoyed a small price premium reflecting its perceived technical superiority and exceptional customer service. Still, the company had long been losing market share due to aggressive price competition from smaller competitors. New management, which took control following a leveraged buyout, was determined to reverse this trend.

Although this company offered standard discounts for volume, quick payment, and so forth, the company had historically been reluctant to negotiate prices with any but its largest customers. Consequently, smaller competitors could predictably set their prices just beneath the leader's price umbrella. To thwart the competition, the new management decided to close the umbrella. Whenever an account seemed seriously threatened by a lower-cost bid, sales managers were authorized to negotiate "special deals" that would retain the business at lower, but still profitable, prices. The effect of this policy was immediate and dramatic; the company effectively stopped the loss of established customers, while continuing to gain new business based on quality and service. Over the next few quarters, market share not only stopped declining but also actually rose by a few points.

Was this a wise strategic move? The company won more pricing battles and, consequently, gained volume and profits. Management was certainly pleased. But

213

how could we expect the market to change as a result of this new pricing policy? What was the predictable long-run impact of this strategy on the nature of competition in the industry? At first, the market changed very little because the company took pains to limit public knowledge of the new policy. Over time, however, customers talked with one another. The company's traditional customers, who willingly had been paying a price premium for the company's product quality and service, began learning that others got the same quality and service for less. Moreover, they learned that others got lower prices because they were tougher negotiators who threatened to give their business to other suppliers.

It is not difficult to imagine what happened next. Previously loyal buyers resolved no longer "to get taken" simply because they hadn't investigated their alternatives. Purchasing authority was moved from users to purchasing departments; doors opened to competitors that had previously been closed; and, instead of giving this company their business, previously loyal customers began giving it only the last look. With more competitors involved in each sale, the sales cycle grew longer and the number of requests for "special deals" grew exponentially. In fact, within two years, management was looking for a way to automate the process of preparing them and billing customers using many different price schedules.

This company inadvertently created a financial incentive for its buyers to become more difficult, and they responded. Although the policy reversed a decline in market share, both industry prices and the company's price premium declined. Management complained about declining profits and loss of customer loyalty, but it made no connection between those changes and its own policies. Management eventually responded to buyers' reluctance to pay the traditional price premium for quality and service by looking for ways to cut costs in those areas.

Although this company achieved immediate benefits from its policy to thwart the competition, it unwittingly undermined the industry price level and the value of its competitive advantage. The lesson here is not that management should avoid defending market share or should never initiate price cuts. The lesson is that before taking such actions, management must anticipate the long-run strategic consequences and weigh them against the short-term benefits. A pricing decision should never be made simply to make the next sale or to meet some short-term sales objective, but rather to enhance the firm's long-term ability to operate profitably. Pricing is like playing chess: Those who make moves one at a time—seeking to minimize immediate losses or to exploit immediate opportunities—will invariably be beaten by those who envision the game a few moves ahead.

Because price changes affect sales more quickly than other marketing decisions, they are often used as a quick-fix solution to short-term problems. Profitable pricing requires, however, that managers also consider how each decision will affect future competitive behavior and profitability. Procter & Gamble, for example, abandoned a decade-long policy of chronic "price promotion," despite the short- term benefits, after realizing that it caused large retailers to adopt purchasing patterns that substantially raised its costs of manufacturing and distribution.

Pricing decisions should always be made as part of a longer-term marketing strategy to generate and capture more profit contribution. Otherwise, it is possible to win many individual battles for market share and still end up losing the war for profitability. This is not to argue that underpricing the competition is never a successful strategy in the long run, but the conditions necessary to make it successful depend critically upon how customers and competitors react to it. The goal of this chapter is to provide guidelines for anticipating those reactions, influencing them, and integrating them into a long-term strategic plan.

UNDERSTANDING THE PRICING GAME

Pricing is a "game," as defined by game theorists, because success depends not only on a company's own pricing decisions but also on how customers and competitors respond to them. Unfortunately, pricing strategically for sustainable profitability is a type of game requiring skills foreign to many marketing and sales managers. What most of us know about competition we learned from sports, academics, and perhaps from intracompany sales contests. The rules for success in these types of competition are quite different from those for success in pricing. The reason, in technical jargon, is that the former are all examples of "positive-sum" games, whereas pricing is a "negative-sum" game. Understanding the difference is crucial to playing the pricing game successfully.[2]

Positive-sum games are those in which the very process of competition creates benefits. Consequently, the more prolonged and intense the game—in sports, academics, or sales—the greater the rewards to the players. The winner always finds playing such games worthwhile, and even the loser may gain enough from the experience so as not to regret having played. In fact, people with a healthy attitude toward these activities often seek opportunities to challenge themselves simply to benefit from the experience. Such a strong competitive spirit is a criterion commonly used to identify job candidates with potential for success in sales.

Unfortunately, that same gung-ho attraction to competition is quite unhealthy when applied to negative-sum games: those in which the process of competition imposes costs on players. Warfare, labor actions, and dueling are negative-sum games because the loser never benefits from participation. The longer the conflict drags on, the more likely it is that even the winner will find that playing was not worth the cost. Price competition is usually a negative-sum game since the more intense price competition is, the more it undermines the value of the market over which one is competing.[3] Price competitors do well, therefore, to forget what they learned about competing from sports and other positive-sum games, and to try instead to draw lessons from less familiar competitions like warfare or dueling.

Students of actual warfare, who are cognizant of its cost, do not make the mistake of equating success with winning battles. Lidell Hart, author of more than 30 books on military strategy, offers advice to political and military leaders that marketers would do well to note:

> Fighting power is but one of the instruments of grand strategy—which should [also] take account of and apply ... financial pressure, diplomatic

pressure, commercial pressure, and . . . ethical pressure, to weaken the opponent's will. . . . It should not only combine the various instruments, but also regulate their use as to avoid damage to the future state of peace.[4]

In short, winning battles is not an end in itself, and warfare is certainly not the only means to an end.

For marketers, as for diplomats, warfare should be a last resort, and even then the potential benefits of using it must be weighed against the cost. Fortunately, there are many positive-sum ways for marketers to compete. Creating new products, creating new ways to deliver service, communicating more effectively with customers about benefits, and reducing the costs of operation are all positive-sum forms of competition. Precisely because they create profits, rather than dissipate them, building capabilities for positive-sum forms of competition is the basis of a sustainable strategy. Competing on price alone is at best a short-term strategy until competitors find it threatening enough to react.

COMPETITIVE ADVANTAGE: THE ONLY SUSTAINABLE SOURCE OF PROFITABILITY

How can companies become strong competitors? Unfortunately, many managers erroneously believe that the measure of competitive success is market share (see Box 10-1). That may be a successful strategy if only one firm attempts to pursue it. When many competitors pursue this same strategy, they engage in negative-sum competition, which does little more than destroy profitability for everyone. Fortunately, there are strategies that promote positive-sum competition. Rather than attracting customers by taking less in profit, these strategies attract customers by creating more value or more operating efficiency. They involve either adding to the value of what is offered without adding as much to cost or reducing costs without equally reducing the value offered.

We call these sources of profitable growth competitive advantages because competitors cannot immediately duplicate them, except at a higher cost. Many managers completely misunderstand the concept of competitive advantage and its importance for long-term profitability. We hear them report that they have a "competitive advantage" in having more stores than the competition, more knowledgeable salespeople, or higher quality. None of these are competitive advantages unless they also enable the firm to deliver value more cost-effectively than one's competitors can. Offering customers a more attractive offer by accepting a lower margin than the competition may be a sales advantage, but it is not a sustainable competitive advantage.

How can a firm achieve competitive advantage? Sometimes it's by luck. Aramco, the Saudi oil company, enjoys oil fields from which oil can be more cheaply extracted than from those in Alaska, the North Sea, or Kazakhstan. Often, advantage comes from moving first on a new idea. By winning a patent, by gaining economies of scale, or by preempting the best locations, a firm may achieve an advantage that would be more costly for a later entrant to match.

BOX 10-1

MARKET-SHARE MYTH

A common myth among marketers is that market share is the key to profitability. If that were true, of course, recent history would have shown General Motors to be the world's most profitable automobile company; United, the most profitable airline; and Philips, the most profitable manufacturer of electrical products ranging from light bulbs to color televisions. In fact, these companies, while sales leaders, have been financial also-rans. The source of this myth—these examples notwithstanding—is a demonstrable correlation between market share and profitability. As any student of statistics should know, however, correlation does not necessarily imply a causal relationship.

A far more plausible explanation for the correlation is that both profitability and market share are caused by the same underlying source of business success: a sustainable competitive advantage in meeting customer needs more effectively or in doing so more efficiently.* When a company has a competitive advantage, it can earn higher margins due to either a price premium or a lower cost of production. That advantage, if sustainable, also discourages competitors from targeting the company's customers or from effectively resisting its attempts to expand. Consequently, although a less fortunate company would face equally efficient competitors who could take market shares

with margin-destroying price competition, a company with a competitive advantage can sustain higher market share even as it earns higher profits. Market share, rather than being the key to profitability, is, like profitability, simply another symptom of a fundamentally well-run company.

Unfortunately, when management misperceives the symptom (insufficient market share) as a cause and seeks it by some inappropriate means, such as price-cutting, the expected profitability doesn't materialize. On the contrary, a grab for market share unjustified by an underlying competitive advantage can often reduce the company's own and its industry's profitability. The ultimate objective of any strategic plan should not be to achieve or even sustain sales volume, but to build and sustain competitive advantage. Profitability and, in many cases, market share will follow. In fact, contrary to the myth that a higher market share causes higher profitability, changes in profitability usually precede changes in market share, not the other way around. For example, Wal-Mart's competitive advantages made it the most profitable retailer in the United States long before it became the largest, whereas Sears's poor profitability preceded by many years its loss of the dominant market share. This pattern of profitability leading, not following, market share is currently
(Continued)

visible in the automobile, steel, and banking industries.

A strategic plan based on building volume, rather than on creating a competitive advantage, is essentially a beggar-thy-neighbor strategy—a negative-sum game that ultimately can only undermine industry profitability. Every point of market share won by reducing margins (either by offering a lower price or by incurring higher costs) invariably reduces the value of the sales gained. Since competitors can effectively retaliate, they probably will, at least partially eliminating any gain in sales while reducing the value of a sale even further. The only sustainable way to increase relative profitability is by achieving a competitive advantage that will enable you to increase sales and margins. In short, the goal of a strategic plan should not be to become bigger than the competition (although that may happen) but to become better. Such positive-sum competition, rather than undermining the profitability of an industry, constantly renews it.**

*Robert Jacobson and David Aaker, "Is Market Share All That It's Cracked Up to Be?," *Journal of Marketing,* 49 (Fall 1985), pp. 11–22; William W. Alberts, "The Experience Curve Doctrine Reconsidered," *Journal of Marketing,* 53 (July 1989), pp. 36–49; Cathy Anterasiun, John L. Graham, and R. Bruce Money, "Are U.S. Managers Superstitious about Market Share?" *Sloan Management Review* (Summer 1996), pp. 67–77; Linda L. Hellofs and Robert Jacobson, "Market Share and Customers' Perceptions of Quality: When Can Firms Grow Their Way to Higher Versus Lower Quality?" *Journal of Marketing,* 63 (January 1999), pp. 16–25.

**For evidence that there are profit leaders in the bottom and middle ranges of market share almost as frequently as in the top range, see William L. Shanklin, "Market Share Is Not Destiny," *Journal of Business & Industrial Marketing,* 4 (Winter–Spring 1989), pp. 5–16.

AOL established a "virtual community" with its proprietary instant messaging and chat rooms, the value of which competitors could not duplicate in the short-term. Google established a dominant position in Internet search by creating an innovative search engine that competitors will take some time to catch up to.

More often, competitive advantages are carved out of the efficient management of the firm's value chain. Michael Porter cites three ways that companies can proactively manage operations to achieve competitive advantage.[5]

- *Needs-Based Positioning*—based on serving only the needs of a particular customer segment or niche, which enables the firm to tailor its operations to meet the unique needs of that segment more cost-effectively.
- *Access-Based Positioning*—based on the company's ability to gain access to customers in unique ways. Access can be a function of geography or customer scale. For example, serving a uniquely wide or narrow geographic market, based on the firm's cost structure, can create a unique cost and service advantage.

- *Variety-Based Positioning*—competing in industries by choosing selected activities as part of strategically designed value chains, including coalitions with strategic partners that coordinate or share value chains to give a company a shared cost or differentiation advantage.

Wausau Paper is one example of a company that successfully pursued the "needs-based positioning" strategy. The company is small by the standards of the industry, but it is more than twice as profitable as the big guys. Its secret is to avoid the high-volume, price-competitive markets and focus on niche markets. One of its focus segments is the market for colored paper. Wausau made the distinctive yellow paper for 3M Post-It notes until other papermakers matched its quality and undercut its price. Rather than compete on price, the company used its experience in making colored papers to create the very bright colors now offered in Kinko's stores. Similarly, the company works closely with food companies to support its innovations. Consequently, it was an early maker of microwave popcorn bags.[6]

The U.S. beer industry offers a classic case of "access-based positioning," both widening and narrowing of geographic reach to achieve competitive advantage. Companies with a national presence, like Anheuser-Busch and Miller, enjoy a huge competitive advantage in purchasing television advertising space at low national rates. They have leveraged that advantage to eliminate smaller, national competitors. Even while smaller national competitors have struggled to survive, microbrewers have multiplied and prospered by pursuing a different geographic strategy. Companies like Smuttlynose Brewing in Portsmouth, New Hampshire, Old Dominion in Northern Virginia, and Elk Grove Brewing in Elk Grove, California, rely on a local cache and word-of-mouth promotion to operate small but profitable businesses.

Microsoft's operating software strategy offers a good example of "variety-based positioning" strategy. As the desktop computer market emerged, Microsoft deliberately chose to focus not on producing complete desktop computer systems, like Apple or IBM, but only on producing the operating system—the strategic gateway to the proper functioning of the computer hardware. As traditional public utilities have come under competitive pressure, they have looked for opportunities to gain cost or product advantages by coordinating activities into combined value chains. The local electric company has become a consolidator of advertising inserts, which it mails along with the monthly bill. Its incremental mailing costs are lower than for traditional mailers (since a bill has to be sent anyway), and it can promise that a higher percentage of recipients will actually open the envelope rather than file it in the wastebasket.

As these examples illustrate, the key to achieving sustainable profitability is to manage the business for competitive advantage. Unfortunately, most companies in competitive markets are driven by a focus on revenue growth, which they pursue by trying to be all things to all people, rather than by a focus on creating value more cost-effectively. Michael Porter, the Harvard competition guru, calls the failure to achieve either a value or a cost advantage "getting stuck in the middle." When such companies are exposed to competitors, some of whom offer higher quality or service while others offer lower prices, the firm's profitability gets squeezed despite its size.[7]

In the absence of a competitive advantage, it is suicidal to drive growth with price. During the internet technology "bubble" of the late 1990s, thousands of Internet retailers and willing investors were hoping to prove this statement wrong. They accepted lower, even negative, margins simply to build share in the belief that ultimately the high value of the Internet would make them profitable. They ignored a simple economic principle: Competition drives out profitability except for those with a source of advantage that prevents competitors from fully matching their costs or their value proposition. As it turns out, the companies with the competitive advantages for competing in Internet space (name recognition, low cost of customer acquisition, economies of scale) are exactly those who have the advantages in bricks and mortar space.

There are a few exceptions, namely, those Internet newcomers who could create advantages that competitors could not duplicate. eBay, for example, enjoys margins and profitability that exceed those of both online and bricks and mortar competitors, not just because of the high value of trading online, but because of the difficulty that price-cutting competitors would face in trying to duplicate its online offerings. The value of an auction is directly related to the size of the base of participants in it (like the value of a telephone network). Once eBay gained a large user base advantage, it became impossible for any competitor to duplicate the value it offers traders. Similarly, Amazon has carefully created profiles of buyer preference along with their credit and mailing information that for many people makes shopping on Amazon a more efficient and pleasant experience than shopping with either an online or traditional competitor.

REACTING TO COMPETITION: THINK BEFORE YOU ACT

Many managers are so fully aware of the risks of price wars and the importance of competing from a position of strength that they think coolly and logically before initiating price competition. It is much harder for most of us to think logically about whether or how to respond when we are already under attack. Consequently, we will discuss in step-by-step detail how to analyze a competitive situation and formulate responses in price-competitive markets that are not of your making.

When is it financially more prudent to accommodate a competitive threat, at least in the near term until you can improve your capabilities, than to retaliate? Thinking through this question does much more than prepare you, intellectually and psychologically, to make the best competitive response. It also reveals weakness in your competitive position. If you do not like how often you must accommodate a competitor because your company cannot fight the threat successfully, you will begin searching for a competitive strategy that either increases your advantage or moves you further from harm's way.

Exhibit 10-1 illustrates the complex flow of thinking required to make thoughtful decisions about reacting to price competition. The exhibit begins with the assumption that one or more competitors have cut their prices or have introduced new products that offer at least some of your customers more value for their money. How should you respond? Some theorists argue that one should never respond since there are better, positive-sum ways to compete on product or service attributes. While that is often true, the time to have explored and implemented those ways was usually long before a competitive price threat. At the time of the threat, a firm's strategic capabilities are fixed in the short run. The question at hand is whether to respond with price when threatened with a loss of sales by a lower-priced competitor. To determine whether a price response is better than no response, one must answer the following questions and explore the interrelationships illustrated in Exhibit 10-1.

1. *Is there a response that would cost less than the preventable sales loss?* Although the need to ask this question might seem obvious, many managers simply stop thinking rationally when threatened. They match any price cut without asking whether the cost is justified by the benefit, or whether the same benefit could be achieved by structuring a more thoughtful response. In Chapter 9, we introduced formulas for financial analysis of a reactive price change. If we conclude that reacting to a price change is cheaper than losing the sales, then it may be a good business decision. On the other hand, if a competitor threatens only a small portion of your expected sales, the sales loss associated with ignoring the threat may be much less than the cost associated with retaliation. Since the threat is small, the cost of cutting the price on all of your sales in order to prevent the small loss is likely to be prohibitively costly. Sometimes the cost of retaliation exceeds the benefits even when the competitor is larger.

It is also important to be realistic about how much of the projected sales loss is really preventable. When a new grocery chain opens with lower prices, the established competitors can surely reduce the sales loss by matching its prices. Still, even if they match, some people will shift to the new store simply because it is newer or more convenient to where they live. They will not return even if the competitor's price advantage is eliminated. Similarly, companies in business markets sometimes unadvisedly delay lowering prices to their most loyal customers even as market conditions are forcing them to lower prices to others. Once those customers learn, often from a competitor's sales rep, that their loyalty has been taken advantage of, matching price is unlikely to win them back. On the contrary, it may simply confirm that they have been gouged.

By constraining an organization's competitive reactions to only those that are cost-effective, managers also force their organizations to think about how to make their price reactions more cost-effective. Following are some principles that can substantially reduce the cost of reacting to a price threat.

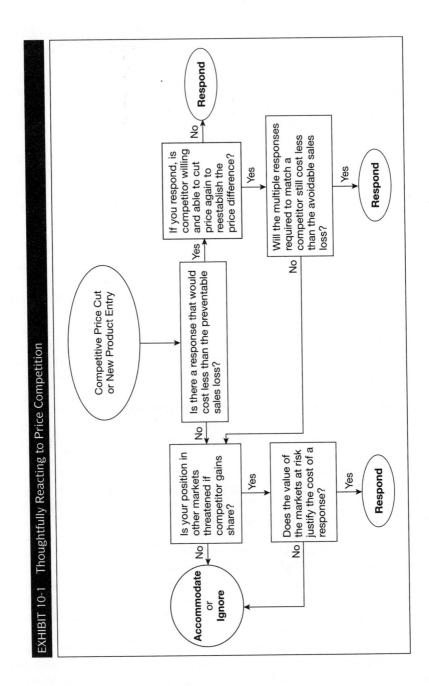

EXHIBIT 10-1 Thoughtfully Reacting to Price Competition

- Focus your reactive price cut on only those customers likely to be attracted by the competitor's offer. This requires developing a "flanking" offer that is attractive or available only to the more price-sensitive buyer. Often, such an offer can be developed in a short period of time since it involves merely eliminating some element of the product or service not highly valued by the price-sensitive segments. When Intel was threatened with lower sales by lower-priced competitors in the personal computer market it employed a flanking brand strategy. Rather than cut the price of its flagship Pentium chip, Intel minimized the cost of responding by creating the Celeron chip. The Celeron involved no additional design or tooling costs, because it was based on the Pentium design, and so could be sold cheaply. To minimize the impact of Celeron pricing on the value of the entire Pentium line, the Celeron chips merely had some Pentium coprocessor capabilities turned off so that they would run poorly on business networks and in data-intensive applications but comparably to a Pentium on home and small-business computers. There are many other flanking brand examples: Sony uses Aiwa as its low-priced "fighting" brand to fight low-cost consumer electronics competitors and maintain the integrity of Sony's premium cutting edge brand position. British Midland Airways uses its "bmibaby" airline—"the airline with tiny fares"—to fight the low-cost competition from no-frills European airlines such as Ryanair and EasyJet.

- Focus your reactive price cut on only the incremental volume at risk. A cheaper competitor will often be unable to entirely replace an incumbent's business, but will be able to gain a share of its competitor's business. For example, if a smaller independent television network, such as WB or UPN in North America cuts its ad rates, advertisers are not going to abandon ABC, NBC, CBS, or Fox. They are, however, going to be more likely to divert some dollars to WB or UPN from the big networks. A big network could neutralize that threat by offering to discount its ad rates to the level of the independent network's rates just for the amount of advertising likely to be diverted. One way this could be structured is as a discount for all purchases in excess of, say, 80 percent of the prior year's purchases or expected purchases. These types of contracts are common not just for advertising, but also for drugs and medical supplies sold to HMOs. Retaliatory discounts applicable only to the incremental volume at risk are also common when pricing to retailers and distributors.

- Focus your reactive price cut on a particular geographic area or product line where the competitor has the most to lose, relative to you, from cutting the price. For example, Kodak may respond to Fuji's retail price promotions in the United States with retail price promotions in Japan, where Fuji has larger market share and margins, and thus more to lose. Remember, the purpose of the retaliation may not be to defend your sales at risk, but to get the competitor to stop the price cutting that puts your sales at risk.

- Raise the cost to the competitor of its discounting. If the competitor's price move is limited only to new customers and the competitor has a market of existing customers, it may be possible to retaliate without cutting your own price at all. Retaliate by educating the competitor's existing customers that they are being treated unfairly. A client of ours did this simply by making sales calls to its competitor's most profitable accounts. In the process of the call, the salespeople casually suggested "You are probably paying about $X for this product now." When the customer questioned this, the salesperson confessed that he really did not know what they were paying but had surmised the figure based on the prices that his competitor offered recently to some other accounts, which he named. In short order, the customer was on the phone demanding similar discounts, and the competitor quickly backtracked on its aggressive offers. Even in consumer markets, it is sometimes possible to appeal to customers' sense of fairness or civic pride to convince them to reject a discounter. Small, local retailers have successfully done this to prevent Wal-Mart from opening stores in Vermont that would no doubt destroy the less efficient, but traditional, local retailers.

Retailers frequently use a related tactic of widely promoting a policy that promises to match the price of low-priced competitors. If a competitor advertises a lower price, then the retailer offers to refund the difference to any of its customers paying a higher price within a reasonable time period, say 30 days following the sale. Only a few very price-sensitive buyers will take the time to gather evidence of the lower advertised competitor prices, and then ensure that the sales receipt for their purchased model matches precisely the competitor's advertised model—all for merely the value of the price differential, often relatively small. However, the price-matching policy is not targeted at all buyers, or even just price sensitive buyers; instead it is a signal to other retail competitors of the futility of aggressive price discounting strategies. After the substantial reduction in margins they incur by heavy discounting, their competitors simply neutralize the advantage by rebating to customers the difference; these deep-discount competitors are better off playing by the rules of established nonprice competition in the category. In North Carolina, Big Star and Winn-Dixie supermarket chains both announced price-matching policies to "meet or beat" the prices of aggressive rival Food Lion. Two years later, the number of products with essentially the same prices across these three competitors increased significantly, and the prices for these products increased as well.[8]

- Leverage any competitive advantages to increase the value of your offer as an alternative to matching the price. The key to doing this without simply replacing a price war with a quality or service war is to make offers that are less costly for you to offer than for your competitor to match. If, for example, you have much better quality, offer a better warranty. If you have more service centers in more locations, offer faster service. Major airlines respond to price competition from smaller upstarts by offering increased frequent flyer miles on newly competitive routes. . Because of their large route systems, frequent flyers miles accumulate miles faster and offer more choices of destinations than anything the small competitors could offer other than price. Moreover, the more sophisticated yield management systems of the large airlines minimized the cost of such programs more effectively than smaller carriers could.

If any of these options is less costly than simply allowing the competitor to take some sales, it is worth continuing to pursue the idea of a response, using the question on the right side of Exhibit 10-1. If, on the other hand, it would cost more to respond than to accept the sales loss, one should continue to examine the option of not responding, using the questions on the left-hand side.

2.   *If you respond, is your competitor willing and able to cut price again to reestablish the price difference?* Matching a price cut will do you no good if the competitor will simply reestablish the advantage. Ask yourself why the competitor chose to compete on price in the first place. If that competitor currently has little market share relative to the share that could be gained with a price advantage, and has no other way to attract customers, then it has little to lose from bringing price down as low as necessary to gain sales. This is especially the case where large sunk costs create substantial "exit barriers."

At one point, we had a pharmaceuticals company ask us to recommend a pricing strategy to defend against a new entrant. Management was initially surprised when we told them that defending their sales with price was foolhardy. Only after thinking about the problem from the competitor's standpoint did they fully understand the competitive dynamics they faced. Customers had no reason to try the competitor's new drug without a price advantage since it offered no clinical advantages. The new entrant had absolutely nothing to lose by taking the price down, since it had no sales anyway. Given that the huge investment to develop and test the drug was entirely sunk but that the manufacturing cost was small, winning sales even at a low price would be a gain. The conclusion was obvious that the competitor would cut price as often as necessary to establish a price advantage.

3.   *Will the multiple responses required to match a competitor still cost less than the avoidable sales loss?* Think about the total cost of a price war, not just the cost of the first shot, before concluding that the cost is worth bearing to defend the sales at risk. If our pharmaceuticals' client had retaliated and closed the price gap enough to keep the competitor from winning sales, the competitor would simply have to cut its price still further. The process would have continued until one or the other stopped it, which was likely to be our client, who had much more to lose from a downward price spiral. If our client was ultimately going to let the competitor have a price advantage, it was better to let them have it at a high price than at a low one. Once the competitor gained some sales, it too would have something to lose from a downward price spiral. At that time, an effort to stop the discount and redirect competition to more positive-sum activities, such as sales

calls, product improvement, and patient education, would be more likely to succeed.

4.   *Is your position in other (geographic or product) markets threatened if a competitor is successful in gaining share? Does the value of the markets at risk justify the cost of a response?* Some sales have a value that far exceeds the contribution directly associated with them. Following Dell's introduction of a new line of computer printers, Hewlett-Packard (HP) immediately severed its relationship to supply HP printers to Dell, signaling the strategic importance to HP of its printer business. HP also retaliated by cutting its PC prices to match Dell's, where Dell had much more to lose. Finally, HP realized that Dell's printer strategy had its own limitations. Dell sources its printers and cartridges from a third-party supplier, Lexmark, limiting Dell's typical cost advantage. So HP defended its lucrative printer business, not with price, but with aggressive product innovations. It introduced new printer models, including digital printing with greater savings for corporate customers; this led to higher revenues and overall printer market share. As a result, HP defended and even expanded its business in printing and copying for major corporations[9].

Retaliatory price cuts are all too often justified by vague "strategic" reasons unrelated to profitability. Before approving any retaliatory price cut for strategic reasons, two things should be required. The first is a clear statement of the long-term strategic benefit and risks. The benefit can be additional sales in this market in the future. It can be additional immediate sales of complementary products, such as sales of software and peripherals if one wins the sale of a computer. It can be a lower cost of future sales because of a competitive cost advantage resulting from the added volume. The risks are that a targeted price cut will spread to other customers and other markets, and that competitors will react, again creating a downward price spiral that undermines profits and any possibility of long-term gain.

The second requirement to justify a strategic price cut is a quantitative estimate of the value of the strategic benefit. This need to quantify often encounters resistance because managers feel that the task is too onerous and will require unnecessary delay. Usually, however, rough estimates are all that is necessary to achieve enough precision to make a decision. A company told us that they always defended price in the institutional segment of their market because sales in that segment drove retail sales. While the relationship was no doubt true, the magnitude of the effect was important given that pricing to the institutional segment had fallen to less than manufacturing cost. A simple survey of retail customers about how they began using the product revealed that only about 16 percent of retail sales were driven by institutional sales. We then estimated the cost of maintaining those sales by retaining all of the client's current institutional sales and compared that with the cost of replacing those sales through expenditures on alternative forms of promotion. That simple analysis drove a complete change in the institutional pricing strategy.

Moreover, as institutional prices rose, "leakage" of cheap institutional product into the retail chain market declined, producing an additional return that had not been anticipated.

HOW SHOULD YOU REACT?

Competitive pricing strategy involves more than just deciding whether or not to react with price. It also involves deciding how to adapt your company's competitive strategy to the new situation. Exhibit 10-2 summarizes the strategic options and when to use them. In addition to the costs and benefits of retaliation that are weighed using the process described in Exhibit 10-1, this exhibit introduces the concept of strategic "weakness" and "strength." These concepts refer to a competitor's relative competitive advantage. Competitive "weakness" and "strength" have little to do with market share, despite the common tendency to equate them. The high cost structure of General Motors makes the company a relatively weak competitor in the automobile market, despite a high market share, because (at least in the North American automobile market) it has higher incremental costs per dollar revenue than its major rivals do. In contrast, the low cost structure of Southwest Airlines makes it a stronger competitor, even when competing against larger airlines, because its low cost per seat mile generates higher profits despite its somewhat lower prices.

When you decide that retaliation is not cost-effective, one option is simply to ignore the threat. This is the appropriate response when facing a "weak"

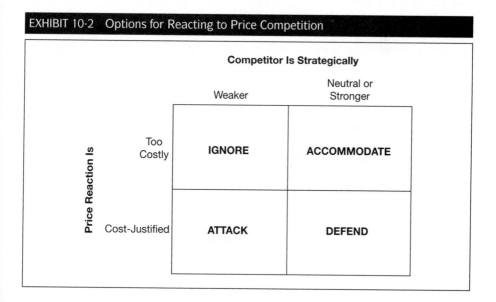

EXHIBIT 10-2   Options for Reacting to Price Competition

		Competitor Is Strategically	
		Weaker	Neutral or Stronger
Price Reaction Is	Too Costly	IGNORE	ACCOMMODATE
	Cost-Justified	ATTACK	DEFEND

competitor, with no competitive product or cost advantages. In that case, the amount of your sales at risk is small and is likely to remain so. In these same circumstances, some authors and consultants recommend a more aggressive option—commonly known as the "deep pockets" strategy—and pursue it to their own detriment. Their logic is that even if retaliation is too costly relative to the immediate sales gained, a large company can win a price war because it can afford to subsidize losses in a market longer than its weak competitor can. Two misconceptions lead people down this dead-end path. One is the meaning of "winning." This is no doubt a strategy to successfully defend market share, but the goal, at least for a publicly owned company, is not market share but profit. The second misconception is that by destroying a weak competitor one can actually destroy competition. Often the assets of the bankrupt competitor are bought cheaply by a new competitor now able to compete from a lower cost base. Even if the assets are not bought, elimination of a weak competitor serving the price-sensitive segment of the market creates the opportunity for a stronger competitor to enter and use that as a basis from which to grow. Consequently, a costly strategy to kill weak competitors makes sense only in an unprofitable industry where a new entrant is unlikely to replace the one eliminated.

When a price-cutting competitor is relatively "strong" and the cost of retaliation is greater than the value of the sales loss prevented, one cannot afford simply to ignore the threat and proceed as if nothing had changed. A strong competitor gaining share is a threat to survival. To maintain a profitable future, one must actively accommodate the threat with changes in strategy. This is what Sears faced as Wal-Mart's network of stores grew to include Sears's traditional suburban markets. There was simply no way that Sears could match Wal-Mart's prices, given Wal-Mart's famously efficient distribution system and Sears' more costly locations.

Sears' only logical response was to accommodate Wal-Mart as a competitor in its markets. Accommodating a threat is not the same as ignoring or confronting it. Accommodating means actively adjusting your own competitive strategy to minimize the adverse impact of the threat while reconciling yourself to live with it. Sears opted to eliminate its lower-margin product lines, remaking its image as a high-fashion retailer that competed less with Wal-Mart and more with traditional department stores.

A European industrial manufacturer took this same tack when it learned that an American company that previously exported product to Europe was about to build production capacity in the United Kingdom, with a generous government subsidy. Realizing that defending its market directly would produce nothing but a bloody price battle, the company refocused its marketing strategy away from the more price-sensitive segments, while creating incentives for less price-sensitive segments to sign longer-term contracts. As a result, the American firm's sales were focused in the least desirable segment where price-sensitive customers made it more vulnerable to a price war than were the traditional European competitors. Accommodating the competitor's entry was costly, but much less so than a futile attempt to prevent the entry with price competition.

The only situation in which it makes sense to use an attack response is when the competitor is weaker and the attack is cost justified. One reason this is rare is that it usually requires a misjudgment on the part of the competitor, who attempts to use price as a weapon from a position of weakness. Still, such misjudgments do occur. The largest U.S. grocery chain at the time, A&P, effectively destroyed itself in the 1970s after initiating a discount pricing strategy to regain market share. Its major competitors initially followed an accommodation strategy, believing that the A&P chain's huge buying power and well-known house brands gave it a cost advantage. When A&P began reporting huge losses, however, its competitors figured out that its high labor costs made the company much more vulnerable than they had thought. They switched to an attack strategy that ultimately forced the company to close half of its stores and sell the others to a more efficient suitor.

More common is the case where the price-cutting competitor is strong, or at least as strong as the defending companies whose sales are under attack. Often because of the attacker's strategic strength, the amount of sales at risk is so great that a vigorous defense is cost justified. The purpose of a "defend" response is not to eliminate the competitor, but rather simply to convince the competitor to back off. The goal is to get the competitor to recognize that aggressive pricing is not really in its financial interest and to refrain from it in the future. This is often the position taken by American Airlines in its competition with other carriers, many of which have lower cost structures. American is careful to limit the time period and the depth of its price responses, signaling a willingness to return prices to prior levels as soon as the competitor withdraws the threat. Sometimes these battles last no more than days, or even hours, as competitors watch to see if American can fashion a cost-effective defense.

Partisans of pricing for market share would no doubt disagree with the restrained approach that we have prescribed. Large market-share companies, they would argue, are often better capitalized and thus better able to finance a price war than are smaller competitors. Although price-cutting might be more costly for the larger firm in the short run, it can bankrupt smaller competitors and, in the long run, reestablish the leader's market share and its freedom to control market prices. Although such a "predatory" response to competition sounds good in theory, there are two reasons why it rarely works in practice. First, predatory pricing is a violation of U.S. and European antitrust laws if the predatory price is below the predator's variable cost. Such a pricing tactic may in some cases be a violation when the price is below the average of all costs.[10] Consequently, even if a large competitor can afford to price low enough to bankrupt its smaller competitors, it often cannot do so legally. Second, and more important, predation is cost effective only if the predator gains some competitive advantage as a result of winning the war. This occurs in only two cases: when eliminating a competitor destroys an important differentiating asset (e.g., its accumulated goodwill with customers) or when it enables the predator to gain such a cost advantage (e.g., economies of experience or scale) that it can profitably keep its prices low enough to discourage new entrants. In the absence of this, new entrants can purchase the assets of the bankrupt competitor, operating at a lower cost base and competing against a large firm now itself financially weakened by the cost of the price war.

A recent example of the long-term futility of price competition occurred in club warehouse segment of retailing. As market growth slowed in the mid 1990s, these retailers all tried to grow by gaining market share, although none had the competitive advantage to justify such growth. For example, Sam's Club (operated by Wal-Mart), Pace (operated by K-Mart), and Costco each opened large warehouse locations within months of each other in El Centro, California, a small city of only 75,000. Costco invaded one of Pace's strongholds in Anchorage, Alaska by building not one, but two club warehouses. Pace retaliated by building another Anchorage club warehouse—leading to significant overcapacity in a minor market. Pace invaded Sam's Club's home turf in Dallas, Texas with plans for a new club warehouse; Sam's Club retaliated immediately by building three more Dallas club warehouses (in addition to six existing locations), locating one next to the Pace store under construction. To attract customers to these new stores, each cut margins precipitously, as charges were filed alleging predatory pricing below cost. By the end of the decade, of eight original club warehouse competitors two to three emerged "victorious"—Sam's (which acquired most of the Pace locations) and Costco (which merged with Price Club; BJ's remained a smaller regional survivor). The exit of the failed club warehouses left behind many huge empty warehouses. It also left a lot of disappointment among the "winners." Even five years later, Sam's Club stores have never recovered their profitability, and have fallen far short of the performance of the traditional Wal-Mart stores.[11]

These guidelines are useful for businesses in hostile competitive environments. Managers must choose their confrontations carefully and structure them to leverage their strengths. Verizon, one of the original regional Bell operating companies, realized that having a national footprint with a single brand and common digital technology in the fractured wireless market would immediately provide a competitive advantage over its other regional rivals. It merged with GTE, a large wireless operator in the United States and abroad. It further filled in its national footprint with an agreement to join forces with Vodafone's wireless assets, including AirTouch in the West and PrimeCo in the Midwest. The new Verizon Wireless brand, at once the nation's largest, leveraged its complete coverage by introducing the "America's Choice" wireless plan in which customers could make unlimited calls anywhere in the continental United States for a flat monthly rate, without incurring roaming fees or network access charges for calls made outside of the customer's local area. At once, Verizon made obsolete the notion of local wireless calling plans with out-of-area "roaming," and erased the distinction between traditional local and long-distance calling plans.

Regional competitors could not match this deal without substantial financial risk since they would need to buy long-distance coverage from other regional carriers.

The key to surviving a negative-sum pricing game is to avoid confrontation unless you can structure it in a way that you can win and the likely benefit from winning exceeds the likely cost. Do not initiate price discounts unless the short-term gain is worth it after taking account of competitors' long-term reactions. Do not react to a competitor's price discounts except with price and nonprice tactics that cost less than accommodating the competitor's behavior would cost. If managers in general were to follow these two simple rules, far fewer industries would be ravaged by destructive price competition.

MANAGING COMPETITIVE INFORMATION

The key to managing competition profitably is diplomacy, not generalship. This does not necessarily mean being "Mr. Nice Guy." Diplomats are not always nice, but they manage information and expectations to achieve their goals without unnecessary confrontation. If they find it necessary to use force, they seek to limit its use to the amount necessary to make their point. In the diplomacy of price competition, the meaning that competitors ascribe to a move is often far more important than the move itself.

The decision to cut price to gain a customer may have radically different long-term effects, depending upon how the competitor interprets the move. Without any other information, the competitor would probably interpret the move as an opportunistic grab for market share and respond with defensive cuts of its own. If, however, the discount is structured to mimic exactly an offer that the same competitor made recently to one of your loyal customers, the competitor may interpret the cut as reflecting your resolve to defend that segment of the market. As such, the cut may actually reduce future opportunism and help stabilize industry prices.

Consider how the competitor might interpret one more alternative: your price cut is totally unprovoked but is exceptionally large, more than you have ever offered before and probably more than is necessary to take the business. Moreover, it is preceded by an announcement that your company's new, patented manufacturing process not only added to capacity but also substantially reduced incremental manufacturing costs. In this case, an intelligent competitor might well interpret the price cut as fair warning that resistance against your grab for market share will be futile.

Managing information to influence a competitor's expectations, and to accurately form your own expectations, is the key to achieving goals without unnecessary negative-sum confrontation. Managing information requires collecting and evaluating information about the competition, as well as communicating information to the market that may influence competitors' moves in ways desirable to your own objectives.

COLLECT AND EVALUATE INFORMATION

Many companies operate while ignorant of their competitors' prices and pricing strategies. Consequently, they cannot respond quickly to changes. In highly competitive markets, such ignorance creates conditions that invite price warfare. Why would an opportunist ever cut price if it believed that other companies were willing to retaliate? The answer is that the opportunist's management believes that, by quietly negotiating or concealing its price cuts, it can gain sufficient sales volume to justify the move before the competitors find out. This is especially likely in industries with high fixed costs (high % contribution margins) and during peak seasons when disproportionate amounts of business are at stake.

To minimize such opportunistic behavior, competitors must identify and react to it as quickly as possible.[12] If competitors can react in 1 week rather than 3, the opportunist's potential benefit from price-cutting is reduced by two thirds. At the extreme, if competitors could somehow react instantly, nearly all benefit from being the first to cut price could be eliminated. In highly competitive markets, managers "shop" the competitors' stores and monitor their advertising on a daily basis to adjust their pricing[13] and the large chains maintain communication systems enabling them to make price changes quickly in response to a competitive threat. As a consequence, by the time most customers even learn what the competition is promoting in a given week, the major competitors have already matched the price.

Knowledge of competitors' prices also helps minimize a purchasing agent's ability to promulgate misinformation. Frequently in business-to-business markets, price wars begin without the intention of any competitor involved. They are caused by a purchasing agent's manipulation of information. A purchasing agent, frustrated by the inability to get a better price from a favored supplier, may falsely claim that he or she has been offered a better deal from a competitor. If the salesperson doesn't respond, a smart purchasing agent may give the threat more credibility by giving the next order to a competitor even without a price concession. Now the first company believes that its competitor is out "buying business" and will, perhaps, match the claimed "lower price" on future orders to this customer, rewarding this customer's duplicitous behavior. If the first company is more skilled in price competition, it will not match the "lower price," but rather will retaliate by offering the same discount to other good customers of the competitor. The competitor will now see this company as a threat and begin its own cuts to defend its share. Without either competitor intending to undermine the industry price level, each has unwittingly been led to do so. The only way to minimize such manipulation is to monitor competitors' prices closely enough so that you can confidently predict when a customer is lying.[14]

Even when purchasers do not lie openly, their selective communication of information often leaves salespeople with a biased perspective. Most salespeople think that their company's prices are too high for market conditions. Think about how a salesperson is informed about price. Whenever the salesperson loses a piece of business, the purchaser informs the salesperson that the price was "too high." When he or she wins the business, however, the purchaser never tells the salesperson that the price was unnecessarily low. The purchaser says the job was won with "the right price." Salespeople get little or no information about how much margin they may have left on the table.

There are many potential sources of data about competitors' prices, but collecting those data and converting the data into useful information usually require a formalized process. Many companies require that the sales force regularly include information on competitors' pricing in their call reports. Having such current information can substantially reduce the time necessary to respond to opportunism since someone collecting information from multiple salespeople and regions can spot a trend much more quickly than can an individual salesperson or sales manager. Favored customers can also be a good source of information. Those that are loyal to the company, perhaps because of its quality or good service, do not want their competitors to get lower prices from another source. Consequently, they will warn the favored company when competitors issue new price sheets or when they hear that someone is discounting to someone else. A partnership with such a customer is very valuable and should be treated as such by the seller.

In highly competitive markets, the information collected should not be limited to prices. Understanding plans and intentions is equally important. We recently worked with a client frustrated by the low profitability in its service industry, despite record revenue growth. In the process, we learned that the industry had suffered from overcapacity but recently had experienced multiple mergers. What was the purpose of those mergers? Was it to gain cost efficiencies in manufacturing or sales that would enable the new company to offer low prices more profitably? Or was it to eliminate some inefficient capacity, enabling the merged company to consolidate its most profitable customers in fewer plants, eliminating the need to win "incremental business." We found answers to those questions in the competitor's briefings to securities analysts, causing our client to rethink its own strategy.

Trade associations, independent industry monitoring organizations, securities analysts, distributors, and technical consultants that advise customers on large purchases are all good sources of information about competitors' current pricing moves and future intentions. Sometimes trade associations will collect information on prices charged in the prior week and disseminate it to members who have submitted their own prices. The airlines' computerized reservations systems give the owners of those systems an advance look at all price changes, enabling them to respond even before travel agents see changes. Monitoring price discussions at trade shows can also be another early tip-off. In retail businesses, one can simply "shop" the competitive retailers on a regular basis. In the hotel industry, nearby competitors regularly check their competitors' prices and room availability on particular nights by calling to make an unguaranteed reservation. If price competition is important enough as a determinant of profit in an industry, managers can easily justify the cost to monitor it.[15]

Selectively Communicate Information

It is usually much easier for managers to see the value of collecting competitive information than it is for them to see the value in knowingly revealing similar information to the competition. After all, information is power. Why should anyone want to reveal a competitive advantage? The answer: so that you can avoid having to use your advantage in a negative-sum confrontation.

The value of sharing information was obvious, after the fact, to a company supplying the construction industry. Unlike most of its competitors as well as most economists, the company accurately predicted a recession and construction slowdown looming on the horizon. To prepare, the company wisely pared back its inventories and shelved expansion plans just as its competitors were continuing to expand. The company's only mistake was to keep its insight a secret. Management correctly felt that by retrenching more quickly than its competitors, it could weather the hard times more successfully, but when competitors desperately cut prices to clear bloated inventories, the entire industry suffered. Had the company shared its insight and discouraged everyone from overexpansion, its own financial performance, while perhaps relatively less outstanding, would have been absolutely more profitable. It is usually better to earn just an average return in a profitable industry than to earn an exceptional return in an unprofitable one.

Even company-specific information—about intentions, capabilities, and future plans—can be useful to reveal unless doing so would preclude achieving a first-mover advantage into a new market. Such information, and the information contained in competitors' responses, enables a company to establish plans "on paper" that are consistent with competitors' intentions, rather than having to reach consistency through the painful process of confrontation.

- *Preannounce price increases.* One of the most important times to communicate intentions is when planning a price increase. Even when a price increase is in the independent interest of all suppliers, an attempt to raise prices will often fail. All may not immediately recognize that an increase is in their interest, and some may hope to gain sales at the expense of the price leaders by lagging in meeting the increase. Other times, an increase may not be in the competitor's interest (perhaps because its costs are lower), meaning that any attempt to raise prices will ultimately fail. Consequently, before initiating a price increase that it expects competitors to follow, a firm's management should publicly explain the industry's need for higher prices and, if possible, announce its own increase far in advance of the effective date. As we discussed in Chapter 5, this "toe in the water" approach enables management to pull back from the price increase if competitors do not join in. This approach can be repeated multiple times until competitors understand that a price increase won't go through without them.

- *Show willingness and ability to defend.* When threatened by the potential opportunism of others, a firm may deter the threat by clearly signaling its commitment and ability to defend its market. For example, Novell, a leader in "open source" computer software, sells a version of Linux and many proprietary products based on open source code. In an attempt to undermine Novell's inroads, proprietary software competitors, including Microsoft, suggested in the press that any products based on open source software might be subject to patent infringement suits by propriety software vendors, with users of the software as potential defendants. Even the hint of potential litigation put fear in the minds of potential customers considering switching to the lower-priced open source platform. But Novell has a competitive advantage that it publicized broadly: 411 patents relating to its proprietary open source products, by far the largest pool of open source patents among computer providers. By contrast, a third-party insurer found 283 relevant registered patents that might be used in a suit against open source products, including 27 held by Microsoft. So Novell published a policy statement describing its intent to defend against potential patent attacks on open source software:

> We believe that customers want and need freedom of choice in making decisions about technology solutions. Those considering Novell offerings, whether proprietary or open source, should be able to make their purchasing decisions based on technical merits, security, quality of service and value, not the threat of litigation. Novell intends to continue to compete based on such criteria. . . .
>
> As appropriate, Novell is prepared to use our patents, which are highly relevant in today's marketplace, to defend against those who might assert patents against open source products marketed, sold or supported by Novell. Some software vendors will attempt to counter the competitive threat of Linux by making arguments about the risk of violating patents. Vendors that assert patents against customers and competitors such as Novell do so at their own peril and with the certainty of provoking a response.[16]

Novell's policy is at the very least a mutually assured destruction policy: If you deploy your patent weapons in a way that threatens Novell's interests, Novell will respond with a large inventory of legal weapons of its own.[17]

Such communications can also be useful even after competitors have started an attack. Such posturing is common in the airline industry. In another airline skirmish, when America West undercut the fare for Northwest Airlines' busy Minneapolis–Los Angeles route, Northwest declined to match the cut. Instead, Northwest struck at America West's Phoenix hub by cutting fares a similar amount on the competitor's profitable Phoenix–New York route. Northwest's response fare was initially available for only a limited time, signaling that this was not a price that Northwest wished to sustain any longer than necessary. It could, however, be extended as long as necessary—if America West failed to back off in Minneapolis.[18]

- *Back up opportunism with information.* While an opportunistic price cut to buy market share is usually shortsighted, it is sometimes an element of a thoughtful strategy. This is most often the case when a company uses pricing to leverage or to enhance a durable cost advantage. Even companies with competitive advantages, however, often win only pyrrhic victories in battles for market share. Although they ultimately can force competitors to cede market share, the costs of battle frequently exceed the ultimate value of the reward. This is especially true when the war reduces customer price expectations and undermines loyal buyer–seller relationships.

The key to profitably using price as a weapon is to convince competitors to capitulate. A Japanese company invited the two top operations managers of its American competitor to the opening of its new plant. After attending the opening ceremony, the company took all guests through the highly automated facility. The American managers were surprised to see the process so highly automated, all the way to final packing, since quality control usually required human intervention at many points in the process. When asked about this, the Japanese hosts informed the guests that this plant was the first to use a new, proprietary process that essentially eliminated the major source of defects. They also indicated that development of the process had taken them more than a decade.

On the way home, realizing now what could be done, the American engineers were eagerly speculating about how this improvement might be achieved and how much they should ask for in a budget to pursue research. They also wondered why their Japanese counterparts would reveal the existence of such an important trade secret. Within a few months they got their answer. The Japanese competitor announced a 20 percent price cut for exports of this product to the American market. If you were the American competitor with a large market share, how would knowledge of this trade secret change your likely response? In this case, the American company wisely chose to "adapt" rather than "defend."

Although the information disclosures discussed here are the most common, they are hardly comprehensive. Almost every public decision a company makes will be gleaned for information by astute competitors.[19] Consequently, companies in price-competitive industries should take steps to manage how their moves are seen by competitors, just as they manage the perceptions of stockholders and securities analysts. For example, will competitors in a highly price-competitive industry interpret closure of a plant as a sign of financial weakness or as a sign that the company is taking steps to end an industrywide overcapacity problem? How they interpret such a move will probably affect how they react to it. Consequently, it is in the company's interest to supply information that helps them make a favorable interpretation. Think twice, however, before disseminating misleading information that competitors will ultimately discover is incorrect. You may gain in the short run; however, you will undermine your ability to influence competitors' decisions and, therefore, to manage price competition in the long run.

WHEN SHOULD YOU COMPETE ON PRICE?

We have been discussing the benefits of avoiding negative-sum competitive confrontation, but some companies clearly benefit from underpricing their competitors. Did not the Japanese automakers in the 1970s, Wal-Mart in the 1980s, and Dell Computer in the 1990s build their strategies around gaining share with lower prices? Yes, and understanding the special circumstances that enabled them to grow using price is necessary for anyone trying to replicate such success. For each of those companies at the times and places they used price to grow, price competition was not a negative-sum game. Every one of these successful price competitors first created business models that enabled them to cut incremental costs below those of their competitors. So long as each could attract customers with a price difference smaller than its cost advantage, it could win customers without reducing industry profitability. In fact, by serving customers more cost-effectively, these companies actually earned profits from each customer in excess of those earned by the competition—making their competitive efforts a positive-sum game.

However, a competitive cost advantage was not by itself enough to succeed. All of these companies also orchestrated a campaign of information to convince their competitors that their cost advantages were decisive. Consequently, their competitors wisely allowed them to maintain attractive price differentials, at least temporarily, until the competitors could figure out how to replicate those costs. Eventually, even these companies recognize that unless they can continue to cut costs faster than competitors, price-cutting cannot be a profitable growth strategy indefinitely. Consequently, they ultimately shift their strategies toward adding more value in ways that enable them to sustain their large market shares without having to sustain a price advantage indefinitely.

Under what conditions are the rewards of aggressive pricing large enough to justify such a move? There are only four:

1. If a company enjoys a substantial incremental cost advantage or can achieve one with a low-price strategy, its competitors may be unable to match its price cuts. Wal-Mart, Dell, and Southwest Airlines created low-cost business models that enabled them to grow profitably using price. In some markets, there may be an "experience effect" that justifies aggressive pricing based on the promise of lower costs. By pricing low and accumulating volume faster than competitors, a firm reduces its costs below those of competitors, thus creating a competitive advantage through low pricing.

2. If a company's product offering is attractive to only a small share of the market served by competitors, it may rightly assume that competitors will be unwilling to respond to the threat. The key to such a strategy, however, is to remain focused. Southwest Airlines began as a small upstart that got little attention. It flew out of little-used airports, such as Hobby Airport in Houston, Texas. Its point-to-point short-hop business model was dramatically different than other established competitors with expensive hub-and-spoke operations in large

airports, and consequently appeared to appeal to only a small niche market. It was easy for bigger competitors to ignore Southwest. That is, until it began to expand to other markets and increasingly take market share away from the major air carriers.

3. If a company can effectively subsidize losses in one market because of the profits it can generate selling complementary products, it may be able to establish a price differential that competitors will be unable to close. Microsoft, for example, priced its Windows software very low relative to value in order to increase sales of other Microsoft software that runs on it. Amazon.com's rationale for its low pricing on books was to build up a body of loyal customers to which it could sell a broad range of other products.

4. Sometimes price competition expands a market sufficiently that, despite lower margins and competitors' refusals to allow another company to undercut them, industry profitability can still increase. Managers who take this course are assuming that they have insight that their competitors lack and are, in effect, leading the industry toward pricing that is, in fact, in everyone's best interest. Before embarking on a price-based strategy, ask which of these your rationale is and recognize that the strategy can rarely be built on price alone or sustained indefinitely.

Summary

No other weapon in a marketer's arsenal can boost sales more quickly or effectively than price. Price discounting—whether explicit or disguised with rebates, coupons, or generous terms—is usually a sure way to enhance immediate profitability. However, gaining sales with price is consistent with long-term profitability only when managed as part of a marketing strategy for achieving, exploiting, or sustaining a longer-term competitive advantage. No price cut should ever be initiated simply to make the next sale or to meet some short-term sales objective without being balanced against the likely reactions of competitors and customers. The key to profitable pricing is building and sustaining competitive advantage. There are times when price-cutting is consistent with building advantage, but it is never an appropriate substitute for it.

Notes

1. Sections of this chapter were first published as an article entitled "Managing Price Competition," *Marketing Management,* 2(1) (Spring 1993), pp. 36–45.
2. For more on the practical applications of game theory, see Adam Brandenburger and Barry Nalebuff, *Competition* (New York: Doubleday, 1996); Rita Koselka, "Evolutionary Economics: Nice Guys Don't Finish Last," *Fortune,* October 11, 1993, pp. 110–114; and Kenichi Ohmae, "Getting Back to Strategy," *Harvard Business Review* (November–December 1988), pp. 149–156.
3. Price competition is a positive-sum

game only when total industry contribution rises as a result. This can happen when market demand is sufficiently stimulated by the price cuts, when a low-cost competitor can win share with a price advantage less than its cost advantage, or when a firm's costs are sufficiently reduced by a gain in market share that total industry profits can increase even as prices fall.

4. B. H. Liddell Hart, *Strategy* (New York: Meridian, 1967), p. 322.

5. Michael E. Porter, "What Is Strategy," *Harvard Business Review* (November–December 1996), pp. 60–78. See also Michael E. Porter, *Competitive Strategy* (New York: The Free Press, 1980), p. 34.

6. Marcia Berss, "Take It or Leave It," *Forbes* (January 1, 1996), pp. 46–47.

7. Porter, *op. cit.,* pp. 41–43. A firm can become large without getting "stuck in the middle" simply by taking on multiple segments. The segments must be managed, however, as a conglomerate of focused businesses rather than as a one-size-fits-all marketing organization. Procter & Gamble is an excellent example of a large company that nevertheless carefully targets each product to meet the needs of a particular focused segment.

8. Akshay R. Rao, Mark E. Bergen, and Scott Davis, "How to Fight a Price War," *Harvard Business Review* (March–April 2000), pp. 11, 107–116.

9. "As Alliances Fade, Computer Firms Toss Out Playbook," *Wall Street Journal* (October 15, 2002), p. A1; "Dude, You're Getting A Printer; Dell's Printer Business Is Puny Next to HP's, But It's Quickly Gaining Ground," Business Week Online, April 19, 2004, p. 12.

10. See the discussion on predatory pricing in Chapter 14.

11. "Store Wars," *Fortune Small Business* (November 2003); "Warehouse Club-War Leaves Few Standing, And They Are Bruised," *Wall Street Journal* (November 18, 1993), pp. A1, 16.

12. Note that this principle applies in the other direction as well. If competitors quickly follow price increases, the cost of leading such increases is vastly reduced. Consequently, companies that wish to encourage responsible leadership by other firms would do well to follow their moves quickly, whether up or down.

13. See Francine Schwadel, "Ferocious Competition Tests the Pricing Skills of a Retail Manager," *Wall Street Journal* (December 11, 1989), p. 1.

14. Another useful tactic that can control such duplicitous behavior in U.S. markets is to require the customer, in order to get the lower price, to initial a clause on the order form that states the customer understands this is "a discriminatorily low price offered solely to meet the price offered by a competitor." Since falsely soliciting a discriminatorily low price is a Robinson-Patman Act violation, the purchasing agent is discouraged from using leverage unless he or she actually has it.

15. For more guidance on collecting competitive information, see "These Guys Aren't Spooks, They're Competitive Analysts," *Business Week* (October 14, 1991), p. 97; and Leonard M. Fuld, *Competitor Intelligence: How to Get It—How to Use It* (New York: Wiley & Sons, 1985).

16. "Novell Statement on Patents and Open Source Software," novell.com.

17. *ComputerWorld,* October 13, 2004; "Novell Waves Its Patent Weapons," LWN.net, October 14, 2004.

18. "Fair Game: Airlines May Be Using a Price-Data Network to Lessen Competition," *Wall Street Journal* (June 28, 1990), p. 1.

19. For a comprehensive and insightful survey of the research on communicating competitive information, see Oliver P. Heil and Arlen W. Langvardt, "The Interface Between Competitive Market Signaling and Antitrust Law," *Journal of Marketing,* 58(3) (July 1994), pp. 81–96.

CHAPTER

11

PRICING
IN CHANNELS
OF DISTRIBUTION

Managing Multiple
Transactions and
Relationships

For products with complex channels to market, including most consumer pack-aged goods and many original equipment manufacturer (OEM) parts, value and pricing is more complex than we have heretofore acknowledged. Channels add multiple transactions, and therefore multiple pricing decisions, as the product moves from the manufacturer to the end-user. For example, although a computer manufacturer can choose to sell its product directly to consumers (as Dell does for many of its computers), most computers are not sold that way. Sometimes, the manufacturer sells directly to a high-volume retailer (like CompUSA). More often, the first sale is to a distributor (such as Ingram Micro or Tech Data), and then from the distributor to a retailer or to value-added reseller who configures a custom solution using the computer as one component. Each time the product is traded to an intermediary, there are pricing challenges somewhat unrelated to the value delivered to the end-consumer but equally important to profitability.

The principles of value-based pricing remain the same when working through channels of distribution, but the sources of value for the within-channel transactions are quite different. For example, when a distributor buys product from a manufac-turer, he does not really care about the features and benefits of the product. He cares about whether or not carrying the manufacturer's brand will enable him to generate incremental volume, or margin, or reduce his cost of sales. The more value the manufacturer's brand generates for the distributor, the higher the wholesale price (the smaller the "trade discount") needed for the distributor to carry the prod-uct. Understanding, communicating, and pricing your economic value to other chan-nel participants is as important as managing your product's value to end-consumers.

The key to understanding channel pricing and price management lies in understanding who generates value for whom. Who is actually the buyer and who is the seller in channel transactions are often ambiguous. A manufacturer may be the seller of product, but the distributor is the seller of services to the manufacturer. The value of both may need to be reflected in just one price, the wholesale price of the product. The amount of the price adjustment is determined, in part, by which channel member has the most power.

As in pricing to end-consumers, the price that the seller can realize for additional profitability is determined by the differentiation value of its total offering. To the extent that the channel partner can offer a manufacturer something unique—such as access to a group of customers only reachable through that partner or unique services that will increase the brand's share—then that "differentiation value" creates the potential for that channel partner to earn a bigger margin. In many markets, such as home improvement products, home appliances, home electronics, and some high-volume consumer packaged goods, the retailers have become more consolidated and powerful. They understand the value that their volume brings to manufacturers and use that to dictate the terms under which they will carry a product.

The key to capturing differentiation value in pricing is to establish appropriate price metrics and policies. The basic job of "moving boxes" has become so competitive that many distributors in markets ranging from medical supplies, to food, to electronics, have gone out of business. Those remaining have not survived solely by cutting costs and becoming more efficient. Their profitability depends on the added services and new sources of revenue they have developed and priced effectively. They have become not only purchasers of product from manufacturers but in many cases suppliers to them of valuable services—such as technical support or inventory management or sales forecasting. They also have increased the service they offer to retailers and value-added resellers (VARs). The balance of this chapter will involve discussion of the various sources of value in channel relationship and the means to price them.

VALUE AND PRICING BETWEEN CHANNEL PARTNERS

Because different segments of end-customers require different levels of service and different manufacturers have different abilities to deliver services, channels are rarely uniform. Large retailers will deal directly with manufacturers, whereas smaller ones will buy from distributors. Some manufacturers will deal exclusively with only one distributor, whereas others in the same industry will sell product to any of them. Some markets will have multiple layers of intermediate distribution whereas others will be flatter. Moreover, some channel partners have backward integrated to serve multiple functions. For example, although Wal-Mart is thought of as a retailer, the competitive advantage on which it built its growth was innovative distribution that enabled it to transfer product from manufacturers to each store more cost effectively than traditional distributors. Similarly, local soft drink bottlers partially manufacture their product as well as distribute it along with various services to retail outlets.

EXHIBIT 11-1   Managing Value Through the Channel

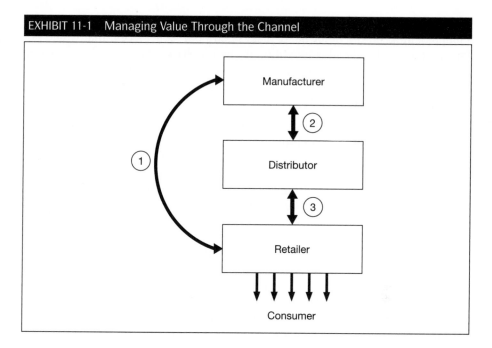

Rather than deal with every combination of channel relationship, we will divide channel relationships into three generic categories: manufacturer–retailer, manufacturer–distributor, and distributor–retailer. Exhibit 11-1 illustrates these. In practice, readers should recognize that within a single market, different combinations of these relationships will apply. In addition, in business-to-business (B-to-B) markets there may be no retail channel at all. Even in these markets, however, the concepts we will discuss are readily applicable.

MANUFACTURER–RETAILER RELATIONSHIPS

The manufacturer–retailer relationship, even if it is not direct because the product flows through distribution, needs to be managed. We use the term *retailer* broadly to define the last channel member selling to the final buyer. Thus the term is meant to include not just traditional retail stores, but the VARs who buy various types of equipment (e.g., electronic controls) to build solutions (e.g., a building security system) for their customers, or the professional (e.g., a dentist) who sells products (e.g., a particular brand of dental implants) along with his or her professional services.

Selecting the right type of channel for your product is essential to leverage its competitive advantage. Brands with different advantages require different channel relationships. For example:

• High-volume watch brands, like Seiko, distribute through mass-market retailers like Sears and Wal-Mart. They produce watches inexpensively and make money by selling a lot of them, despite a small margin per unit. They do not want retailers who add high markups, but rather ones that make money by driving volume. Philippe Patek, on the other hand, makes heirloom "timepieces" that would not fare well in head-to-head competition in the jewelry case at Wal-Mart. A Patek Philippe watch is a work of art that must be displayed and sold like art or expensive jewelry. Consequently, it selects a retail channel—high-end jewelry stores—that provide the sales support and retail environment to sell few at high margins.

• Companies that manufacture high-end cosmetics have a unique distribution system. They distribute in high-quality department stores, but they do not sell their products to these stores. Instead, they rent display space and staff it with their own sales representatives. They do so because much of the differentiation value of their products stems from augmentation. Each company's representative is trained as a cosmetologist to help a woman select cosmetics appropriate for her and to teach her how to use them most effectively. At the same time, the cosmetologist makes the connection between the customer's enhanced beauty and the particular brand of cosmetics that is sold. Other cosmetic companies employ agents as their sales representatives. Avon and Mary Kay cosmetics are sold by agent "beauty consultants" who consult directly with customers. This approach gives the supplier high levels of control over the distribution channel. Low-priced cosmetics need only market access, since they sell on price. Consequently, they buy distribution from drug stores with much smaller margins.

• Caterpillar Tractor is legendary for the quality of its exclusive dealer network. Caterpillar selects its dealers carefully and treats them royally in order to instill a feeling that they are part of a family of Caterpillar employees. This is because Caterpillar's reputation for reliability enables it to charge a substantial price premium. Although that reputation stems in part from the high quality of the physical product, it could be quickly destroyed if a dealer is not quick to come to a customer's aid when inevitable breakdowns occur. Caterpillar dealers, however, view a breakdown as a potential blight on their family name and will go to unusual extremes to correct it. Such commitment is well worth the extra cost to Caterpillar of maintaining its exclusive distribution network.

• When companies use different pricing strategies for different versions of their products, they need to coordinate those strategies with different distribution channels. Despite the success of L'eggs pantyhose in supermarkets, Hanes continues to sell higher-quality, higher-priced hosiery through department stores. Pitney Bowes continues to sell the bulk of its office equipment through its sales force but uses direct mail to sell its lowest-priced scales and postage meters to small buyers. In each of these cases, low-priced products are appropriately distributed through low-cost channels that preserve their price advantage, whereas higher-priced products justify the higher cost of distribution methods that can enhance the pricing relationship between the manufacturer and the end-retailer, who can influence perceptions of the product's differentiating attributes.

Having selected or designed a strategically complementary means of retail distribution, one factor determines first and foremost the power to define the pricing: who can influence the customers' purchase behavior for the benefit or loss of the other. If customers are brand loyal and a retailer does not carry a customer's preferred brand, the retailer may lose not only that customer's business for that product but for other products as well. Few supermarkets could afford not to carry Coca-Cola. Supermarkets will often put it on their shelves at zero margin as a "loss leader" just to drive store traffic. On the other hand, if customers are store loyal, manufacturers will be unable to reach certain consumers unless that retailer carries their product. The Whole Foods Supermarket chain has such customer loyalty and broad reach among the rapidly growing, high-income market of natural food enthusiasts that natural food manufacturers have little choice but to buy their way onto its shelves.

These illustrate the two clearly delineated extremes of manufacturer–retailer relationship called "pull" and "push" marketing—with loyal customers "pulling" preferred, known brands through the retailer, and marketers of unknown brands "pushing" the retailer to get their brands in front of customers. More specifically, a *pull strategy* involves heavy manufacturer advertising, personal selling, and/or other promotional expenditures to create end-customer preference for a brand. The goal is to motivate customers to seek out the brand, even if they must make other trade-offs, including switching to another retailer, to do so. Intel Inside® illustrates a phenomenally successful pull campaign in a category where end-consumers traditionally knew or cared little about the semiconductor chip within their computer. Every competitor of Intel used a push strategy. However, Intel successfully reached past computer manufacturers and retailers to create a preference for computers with its chip inside. That preference enables Intel to command a wholesale price premium and larger market share, and to more effectively execute a segmented pricing strategy across end-use applications.

Conversely, a *push strategy* involves relying on the channel partners to create a market for the manufacturer's product. Push strategies enable manufactures to delegate marketing, including the advertising and/or personal selling, of their product. That may involve the retailer promoting the brand or, at the extreme, allowing it to become just an invisible part of the retailer's promoted final offering. For example, the suppliers of coffee and pastries to Starbucks have no brand identity, even though the customer may have a preference for their product. Exhibit 11-2 summarizes the economics of the choice between a pull and a push approach.

CHANNEL PRICING FOR PULL BRANDS

Obviously, the pricing challenge is quite different for both the manufacturer and the retailer between pull and push marketing. When a pull strategy works well, the manufacturer is in the position to dictate the terms. Retailers need and want the brand to drive store traffic. A retail grocer's margins for leading brand name products are lower, despite higher retail prices, than for second tier and house brands. The pull effect reaches back though the distributor, who will carry a popular brand at a lower margin because retailers are demanding it. The cost of not having the pull brand is the potential to lose all of a customer's business.

	Push Channel Strategy	Pull Channel Strategy
EXHIBIT 11-2 Push Versus Pull Distribution Strategies		
Manufacturer economics	Deep wholesale discounts and promo fees are "variable" costs, which favor small-volume brands	Heavy advertising and mass marketing create high "fixed" costs, which favor high-volume brands
Channel member economics	High margins, high costs of sales, advertising, and/or service are shared by multiple brands	Low margins require making money by efficiently moving volume at minimum cost
Market types, ease of communication	Niche and diffuse markets difficult to target with mass communication	Mass-market appeal, or easily targeted (e.g., 18–24 years old) with mass communications
On-site augmentation required by channel	Moderate to high	Low to none
Distribution intensity	Selective	Intensive

Moreover, both the retailer and the distributor benefit from the faster turnover of inventory for a widely demanded pull brand.

A pull brand marketer can squeeze the retailer's margin both by offering a lower wholesale discount and by promoting the suggested retail price widely enough that retailers cannot easily exceed it. However, it makes sense to create volume and promotional incentives even while squeezing the channel margin. Otherwise, a retailer has the incentive to carry a brand, and even to advertise its availability, to attract customers to the store, but then to actively promote switching to push brands that have a higher margin. Fortunately, pull marketers can structure promotional incentives in ways that neutralize the retailer's incentive to "bait and switch," while costing much less than matching the margins of push brands. There are two options to structure volumes incentives for pull brands to match push brand margins.

The first option is the use of a step discount. Pull marketers often create step price discounts, or other incentives, based on the brand's share of a retailer's (or a distributor's) volume, rather than the absolute volume. For example, if the brand's share at a retailer exceeds 50 percent, its wholesale price is discounted to increase the retail margin by 1 percent; if brand share exceeds 70 percent, there may be an additional adjustment to increase the retail margin by 2 percent. Alternatively, these volume incentives can be in the form of added services. For example, the pull brand's advertising might mention the names of retailers that carry its product if the brand's share at that retailer exceeds 50 percent. The key is to set the hurdle to begin receiving these discounts at or just below the brand's average market share across retailers. This volume incentive structure enables the brand to captures a higher margin for the volume that loyal customers would have bought anyway, while creating an incentive for the retailer to encourage switching to the brand. For example, a brand with an incremental incentive may get better shelf space or be suggested by the retailer's sales associates.

The second option is a "back-end" rebate incentive. Pull marketers often create retailer-specific back-end rebate incentives to gain or defend share. Rebated volume incentives have advantages over wholesale step discounts. With step discounts, the retailer has the incentive to promise more volume than he can deliver to get a lower price. With rebates, the retailer must deliver on and document the brand share before receiving the rebate. The volume target for the rebate can also be made retailer specific, facilitating adjustment to differences such as the strength of competition in different regions, while still maintaining a uniform pricing policy and the appearance of price integrity. Finally, rebating facilitates focusing the discount on the incremental volume, thus reducing the total cost while maximizing the incentive.

For example, the manufacturer might offer a rebate equal to 1.5 percent of sales if the retailer can increase sales by at least 20 percent over quarter. This seems like a push tactic, and is, but only on the margin. The pull marketer who currently gets a 25 percent share of a retailer's or distributor's business simply because of end-consumer brand loyalty does not want to match push brand wholesale discounts for that volume. He wants to focus incentives on volume retention and growth. If the retail margin differential between a well-known pull brand and a push brand competitor were 4 percent, the pull brand manufacturer does not need to offer anything close to a 4 percent price cut to induce the retailer to favor the pull brand. Instead, offering a rebate of 1.5 percent only if the retailer increases the brand's share to 30 percent effectively gives the retailer a 9.0/5 percent margin increase on the incremental sales (1.5 percent $\times$ 30/5 = 4.5 percent), enough to counter the 4 percent advantage of the push brand. To use this as a defensive strategy for a brand under attack, simply set the rebate goal at or slightly below the brand's current share, making it very costly for the retailer to shift share to a lower cost competitor.

CHANNEL PRICING FOR PUSH BRANDS

When marketers rely on push marketing, they lack the leverage that pull marketers have in dictating their pricing to their channel partners. There are, nevertheless, strong reasons why many products—including some that are financially very successful—rely on a push strategy.

1. The costs are largely variable—being proportionate to the amount of sales and the number of retail distribution outlets. This is a big advantage for a product that is starting out small. The cost of an effective advertising campaign could be prohibitive.

2. The retailers have already targeted a diffuse market. In markets where demand is diffuse—few people are potential purchasers—the retailer (which may be a catalog or e-commerce company) has already identified

them. Either the target consumers already know where to buy or retailers own a highly coveted customer list. For sales of scuba equipment, aids to the physically impaired, and materials to people interested in do-it-yourself home repair, no advertising outlets exist to reach a majority of the potential buyers. All of the potential purchasers, however, will eventually need to visit a retailer or Web site, or read a catalog which, given an adequate incentive, can promote the product.

3. The retailers or others in the chain "augment" the product. Few people would pay the prices for Mary Kay cosmetics if they were available on a rack in a drug store. The value is in the Mary Kay experience of being "made up" in the privacy of one's home. Mary Kay creates that experience with a team of independent distributors who are motivated by, among other things, high margins.

4. Pull strategies require a broader range of sophisticated marketing expertise that a firm may lack. Pull brand managers must know not only who their end-customers are, but also understand why they buy. They must connect their offerings to benefits and communicate the value to end-customers, and they must create messages that can be indirectly communicated convincingly in limited space or time. It is simply a lot easier to understand the value your brand delivers to a much smaller number of channel members whom you can meet personally.

Given these considerations, it is not difficult to understand why manufacturers of products selling at the high end of a market often rely on a push strategy. Grohe sells faucets with unique style and durability, but does little advertising. Most people building their dream home, having never done it before, do not know why they should want a Grohe faucet selling at two or more times the retail price of a generic brand faucet. But Grohe would have a difficult time targeting advertising at people ready to make such a decision. However, a plumber or plumbing supply house can identify them. By establishing a retail margin that makes it much more profitable for the plumber to sell and install a Grohe than a generic faucet, they win the sales support they need to justify the price differential.

For push brands that simply require having access to the store where the customers are, manufacturers usually set a margin reflecting the industry standard for the type of retailer. Undifferentiated retailers receive that margin and nothing more. Large, high-volume retailers that control access to a lot of customers and whose support push brands need, unbundle their services and add charges to capture the value of their differentiation. Unless the brand is one of the share leaders in a push category, the retailer might charge a "slotting fee" even to reserve shelf space for the product. Otherwise, since consumers have little brand preference, it makes sense for retailers to limit the number of brands they carry to only the market leaders. Retailers also expect co-op advertising dollars to feature a push brand in the store's print advertising.

To motivate the retailer's individual sales employees, the manufacturer might offer "SPIFF," or incentive payments for the retailer's employees, to more aggressively promote their brand. This is common in businesses where customers require a lot of one-to-one sales support in making a decision, such as when selecting flooring or lighting products for a new home. So long as the brand also has a high retail margin, management of the retailer is happy for the manufacturer to pay SPIFF as the sales effort can increase what customers spend overall. Finally, large chains like Jewel and Walgreens, sell sales data—either directly to manufacturers or to intermediaries who pool and process it—enabling them to track their market shares.

While all the retail charges for push brand marketing can become substantial, the manufacturer is simply buying marketing services all in one place that pull brands buy elsewhere. If retailers can target the customers in ways that national brand advertising could not, and enable the manufacturer to share the cost of advertising across brands, the ability to market a brand by paying for "push" is still a good deal. That is why one of the premium brands of cosmetics, Kiehl's, does little advertising and instead chooses to market its products directly or through high-end retail channels such as Neiman-Marcus and Saks Fifth Avenue. The cost of reaching their small, but dedicated customer base through advertising would be prohibitive. The success of their high-end push strategy is evidenced by the fact that the company has been in existence for over 150 years. Still, the fact that push marketers buy marketing services from retailers does not mean that they do not need to think strategically about marketing, as the following discussion illustrates.

Resale Margin Maintenance

A key pricing challenge for push marketers is managing the inherent conflict between two drivers of volume: breadth of distribution and the motivation of the individual retailer to push the brand. Because buyers don't go looking to find a particular push brand, exposure to more of the potential buyers requires distribution in more of the possible retail outlets. So long as all that the push brand requires is exposure, like the house brands in a retail grocery, maximizing exposure only is fine. The conflict arises when push brands require more than just exposure. Many push brands require active sales or technical support (think high-end home entertainment systems, jewelry, or replacement storm windows).

Retailers are motivated to supply that support to the extent that, by raising consumers' perception of the product's value, they can earn higher margins from doing so. The conflict occurs because retailers can only expect to capture higher margins when they sell value if the customer is unable to buy the same brand at a discount from a retailer down the street or on the Internet. Customers could go to their local electronics retailer to compare the sound of different stereo speakers or view the picture quality of different large-screen TVs and thus learn of the superiority of some brands over others. Then, having made their decision that a better quality push brand is worth the price, they could go online to find someone who will discount the retail price. If the Internet marketer does not have the cost of displays, listening rooms, and knowledgeable salespeople, he can easily give away much of the high retail margin and still make a very profitable sale.

Obviously, the more this happens, the less likely it is the high-service retailer will display, push, or even continue to carry the brand.

To avoid this problem, manufacturers of such products would like to make their products widely available but then set minimum resale prices, ensuring each reseller a large enough margin to support services that enhance the product's value. Before 1976, manufacturers could legally set minimum resale prices in any state that passed a fair-trade law endorsing the practice. Since federal antitrust law no longer condones contracts enabling manufactures to dictate resale prices, they must either severely limit distribution or find a noncontractual way to enforce resale pricing and discounting policies.[1] Failure to do so results in manufacturers being under constant pressure from high-service retailers to lower wholesale prices so that the retailer can maintain margins. Without a price maintenance strategy, however, that margin gets quickly passed on to consumers by low-service retailers as more deeply discounted retail prices.

To maintain resale prices and the retailer's incentive to carry and promote a brand, a manufacturer can select the channel intermediaries with whom it will deal, and can make the resale price that they charge a criteria for continuing to ship product to them.[2] When a manufacturer offers co-op advertising dollars, it can specify that those dollars can be used only for advertisements that do not undercut the manufacturer's resale price policy. A manufacturer can also establish criteria for retailers that carry their products, such as that the retailer must devote some minimum amount of display space to the product or have an on-site repair facility. All these criteria are appreciated by those retailers who are effective push marketers because they discourage those that are not from carrying the push brand.

DISTRIBUTOR RELATIONSHIPS

As rapid transportation options have improved and large retailers have developed their own logistics capabilities, the traditional need for distributors to hold inventory and move boxes has declined. As a result, many have gone out of business. Survivors in many markets are thriving, however, because they offer additional services more efficiently than manufacturers or retailers can offer them on their own.

For example, as technologies evolve rapidly, many companies that develop them lack the expertise to understand where and how their products could be used by end-customers. They know simply that, for example, they have made a data storage device that is cheaper or that accesses data faster. On the other end, retailers and VARs often specialize in meeting the needs of narrow market segments; they are not experts in all the latest technological breakthroughs. A technology distributor can fill the gap with experts who try new products, figure out how to make them work together, and offer that knowledge to VARs who buy the components from them. They may also staff the telephone help line to support end-consumers having problems with the product.

Another example of a successful distributor who augments products with different services is Cardinal Health. Cardinal will take products from various medical manufacturers to make up a customized tray of medical items required at various points in a hospital. The tray might include all the items that Dr. Smith, a surgeon, has specified that he prefers to use when doing an appendectomy. If Dr. Jones prefers a different type of dressing or has different size hands, her tray will have different items. The cost of customized trays is not cheap, but saves the hospital more than the added cost because it does not have to store boxes of inventory, invest time pooling the items, and deal with the implications of mistakes.[3]

Distributors, because they can pool data from many transactions, are also often the first to see trends in product usage, which is valuable information to manufacturers, and to spot new sales opportunities, which is valuable to retailers and VARs. Small manufacturers and small retailers sometimes turn over their entire inventory management to a distributor. The distributor tells the manufacturer what models, sizes, or colors to make next and takes the entire run into its warehouse. On the other end, it monitors a retailer's inventories and, based on usage, decides what and how much of each item the retailer should stock locally and what it should not stock, but instead take orders for, that the distributor can ship directly to the customer on the retailer's behalf.

While some distributors in every market have been successful in finding valuable services that justify their existence, a smaller subset have priced those services effectively. The common mistake is to keep adding services of value to both manufacturers and retailers, but attempting to capture the value of those services in the product margin alone. The problem is that those who use the services most intensely are not necessarily those who buy the most product. High-service users therefore often drive more costs than revenues, while low-service users balk at paying premium margins. A common, and understandable, phenomenon is the retail customer who orders from a high-service distributor only products that require technical help to understand, that need to be shipped immediately, or that are not available elsewhere.

It is almost impossible for a distributor to capture the value of such services by simply asking the manufacturer to give a bigger wholesale discount, or asking the end-customer to pay a higher price. The value of services simply does not track closely enough with the value of product sales. The key to distributor profitability is in unbundling services and in rewarding customer behaviors that reduce the cost to serve them. It also lies in using services to build customer loyalty. Technology distributors charge the manufacturers of innovations to find end-use applications of their products and to support customers in adopting products for those applications. They may charge by the hour or for dedicated head count. By doing so, they need not worry that the customer may take their time and then ultimately buy the product through another distributor. They still get paid for the service from the manufacturer who still gets the sale. They are more likely to make the product sale as well because they can make it easier for customers to order from the distributor where they get technical advice.

Even when services are integrally tied to the product sale, the cost of the service can be unbundled. Distributors can charge a premium for rush orders, which retailers are usually willing to pay lest they lose a sale. They can add an optional premium to the price for inventory management—enabling the retailer not only to save the cost of ordering but also to optimize the profitability of their product mix. Small retailers are often willing to do this because the distributor's ability to learn from the experience of a large sample of retailers enables the distributor to predict better what mix of product will maximize the retailer's store traffic and the return on it's shelf space.

DRIVING VOLUME WITH CHANNEL PARTNERS

Complex channels create challenges and opportunities to use price to drive volume. Some involve using price to stimulate consumer trial, to change dealer behavior, and to gain access to high-volume power buyers who demand the lowest prices in return. In this section, we'll describe the risks and benefits of each option and suggestions for managing them.

DEALING TO INDUCE TRIAL

One of the most important strategic uses of pricing, especially when the product is new, is to induce trial. A buyer's first purchase represents more than just another sale; it is an opportunity to educate him or her about the product's attributes.[4] Since only people who are familiar with a product can become loyal repeat purchasers, inducing potential buyers to make their first purchase is a critical step in building sales. Although new products need to build sales quickly, even companies marketing established products face the problem that some educated buyers leave the market, some switch to other brands, and some simply forget what they have learned. Consequently, to maintain a fixed market share, manufacturers must regularly induce trial by new buyers.

A common tactic for inducing trial of repeat-purchase products is a promotional price deal. It makes sense for a firm to cut its price, even to an unprofitable level, for a first-time buyer because the firm benefits from a first purchase by much more than the revenue from that sale. A buyer who likes the brand becomes a repeat purchaser at its regular price, thereby beginning a stream of future income for the seller. The price deal is an investment in future sales.

Price deals through channels normally take one of four forms: trial offers, coupons, rebates, or free samples. To understand why manufacturers use these methods rather than simply cutting the explicit prices of their products, one needs to understand the objectives of the dealing firm. First, the manufacturer wants the promotional price cut to benefit the end-customer, not to add to the margin of a distributor or retailer. Even in categories with high promotional price elasticities, there must be a high likelihood of retailer pass-through and a low likelihood of forward buying for promotional pricing to be profitable.[5] Second, the manufacturer wants the end-consumer to perceive the price cut as a special, exceptional offer in order to minimize the perception that the product may be of lower quality because it is offered at a lower price. Third, the manufacturer wants to direct the price cut to first-time buyers and minimize the extent to which repeat buyers can take advantage of it to make multiple purchases. An explicit price cut usually fails to achieve these objectives, whereas one of the four common dealing tactics often can.

Trial offers are simple price cuts that the seller makes clear are temporary. Although trial offers are the cheapest way to offer a price promotion, the trick to making them successful is ensuring that the temporary wholesale price cut to the trade, usually in the form of an off-invoice allowance, actually gets passed through to the end-consumer and that the end-consumer actually perceives the lower price as a special deal. Usually these two objectives are accomplished with special packaging. When the package says in banner print "20¢ Off Regular Price" or "Special $1.99," consumer pressure compels the retailer to pass on the promised savings. Consumers are unlikely to interpret the low price as a signal of low quality when it reflects a discount that is clearly temporary. Sometimes, a trial offer can also meet the third objective, excluding repeat buyers. Magazines, for example, offer discount trial subscriptions at rates unavailable to current subscribers. For most products, however, separating new from repeat purchasers is not easy. Since this is not a major problem for new products, trial offers are used primarily for new product introductions.

Coupons meet all three of the objectives effectively, which explains their popularity as a method of dealing.[6] Not only does the consumer receive the discount while seeing clearly that the regular price is higher, but the coupon also limits the number of discounted purchases that repeat buyers can make. Moreover, coupons can often be distributed in ways that increase the probability that only first-time users will redeem them. For example, coupons for automatic dishwasher detergent are placed inside new dishwashers, and coupons for disposable diapers and other baby products are mailed to new parents.[7] Finally, a coupon makes buyers aware of a deal even when the product is not yet stocked in the store where they shop. Their desire to redeem the coupons can then pressure the store into placing an order.[8]

Coupons do have their drawbacks. Because they are inconvenient, coupon redemption rates are low among families in some demographic groups (those with high incomes or with both spouses working).[9] Moreover, the manufacturer's cost of coupons greatly exceeds the amount of the discount that the consumer receives. In addition to the cost of printing and distributing coupons, retailers must be paid for handling them, and clearinghouses must be paid for redeeming them. Finally, a high rate of fraudulent redemption, 20 percent on average but as much as 80 percent in some cases, adds to coupons' cost.[10]

Rebates have grown popular in recent years as a substitute for couponing. Rebates can meet all three objectives of dealing, but they have the disadvantage of being more costly to the consumer. The average value of a coupon is less than 50 cents. Few people would invest the time and postage to claim a rebate of the same value. Consequently, rebates are effective only when the dollar amount of the discount is large. Companies that sell multiple products, however, can often overcome this problem by requiring the purchase of a number of different products to claim a single large rebate. In addition to meeting all three of a manufacturer's objectives in dealing, the advantages of rebates are as follows:

- They avoid the problem of coupon counterfeiting and fraudulent redemption by retailers.
- They enable the firm to limit the offer to one per family, thus controlling the benefit to repeat purchasers.
- They often involve lower administrative costs than couponing, particularly when they cover multiple products.
- They enable the firm to develop a mailing list of deal-prone consumers that can be used for future promotions.
- Many consumers buy a product because of the rebate, but then fail to redeem it.[11]

The most effective and most costly deal is the *free sample*. A much larger percentage of consumers will use a free sample than will redeem a coupon, enabling the manufacturer to induce trial far more quickly and with broader coverage of the various demographic groups.

For example, when Lever Brothers introduced its Sunlight dishwashing detergent, it used free samples to gain trial in 70 percent of all households. In contrast, a typical coupon or rebate offer is redeemed by only about 5 percent of the targeted households. Nevertheless, the high cost of free samples makes them a profitable promotional tactic only for products that are purchased frequently, such as soaps or cigarettes, or those with very high contribution margins, such as computer software.[12]

DEFENSIVE DEALING

Over the past two decades, most consumer markets have moved from growth to maturity. Companies with strong brand images and profitable market shares should have recognized the need to change from growth-oriented to value-preserving strategies. Instead, many companies have offered larger and more frequent deals to sustain sales growth. Both researchers and managers have begun to suspect that such chronic dealing undermines consumer loyalties and increases marketing costs. Moreover, when the dealing is financed at the expense of advertising, the short-term boost to sales is often more than balanced by a long-term loss in brand equity.[13] Recent research suggests that promotions and dealing need to consider the type of product being promoted. For example, one study found that nonmonetary promotions, such as free gifts or sweepstakes, were particularly effective in increasing market share for high-end leisure products; the effect was smaller, but positive for low-end leisure products and high-equity utilitarian products. By contrast, monetary promotions, such as price cuts or free product, were particularly effective in increasing market share for high-end utilitarian products; the effect was smaller, but positive, for low-end leisure products.[14]

Although dealing is still a useful tactic for new brand introductions in mature markets, it generally does not make sense for established brands to meet the price deals of new competitors. There are three reasons for this. First, only part of an established brand's buyers will actually respond to a dealing firm's inducements to try its brand. Unfortunately, the firm defending an established brand does not know who among its buyers are potentially disloyal. It must offer all of them the defensive price cut in order to neutralize a competitor's deal. This puts the defending brand at a cost disadvantage if the dealing competitor has a smaller market share. Consider the case where the dealing brand has a 10 percent market share and the defending brand has a 90 percent market share, 5 percent of which is disloyal when presented with a deal. The dealing brand must offer the deal on two sales it would have made anyway in order to induce the switch of each additional sale from the established brand. This is because its current market share is twice the additional market share that it can induce to try its brand. In comparison, the defending firm must offer a defensive deal on seventeen sales that it would have made anyway in order to prevent disloyal buyers from trying the competing brand. This is because the loyal market share of the defending firm is seventeen times the share that it would lose if it did not meet the deal. Consequently, the defending firm must give up 8.5 times as much revenue to neutralize a deal as the dealing firm gives up to offer it.

Second, when a product's costs are primarily incremental and avoidable, firms can offer deals on small-share brands at little cost until customers respond to the deal and try the product. The defending firm, however, must bear the cost of a defensive deal each time it offers the deal to retain buyers' loyalty. Consequently, to the extent that costs are incremental and avoidable, a firm marketing a new brand can repeatedly offer attractive deals at little cost until it succeeds, whereas the established firm bears significant cost in repeatedly defending against it.

Third, as mentioned above, frequent dealing can tarnish a brand's image, thus reducing consumers' loyalty. Unless the established brand was already positioned as an economy product, the firm may have difficulty reestablishing its regular price without losing some previously loyal buyers.

Because of these disadvantages, price dealing is generally much more cost effective to induce trial for new brands or for those with small market shares than for established brands trying to prevent it. One exception to this is defensive deals that motivate end-users to stockpile inventories and thereby remove the end-user from the market for a sustained period of time. Packaged-goods marketers frequently use bonus packs, which contain significantly greater quantities of the product for the same price to thwart the price deals of competitors. These bonus packs appeal to already loyal customers, who have less incentive to pay attention to competitive price deals because the deal not only reduces the price per unit but also causes them to stock up with extra product from their regular brand.[15] Established brands can also use other marketing instruments with which they have a greater advantage. In the beer industry, for example, Heileman, Stroh, and Pabst found couponing an effective marketing tool for entering new geographical markets where their beers were unknown. But Anheuser-Busch and Miller, brewers of the most popular national brands, wisely chose not to respond with deals of their own. Instead, they recognized that they could defend market share more cost-effectively by increasing their advertising and distribution efforts because they enjoyed superior economies of scale in those activities.[16]

Defensive deals are occasionally advisable. Because costs in some markets are overwhelmingly fixed, a new firm offering a promotional deal on a new brand bears costs comparable to those of the defending firm, even if it makes no sales. In many markets, a premium image has so little effect on price sensitivity that the defending firm need not worry about cheapening it. In the airline industry, for example, costs are overwhelmingly fixed and buyers select flights more for convenience and service than for image. As a result, established firms on many routes successfully defend their markets by matching the promotional fares of new entrants.

Defensive dealing may also prove useful as a temporary segmentation technique during recessions. Coupon redemption rates increase during recessions and decline during recoveries.[17] In Chapter 4, we discussed how coupons offer one way to separate the price-sensitive segment for discounting. Often this can be done very cost-effectively by printing a coupon or rebate certificate on the package for use by consumers willing to take the time to redeem them. Since the price-sensitive segment grows during recessions, these deals can maintain the brand loyalty of customers who are temporarily more price sensitive, without undercutting margins to all customers. Prices can then be increased more easily after the recession simply by dropping the deal.

TRADE DEALING

A channel pricing tactic commonly used in push marketing, and occasionally in pull marketing as well, is the trade deal. *Trade deals* are temporary wholesale discounts to retailers from a product's regular wholesale price to achieve a specific short-term objective. Most often, they are used to gain the retailers' support during a promotional campaign. A push brand manufacturer may offer a trade deal in return for putting the product on an end-of-aisle display. Prominent displays can multiply the impact of a price promotion by a multiple of two to six times for frequently purchased products.

Both push and pull brand manufacturers wisely offer trade deals on products that they produce seasonally in order to induce retailers to stock up at the time of production. Canned foods, such as salmon, fruits, and some vegetables, are packed by manufacturers at one time of the year and then must be stored at significant cost for sales in the off-season. If retailers are willing to stock up during the production season in return for a discount less than the manufacturer's cost of holding inventory, such trade deals are a profitable tactic. Retailers are often willing to take advantage of such deals because (1) their inventory holding costs are sometimes lower than those of manufacturers since they fully utilize their storage space by purchasing different products on deal in different seasons, and (2) they can often induce consumers to stock up as well by passing on part of the trade deal as a price promotion of their own.[18] Occasionally, leading manufacturers also use trade dealing as a defense against the introduction of competing brands. If a temporary trade deal prompts retailers and consumers to load up with inventories of the leading brand, they will be more reluctant to take on still more inventories of a new brand. One advantage of defensive trade deals is that they are easier to adjust to reflect the precariousness of a brand's position in different stores and geographical areas.

Sometimes, however, increased inventory holding by retailers results in an unintended and undesirable effect of trade dealing. If a manufacturer offers retailers a trade deal to discount and advertise a product for 1 week, they may order more of the product than they can actually sell that week, enabling them to reduce their purchases in later weeks at the regular wholesale price. In fact, retailers are notorious for effectively converting manufacturers' trial offers and periodic sales into trade deals by ordering more than they can sell during the period of the retail price cut. This "forward buying" can unnecessarily raise distribution cost for both retailers and distributors by a combined 1 to 2 percent of sales.

Top management must also be wary of the effect that trade dealing has on incentives for product managers. Trade deals, like end-consumer price promotions, are sometimes used to meet short-term goals that arguably are not in the firm's long-run interest. When brand managers are rewarded for meeting sales quotas, they may use quick end-of-quarter trade promotions to reach their goals. Although the resulting stocking up by retailers depresses later sales at higher prices, that may be of little concern to some brand managers who may hope to be promoted before the effects of overdealing catch up with them. The money for these trade deals is often diverted from the advertising budget. Although advertising has less of a short-term effect on sales than a trade deal, it probably has a much larger impact on long-term brand equity with consumers. Moreover, as discussed below, the demand "pull" from a manufacturer's advertising reduces a retailer's power to set prices and dictate terms. Such short-run thinking is probably not typical in most firms, but it is sufficiently widespread to cause experts in industry, academia, and government to express alarm.[19]

NEGOTIATING WITH POWER BUYERS

Big retailers have used the promise of volume to get a better deal and manufacturers have complained about them since the early days of the supermarket and the Sears catalog. Over the past decade, however, the power to negotiate channel prices has shifted strongly toward a small subset of retailers accounting for a large amount of share. Just since the mid 1990s, the "big box" retailers like Wal-Mart, Target, Home Depot, and Lowes have increased their total dollar share of North American retail sales from 10 to over 25 percent.[20] Smaller but equally powerful retailers, like CompUSA and Staples, dominate access to particular submarkets. Even in markets where the end-customer is a business, a few buyers have come to control large amounts of volume. Most hospitals belong to one of two large "buying groups" that extract price concessions before a manufacturer can become an approved supplier to group members. Carpet buyers have similarly formed groups to pool volume and extract discounts. While the trend began in North America, it has become a worldwide phenomenon, with discounters consolidating volume even in formerly restrictive markets like Germany and Japan.

Initially, many power buyers gained share by merging retail and distribution functions and, by coordinating them better, radically cutting inventory management and transportation costs. By passing those savings on to consumers, they drove volume for the benefit of everyone but their less efficient competitors. As their shares have grown larger, however, they have gained an additional advantage—the ability to negotiate differentially lower pricing from manufacturers. As destination stores, separate from competitors and covering an ever broader range of items, they are more likely to be the only store that a consumer will visit. With more customers shopping at Wal-Mart and Home Depot as their only store, the power of even a strong brand to drive store traffic is diminished. A highly advertised brand will be preferred once someone is in the Wal-Mart but, as Wal-Mart carries more and more leading brands, it becomes less likely that a Wal-Mart shopper will make a second stop elsewhere just to pick up a preferred brand that Wal-Mart does not carry. High-quality brands still need to bear the cost of advertising to justify their premium retail prices, but they cannot automatically expect the big box stores to pay for part of that cost with a smaller retail margin.

Wal-Mart, Home Depot, and the like know they have that power and use it in negotiations. As one supplier reported being told by a big box purchasing agent, "We expect your price to us to cover your costs. Earn your profits from somebody else." Obviously, with these stores continuing to broaden their product line and to increase the number of locations, it will remain increasingly difficult for manufacturers to try to grow profitably. So what can and should they do? First, stay realistic. The effect of big box retailers is to reduce the value of brands, and nothing that a manufacturer can do is going to turn back the clock. The goal is to find the most viable, profitable strategy for your brand within a world of bigger customers who can control more volume.

Many companies that were seduced by the big volume of power buyers have lost their profitability as a result. Their mistake was to think of power buyer volume as purely incremental. While for push brands it may be, for pull brands it definitely is not. Pull brands have value for retailers competing with the big box stores precisely because some people who shop at Wal-Mart or Home Depot will still go to another store to get a preferred brand of cosmetics, paint, or whatever. Other stores will pay more than the power buyers precisely because the brand can draw a buyer to them. For example, Benjamin Moore paints have high value to local hardware stores and home centers not just because they have high customer loyalty, but also because they are not available at Home Depot or Lowes.

Some companies initially seduced by the volume in the power buyers ultimately found better profits among retailers who support their differentiation. Timbuk2, a small manufacturer of unique and well-made laptop and other shoulder bags, began selling through big volume computer stores like CompUSA at lower margins. While volume increased, it was not enough to justify the loss of margin and volume from specialty stores. After just one holiday season, Timbuk2 withdrew from its mass-market channels and instead strengthened its relationships with higher-priced specialty retailers—Urban Outfitters, the Discovery Channel Store, REI, and the Apple Store, where its margins and theirs were much higher. It then looked elsewhere for growth, developing line extensions into women's specialty fashion stores, sporting goods stores, and other stores frequented by fashion conscious, more affluent customers.[21]

When the retail "buyer" is nothing more than a buying group, which qualifies and approves sellers to members but does not actually make purchases, the real value is even less. Unless the product is a commodity with no end-customer preference, a seller can win business from buying group members even if not "approved." The members that will continue to purchase are the largest buyers whom the buying group can least afford to exclude but with whom the seller can most cost effectively negotiate without the group. Moreover, without the constraints of the buying groups' rules and the cost of its fees, the manufacturer can offer even better deals to its members. Buying groups provide a lot of value to small brands trying to become known, but have profited from established brands usually just by being smarter negotiators.

Still, in many markets, power buyers control so much volume that one cannot grow without them. For push brands, without the volume to justify large marketing expenditures, the broad distribution and access to volume that power buyers offer may be the key to profitable growth. Here is how others have made that choice and still preserved profitability.

MAKE POWER BUYERS COMPETE

Many companies with strong brand preference miss a big opportunity by framing the strategic issue poorly. They ask themselves whether they should continue with their traditional retail channel targeting less price-sensitive customers or sell to power buyers with their high volumes at lower margins. This misses a third option: sell to one power buyer in a segment exclusively giving it a pull advantage over competing power buyers. Martha Stewart certainly got higher margins from Kmart because of her exclusive contract than she would have gotten from selling Martha Stewart products to all big chains. The attached sidebar describes how an interesting small company called Imagitas is beating power buyers at their own game by exploiting the power of its product to give a competitive advantage to whichever buyer has it exclusively.

IMAGITAS GETS PAID FOR ITS UNIQUE VALUE

Every year approximately 44 million households move in the United States. They spend more money in 3 months on their new home ($7,100 on average, excluding real estate fees) than established residents spend in a 4-year period. Most of this "new nest hyperspending" occurs within 1 to 4 weeks following the move. Moreover, new household members identify and become loyal to new and more convenient stores: 30 percent change health clubs, 35 percent change garden shops or nurseries, 36 percent change banks, 50 percent change dry cleaners, 44 percent change grocery stores, and 31 percent change hardware stores. Tapping this lucrative market is extremely valuable to a broad variety of retail merchants.

Imagitas, a fast-growing marketing service company, controls the channel gateway to the movers market via an exclusive relationship with the U.S. Postal Service. Imagitas prints and distributes the official change-of-address form and confirmation letter on behalf of the U.S. Postal Service. Through these "products" they can deliver advertisements, offers, and opt-in services to valuable moving consumers immediately before and after their move. Essentially, if you want to sell to recent movers, the best way to do so is through Imagitas.

Imagitas creates value for advertisers by efficiently channeling customer sales volume through its exclusive channel partners, and sets prices based on this exclusive value. For example, for a national retail client Imagitas identified and quantified the following key value drivers:*

Retained Customers–Move Related Spending	$9 million in post-move gross sales, $1,170,000 in profit contribution	Ensure existing customers don't switch to a competitor during the move. Retain customers entering the hyper-spend period after the move (Weeks 1-4)
Acquired Customers–Move Related Spending	$11 million in post move gross sales, $1,430,000 in profit contribution	Steal consumers away from competitors during the hyper-spend period after the move (Weeks 1-4)
Loyal Customers– Annual Spending	$35 million in annual gross sales, annual profit contribution of $4,550,000	Lock-in recurring revenue from consumers who establish entrenched shopping habits & loyalties shortly after the move

*Values are disguised.

Imagitas then estimates total economic value ($7,150,000 for this partner), converts to per household terms, and sets price relative to the value actually driven to the channel partner. Partners pay higher rates per household for higher actual response rates (more customers and conversions), and lower rates for lower response rates.

Imagitas has defined its own pricing policy that maximizes the value of its franchise. It avoids having its value diminished through negotiations with power buyers, although its client base includes many of the power buyers in their categories including Home Depot, Bank of America, and CVS. Its pricing policy involves giving category exclusivity for 1 to 3 years to the highest bidder when a contract comes up for renewal. For example, a national retailer such as Linens-n-Things can lock out competitors by buying a category exclusivity contract for either 1 year, or 1 year plus an option for an additional 1 or 2 years. Because all contracts expire at the latest in 3 years, the category is constantly put up for solicitation among category competitors, causing them to consider carefully and regularly the value to them of Imagitas' access to this key channel. The prices competitors pay to access the Imagitas' service keep going up. The company grew revenues from this product by 40 percent over the last decade, with an average renewal rate of 90 percent.

QUANTIFY THE VALUE TO THE RETAILER
Imagitas also illustrates how to quantify and communicate the value of differentiation. There are many ways that a brand can bring differential value to a big box retailer. Even if the retailer already has someone as a customer, the brand can drive store visit frequency. Disposable diapers are very valuable to Wal-Mart because their bulk requires frequent visits from a valuable, high-spending demographic group. A large manufacturer that is capable of serving power buyers everywhere it operates also reduces acquisition costs for such buyers.

ELIMINATE UNNECESSARY COSTS
The most difficult challenge to manage is trying to serve both high-volume power buyers who are unwilling to pay for your pull marketing efforts, and non-power buyers who value your brand because you support its marketing. Companies that profitably serve power buyers often specialize in doing so, eliminating costs of marketing and distribution. Shaw Industries, the largest carpet supplier in North America, squeezed costs from fiber production, carpet manufacture, and distribution by aligning itself totally to sell massive volume though Home Depot, Lowes, and large retail carpet buying groups.

SEGMENT THE PRODUCT OFFERING
There is no need to offer exactly the same product through a power buyer and through traditional channels where there is a conflict. Although John Deere sells products through Home Depot, it does not sell exactly the same products as through distributors. In the case of some packaged goods, only large sizes are available though Wal-Mart, Target, and other big box retailers. These steps obviously do not entirely prevent the potential cannibalization, but they do reduce it.

RESIST "DIVIDE AND CONQUER" TACTICS
Power buyers get their power from their ability to deny a brand or product line any volume through their stores or buying group. The key to their success is to structure the discussion as being about the pricing of each of the manufacturer's products individually. As a result, they maximize the competition for each product line and minimize any negotiating benefit that the supplier gets from offering a full line. Thus a medical buying group will tell a medical products manufacturer with nine product lines that there will be nine separate buying decisions, occurring at different times, for each product line. The implication for the seller is that, in the absence of the best price for each, it could end up with a few orphaned products that are excluded from the buying group's distribution channel.

Recall our discussion of pricing policies in Chapter 6, and do not react passively to purchasing policies that undermine your advantages; proactively set policies of your own. When a large medical products company was confronted with these divide and conquer tactics, it simply returned multiple bid forms for each product with different prices, adding a line to the top margin of each specifying the conditions under which those prices would apply. The lowest applied only if all the manufacturer's products were approved by the buying group, while the highest would apply if only a subset were approved. The buying group hated this tactic, but the seller maintained its response, explaining how the value of the channel to the seller was vastly reduced without complete acceptance. Recognizing the cost of losing all the seller's products, some of which had large market share among members, the buying group approved all the products.

Summary

Although the principles of value-based pricing remain the same within channels, channel relationships add complexity to all elements of the pricing problem. The value that a seller need consider and communicate to a buyer is more than just the value of the product to the ultimate user. It is also the value represented by one channel partner over another in revenues that can be achieved because of increased access to a market and in costs that can be avoided because of services that the channel partner delivers. Such value may go both ways in a single transaction, making ambiguous who is really the buyer and who the seller.

The pricing challenge is quite different for the manufacturer selling a pull brand, whose brand has a reputation supported by a marketing effort from which channel partners want to benefit, and a push brand for which the manufacturer is buying access and marketing from the channel partners. For pull brands, the goal of pricing is to ensure that the manufacturer captures the value in sales despite its lower margins for the channel. For push brands, the goal is to create incentives for sellers to carry and promote the brand, ideally while still distributing the brand widely through competitive channels. When the push brand requires more than just in-store availability, the key to making that strategy work is usually a plan to maintain resale margins.

Channels also create opportunities for using price deals to achieve objectives, such as filling the channel to block a competitor or inducing the channel to absorb the cost of holding inventories during peak production. Channels also create challenges in using price to influence the behavior of end-customers, such as inducing them to try a new brand. The risk is always that the distributor or retailer will absorb the deal itself, increasing its margin without driving more sales. Various tactics for dealing can overcome these and other challenges in offering deals.

Finally, growing market share of power buyers creates new challenges for manufacturers. Power buyers expect to negotiate lower wholesale prices than their competitors receive even from the sellers of pull brands. Power buyers have buyers trained in ways to manage the buying process to their benefit. Surviving in a market with such a channel requires dispassionately evaluating whether the access such power buyers offer is really consistent with a brand's value proposition, and rejecting the power buyer path if it is not, despite the potential volume. If one decides that such a channel is compatible with the brand's marketing, then the manufacturer must have a strategy to preserve its profitability despite the power and negotiating tactics of those buyers.

Notes

1. For a summary of the legal status of resale price management at the time of this publication, and the steps needed to keep any restrictions within the law, see section entitled Vertical Price Fixing in Chapter 14. Since case law changes, it is always wise to get a legal opinion before initiating a strategy.

2. Resale price was not an acceptable criterion for cutting off supply to a retailer or distributor until the Supreme Court overturned that precedent in a landmark case in 1988. See *Business Electronics Corp. v. Sharp Electronics Corp.*, 488 U.S. 717 (1988).

3. For more discussion of the different types of innovative services that Cardinal Health offers, enabling them to grow profitably while competitors have failed, see Adrian Slywotzky and Richard Wise, *How to Grow When Markets Don't* (New York: Warner Books, 2003), pp. 18–40.

4. Of course, this is only true to the extent that a brand actually has differentiating attributes that a buyer can learn by sampling. House brands and generic groceries, for example, do not have price promotions precisely because they lack differentiating attributes that buyers could learn enough about through sampling. Their appeal is their price.

5. Chakravarhi Narasimhan, Scott A. Neslin, and Subrata K. Sen, "Promotional Elasticities and Category Characteristics," *Journal of Marketing*, 60 (April 1996), pp. 17–30.

6. See Russell Bowman, *Couponing and Rebates: Profit on the Dotted Line* (New York: Lebhar-Friedman Books, 1980), pp. 2–3.

7. Checkout coupon systems also, such as Checkout Coupon of Catalina Marketing, automatically issue coupons during supermarket-check-out activities to purchasers of competing products.

8. See William Nigut, Sr., "Is the Boom in Cents-Off Couponing Going to Burst?" *Advertising Age* (December 15, 1980), pp. 41–44.

9. Robert C. Blattberg and Scott A. Neslin, *Sales Promotion: Concepts, Methods, and Strategies* (Upper Saddle River, NJ: Prentice Hall, 1990); William Massy and Ronald Frank, "Short-Term Price and Dealing Effects in Selected Market Segments" *Journal of Marketing Research*, 2 (May 1965), pp. 175–185; David Montgomery, "Consumer Characteristics Associated with Dealing: An Empirical Example," *Journal of Marketing Research*, 8 (February 1971), pp. 118–120: Robert Blattbert et al., "Identifying the Deal-Prone Segment," *Journal of Marketing Research*, 15 (August 1978), pp. 369–377.

10. "Coupon Scams Are Clipping Companies," *Business Week* (June 15, 1992), pp. 110–111.

11. See Toni Mack, "Rebate Madness," *Forbes* (February 13, 1984), pp. 76–77.

12. Software suppliers for mainframe computers sell systems for tens of thousands of dollars. They can produce copies, however, for only a few hundred dollars. To enable potential buyers to learn the value of these systems, they sometimes offer free samples of the software, but with a built-in subroutine that destroys the program after a limited time.

13. Charles Hinkle, "The Strategy of Price Deals," *Harvard Business Review*, 43 (July–August 1965), pp. 75–85; C. A. Scott, "The Effects of Trial and Incentives on Repeat Purchase Behavior," *Journal of Marketing Research*, 13 (August 1976), pp. 263–269; Joe Dodson, Alice Tybout, and Brian Sternthal, "Impact of Deals and Deal Retraction on Brand Switching," *Journal of Marketing Research*, 15 (February 1978), pp. 72–78; John Philip Jones, "The Double Jeopardy of Sales Promotions," *Harvard Business Review* (September–October 1990), p. 146; David A. Aaker, *Managing Brand Equity* (New York: Free Press, 1992).

14. Pierre Chandon, Brian Wansink, and Gilles Laurent, "A Benefit Congruency Framework of Sales Promotion Effectiveness," *Journal of Marketing*, 64 (October 2000), pp. 65–81.

15. Kusum L. Ailawadi, Scott A. Neslin, and Karen Gedenk, "Pursing the

Value-Conscious Consumer; Store Brands Versus National Brand Promotions," *Journal of Marketing,* 65(1) (January 2001), pp. 71–89; Brian Wansink, R. J. Kent, and S. J. Hoch. "An Anchoring and Adjustment Model of Purchase Quantity Decisions," *Journal of Marketing Research,* 35 (February 1998), pp. 71–81.

16. Robert Reed, "Beer Couponing Foams to the Top," *Advertising Age* (February 21, 1983), pp. 10, 71.

17. Scott Hume, "Coupons Set Record But Pace Slows," *Advertising Age,* 64 (February 1, 1993), p. 25; Elliot Zweibach, "Coupon Redemptions Increase 10 Percent."

18. Even when retailers do not receive manufacturer trade deals, they may still offer deals to get consumers to stock up on certain items. This can pay if it reduces a retailer's inventory cost by more than the cost of the deal. See Robert C. Blattberg, Gary D. Eppen, and Joshua Lieberman, "A Theoretical and Empirical Evaluation of Price Deals for Consumer Nondurables," *Journal of Marketing,* 45 (Winter 1981), pp. 116–129.

19. Monci Jo Williams, "The No-Win Game of Price Promotion," *Fortune* (July 11, 1983), pp. 93–102; Robert D. Buzzell, John A. Quelch, and Walter J. Salmon, "The Costly Bargain of Trade Promotion," *Harvard Business Review* (March–April 1990), pp. 141–149; Jakki J. Mohr and George S. Low, "Escaping the Catch-22 of Trade Promotion Spending," *Marketing Management* 2(2) (1993), pp. 31–39.

20. Robert J. Frank et al., "Competing in a Value-Driven World," McKinsey & Company North American Retail Practice (February 2003); Tekla Back, Kelly Haveron et al., "Winning in a Value-Driven World," McKinsey & Company North American Retail Practice (February 2005).

21. Andrew Tilin, "Bagging the Right Customers," *Business 2.0* (May 2005), pp. 56–57.

12

PRICING OVER THE PRODUCT LIFE CYCLE

Adapting Strategy in an Evolving Market

Products, like people, typically pass through predictable phases. A product is conceived and eventually "born;" it "grows" as it gradually gains in buyer acceptance, eventually it "matures" as it attains full buyer acceptance, and then it ultimately "dies" as it is discarded for something better. There are, of course, exceptions to this process. Death sometimes comes prematurely, dashing expectations before they even begin to materialize; youth sometimes extends inordinately, deceiving the unwary into thinking it can last forever. Still, the exceptions notwithstanding, the typical life pattern affords one a chance to understand the present and anticipate the future of most products. Such understanding, anticipation, and preparation make up a firm's long-run strategic plan. Profitable pricing is the bottom line measure of that plan's success.

The market defined by the introduction of a new product evolves through four phases: development, growth, maturity, and decline, as Exhibit 12-1 illustrates.[1] In each of its phases, the market has a unique personality. Accordingly, one's pricing strategy must vary if it is to remain appropriate, and one's tactics must vary if they are to remain effective.

NEW PRODUCTS AND THE PRODUCT LIFE CYCLE

New products play an integral, albeit frequently misunderstood, role in the product life cycle. Every product life cycle begins with the launch of an innovative new product. When the Apple iPod first hit store shelves in 2002, it transformed the way that consumers purchased, stored, and consumed music. Today, the market for portable music players with electronic storage capacity is in the growth stage of the product life cycle with few signs of reaching maturity any time soon. Whereas all product life cycles begin with the launch of a new product, the converse is not always true—not all new products start a new life cycle. Companies

EXHIBIT 12-1 Sales and Profits over the Product's Life from Inception to Demise

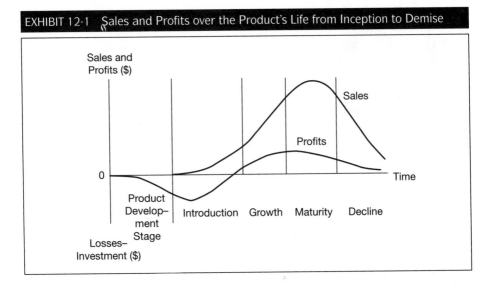

frequently launch new products at the maturity stage to refine their differentiation relative to the many competitors in the market. Even when a new product provides a completely new benefit, it may not be an innovation from the standpoint of buyers. For example, drugs are so readily accepted as cures in our culture that new ones are generally adopted with little hesitation by both doctors and patients. Similarly, most new consumer package goods products and business manufacturing products represent incremental improvements to existing products in a mature product category. This distinction between innovative new products early in the life cycle versus incremental improvements to existing products in mature markets is an important one because the focus for pricing strategy changes depending on the stage.

Understanding the unique aspects of pricing new products, regardless of the stage of the life cycle, is crucial for a number of reasons. First, new products represent a primary source of organic volume and profit growth and avoiding pricing mistakes can have both short and long-term impact on financial performance. If priced too high at launch, a new product will fail to achieve the volume necessary to maintain short-term profitability. Conversely, if priced too low, a new product *may* achieve its volume targets while failing to deliver sufficient profits. The later scenario, pricing too low at launch, can have long-term implications for future profit growth because existing products are the primary reference price for future products. As we explained in Chapter 7, customers with a low reference price will frame the purchase as a loss, leading to greater price sensitivity and lower willingness-to-pay.

A second reason that makes new product pricing especially important is that new product launch creates an excellent opportunity to reengage with customers to change what and how they purchase. Customers are less knowledgeable about new products and, hence, must educate themselves about new features, benefits, and ultimately value that the product might deliver. This lack of knowledge represents an opportunity and a challenge for marketers. The opportunity stems from the fact that customers are more receptive to new value communications, price metrics, policies, and price points. As a result, new product launches represent one of the best opportunities to introduce value-based pricing to a market because customers are prepared for and, even expecting, change. The challenge stems from the fact that customers are less knowledgeable about the value of the product and, hence, have higher perceived risk and greater price sensitivity. Striking a balance between higher price sensitivity due to perceived risk and the importance of maintaining appropriately high prices to maximize profits makes new product pricing challenging. Moreover the balance changes over the product life cycle. Marketers who do not understand how to manage this balancing act risk lower profits and lower revenue growth.

PRICING THE INNOVATION FOR MARKET INTRODUCTION

An innovation is a product so new and unique that buyers find the concept somewhat foreign. It does not yet have a place in buyers' lifestyles or business practices. The first automobiles, vacuum cleaners, and prepackaged convenience foods initially had to overcome considerable buyer apathy grounded in a lack of awareness of the benefits offered. The first business computers had to overcome skepticism bordering on hostility. Today, innovations from wireless Internet to hybrid fuel vehicles have encountered similar consumer reluctance, despite their legitimate promise of substantial value. An innovation requires buyers to alter the way they evaluate satisfying their needs. Consequently, before a product can become a success, its market must be developed through the difficult process of buyer education.

By definition, most customers know little about an innovative product and how it might meet their needs in new ways. Hence, successful launches of innovations hinge upon the education process that customers undergo. An important aspect of that educational process is called information diffusion. Most of what individuals learn about innovative products comes from seeing and hearing about the experiences of others.[2] The diffusion of that information from person to person has proved especially influential for large-expenditure items, such as consumer durables, where buyers take a significant risk the first time they buy an innovative product. For example, an early study on the diffusion of innovations found that the most important factor influencing a family's first purchase of a window air conditioner was neither an economic factor such as income nor a need factor such as exposure of bedrooms to the sun. The most important factor was social interaction with another family that already had a window air conditioner.[3] This finding has been replicated in dozens of markets ranging from consumer electronics to business computers.

Recognition of the diffusion process is extremely important in formulating pricing strategy for two reasons: First, when information must diffuse through a population of potential buyers, the long-run demand for an innovative product at any time in the future depends on the number of initial buyers. Empirical studies indicate that demand does not begin to accelerate until the first 2 to 5 percent of potential buyers adopt the product.[4] The attainment of those initial sales is often the hardest part of marketing an innovation. Obviously, the sooner the seller can close those first sales, the sooner he or she will secure long-run sales and profit potential.

Second, the "innovators," people who try the new product early, are not generally a random sample of buyers. They are people particularly suited to evaluate the product before purchase. In many cases, they are also people to whom the later adopters, or "imitators," look for guidance and advice. However, even innovators know little about how attributes or major attribute combinations should be valued. Value communications and effective promotional programs can, therefore, readily influence which attributes drive purchase decisions and how those attributes are valued. Identifying the innovators and making every effort to ensure that their experience is positive is an essential part of marketing an innovation.[5]

What is the appropriate strategy for pricing an innovative new product? To answer that question, it is important to recognize that consumers' price sensitivity when they first encounter an innovation bears little or no relationship to their long-run price sensitivity. Most buyers are relatively price sensitive when facing a new innovation because they may not even recognize the need for it until they learn of the product's benefits. Moreover, they lack a reference for determining what would constitute a fair or bargain price and this uncertainty leads to higher price sensitivity. While most potential customers are price sensitive at the introductory stage of the life cycle, there generally is a small group of well-informed consumers, called innovators, which are generally not deterred by high prices.

Given the problem of buyer ignorance, the firm's primary goal in the market development stage is to educate potential buyers concerning the product's worth through effective price and value communications as described in Chapter 5. Thus it is important to consider the value message that various list price strategies send to the market. If the seller plans a skim-pricing strategy, the list price should be near the relative value that price-insensitive buyers will place on the product. If the seller plans a neutral strategy, the list price should be near the relative value for the more typical potential user. The seller of an innovation should not set a list price for market penetration, however, since the low price sensitivity of uninformed buyers will make that strategy ineffective and may, due to the price–quality effect, damage the product's reputation. In addition to using list price, marketers must consider other value communication approaches.

Communicating Value with Trial Promotions

Deciding what the list price should be and what price first-time buyers actually pay are entirely separate questions. Determining the actual price that first-time buyers pay depends on the relative cost of different methods for educating buyers about the product's benefits. If the product is frequently purchased, has a low incremental production cost, and its benefits are obvious after just one use, the cheapest and most effective way to educate buyers may be to let them sample the product. For example, America Online built its commanding market share by sending every family in America a mailing, including a diskette, for a 30-day, free trial membership.

Not all innovative products can be economically promoted by price-induced sampling, however. Many innovations are durable goods for which price-cutting to induce trial is rarely cost-effective. A seller can hardly afford to give the product away and then wait years for a repeat purchase. Moreover, many innovative products, both durables and nondurables, will not immediately reveal their value when sampled once. Few people who sampled smoke alarms, for example, would find them so satisfying that they would yearn to buy more and encourage their friends to do the same. And many innovations (e.g., web-enabled cell phones) require that buyers learn skills before they can realize the product's benefits. Without a marketing program to convince buyers that learning those skills is worth the effort and strong support to ensure that they learn properly, few buyers will sample at any price, and fewer still will find the product worthwhile when they do. In such cases, price-induced sampling does not effectively establish the product's worth in buyers' minds. Instead, market development requires more direct education of buyers before they make their first purchases.

COMMUNICATING VALUE WITH DIRECT SALES

For innovations that involve a large dollar expenditure per purchase, education usually involves a direct sales force trained to evaluate buyers' needs and to explain how the product will satisfy them. The first refrigerators, for example, were sold door-to-door to reluctant buyers. The salesperson's job was to help buyers imagine the benefits that a refrigerator offered, beyond those that an ice chest was already capable of providing. Only then would those first buyers abandon tradition to make a large capital expenditure on new, risky technology. Business buyers are equally skeptical of the value of new innovations. In the 1950s, most potential users of airfreight service thought they had no need for such rapid delivery. American Airlines built the market for this new innovation by offering free logistics consultation. American's sales consultants showed potential buyers how this high-priced innovation in transportation could replace local warehouses, thereby actually saving money.[6] They taught the shippers how to see their distribution problems differently, from a perspective that revealed the previously unrecognized value of rapid delivery by American's planes.

When the innovation is more complicated than refrigeration or airfreight, even a convincing evaluation of buyers' needs may leave them too uncertain about the product's benefits to adopt it. For example, in the early 1990s enterprise software was considered quite a risky purchase because of the high degree of uncertainty about the ability to integrate the software into the company's IT architecture to do the billing, payroll, and production scheduling that the salesperson claimed it could do. SAP, a market leader in enterprise software, increased the business adoption rate of enterprise software by mitigating this source of uncertainty. SAP did so by providing new customers access to successful installations and by partnering with integration firms to ensure successful implementation. The result was that sales of SAP's enterprise software increased ninefold in the mid-nineties.

Neither American Airlines nor SAP priced their products cheaply despite their desire for rapid sales growth. Instead, they educated their markets, showing why their products were worth the price, and they aided buyers' adoption to minimize the risk of failure. They funded these high levels of education and service with the high prices buyers paid for the perceived value of the products. DuPont has employed this same high-price, high-promotion strategy in introducing numerous synthetic fabrics and specialty plastics. Apple employed it in developing the market for personal computers and storable digital music devices and the most successful marketers of industrial robots are using it today.[7]

MARKETING INNOVATIONS THROUGH DISTRIBUTION CHANNELS

Not all products have sufficiently large sales per customer to make direct selling practical. This is particularly true of innovative products that are sold indirectly through channels of distribution. However, the problem of educating buyers and minimizing their risk does not go away when the product is handed over to a distributor. It simply makes the need to rely on an independent distribution network problematic. The innovator must somehow convince the distributors who carry the product to promote it vigorously. One way to do this is with low wholesale pricing to distributors. The purpose of the low wholesale prices is not for distributors to pass the discounts on to consumers. The purpose is to leave distributors and retailers with high margins, giving them an incentive to promote the product with buyer education and service. While that works whenever distribution is relatively exclusive, there is the risk whenever distribution is less restricted that competition will simply cause the extra margin to be passed on in price discounts, thus losing the promotional incentive. To overcome that challenge, innovators may keep the margins at normal levels but pay incentive fees for stocking new products, for co-op advertising, for in-store displays, for premium shelf space, and for on-site service and demonstration. They may also offer incentives directly to the middleman's salespeople for taking the time to understand and promote the product. For example, telecommunications companies successfully introduced cell phone service by giving end-customers and retailers substantial discounts on the phones (often the discount was 100 percent) in exchange for 1- to 2-year service subscriptions. Today, cell phone penetration is over 65 percent in Europe with that rate expected to near 100 percent within 5 years.

PRICING NEW PRODUCTS FOR GROWTH

Once a product concept gains a foothold in the marketplace, the pricing problem begins to change. Repeat purchasers are no longer uncertain of the product's value since they can judge it from their previous experience. First-time buyers can rely on reports from innovators as the process of information diffusion begins. In growth, therefore, the buyer's concern about the product's utility begins to give way to a more calculating concern about the costs and benefits of alternative brands. Unless a successful innovation is unusually well protected from imitation, the market is ripe for the growth of competition. As competition begins to break out in the innovative industry, both the original innovator and the later entrants begin to assume competitive positions and prepare to defend them. In doing so, each must decide where it will place its marketing strategy on the continuum between a pure differentiated product strategy and a pure cost leadership strategy.[8]

With a differentiated product strategy, the firm focuses its marketing efforts on developing unique attributes (or images) for its product. In growth, the firm must quickly establish a position in research, in production, and in buyer perception as the dominant supplier of those attributes. Then, as competition becomes more intense, the uniqueness of its product creates a value effect that attenuates buyers' price sensitivity, enabling the firm to price profitably despite increasing numbers of competitors. Apple created such a reputation during the growth stage of computers with its use-friendly user interface, proprietary operating system, and distinct product designs. As a result, Apple has always carried a premium relative to Windows-based machines with similar capabilities. Intel did this for its chips, creating a customer perception that a computer was more reliable with "Intel inside." Paccar's heavy-duty trucks carry a premium from the reputation the company built for exceptional reliability and style. With a cost leadership strategy, the firm directs its marketing efforts toward becoming a low-cost producer. In growth, the firm must focus on developing a product that it can produce at minimum cost, usually but not necessarily by making the product less differentiated. The firm expects that its lower costs will enable it to profit despite competitive pricing. EMC established this position in data storage by getting ahead of competitors in cost-cutting technology. Thus when price warfare broke out during a slowdown in demand, EMC was able to cut its prices by more than 50 percent over 12 months, yet still report growth in earnings per share.

Pricing the Differentiated Product

A differentiated product strategy may be focused on a particular buyer segment or directed at multiple segments. In either case, the role of pricing is to collect the rewards from producing attributes that buyers find uniquely valuable. If the differentiated product strategy is focused, the firm earns its rewards by skim pricing to the segment that values the product most highly. For example, Godiva (chocolate), BMW (automobiles), and Gucci (apparel) use skim pricing to focus their differentiated product strategies. In contrast, when the differentiated product strategy is more broadly aimed at multiple segments, companies should set neutral or penetration prices and earn rewards from the sales volume that its product can then attract. Kodak (photographic film and paper), Toyota (automobiles), and Caterpillar (construction equipment) use neutral pricing to sell their differentiated products to a large share of the market.

Penetration pricing is also possible for a differentiated product. This is common in industrial products where a company may develop a superior piece of equipment, computer software, or service, but price it no more than the competition. The price is used to lock in a large market share before competitors imitate, and therefore eliminate, the product's differential advantage. Although the Windows operating system is clearly a unique product, Microsoft used penetration pricing to ensure that its product became the dominant architecture and default standard for software application programmers. Penetration pricing is less commonly successful for differentiated consumer products, since buyers who can afford to cater to their desire for the attributes of differentiated products can often also afford to buy them without shopping for bargains.

PRICING THE LOW-COST PRODUCT

Like the differentiated product strategy, a cost leadership strategy can also be either focused or more broadly based. If a firm is seeking industrywide cost leadership, penetration pricing often plays an active role in the strategy's implementation. For example, when the source of the firm's anticipated cost advantage depends on selling a large volume, it may set low penetration prices during growth to gain a dominant market share. Later, it maintains those penetration prices as a competitive deterrent, while still earning profits due to its superior cost position. Wal-Mart uses this strategy successfully to achieve substantial cost economies in distribution and high sales per square foot. Even when the source of the cost advantage is not a large volume but a more cost-efficient product design, the firm may set low penetration prices to exploit that advantage. Japanese manufacturers used penetration pricing to exploit their cost advantages and dominate world markets for TV sets after extensively redesigning the manufacturing production process with automated insertion equipment, modular assembly, and standardized designs.

At this point a definite word of warning is in order. Much of the business literature implies that penetration pricing is the only proper strategy for establishing and exploiting industrywide cost leadership. That literature is dangerously misleading. If a market is not particularly price sensitive, penetration pricing will not enable a firm to gain enough share to achieve or exploit a cost advantage. In that case, neutral pricing is the most appropriate pricing strategy and can still be quite consistent with the successful pursuit of cost leadership. The marketing histories of many cost leaders (e.g., Honda in electric generators and R. J. Reynolds in cigarettes) confirm that industrywide cost leadership is attainable without penetration pricing. The battle for the dominant share and cost leadership in those markets and many others is fought and won with weapons such as cost-efficient technological leadership, advertising, and extensive distribution. In many cases, the battle is won against competitors with lower prices.

Penetration pricing is not always appropriate when cost leadership is based on a narrow customer focus. If the focused firm's cost advantage depends directly on selling to only one or a few large buyers, penetration pricing may be necessary to hold their patronage. For example, suppliers that sell exclusively to Wal-Mart or to the auto industry enjoy lower costs of selling and distribution but usually have to charge penetration prices to retain that business. When, however, the firm's cost advantage is derived simply from remaining small and flexible, neutral pricing is compatible with focused cost leadership. For example, specialized component assembly is often done by small contract manufacturers that are cost leaders because their small size enables them to maintain nonunion labor, low overhead, and flexibility in accepting and scheduling orders. Since those cost advantages do not depend on maintaining a large volume of orders, and since the buyers that those companies serve are more concerned about quality and reliability than about price, their pricing strategy is usually neutral. When an order requires an especially fast turnaround and the buyer has little time to look for alternatives, those same manufacturers will occasionally even skim price their services.

PRICE REDUCTIONS IN GROWTH

The best price for the growth stage, regardless of one's product strategy, is normally less than the price set during the market development stage. In most cases, new competition in the growth stage gives buyers more alternatives from which to choose, while their growing familiarity with the product enables them to better evaluate those alternatives. Both factors will increase price sensitivity over what it was in the development stage. Moreover, even if the firm enjoys a patented monopoly, reducing price after the innovation stage can speed the product adoption process and enable the firm to profit from faster market growth.[9] Such price reductions are usually possible without sacrificing profits because of cost economies from an increasing scale of output and accumulating experience.

Pricing in the growth stage is not generally cutthroat. The growth stage is characterized by a rapidly expanding sales base. New firms can generally enter and existing ones expand without forcing their competitors' sales to (correspondingly) contract. For example, sales of Apple's Ipod continue to grow rapidly despite loss of some market share to new entrants. Because new entrants can grow without forcing established firms to contract, the growth stage normally will not precipitate aggressive price competition. The exceptions occur in the following situations:

1. The production economies resulting from producing greater volumes are large and the market is price-sensitive. Consequently, each firm sees the battle for volume as a battle for long-run survival (as often occurs in the electronics industry).

2. Sales volume determines which of competing technologies becomes the industry standard (as occurred in the market for digital music players).

3. The growth of production capacity jumps ahead of the growth in sales (as occurred in the cell phone market).

In these cases, price competition can become bitter as firms sacrifice short-term profit during growth to ensure their profitability in maturity.

Whether or not pricing competition becomes intense, the most profitable pricing strategies in growth are usually segmented. The logic for this is simple. In the introduction phase, all customers are new to the market and technology is simple. In growth, customers naturally segment themselves between those who are coming new to the market and those who are knowledgeable and experienced purchasers. That by itself may call for a segmented strategy. IBM and Compaq faced this challenge when a growing segment of knowledgeable buyers began purchasing exactly what they wanted at lower cost from Dell, Gateway, and local generic assemblers. IBM and Compaq's bundled packages purchased through computer stores at higher prices remained the preferred channel for new and less knowledgeable buyers. With some difficulty (see Chapter 11), these companies were forced to develop dual pricing and distribution systems to accommodate those different segments.

PRICING THE ESTABLISHED PRODUCT IN MATURITY

A typical product spends most of its life in maturity, the phase in which effective pricing is essential for survival, although latitude in decision making is far more limited. Without the rapid sales growth and increasing cost economies that characterize the growth phase, earning a profit in maturity hinges on exploiting whatever latitude one has. Many products fail to make the transition to market maturity because they failed to achieve strong competitive positions with differentiated products or a cost advantage.[10] Firms that have successfully executed their growth strategies are usually able to price profitably in maturity, although rarely as profitably as at the height of industry growth.

In the growth stage, the source of profit was sales to an expanding market. In maturity, that source has been nearly depleted. A maturity strategy predicated on continued expansion of one's customer base will likely be dashed by one's competitors' determination to defend their market shares. In contrast to the growth stage, when competitors could lose share in an expanding market and suffer only a slower rate of sales increase, competitors that lose share in a mature market suffer an absolute sales decline. Having made capacity investments to produce a certain level of output, they will usually defend their market shares to avoid being overwhelmed by sunk costs.[11] Pricing latitude is further reduced by the following factors increasing price competition as the market moves from growth to maturity:

1. The accumulated purchase experience of repeat buyers improves their ability to evaluate and compare competing products, reducing brand loyalty and the value of a brand's reputation.

2. The imitation of the most successful product designs, technologies, and marketing strategies reduces product differentiation, making the various brands of different firms more directly competitive with one another. This homogenizing process is sometimes speeded up when product standards are set by government agencies or by respected independent testing agencies like Underwriters Laboratories.

3. Buyers' increased price sensitivity and the lower risk that accompanies production of a proven standardized product attract new competitors whose distinctive competence is efficient production and distribution of commodity products. These are often foreign competitors but may also be large domestic firms with years of experience producing or marketing similar products.

All three of these factors worked to reduce prices and margins for photocopiers during the early 1980s and for personal computers and peripherals during the 1990s, as those markets entered maturity.

Unless a firm can discover a marketing strategy that renews industry growth or a technological breakthrough that enables it to introduce a more differentiated product, it must simply learn to live with these new competitive pressures.[12] As we discussed in Chapter 10 on competition, effective pricing in maturity focuses not on valiant efforts to buy market share but on making the most of whatever competitive advantages the firm has. Even before industry growth is exhausted and maturity sets in, a firm does well to seek out opportunities to improve its pricing effectiveness to maintain its profits in maturity, despite increased competition among firms and increased sophistication among buyers. Fertile ground for such opportunities lies in the following areas:

UNBUNDLING RELATED PRODUCTS AND SERVICES

The goal in the market development stage is to make it easy for potential buyers to try the product and experience its benefits. Consequently, it makes sense to sell everything needed to achieve the benefit for a single price. During the early years of office automation, IBM sold the total office solution, bundling hardware, software, training, and ongoing maintenance contracts. In growth, it makes sense for the leading firms to continue bundling products for a different reason: the bundle makes it more difficult for competitors to enter. When all products required for a benefit are priced as a bundle, no new competitor can break in by offering a better version of just one part of that bundle.

As a market moves toward maturity, bundling normally becomes less a competitive defense and more a competitive invitation. As their number increases, competitors more closely imitate the differentiating aspects of products in the leading company's bundle. This makes it easier for someone to develop just one superior part, allowing buyers to purchase other parts from the leading company's other competitors. If buyers are forced to purchase from the leading company only as a bundle, the more knowledgeable ones will often abandon it altogether to purchase individual pieces from innovative competitors. Unless the leading company can maintain overall superiority in all products, it is generally better to accommodate competitors in maturity. This is accomplished by selling many buyers most of the products they need for a benefit rather than selling the entire bundle to ever fewer of them. An example of this tactic can be seen in the desktop computer industry, when experienced buyers seeking increased performance and customized configurations chose to satisfy their unique performance needs by purchasing options provided by innovative specialized suppliers. To avoid losing part of their sales, the dominant manufacturers were forced to unbundle the packages they had offered successfully during growth.

IMPROVED ESTIMATION OF PRICE SENSITIVITY

Given the instability of the growth stage of the life cycle, when new buyers and sellers are constantly entering the market, formal estimation of buyers' price sensitivity is often a futile exercise. In maturity, when the source of demand is repeat buyers and competition remains more stable, one may better gauge the incremental revenue from a price change and discover that a little fine tuning can significantly improve profits. The techniques for making such estimates of price sensitivity are outlined in Chapter 13.

IMPROVED CONTROL AND UTILIZATION OF COSTS

As the number of customers and product variations increases during the growth stage, a firm may justifiably allocate costs among them arbitrarily. New customers and new products initially require technical, sales, and managerial support that is reasonably allocated to overhead during growth, since it is as much a cost of future sales as of the initial ones. In the transition to maturity, a more accurate allocation of incremental costs to sales may reveal opportunities to significantly increase profit. For example, one may find that sales at certain times of the year, the week, or even the day require capacity that is underutilized during other times. Sales at these times should be priced higher to reflect the cost of capacity.

More important, a careful cost analysis will identify those products and customers that are simply not carrying their weight. If some products in the line require a disproportionate sales effort, that should be reflected in the incremental cost of their sales and in their prices. If demand cannot support higher prices for them, they are prime candidates for pruning from the line.[13] The same holds true for customers. If some require technical support disproportionate to their contribution, one might well implement a pricing policy of charging separately for such services. While the growth stage provides fertile ground to make long-term investments in product variations and in developing new customer accounts, maturity is the time to cut one's losses on those that have not begun to pay dividends and that cannot be expected to do so.[14]

EXPANSION OF THE PRODUCT LINE

Although increased competition and buyer sophistication in the maturity phase erode one's pricing latitude for the primary product, the firm may be able to leverage its position (as a differentiated or as a low-cost producer) to sell peripheral goods or services that it can price more profitably. Novartis, a Swiss pharmaceutical maker, recognized the need for broader and more flexible product lines to meet the needs of smaller market niches in 2004 and committed to invest $60 million in new packaging and production capabilities to support them.[15] The flexibility not only reduces inventory costs, but also enables the drugmaker to better execute a segmented pricing strategy in an increasingly fragmented market.

REEVALUATION OF DISTRIBUTION CHANNELS

Finally, in the transition to maturity, most manufacturers begin to reevaluate their wholesale prices with an eye to reducing dealer margins. There is no need in maturity to pay dealers to promote the product to new buyers. Repeat purchasers know what they want and are more likely to consider cost rather than the advice and promotion of the distributor or retailer as a guide to purchase. There is also no longer any need to restrict the kind of retailers with whom one deals. The exclusive distribution networks for Apple, Compaq, and even IBM have given way to low-service, low-margin distributors such as discount computer chains, off-price office supply houses, and even warehouse clubs. The discounters who earlier could destroy one's market development effort can in maturity ensure one's competitiveness among price-sensitive buyers.

PRICING A PRODUCT IN MARKET DECLINE

A downward trend in demand driven by customers adopting alternative solutions characterizes the market in decline. The effect of such trends on price depends on the difficulty the industry has in eliminating excess capacity. When production costs are largely variable, industry capacity tends to adjust quickly to declining demand and there can be little or no effect on prices. When production costs are fixed but easily redirected, the value of the fixed capital in other markets places a lower boundary on prices. When an industry's production costs are largely fixed and sunk because capital is specialized to the particular market, the effects of market decline are more onerous. Firms in such industries face the prospect of a fatal cash hemorrhage if they cannot maintain a reasonable rate of capacity utilization. Consequently, each firm scrambles for business at the expense of its competitors by cutting prices. Unfortunately, since the price cuts rarely stimulate enough additional market demand to reverse the decline, the inevitable result is reduced profitability industrywide. The goal of strategy in decline is not to win anything; for some it is to exit with minimum losses. For others the goal is simply to survive the decline with their competitive positions intact and perhaps strengthened by the experience.

ALTERNATIVE STRATEGIES IN DECLINE

There are three general strategic approaches that can be adopted in a declining market: retrenchment, harvesting, or consolidation. In most declining markets, each of these strategies will be adopted by various competitors. The conventional camera market, which went into decline in the late 1990s and early 2000s is a good case in point. For example, Kodak adopted a retrenchment strategy in which it intentionally exited the broad conventional camera market while maintaining a position in the conventional disposable market as long as it remains viable. A retrenchment strategy involves either partial or complete capitulation of some market segments to refocus resources on others where the firm has a stronger position. The firm deliberately forgoes market share but positions itself to be more profitable with the share it retains. Not all firms that forgo market share in a declining market do so as a deliberate strategic decision. Some are forced to sell out to satisfy creditors or for other reasons. Retrenchment, in contrast, is a carefully planned and executed strategy to put the firm in a more viable competitive position, not an immediate necessity to stave off collapse. The essence of a retrenchment strategy is liquidation of those assets and withdrawal from those markets that represent the weakest links in the firm's competitive position, leaving it leaner but more defensible. In the case of Kodak, the retrenchment strategy has proven effective as it enabled the firm to invest more heavily in the digital camera market where it took the number one market share position in 2005.[16]

In contrast to retrenchment, a harvesting strategy is a phased withdrawal from an industry. It begins like retrenchment with abandonment of the weakest links. However, the goal of harvesting is not a smaller, more defensible competitive position but a withdrawal from the industry. The harvesting firm does not price to defend its remaining market share but rather to maximize its income. The harvesting firm may make short-term investments in the industry to keep its position from deteriorating too rapidly, but it avoids fundamental long-term investments, preferring instead to treat its competitive position in the declining market as a "cash cow" for funding more promising ventures in other markets. Polaroid was forced into a rapid harvesting strategy that ultimately led to the demise of the company in 2002 because it failed to respond to the emergence of the digital technologies in time.

A consolidation strategy is an attempt to gain a stronger position in a declining industry. Such a strategy is viable only for a firm that begins the decline in a strong financial position, enabling it to weather the storm that forces its competitors to flee. A successful consolidation leaves a firm poised to profit after a shakeout, with a larger market share in a restructured, less-competitive industry. Consolidation is the approach adopted by Nikon and Canon that recognized that the high-end market for art photography is likely to remain viable for many years. Although most of their product development investments are focused on the growing digital market, they recognize that the art market is likely to remain viable for years and have restructured their business to enable them to continue to serve those markets profitably.

The lesson from the camera industry is that there are strategic choices that can improve even the worst phases of life cycles, but the choice is not arbitrary. It depends on a firm's relative ability to pursue a strategy to successful completion, and it requires forethought and planning. For any of the strategic choices during the decline phase, timing, foresight, and creativity are crucial for successful implementation. It is crucial that companies in declining markets act decisively. The sooner managers face market realities, the more time they have to craft strategies appropriate for their firms.

Summary

The factors that influence pricing strategy change over the life of a product concept. The market defined by a product concept passes through four phases: development, growth, maturity, and decline. Briefly, the changes in the strategic environment over those phases are as follows:

MARKET DEVELOPMENT
Buyers are price insensitive because they lack knowledge of the product's benefits. Both production and promotional costs are high. Competitors are either nonexistent or few and not a threat since the potential gains from market development exceed those from competitive rivalry. Pricing strategy signals the product's value to potential buyers, but buyer education remains the key to sales growth.

MARKET GROWTH

Buyers are increasingly informed about product attributes either from personal experience or from communication with innovators. Consequently, they are increasingly responsive to lower prices. If diffusion strongly affects later sales, price reductions can substantially increase the rate of market growth and the product's long-run profitability. Moreover, cost economies accompanying growth usually enable one to cut price while still maintaining profit margins. Although competition increases during this phase, high rates of market growth enable industrywide expansion, generally limiting price competition. Price-cutting to drive out competitors may occur, however. Cost advantages associated with sales volume are substantial if current market share is expected to determine which competing technology becomes the industry standard, or if capacity outstrips sales growth.

MARKET MATURITY

Most buyers are repeat purchasers who are familiar with the product. Increasing homogeneity enables them to better compare competing brands. Consequently, price sensitivity reaches its maximum in this phase. Competition begins to put downward pressure on prices since any firm can grow only by taking sales from its competitors. Despite such competition, profitability depends on having achieved a defensible competitive position through cost leadership or differentiation and on exploiting it effectively. Common opportunities to maintain margins by increasing pricing effectiveness include unbundling related products, improved demand estimation, improved control and utilization of costs, expansion of the product line, and reevaluation of distribution channels.

MARKET DECLINE

Reduced buyer demand and excess capacity characterize this phase. If costs are largely variable or if capital can be easily reallocated to more promising markets, prices need fall only slightly to induce some firms to cut capacity. If costs are largely fixed and sunk, average costs soar due to reduced capacity utilization, while price competition increases as firms attempt to increase their capacity utilization by capturing a larger share of a declining market. Three options are available: retrench to one's strongest product lines and price to defend one's share in them, harvest one's entire business by pricing for maximum cash flow, or consolidate one's position by price-cutting to drive out weak competitors and capture their markets.

Notes

1. See Theodore Levitt, "Exploit the Product Life Cycle," *Harvard Business Review,* 43 (November—December 1965), pp. 81–94; John E. Smallwood, "The Product Life Cycle: A Key to Strategic Market Planning," *MSU Business Topics* (Winter 1973), pp. 29–35; and George Day, "The Product Life Cycle: Analysis and Applications," *Journal of Marketing,* 45(4) (Fall 1981), pp. 60–67. For a criticism of the life-cycle concept, especially when applied to individual brands, see Nariman K. Dhalla and Sonia Yosper, "Forget the Product Life Cycle Concept," *Harvard Business Review,* 54 (January–February 1976), pp. 102–112.

2. See Everett M. Rogers and F. Floyd Shoemaker, *Communication of Innovations,* 2nd ed. (New York: The Free Press, 1971); Frank M. Bass, "A New Product Growth Model for

Consumer Durables," *Management Science,* 15 (January 1969), pp. 215–227.

3. William H. Whyte, "The Web of Word of Mouth," *Fortune,* 50 (November 1954), pp. 140–143, 204–212.

4. Rogers and Shoemaker, *op. cit.,* pp. 180–182.

5. See Everett M. Rogers, *Diffusion of Innovations* (New York: The Free Press, 1962), Chapters 7 and 8; Rogers and Shoemaker, *op. cit.,* Chapter 6; Gregory S. Carpenter and Kent Nakamoto, "Consumer Preference Formation and Pioneering Advantage," *Journal of Marketing Research,* 26 (August 1989), pp. 285–298.

6. Theodore Levitt, *The Marketing Mode* (New York: McGraw-Hill, 1969), pp. 7–8.

7. See Philip Maher, "Coming to Grips with the Robot Market," *Industrial Marketing* (January 1982), pp. 93–98.

8. Porter, *Competitive Strategy,* pp. 34–41.

9. See Abel P. Jeuland, "Parsimonious Models of Diffusion of Innovation, Part B: Incorporating the Variable of Price," University of Chicago working paper (July 1981).

10. See Hall, "Survival Strategies," pp. 75–85.

11. This problem can even result in a period of intensely competitive, unprofitably low pricing in the maturity phase if, as sometimes happens, the industry fails to anticipate the leveling off of sales growth and thus enters maturity having built excess capacity.

12. See Porter, *op. cit.,* pp. 247–249, for a discussion of the problems faced by firms that do not acknowledge the transition to maturity.

13. See Philip Kotler, "Phasing Out Weak Products," *Harvard Business Review,* 43 (March–April 1965), pp. 107–118.

14. Theodore Levitt, "Marketing When Things Change," *Harvard Business Review,* 55 (November–December 1977), pp. 107–113; Porter, *op. cit.,* pp. 159, 241–249.

15. Lisa McTigue Pierce, "Novartis Advances with Bold Steps," www.looksmart.com. 2005.

16. Ken Dobbin, "Kodak Moves Ahead of Japanese Giants in US Digital Camera Market," *The Detroit News* (February 3, 2005).

13

PRICE AND VALUE MEASUREMENT

Research Techniques to Supplement Judgment

Estimates of customer price sensitivity and willingness-to-pay can sometimes substantially improve both price setting and segmentation. Indeed, some estimate of price sensitivity, whether it be quantitative or qualitative, is required for the price setting process described in Chapter 7. Sometimes research can provide very specific estimates of the impact of prices on sales volume. Other times estimates provide only a rough indication of a customer's willingness-to-pay given a set of circumstances. At their worst, estimates of price sensitivity fail to reflect the real nature of the buying decision, misleading management into making ineffective pricing decisions. This is often the case when a research design causes respondents to pay much more attention to price than real customers would. Fortunately, in almost all cases it is possible to develop an estimate of price sensitivity; the key to doing this successfully is to recognize that as with any estimate, one needs to be cognizant of the accuracy of the estimate. Specifically, it is important to consider that the estimate is only an approximation of the actual value, and we need to recognize the level of accuracy of the estimate, as well as how any changes in assumptions can change the estimate.

There are numerous procedures for measuring and estimating price sensitivity. Each procedure offers particular advantages over the others in terms of accuracy, cost, and applicability, so the choice is not arbitrary. One must think carefully about the appropriate procedure for any particular product before beginning research. In no case should a manager use a particular technique just because it is cheap, convenient, or fast. Instead, managers need to carefully assess their needs and adopt techniques that are most appropriate for the given situation. Even if the cost for those techniques is high, the benefit is often sufficiently large to justify the expense.

281

TYPES OF MEASUREMENT PROCEDURES

Procedures for estimating price sensitivity differ on two major dimensions: the conditions of measurement and the variable being measured. Exhibit 13-1 classifies the various procedures according to these two dimensions. The conditions of measurement range from a completely uncontrolled to a highly controlled research environment. When making uncontrolled measurements, researchers are only observers. They measure what people actually do, or say they would do, in a situation not of the researcher's making. For example, marketing researchers might collect data on consumer purchases of laundry detergent in a grocery store, but the prices and other variables that influence those purchases are beyond their control. This is often the case in the analysis of historical data of product sales from retail-scanner data.

In contrast, when making controlled measurements, researchers manipulate the important variables that influence consumer behavior to more precisely observe their effect. Researchers conducting an experimentally controlled study of price sensitivity for a laundry detergent could select the prices as well as the advertising and shelf placement of various brands in order to make the data more useful. They might attempt to gain even more control by conducting a laboratory experiment in a simulated store, carefully selecting the individuals whose purchases would be recorded. Participants for the experiment could be chosen to represent various demographic variables (such as race, sex, income, and family size) in proportions equal to those of the product's actual market or to represent a particular group (such as mothers with children) to whom the product was intended to appeal. Generally, controlled research produces more accurate estimates of the effects of the controlled variables on price sensitivity, but depending on the level of realism, it is often costly to implement in a "real-world" setting. A laboratory setting is often used to better control other factors that may affect

EXHIBIT 13-1 Techniques for Measuring Price Sensitivity		
	Conditions of Measurement	
Variable Measured	**Uncontrolled**	**Experimentally Controlled**
Actual purchases	• Historical sales data • Panel data • Store scanner data	• In-store experiments • Laboratory purchase experiments
Preferences and intentions	• Direct questioning • Buy-response survey • Depth interview	• Simulate purchase experiments • Trade-off (conjoint) analysis

price sensitivity as well as to reduce costs, but these improvements come at the expense of realism.

The dependent variable for estimating price sensitivity is either actual purchases or purchase preferences and intentions. Actual-purchase studies measure behavior, whereas preference-intention studies measure the intended choices that people claim they would make in a hypothetical purchase situation. Since the ultimate goal of the research is to estimate how people respond to price changes in actual-purchase situations, research that measures actual behavior is generally more desirable, but it is also more costly, time-consuming, and sometimes impractical, given the need to move products to market quickly. The following discussion summarizes these research techniques and some of the trade-offs of choosing one method over another.

UNCONTROLLED STUDIES OF ACTUAL PURCHASES

One way to estimate price sensitivity is to analyze past sales data. Naturally, one would expect this to work well in assessing the price sensitivity of customers for existing products in which consumers have prior-use experience. Given the increased use of scanners in supermarkets and mass merchandisers, and the databases maintained on their most frequent customers by hotels, airlines, and web sites, analysis of historical data is becoming an increasingly important source of information to model customer sensitivity to prices and price deals. Still, changes in (1) the number of brands on the market, (2) how recently competitors offered price promotions, (3) the amount and effectiveness of advertising by each brand, (4) increased price sensitivity of more-educated consumers, and (5) general economic conditions can undermine the ability of historical data analysis to diagnose the true effects of a price change.

There are three types of past sales data from which a marketing researcher might attempt to estimate price sensitivity: (1) historical sales data—sales reports from a company's own records or from a sales-monitoring service, (2) panel data—individual purchase reports from members of a consumer panel, and (3) store scanner data—sales data for an individual retail outlet.

Historical Sales Data

Sales data collected as part of a company's regular operation are cheap and available for all products that have prior sales histories. Given the ability to actually track data on a minute-to-minute basis, marketers are able to analyze trends and project future movement of product sales. One needs to be careful in recognizing that sales data only allow for the estimation of price elasticity of the next level in the channel. For example, in a retail environment, unless a manufacturer sells directly to the end-user, its sales data reflect shipments to retailers, not actual retail sales during the period. Retailers will often stockpile, with no intention of passing the savings on to the consumer, to take advantage of short-term promotions on the part of the retailer or in anticipation of increases in demand on the part of consumer. Understanding this, some marketers have direct links with the inventory movement of their retail outlets, combined with up-to-date retail price data. While this is generally part of the inventory-management system to facilitate timely replacement of stock, it also provides the marketer with instant data that can be analyzed for important trends in demand.

Good estimates of actual retail sales are available for some products from companies that survey retail stores (e.g., A. C. Neilsen).[1] Also, for some factors—such as product reformulations, changes in consumer tastes, and changes in distribution—there is simply no way to take out the effect. For others, such as recessions or changes in the level of advertising, the researcher can statistically control the estimation process to take out their effects.

Another problem with sales data is that it is frequently available only at an aggregated level. In any given week, some stores will charge higher prices than others. Over time, the same store will put the product on sale for a week and then return its price to the regular level. These price variations influence sales and, therefore, could provide useful information about price sensitivity. Unfortunately, data that aggregate sales for all stores over a number of weeks conceal these individual price differences. Given the aggregation in the data, the researcher is forced to explain sales variations by looking at only the average retail price across stores and throughout the time period. Since average prices have less variation and fewer observations than actual prices at individual stores in particular weeks, the data have less statistical power than data on individual purchase prices. In addition, some stores serve segments that are substantially more price responsive than others; aggregated sales data will mask these differences and will lead to price elasticity estimates that may, on average, be correct, but do not really apply to any single store setting.

Panel Data

A number of marketing research companies collect individual purchase data from panels of a few thousand households. Each household keeps a daily record of all brands purchased and price paid or uses a special credit card that tracks purchases. Since products are purchased daily, the data for each household must be aggregated to produce a series on weekly or biweekly purchases. Such data have a number of advantages:

1. One can accumulate observations more quickly with weekly panel data than with bimonthly or quarterly sales data, reducing the problem that other factors may change and reduce the comparability of the data.
2. One can observe the actual price paid, rather than an average of the retail prices that different stores charge, and one can identify sales that were made with coupons or promotions that alter the price actually paid.[2] This captures more price variation in the data, making the effects of price changes easier to detect.
3. One can get data on the sales and prices of competing products (provided someone in the panel bought them), as well as on sales of one's own product.
4. One can correlate price sensitivity with various demographic classifications of consumers and possibly identify opportunities for segmentation.[3]

One potential drawback is that panel data may not be adequately representative of the market as a whole. Of all households invited to join a panel, fewer than 5 percent accept the offer and accurately record their purchases. There is reason to suspect, therefore, that panel members are a biased sample of the population. Moreover, the fact that panel members must record their purchases tends to make them more price aware, and thus more price sensitive. This problem increases the longer a household participates in a panel. Fortunately, technological advances have enabled some research companies to develop panels that do not require consumers to record their purchases.[4] Instead, in-store scanners record purchases automatically whenever panel members identify themselves in the store's checkout line. This vastly simplifies panel membership, increasing the panel participation rate to over 70 percent and attenuating the problem of heightened price awareness. Further, the data tend to be more representative of real purchasing behavior of consumers without the bias that has been problematic in the past.

A second potential drawback to panel data is that typically only one member of the household agrees to participate in the panel, yet in most households multiple people perform shopping duties. As a result, it is easy to miss purchase data from the nonparticipating member(s) of the household who often have very different criteria for making purchase decisions. For example, if the nonparticipating family member joins Costco and purchases cereal by the bushel, the family is essentially out of the cereal market for a while, no matter how substantial a discount is offered to the participating panel member. Given the ever-widening use of scanners and the ability to link scanner data with panel data, increasing numbers of consumer products can be analyzed using this type of analysis. The superiority of panel data estimates over those from aggregate sales data is due to the availability of more observations from a shorter and more comparable time period. With the availability of advertising and other promotional data, researchers are able to estimate price sensitivities for different customer groups with a reasonable degree of reliability (Box 13-1). Since multiple companies share the cost of the same ongoing research, estimates based on panel data are also less expensive than estimates based on an equal number of observations from proprietary research.

Store Scanner Data

An alternate source of actual sales comes from auditing price transactions and sales at individual retail stores. Modern technologies have made accurate weekly sales and price data available at reasonable cost. Any store that uses scanners can generate such data as part of its normal operations. The weekly frequency of scanner data makes it vastly superior to aggregate sales data. Fortunately, the availability of scanner data, which is used in more than 90 percent of department, grocery, and mass-merchandise stores, provides marketers with almost immediate information on the movement of their product. Some questions have arisen as to the accuracy of pricing information of scanner data, but, for the most part, those inaccuracies have been in less than 10 percent of the cases.[5] Although it lacks the corresponding demographics of consumer panel data, it also costs

BOX 13-1

USING PANEL DATA TO MEASURE THE IMPACT OF PROMOTION ON CHOICE

In a recent study, the authors asked two important questions: whether consumers are getting more price sensitive and whether the group of price-sensitive consumers is growing. To evaluate these and other questions, they examined more than eight years of usage data from a panel of consumers and were able to compare those data with quarterly advertising data from producers within a household nonfood product category. They were able to evaluate three different types of price promotions: temporary price reduction, price feature of the product, or the offering of a coupon. For their analysis, they used a multinomial logit model to evaluate the impact of the promotional (price and nonprice) activities on the consumer's choice of a product. Further, they were able to segment users into loyal and nonloyal segments and compare the price sensitivities of the two groups. The summarized results indicated the following:

Consumer's Sensitivities to:	Average Price Sensitivities	Changes Over Time
1. Loyal segment		
Price	−.28	Increase
Price promotion	.02	Increase
Nonprice promotion	.03	Decrease*
2. Nonloyal segment		
Price	−1.70	Increase
Price promotion	.04	Increase
Nonprice promotion	.09	Decrease*
Nonloyal segment size		Increase*

*Indicates significant at $p < .05$, all else $p < .001$.

The price sensitivities are shown across all of the periods analyzed. Based on the elasticities, the loyal segment showed little price sensitivity, but it did increase over time. The nonloyal, price-oriented segment showed higher price sensitivities that increased over time as well. They did note that the size of the nonloyal segment increased over time, indicating that "an increasing proportion of consumers have become more price and promotion sensitive over time."

Source: Carl F. Mela, Sunil Gupta, and Donald R. Lehmann, "The Long-Term Impact of Promotion and Advertising on Consumer Brand Choice," *Journal of Marketing Research,* May 1997, pp. 248–261.

substantially less. When store scanner data can be combined with panel data that track the demographic and broader behavioral characteristics of consumers, researchers often get huge bonuses in insights into price sensitivity and purchasing behaviors. Scanner data have become a major source of information on the price sensitivity of consumer-packaged goods.[6]

While sales data—in the form of panels and scanner data—are quite prevalent in the consumer package goods industry, in many business-to-business markets there are simply too few transactions and market oversight to develop similar data sets. However, not all is lost. We recently spoke with a firm that created a competitive sales database. Specifically, the firm (a tractor manufacturer) created an internal database in which its sales force would register any competitive bid information. Over time the company built a database of competitive price information, which, combined with the record of its own bid outcome history allows the firm to estimate the price sensitivity of customers, by segment if necessary, as well as to estimate the incremental value its tractors offered over the competition. The total investment for this multi-billion-dollar firm was on the order of $50,000.

There is some level of bias in the data that one needs to be aware of—the competitive quotes are being obtained from customers who have an incentive to provide low prices. One thus needs to adjust the distribution to reflect the bias; the level of bias can be estimated if one can confirm actual quotes for a sample of transactions and measure the actual level of bias. One also needs to be careful to "normalize" competitive quotes so that equivalent comparisons are being made. Are after-sale services, special financing terms, or training included, for example?

Further, when the quote history is overlaid with actual sales success data, it is possible to estimate the probability at which a sale is imminently likely, as well as the decline in the probability in a sale as price increases—a form of estimating price sensitivity as well as a way to estimate the amount of "money left on the table" in successful bids.

Finally, as firms update their pricing capabilities, many are discovering new opportunities to study responses to pricing actions. For example, as companies invest in technologies that allow for rapid and frequent price changes, they can look to yield management techniques that allow for the study of demand changes in response to pricing actions. Motel 6 for example, has the ability to post prices electronically on its billboards and can change these prices—at nearly no cost—by the hour. In only a short span of time, this company can study the price responsiveness of its customers by location, by day of week, and indeed even by time of day. As companies add to their ability to set and manage prices, new opportunities will become available to create "natural experiments" to allow for the study of price reactions at relatively low cost.

Analyzing Historical Data

Analysis of historical sales data often involves application of linear regression analysis. This statistical technique attempts to show how much of the historical variation in a product's sales can be explained by each of the explanatory variables, including price, that the researcher includes in the analysis. One should not expect, however, that the researcher will necessarily succeed in identifying the effect of price with such an analysis. If there has been little historical variation in a product's price, then no statistical technique applied to its sales data can reveal the effect of price changes. Moreover, if every time price was changed and some other variable—such as advertising—was also changed, the best one can do is discover the joint effect of such a simultaneous change on sales. Fortunately, the use of more sophisticated multivariate techniques such as time series analysis or structural equations modeling can often provide estimates of their cross-impacts on demand.

In any case, one must be careful to recognize the limits of a successful analysis of historical data. To estimate any equation, the researcher must develop a mathematical form for the relationship between price and sales. To the extent that the assumed form incorrectly specifies the relationship, estimates of price sensitivity may be misleading. Moreover, the researcher's estimate of price sensitivity is valid only over the range of price and advertising levels used to estimate it. There is no reason to believe that the same relationship would necessarily apply to price changes outside that range. One also needs to be careful to recognize that it is not enough to consider just a point estimate of price sensitivity; one needs to also look at the size of the corresponding error terms to understand the quality and accuracy of the estimate. Finally, regardless of how well an estimated equation fits past data, its value in predicting the effect of future price changes rests on the assumption that the future is like the past. The more other factors change, the less the past can predict the future. Despite these limitations, if a researcher has a lot of historical data with enough price variation in it, useful estimates of price sensitivity are possible.[7] For multiproduct companies, an understanding of price responsiveness can be used to help optimize demand flow across a product line. Specifically, prices can be adjusted to direct demand to specific products to better manage inventories, obtain better leverage with suppliers, yet at the same time allow a wide product selection for customers who require specific items.

Exhibit 13-2 shows the results of research that utilized regression analysis to evaluate the importance of various product attributes to two groups of customers: those who are loyal (more than 1 year of ownership) and those who are new (less than 1 year). The categorization of customers as new or loyal was based on input from the managers of the credit-card company who found that people who used their card for at least 1 year tended to stay users for an extended period of time. Of interest is the marginal increase in price sensitivity as measured by sensitivity to interest rates, for nonloyal customers (attribute importance of 0.16 compared to 0.14 for loyal customers) and the very large difference in needs for service. The researchers were also able to run regression equations for different time periods and determine how attribute importance was changing over time.

EXPERIMENTALLY CONTROLLED STUDIES OF ACTUAL PURCHASES

A researcher might attempt to estimate price sensitivity by generating experimental purchase data. Such data may come from pricing experiments conducted in a store without the buyers' knowledge or from pricing experiments conducted

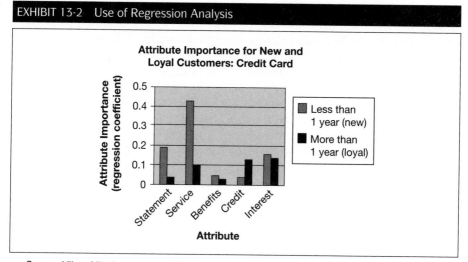

EXHIBIT 13-2 Use of Regression Analysis

Attribute Importance for New and Loyal Customers: Credit Card

Less than 1 year (new)

More than 1 year (loyal)

Attribute

Source: Vikas Mittal and Jerome M. Katrichis, "Distinctions Between New and Loyal Customers," *Marketing Research,* Spring 2000, pp. 27–32.

in a laboratory. Since the researcher controls the experiment, price variations can be created as desired to generate results while holding constant other marketing variables, such as advertising levels and in-store displays, which often change with price variations in uncontrolled sales data. The researcher can examine the effect of a number of different prices quickly and either (1) exclude many unwanted external effects in the laboratory experiment or (2) establish a control for the in-store experiment that will take account of them. Moreover, all this can be done while still providing buyers with purchase decisions that are comparable to those they make under normal conditions. As a result, to the degree that the experimental setting reflects the actual purchase environment, experimental research provides fairly reliable estimates of price sensitivity.

In-Store Purchase Experiments

An in-store purchase experiment relies on actual purchase data collected when buyers are unaware they are participating in an experiment. Although the term "in-store" reflects the fact that most such experiments are conducted in stores, the principles of in-store experimentation are equally applicable to any natural purchase environment. Such experiments are often easier to conduct for products sold through more controlled direct-retail methods, such as mail-order catalogs, than for those sold in traditional retail stores. For example, the researcher can select a subset of the mailing list to receive catalogs with experimental prices that differ from those in the regular catalog. Even in direct sales to business, one can sometimes select a representative sample of customers from one sales area, offer them an experimental price, and monitor the difference between sales to those buyers and to those in other regions where sales are made at the regular price.

The simplest design for an in-store pricing experiment involves monitoring sales at the historical price to obtain a base level of sales and then initiating a price change to see how sales change from that base level. In practice this is a very common experimental design that can yield useful information; however, it fails to exploit one of the major advantages of experimentation: the ability to control for external factors. Without such control, the researcher is forced to make the tenuous assumption that any sales change from the base level resulted from the price change alone, not from changes in other factors. Fortunately, the addition of an experimental control store (or mail sample or sales territory) can reduce this problem substantially. To establish such a control, the researcher finds a second store in which sales tend to vary over the base period in the same way that they vary in the first store, indicating that factors other than price influence both stores' sales in the same way. The researcher then changes price only in the first store, but continues to monitor sales in both stores. Any change in sales in the control store indicates to the researcher that some factor other than price is also causing a change in sales. To adjust the results, the researcher subtracts from the sales in the experimental store an amount equal to the change in sales in the control store before determining the effect of the price change alone.[8]

One of the greatest benefits of in-store experimentation is the ability to test for interactions between price and other marketing variables that, in historical data, tend to change together. Unfortunately, the cost of such experimentation is very high because each additional factor studied requires the inclusion of more stores. The experimental design with the greatest amount of information, called a full factorial design, would require enough stores to match every level tested for each marketing variable with every level of the other variables. Usually, the researcher is forced to use a less-than-perfect experiment, called a fractional factorial design, that sacrifices some precision (generally by assuming away interaction effects) in order to reduce the number of stores required.[9]

There are a number of studies on price sensitivity, shelf management, and other retail marketing activities that are based on the data collected by the University of Chicago in a collaborative arrangement with Dominick's Finer Foods, a Chicago-area grocery retailer with 86 stores and $435 billion in sales in 1999. The database contains store-level weekly price and wholesale cost data for all stores, as well as other information on marketing and promotional activities. The database of historical data is available for public use, and can be accessed through the Internet.[10]

Although many articles illustrate the successful application of in-store experimentation to estimate price sensitivity, the greatest impediment to using in-store experiments is the high cost of monitoring sales, analyzing the data, and securing the cooperation of retailers.[11] Although in theory this is an inexpensive experiment because as few as two stores for 1 week could constitute a test, accurate tests require many stores and last for months. A large number of stores are necessary to reduce the problem of an external factor influencing just one store and to obtain a representative sample of consumers whose behavior can reasonably be generalized to the market as a whole. It is often necessary to set a long time period for an in-store test in order to get past the short-run inventory effect on price sensitivity that initially masks the long-term effect. Consequently, a good in-store experiment is very expensive. When, for example, Quaker Oats conducted an in-store experiment that focused on the effect of price alone, the study required 120 stores and ran for 3 months. Such a study can easily cost several million dollars.[12]

In addition to the financial and time cost of in-store experiments, there are other drawbacks. There is the potential loss of consumer goodwill when some buyers are charged higher prices than others. On the other hand, charging prices below normal can become too costly when the product is a large-expenditure durable good such as an automobile or a piece of industrial equipment. An in-store test also involves the very real risk of being discovered by a competitor. If the product is new, a company may not wish to give its competitors an advance look. Moreover, when competitors find out about a test market, they often take steps, such as special promotions or advertising in selected areas, to contaminate the results.[13] Thus, although in-store experiments have the potential for yielding very high-quality estimates, market researchers are more often forced to use alternatives. The closest of those alternatives is a laboratory purchase experiment.

Laboratory Purchase Experiments

Laboratory purchase experiments attempt to duplicate the realism of in-store experimentation without the high cost or the possible exposure to competitors. A typical laboratory experiment takes place in a research facility at a shopping mall. Interviewers intercept potential participants who are walking by and screen them to select only those who are users of the product category being researched. Based on information from a short pretest questionnaire, the researchers can control the proportion of participants in each demographic classification (e.g., sex, age, race, income, or family size) to ensure that the experimental population is representative of the actual population of buyers, a technique known as proportionate sampling. If members of some demographic categories cannot be found in adequate numbers in the mall, telephone interviews may be used to contact such people and offer them an incentive to come and participate in the experiment.

The laboratory researcher can control who participates and can quickly manipulate prices and other elements in the purchase environment (such as shelf location and point-of-purchase displays), all at a single location. Moreover, the researcher can almost entirely eliminate external factors such as changes in competitors' prices, stock-outs of competing products, or differences among stores that may contaminate the results of an in-store test. Participants exposed to different prices see exactly the same display at the same location in the laboratory experiment. Even effects associated with the time of day can be controlled by constantly changing prices for each new participant in the experiment. Thus, if testing three different price levels, approximately one third of the consumers who take the test at any hour can be exposed to each price level. This ability to control the experiment so closely enables the researcher to draw inferences from far fewer purchases in much less time than would be possible with an in-store experiment.

Laboratory research facilities vary greatly depending on the sophistication of the research organization and the budget of the client company. The simplest facilities may consist of an interviewing room with a display of products from a single product category. The price for each brand is clearly marked, and the participant is invited to make a purchase. In theory, since the consumer is actually making a purchase, or can choose not to buy at all, the purchase decision in a simple laboratory experiment is the same one that the consumer would make shopping in an actual retail store. In practice, however, that conclusion may not be true. The problem lies in the artificiality of a simple laboratory environment. First, a single display in a laboratory encourages the consumer to give the purchase decision much more attention than would be typical in an actual shopping situation. Research indicates that most grocery shoppers do not even look at most prices when actually shopping in a supermarket. In a laboratory, however, consumers do not want to appear careless. They are, therefore, much more likely to note and respond to price differences. Second, when consumers know they are being watched from behind one-way mirrors, they may act as they think they should rather than as they would in real life. Thus some consumers may buy the low-priced brand just to appear to be smart shoppers, or the high-priced brand so as not to appear stingy. They may also buy something from the category out of a feeling of obligation to the researcher who gave them the money, even though they would not buy from that category in a store.

To overcome these limitations, a few research companies offer highly sophisticated laboratory research facilities. The most elaborate facilities attempt to duplicate as closely as possible the actual conditions under which consumers buy the product. These facilities contain complete simulated stores the size of small convenience stores. Before entering the simulated store, consumers may view reruns of television programs within which are embedded television commercials for the research product, or they may read magazines within which are print advertisements for the product. When consumers finally enter the store, they are invited to do all their shopping, purchasing whatever they want, just as they would on a regular shopping trip. They do not know what products or what product categories are subjects of the research. They use their own money to make their purchases. Their reward for participation is a substantial discount off their total when they check out at the cashier. Box 13-2 describes such a laboratory experiment.

Even the best laboratory experiment is somewhat artificial, introducing some bias into the results. Still, companies that do this research argue convincingly that the problem of bias is not as great as the problems of in-store experimentation and that they can accurately adjust the results of their laboratory experiments, based on their past experience with similar product categories, to take out the effects of any biases inherent in the experimental process.[14] Moreover, one cannot argue with the economics. The cost of even the most

BOX 13-2

MEASURING PRICE SENSITIVITY FOR A COMPUTERIZED CLOCK RADIO: A LABORATORY PURCHASE STUDY

A major Japanese electronics manufacturer was interested in assessing how different advertising and pricing strategies would affect market demand for a new multifunction product (a combination digital clock, AM/FM radio, and cassette player with built-in memory calendar–date book). In addition to being a high-quality clock radio, the product enjoyed several unique features. The clock alarm could activate either a buzzer, the radio itself, or a cassette tape. (A demonstration tape played the old lyric "When the red, red robin comes bob, bob, bobbing along/Get up, you sleepy head/Get up, get out of bed.") Another unique feature was the computer memory, which permitted the user to program up to 500 key dates and/or times. With this system the user could peek ahead in a given month or week to see key dates coming up, and/or wait until the morning of the date when the preprogrammed information would appear on a small screen.

The key questions asked by the manufacturer were twofold. First, how should the product be positioned in television advertising, as an advanced clock radio or as a table-top time-management computer? Second, should the product be priced at $59 to attract a large share of the high-volume radio market; at $79 to compete with high-quality AM/FM radio-cassette players; or at $99 to signal the product's uniqueness and skim the segment that valued those unique features most highly? To address this problem, the manufacturer contracted with Yankelovich, Clancy, Shulman (now Yankelovich Partners) to conduct a laboratory purchase experiment.

In each of four markets, 300 prospective buyers (men and women, aged eighteen and over) were randomly recruited. They were invited to the company's laboratory facilities for the apparent purpose of previewing a new television program and seeing new home electronic products. The design for the study was very simple. Each participant was randomly assigned to a treatment group for exposure to one of the two possible positionings and three possible prices. Thus, at each location, six groups of the fifty participants each were exposed to a different positioning/price combination.

The groups were first exposed to a new half-hour television program in which was embedded advertising for the new product, for competitive products, and for control products. Following this, participants were invited into an adjoining simulated electronics store where they had the opportunity to see the new product along with many competitive products, priced as they would be at local

(Continued)

stores. They could ask questions of store salespeople and read available literature about the products.

All products in the store were for sale at a 30 percent discount off the listed price. Approximately 40 percent of all participants actually made a purchase. The nonbuyers were asked a set of questions to estimate what they would have purchased if they had made a purchase.

The results of the study showed significant effects of both positioning and price on demand. Overall, 14 percent of all prospective purchasers were buyers of the new product. Demand varied with positioning and price in the following way:

Percentage of Purchasers Under Different Conditions

Price	Advanced Clock Radio (%)	Time Management Computer (%)
$59	25	20
79	19	11
99	8	1

Source: Provided by Yankelovich, Clancy, Shulman (now Yankelovich Partners), a marketing research, modeling, and consulting firm in Westport, Connecticut. (Although this description is based on an actual study, some details have been masked to maintain confidentiality.)

sophisticated laboratory experiment is only a small fraction of the cost of in-store testing. As a result, the leading marketers of consumer packaged goods and small appliances rely extensively on this research technique when making pricing decisions.[15]

UNCONTROLLED STUDIES OF PREFERENCES AND INTENTIONS

The most common research technique for directly estimating price sensitivity is the survey of brand preferences or purchase intentions. Companies prefer to measure preferences or intentions, rather than actual purchases, for a number of reasons:

1. Survey data cost much less to collect than purchase data.
2. Survey data can be measured for large durable goods, such as automobiles or photocopiers, for which in-store or laboratory experiments at various prices are impractical.
3. Survey data can be collected even before a product is designed, when the information is most valuable in directing product development.
4. The results can be collected quickly.

Unfortunately, the problem with survey research is that many consumers do not provide answers that are a reliable guide to their actual purchase behavior. The reasons are varied, but one of the main issues is that surveys require a level of abstraction that the respondent may or may not be able to perform. This is especially true of new products that are wholly unfamiliar or whose application is not readily apparent. As a result, determination of value delivered, or willingness-to-pay, are difficult to arrive at even for a committed respondent. In order to solve this problem, some research companies cross-validate the results of one survey with the results of another, often using slightly different methods of data collection and questioning. For example, a firm might collect data using personal interviews and validate the results by telephoning a different group of respondents and asking the same set of questions. The closer the results are from the two samples and methods, the more valid and accurate the final results.

Direct Questioning

Very early in the development of survey techniques for marketing, researchers learned that it was futile to ask consumers outright what they would be willing to pay for a product. Direct questioning sometimes elicits bargaining behavior, with consumers stating a lower price than they would actually pay. Other times, it elicits a desire to please the researcher or to not appear stingy, prompting consumers to state a higher price than they would actually pay. Frequently, it simply elicits a cursory answer that consumers would change were they to give the question the same thought as an actual purchase decision. Consequently, uncontrolled direct questioning as a research technique to estimate price sensitivity should never be accepted as a valid methodology. The results of such studies are at best useless and are potentially highly misleading.

Buy-Response Surveys

A slight variant of the direct-question survey involves showing consumers a product at a preselected price and asking if they would purchase at that price. Surprisingly, although directly asking consumers what they would pay usually yields meaningless answers, asking them if they would buy at a preselected price yields answers that are at least plausible. When the answers given by different consumers for different price levels are aggregated, they produce what looks like a demand curve for market share, sometimes called a purchase probability curve (Box 13-3). Presumably, questioning willingness-to-buy generates better responses simply because it is structured more like an actual purchase decision than as an open-ended question about what the consumer would pay. Also the consumer has no opportunity to bargain with the researcher.[16] Interestingly there are a number of studies that have documented cultural differences that lead to large amounts of substantial and systematic variation in the accuracy of buy-response surveys across countries such as the United States, Germany, and Japan, among others.

Attribute Positioning

Another method for evaluating price sensitivity is to include price as one of the attributes describing a product or a purchase situation. Consumers rate the importance of each attribute using a variety of scaling techniques. Those scales

BOX 13-3

PURCHASE PROBABILITY CURVES: A SIMPLE BUY-RESPONSE STUDY—OPPORTUNITY FOR A HIGHER PRICE

A software firm developed a product for law firms that would easily produce high-quality legal documents and would manage document storage and billing of time for both small and large offices. The original estimates of price were $500 per unit. Chadwick Martin Bailey, Inc., conducted a national study to measure price sensitivity for the product. It began the process by conducting extensive exploratory research, including focus groups and semi-structured interviews. This phase of the research initially indicated that prices in the range of $6,000 might be perfectly acceptable to a large segment of attorneys. A random sample of 603 attorneys was contacted by telephone and asked the likelihood of purchase at either $2,000, $4,000, $6,000, or $8,000, yielding about 150 responses per price point. Probability of purchase was measured using a 0–10 likelihood of purchase scale, and all responses in the 8–10 range were used as a basis for assessing price sensitivity. At $2,000, 49 percent of the firms would have bought the package. Demand was found to be very inelastic for higher prices, as shown in Figure A. Movement from $4,000 to $8,000 in price made little difference in the proportion of law firms willing to buy the product, but produced large differences in revenue from sales, as shown in Figure B.

FIGURE A   Purchase Probability Curve

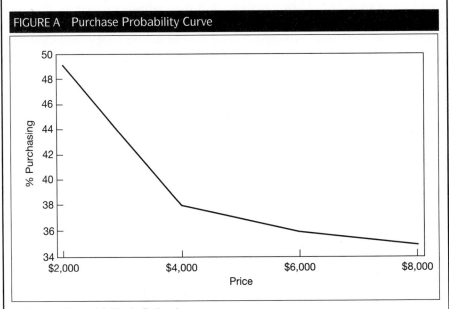

Source: Chadwick Martin Bailey, Inc.

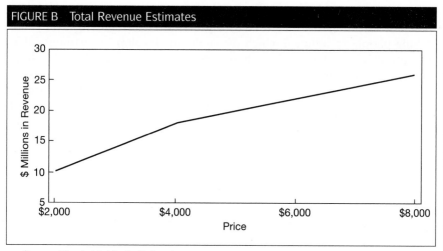

FIGURE B   Total Revenue Estimates

Source: Chadwick Martin Bailey, Inc.

This study was provided by Chadwick Martin Bailey, Inc., a planning and market research firm located in Boston, Massachusetts.

One cannot, however, treat buy-response data as directly comparable to or directly predictive of the sales that would actually occur at the corresponding prices in a store. Most problematic is the fact that consumers' answers depend on their recollection of the actual prices of competing products. To the extent that they overestimate or underestimate competing prices, they will misjudge their willingness-to-buy. Even with this form of the question, some consumers will still want to please the researcher, or will fear appearing stingy, and so will falsely claim a willingness-to-buy the brand over competing brands regardless of the price.

Nevertheless, such research is useful (1) as a preliminary study to identify a range of acceptable prices for a new product and (2) to identify changes in price sensitivity at different points in time or place, assuming that the biases that affect these studies remain the same and so do not affect the observed change. For example, recall that in Chapter 4 (Exhibit 4-4), we saw a buy-response survey for a new food product that showed no difference in consumers' willingness-to-buy at different prices when they knew only the product concept, but a significant difference after they had tried the product. In interpreting the study, one would not want to take the absolute percentage of consumers who claimed they would buy as an accurate prediction of the percentage of consumers who would actually buy at the different prices. However, differences in the stated probability of purchase before and after trial may reliably predict the change in price sensitivity caused by the product trial.

Intention measurement is also sometimes used successfully to predict actual purchases when researchers have past experience that allows them to adjust for the bias in

(Continued)

subjects' stated intentions. Typically, purchase intentions are measured by asking people to indicate which of the following best describes their likelihood of purchase:

> Definitely would buy
> Probably would buy
> Might/might not buy
> Probably would not buy
> Definitely would not buy

The leading survey research firms have asked such questions of millions of buyers for thousands of products. Consequently, they are able to develop adjustments that reflect the average bias in these answers for various product classes. Thus, an experienced researcher might expect that only 80 percent of people answering "definitely would buy," 50 percent answering "probably would buy," 25 percent answering "might/might not buy," and 10 percent answering "probably would not buy" will actually purchase.

---

can be a 1 to 5 or a 1 to 10 importance rating or simply an evaluation of the percent of respondents mentioning the attribute as being important.[17] This approach is problematic because responses tend to be offhand and overly positive, due to halo effects, where respondents tend to not carefully discriminate among listed attributes and give similar ratings or responses to many attributes, especially those adjacent to each other.

Depth Interviews

A depth interview is a "semistructured" method that is used to elicit responses from customers on how they use products and services, from which the research infers value rather than asking about value directly. The interview is often conducted one on one with a respondent and lasts for 1 to 2 hours. In a consumer environment, it is used to understand how individuals and families use products and how they might value different features or positioning approaches. In a business-to-business environment, the interviewer attempts to understand how businesses gain revenues or reduce costs by using a specific product or service; to do this successfully one needs to have a deep understanding of the respondent's business. Depth interviews in pricing research are useful in (1) understanding which product or service features and benefits are important to a customer, (2) assessing the monetary or psychological value of these features and benefits that a customer receives as a result of using the product or service, and (3) assessing roughly what a customer might be willing to pay to obtain these features and benefits. Depth interviews are also used to develop economic-value models of how much a customer could gain in monetary terms from purchase of the product. The model then becomes part of a promotional campaign to increase customers' willingness-to-pay. Such models work well for business customers, where most benefits can be translated into additional revenues or costs saved. It works well in consumer markets where the benefit is a cost saving (e.g., the value of buying a more efficient refrigerator).

EXHIBIT 13-3   Effectiveness of Focus Groups vs. Depth Interviews

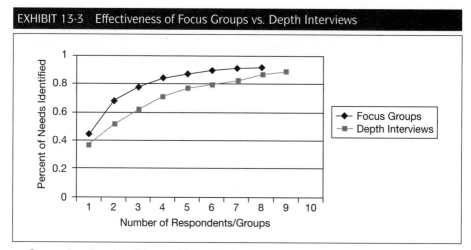

Source: Jonathan Alan Silver and John Charles Thompson Jr., "Understanding Customer Needs: A Systematic Approach to the 'Voice of the Customer,'" Master's Thesis, 1991, Cambridge, MA, Sloan School of Management, Massachusetts Institute of Technology.

Similar to a focus group (Exhibit 13-3), a depth interview is relatively unstructured and is usually conducted by an experienced interviewer who has a specific interview guide and objective, such as to quantify the value of differentiating features. Depth interviews are used less frequently in market research due to the need for highly specialized interviewers, the expense per interview, and the small sample size.[18] This is especially true for consumer pricing research for mass-market products and services. However, for more complex business-to-business pricing research, the quality of information obtained with regard to customer value and willingness-to-pay often yield much more fruitful insights and analysis. For example, in business markets, depth interviews enable the interviewer to probe customer needs, customer experiences, how they attempt to deal with problems, how the supplier's products or services could solve these problems, and the value to the customer of the consequent savings or gains they would realize from using the firm's products or services.

Depth interviews do not ask customers directly how much they would be willing to pay. Instead, the interview focuses on the financial benefits to the customer that a product or service could influence. It is also possible to get a sense of perceived value by identifying other items that the customer buys to achieve the same benefit. For example, *evoked anchoring,* one method used successfully in business-to-business markets, asks respondents to identify items in their budget that they might consider a trade-off in order to obtain the value and benefits promised by a supplier's proposed product or service solution. For example, when helping a software client to price relationship–management software, we identified that one benefit was reduced customer turnover. By asking potential buyers of the software to identify the costs to acquire new customers, we could infer the value to retain them.

Depth interviews enable marketers to understand not only what someone might perceive their product or service to be worth, but also why it is worth that much. The depth interview attempts to understand the needs that the product addresses and how the product or service addresses them. The process often uncovers ways that suppliers can enhance their current product or service offerings and, in doing so, provide the basis for creating more differentiated products that can be sold at higher prices. It also exposes who in the buying organization has goals that are likely to benefit from purchase of the product.[19]

The interview must be conducted outside the context of a selling opportunity or a negotiation, since customers are unlikely to reveal value at such times. However, the data garnered often form the basis of a value-based selling approach in which salespeople, armed with an understanding of how their products differ from those of competitors and how those differences create value for customers, can justify their pricing to the customer and to themselves. Companies often can use the information gained from depth interviews to develop "value case histories." These case histories describe the experience of a particular customer in using a firm's products and the specific value that the customer received. These case histories eventually become a sales support tool.[20]

The depth interview is an excellent method for developing a better understanding of how different product and service features create value for customers, especially customers in a business-to-business environment. It is especially useful in moving beyond the core product and understanding how different service and support elements can create incremental value for a user and provide insights into how a product might be priced to capture that value. It often identifies similar service and support characteristics that can successfully differentiate what are often thought of as commodity products.[21] A common concern is that customers won't provide the data. However, our experience is that most customers are quite willing to share insights and data that will help suppliers serve them better.

EXPERIMENTALLY CONTROLLED STUDIES
OF PREFERENCES AND INTENTIONS
To solve some of the problems of bias and extraneous factors when measuring preferences and intentions, researchers try to exercise some control over the purchase situation presented to respondents.

The questions must be designed to make the survey respondents consider the questions in the same way they would consider an actual purchase decision. The extent to which that can ever be fully accomplished is still an open question, but marketing researchers, recognizing the potential value of accurate survey information, are certainly trying.

Simulated Purchase Experiments
Many researchers believe that the best way to get consumers to think about a survey question and to respond as they would in a purchase situation is to simulate the purchase environment as closely as possible when asking the survey questions. With this type of research, the researcher asks the consumers to

imagine that they are on a shopping trip and desire to make a purchase from a particular product class. Then the researcher shows the consumers pictorial representations, descriptions, or sometimes actual samples of brands along with prices and asks the consumers to choose among them, given various prices. Since actual products need not be used, this technique enables one to test pricing for new product concepts, as part of a general concept test, before the concepts are actually developed into products.

The primary difference between such a simulated purchase experiment and a laboratory purchase experiment is that participants only simulate the choice decision to purchase a product and so do not get to keep their choices.[22] The simulated purchase experiment is a widely used tool in pricing research that overcomes two important drawbacks of other types of surveys. If it is structured as a choice task among alternative brands, a consumer's thought process should more closely approximate the process actually used when making a purchase. Also, since consumers have no way of knowing which brand is the one of interest to the researcher, they cannot easily think of the choice as a bargaining position or as a way to please the researcher. Thus, simulated purchase experiments can sometimes predict price sensitivity reasonably well.[23]

While any type of research is prone to bias, the simulated purchase experiments can often be an acceptable method for gaining quick and low-cost information on the buying behavior of consumers. If, for example, a company wants to estimate the price sensitivity of a product sold nationally, the cost of hundreds of in-store experiments throughout the country would be prohibitive. If the company conducted both an in-store experiment and a simulated purchase experiment in a few locations and found them reasonably consistent, it could confidently use the latter to cover the remaining locations and to conduct future research on that product class. Even if the experiment showed a consistent tendency to be biased, simulated purchase experiments could still be used successfully after the results had been adjusted by the amount of that previously identified bias.

Trade-Off (Conjoint) Analysis

An experimental technique, called trade-off (or conjoint) analysis, has become popular for measuring price sensitivity as well as sensitivity to other product attributes.[24] The particular strength of trade-off analysis is its ability to disaggregate a product's price into the values consumers attach to each attribute. Consequently, trade-off analysis can help a company identify the differentiation value of unique product attributes and, more important, design new products that include only those attributes that consumers are willing to pay for as well as how much they are likely to pay for the entire product and service package. Currently, trade-off analysis aids in the design of a range of products, from automobiles and office equipment to household cleaners and vacation packages.

The basic data for trade-off analysis are consumers' answers to questions that reveal not their directly stated purchase intentions, but rather the underlying preferences that guide their purchase intentions. The researcher collects such data by asking respondents to make choices between pairs of fully described products or between different levels of just two product attributes. The products are typically designed to systematically vary in the levels of certain attributes that define the product. When multiple levels of price are included in the study design, it is possible to not only assess the value assigned to certain product attributes, but one can also arrive at an estimate of price elasticity. The data are collected with a questionnaire or online.

After obtaining a consumer's preferences for a number of product or attribute pairs, the researcher then manipulates the data to impute the value (called utility) that each consumer attaches to each product attribute and the relative importance that each attribute plays in the consumer's purchase decision.[25] With these data, the researcher can predict at what prices the consumer would purchase products containing various combinations of attributes, including combinations that do not currently exist in the marketplace. The researcher can also estimate how much of one attribute the consumer is willing to trade off in order to obtain more of another attribute—for example, how much more price a consumer is willing to trade off in order to obtain more fuel efficiency in a new automobile.

With similar data from a number of consumers who are representative of a market segment, the researcher can develop a model to predict the share of a market that would prefer any particular brand to others at any particular price. Since the researcher has collected data that reveal underlying preferences, consumers' preferences can be predicted, or interpolated, even for levels of price and other attributes not specifically asked about in the questionnaire, provided the attributes are continuously measurable and bounded by the levels that were asked about in the survey. Box 13-4 provides an example of such a process. Readers should note how the basic features were varied along with price in order to develop a relationship between features and value, here termed "feature utility." Segmentation in the sample of respondents is needed to understand how some groups of individuals have higher values for some attributes than others. In this study, those segmented ratings were used as the basis for successfully predicting the probable market share for a new hotel, given careful analysis of how existing hotels matched the needs of different consumers. Failure to segment the respondents into high- and low-value groups often hides the true nature of price and value sensitivity in the population.

It is useful to contrast trade-off analysis with direct questioning methods. By having respondents evaluate a product in its entirety rather than in the more abstract form of individual attributes, responses are more likely to mimic actual choices. For example, in a study of recent MBA graduates, when asked about individual job attributes, the most important was the people and culture of the company. Salaries were rated low on the list of attributes under consideration. However, when studied in a conjoint environment where respondents were given job descriptions to choose from, analysis revealed that salary was the most important job attribute, followed by the region and location of job; people and workplace culture only ranked fourth most important. Perhaps the respondents

BOX 13-4

A CONJOINT STUDY: NEW HOTEL'S BEST PRICE AND ATTRIBUTES

The Greater Southern Development Authority of Western Australia commissioned a conjoint study into the feasibility of building a new resort hotel in Australia's southwest region. The objective of the study was twofold: (1) to verify whether the demand was adequate to justify the project and (2) to determine the optimal features that the hotel should offer. Important hotel attributes—*cost per night, site* (view), *town center* (nearness to town)—and feasible "levels" of those attributes were identified by reviewing current hotels and developer proposals for new hotels and by interviewing possible users of the proposed facility.

Using these attributes levels, sixteen feasible hotel profiles were developed and consumer preferences for them were tested. Telephone interviews were used to identify tourists likely to visit the area. A questionnaire was mailed to 300 potential tourists who were asked to rate the sixteen alternative hotel configurations. Eighty-one percent of the questionnaires were returned and included in the analysis.

Respondents rated the alternative configurations using an eleven-point "likelihood of purchase" scale. Average scores for each attribute level were compared to determine their overall value in the purchasing decision. The initial results of the analysis included an evaluation of

the importance of each attribute and the value or utility that each of the attribute levels had relative to one another. Those utility values were then interpreted relative to the utility of the price of the hotel room in order to develop a dollar (Australian) value for the nonmonetary attributes. Table A lists the results for the attributes reported here. Because of the high negative utility associated with higher price points, the data suggest the market is too price sensitive for a high-priced resort hotel.

Unfortunately, many analysts using conjoint data would stop at this point. In fact, Table A shows only the price sensitivity for a mythical "average" consumer who may be unlike any in the marketplace. Different consumers often have very different price sensitivities for various products and their attributes. To understand these differences, the data for this study were analyzed by applying cluster analysis to individual utilities. This analysis resulted in the identification of four customer segments, each with differing values for the product attributes (see Table B).

Only when the attribute values of the individual segments are evaluated can we find a segment of "active water seekers" for whom price is relatively unimportant. Once this segment was found, the data were analyzed to predict the market share that

(Continued)

Attribute and Levels	Importance	Utility	Value*
Cost per night	56		
40*		1.86	
60		0.28	
80		−0.45	
100		−1.99	
Site	6		
View		−0.01	$−0.16
Harbor		−0.19	−2.96
Mountains		−0.07	−1.09
Beach		0.25	3.89
Town center	7		
Short walk		0.05	$0.78
5 minutes		0.21	3.27
20 minutes		−0.26	−4.05

*Values are in Australian dollars.

TABLE B Attribute Importance and Utilities for Different Hotel Segments

Attribute and Levels	Convenience Seekers Impor-tance	Utility	Basics Seekers Impor-tance	Utility	Active Water Seekers Impor-tance	Utility	Passive Viewers Impor-tance	Utility
Cost per night	31		73		14		41	
40*		0.87		3.14		0.09		1.44
60		0.35		0.89		−0.05		0.64
80		0.15		−1.15		0.23		−0.12
100		−1.27		−3.89		−0.09		−2.17
Site	16		3		29		14	
View		0.16		−0.04		−0.35		0.19
Harbor		0.01		−0.10		0.22		0.31
Mountains		0.37		0.07		−0.30		0.31
Beach		0.28		0.14		0.30		0.47
Town center	18		1		3		9	
Short walk		0.15		0.01		0.04		−0.03
5 minutes		0.39		0.04		−0.02		0.26
20 minutes		−0.74		−0.05		−0.02		−0.34

*Values are in Australian dollars.

Source: Chadwick Martin Bailey, Inc., a planning and market research firm located in Boston, Massachusetts. The results of this study were reported in complete form at the Second International Conference on Marketing and Development, Budapest, July 10–13, 1988, in a paper entitled "Regional Planning for Resort Hotels: A Conjoint Application" by John Martin and David Blackmore.

the "ideal" hotel could obtain for this segment. The results: A hotel on the beach and a short walk to the town center could capture a 16.4 percent market share at a price of $80, with most of the potential customers coming from the active water seekers segment. The fact that most of the customers in this market would deem this hotel a poor value is irrelevant.

behaved more altruistically when attributes were evaluated—and recorded—separately, but when presented with more realistic job choices, conjoint analysis allows for an accurate evaluation of preferences.

Of all methods used to estimate price sensitivity from preferences or intentions, trade-off analysis promises the most useful information for strategy formulation. The researchers can do more than simply identify the price sensitivity of the market as a whole; they can identify customer segments with different price sensitivities and, to the extent that those differences result from differences in the economic value of product attributes, can also identify the specific product attributes that evoke the differences. Consequently, researchers can describe the combination of attributes that can most profitably skim or penetrate a market. The economic value of a product can also be identified even when the product is not yet developed by presenting consumers with different experimental product combinations in the form of pictorial and descriptive product concepts, or new product prototypes.

With the use of more advanced modeling techniques, researchers are able to use an adaptation of conjoint analysis, discrete choice analysis, in which consumers are given either a limited number of choices or a wide range of choices of different product packages from different competitors, all often at different prices. Based on the analysis of their choices, researchers are then able to form segments by grouping consumers based on the similarity of their responses and develop estimates of market share based on the size and responsiveness of the different segments (Box 13-5). Given internal costs and external promotions, the models can predict likely levels of profitability given those customer and competitive responses.

As a result of these promised advantages, the use of trade-off analysis by both market research firms and internal research departments has grown rapidly, but the performance of trade-off analysis is only as good as its ability to predict actual purchase behavior. There are, however, a number of reasons why a prudent manager might suspect the reliability of this technique for some markets. Trade-off analysis is an experimental procedure that introduces bias to the extent that it does not simulate the actual purchase environment. The respondent taking a conjoint test is encouraged to focus much more attention on price and price differences than may occur in a natural purchase environment. Thus, while trade-off analysis is still useful for studying non-price trade-offs, it should not be trusted in situations where there is little evidence that the purchaser evaluates prices when actually making a decision. For example, research companies have compared the predicted effects of price on physicians prescribing decisions with data on the actual price of the pharmaceuticals they prescribed. The conjoint tests predicted much higher price sensitivity than in fact was the case. Also, if respondents have little experience with the product as is usually the case with innovative product categories, the technique poorly predicts the trade-offs that customers will make.

Because trade-off analysis measures underlying preferences, the researcher has the ability to check if an individual consumer's responses are at least consistent. Consumers who are not taking the survey seriously, or who are basically irrational in their choice processes, are then easily identified and excluded from the

---

BOX 13-5

PROFITABILITY OPTIMIZATION MODEL USING DISCRETE CHOICE SURVEY

Alltel, a telecommunications provider, was trying to determine the appropriate bundles of offerings and prices for a broad range of telecommunications services. They used an outside market research firm to develop a model from conjoint-like data that allows scenario testing for specific product/service offerings in terms of price, product features, and packaging of those features.

The research firm needed to model the complex elements of the wireless industry (access, per minute fees, roaming, toll, and features), wireline (access, interstate toll, intrastate toll, optional call plans, and features), and several others. They knew that prices in all sectors would continue to decline quickly and that they could expect a response to any move by all of the competitors in each area. The business questions they faced were these: (1) Would consumers choose Alltel over the dominant local provider? (2) Would they want bundles rather than individual services and at what price? (3) What prices would optimize Alltel's market share/sales/contribution? (4) What would happen when competitors responded?

The market researcher surveyed a large number of potential customers using the survey instrument in Table A. Analysis of the data revealed six very distinct segments in the respondent population, so a separate model was developed for each segment that analyzed expected demand, price elasticity for each product/service, cannibalization of existing products, and possible competitive responses. The resulting model permitted the real-time input of competitive prices (Table B) and provided expected market share, sales volume, and subsequent profit contribution for the client and its competitors (Table C).

Source: This research was performed and provided by SDR Consulting, a market research/modeling firm located in Atlanta, Georgia.

Please indicate which individual services or packages you would prefer.

Individual Services	Alltel	Bell South	AT&T	Cable Provider	Regional Bell	Other
Wireless (Cellular/Mobile) Service						
No free local minutes	$14.95	$19.95	$19.95	$14.95	$19.95	$19.95
200 free local minutes	n/a	$39.95	$39.95	$39.95	$39.95	$39.95
400 free local minutes plus 5 calling features*	$49.95	$49.95	$49.95	$49.95	$49.95	$49.95
1,000 free local minutes plus 5 calling features*	$89.95	$99.95	$99.95	$89.95	$89.95	$89.95
Wireline (Local) Service						
Single-line basic service	n/a	$22.95	n/a	n/a	n/a	n/a
Single line with all calling features*	n/a	$28.95	$26.95	$26.95	$29.95	$28.95
Single line with all calling features plus Voice Mail	$34.95	$34.95	$31.95	$31.95	$31.95	$33.95
Second line, no features	$19.95	$13.95	$12.95	$12.95	$19.95	$13.95
Long Distance						
Wireline	$0.08	$0.13	$0.13	$0.13	$0.10	$0.13
Wireless	$0.09	$0.15	$0.15	$0.15	$0.13	$0.15
Internet						
Unlimited online access	$19.95	$19.95	$21.95	$34.95	$19.95	$21.95
		OR				
Packages	1 year contract	1 year contract	1 year contract			
Bronze*	$49.95	$79.95	$79.95			
Silver*	$109.95	$114.95	$114.95			
Gold*	$149.95	$209.95	$209.95			

*See handout for explanation of Bronze, Silver, and Gold packages, along with special calling features.

TABLE B Market Response Simulator

	Alltel	Local Bell (ILEC)	AT&T	Cable Provider	Regional Bell	Other
Wireless						
No free local minutes	$14.95	$19.95	$19.95	$14.95	$19.95	$19.95
200 free local minutes	$29.95	$29.95	$29.95	$29.95	$29.95	$29.95
400 free local minutes	$49.95	$49.95	$49.95	$49.95	$49.95	$49.95
1000 free local minutes	$89.95	$99.95	$99.95	$89.95	$89.95	$89.95
Local Service						
Single-line basic service	n/a	$22.95	n/a	n/a	n/a	n/a
Single line w/features	n/a	$28.95	$26.95	$26.95	$29.95	$28.95
Single line w/features plus Voice Mail	$34.95	$34.95	$31.95	$31.95	$31.95	$33.95
Single w/features plus second line	$19.95	$13.95	$12.95	$12.95	$19.95	$13.95
Long Distance						
Wireline	$0.10	$0.13	$0.13	$0.13	$0.10	$0.13
Wireless	$0.13	$0.15	$0.15	$0.15	$0.13	$0.15
Internet						
Unlimited online access	$19.95	$19.95	$19.95	$19.95	$19.95	$21.95
Packages						
Alltel	1 year contract	1 year contract	1 year contract	1 year contract	1 year contract	n/a
Bronze	$44.95	$69.95	$69.95	$62.95	$69.95	n/a
Silver	$99.95	$99.95	$99.95	$99.95	$99.95	n/a
Gold	$179.95	$184.95	$184.95	$179.95	$179.95	n/a

TABLE C Market Response Simulator Summary Output

Customer Share Total Model	Alltel Test	Local Bell (ILEC) Test	AT&T Test	Cable Provider Test	Regional Bell Test	Other Test	Total Test	
Wireless	46.8%	9.8%	11.7%	6.8%	0.8%	8.8%	84.7%	Shows the provider's customer share of each service and percentage of customers buying packages
Local service	3.3%	52.4%	23.6%	2.5%	0.8%	2.0%	84.7%	
Long distance	16.4%	7.4%	45.7%	2.8%	4.3%	8.1%	84.7%	
Internet	7.8%	31.7%	9.1%	1.6%	1.4%	8.2%	59.8%	
Packages	15.3%	0.0%	0.0%	0.0%	0.0%	n/a	15.3%	

Total Annual Dollars (million $) Total Model	Alltel Test	Local Bell (ILEC) Test	AT&T Test	Cable Provider Test	Regional Bell Test	Other Test	Total Test	
Wireless	$49.47	$13.19	$14.42	$7.02	$1.36	$10.45	$95.91	Shows the provider's total annual revenue for each service and package offering
Local service	$6.05	$78.15	$36.76	$3.93	$1.39	$3.30	$129.58	
Long distance	$15.02	$8.58	$51.84	$3.25	$3.75	$9.32	$91.75	
Internet	$6.64	$27.10	$7.81	$1.38	$1.21	$7.71	$51.85	
Packages	$74.58	$0.00	$0.00	$0.00	$0.00	n/a	$74.58	
Total	$151.76	$127.02	$110.83	$15.58	$7.70	$30.78	$443.67	

Total Annual Contribution (million $) Total Model	Alltel Test	
Wireless	$31.76	Shows Alltel's total contribution (revenue-cost) for each service and package offering
Local service	$2.41	
Long distance	$3.31	
Internet	$1.90	
Packages	$21.10	
Total	$60.47	

sample. Even more comforting are three separate studies that show a high degree of consistency, or reliability, when subjects are asked to repeat a trade-off questionnaire a few days after having taken it initially.[26] Since the subjects are unlikely to remember exactly how they answered the questions in the earlier session, the consistency of the answers over time strongly suggests that they do accurately reflect true underlying preferences. More comforting yet is the result of a study showing that the exclusion from the questionnaire of some product attributes a subject might consider important does not bias the subject's responses concerning the trade-offs among the attributes that are included.[27] Although trade-off analysis is more costly than a simple survey, it also provides much more information. Given its relatively low cost and the fact that it has met at least some tests of reliability, it certainly warrants consideration when seeking to develop a product with features that can be priced most profitably.

USING MEASUREMENT TECHNIQUES APPROPRIATELY

Numerical estimates of price sensitivity can either benefit or harm the effectiveness of a pricing strategy, depending on how management uses them. This is especially true when respondents have considerable experience with the use and purchase of a product. If managers better understand their buyers and use that knowledge to formulate judgments about buyers' price sensitivity, as discussed in Chapter 5, an attempt to measure price sensitivity can be very useful. It can give managers new, objective information that can either increase their confidence in their prior judgments or indicate that perhaps they need to study their buyers further. An understanding of price sensitivity also provides a reference by which to judge proposed price changes—how will sales respond as we increase or decrease prices? Combined with variable cost data, it is possible to judge whether proposed changes in price will have the desired effect on profits.

Integrating soft managerial judgments about buyers and purchase behavior with numerical estimates based on hard data is fundamental to successful pricing. Managerial judgments of price sensitivity are necessarily imprecise while empirical estimates are precise numbers that management can use for profit projections and planning. However, precision doesn't necessarily mean accuracy. Numerical estimates of price sensitivity may be far off the mark of true price sensitivity. Accuracy is a virtue in formulating pricing strategy; precision is only a convenience.

No estimation technique can capture the full richness of the factors that enter a purchase decision. In fact, measurements of price sensitivity are precise specifically because they exclude all the factors that are not conveniently measurable. Some estimation techniques enable the researcher to calculate a confidence interval around a precise estimate, indicating a range within which we may have some degree of statistical certainty that the true estimate of price sensitivity lies. That range is frequently wider than the interval that a well-informed manager could specify with equal confidence simply from managerial judgment. Unfortunately, researchers often do not (or cannot) articulate such a range to indicate just how tenuous their estimates are. When they do, managers often ignore it. Consequently, managers deceive themselves into thinking that an estimate of price sensitivity based on hard data is accurate when in fact it is only a point estimate of something we can rarely predict with 100 percent accuracy. Fortunately, a manager does not have to make the choice between judgment and empirical estimation. Used effectively, they are complementary, with the information from each improving the information that the other provides.

USING JUDGMENT FOR BETTER MEASUREMENT

Any study of price sensitivity should begin with the collection of information about buyers—who they are, why they buy, and how they make their purchase decisions—since those are the essential inputs in the formulation of judgment. At the outset, this information should come from open-ended, qualitative, or exploratory research that enables managers to discover facts and formulate impressions other than those for which they may have been specifically looking.[28] In industrial markets, such research may consist of accompanying salespeople to observe the purchase process. After a sale, managers might follow up to ask how and why the purchase decision was made. One can also look at past bid histories to see the correlation between various price levels and the likelihood of winning the bid. In many cases, managers can interview important customers and intermediaries by telephone to gain their impressions about a variety of price and marketing issues.[29] In consumer markets, such research may consist of observing consumers discussing their purchase decisions in focus groups or depth interviews as previously discussed. Insights generated from such informal observation could then be confirmed with more formal research in the form of a survey administered to a larger number of buyers.

Having formed judgments about buyers based on qualitative impressions developed from observing them, a manager will often find it practical and cost-effective to expand this understanding through original primary research that attempts to measure certain aspects of buyer behavior, such as price sensitivity. That attempt is far more likely to produce useful results, to the extent that management already understands the way buyers make their purchase decisions and uses that information to help structure the attempt at measurement. There are a number of ways that managerial judgment can, and should, guide the measurement effort.

1. For experimentally controlled data estimation, managerial judgment should determine the focus of the research on certain target demographic groups and provide guidance for generalizing from those groups to the population as a whole.

   • Management may know that 80 percent of its product's buyers are women who are employed full-time. That information is important if the researcher plans to measure price sensitivity with an in-home

survey or an experiment in a shopping center. On a typical day between 9:00 A.M. and 5:00 P.M., few of the experimental subjects at home
or in the shopping center would be representative of that product's
buyers. To get a representative sample, the researcher might need to
conduct the in-home survey in the evenings or the experiment only
during the lunch hour at locations near where many women work. He
or she might also ask a prescreening question (Are you employed
full-time?).

- If management also knows that different demographic groups buy the
product in different quantities, that information can be used to scale
the survey results differently for different subjects in the sample to
reflect their relative impact on the product's actual sales.

2. For historical data estimations, the intervention of informed managerial
judgment into the analysis is even more essential, since the lack of any
experimental control invariably results in data that are full of potential
statistical problems. Managerial judgment should be used to reduce
random error and solve statistical problems.

- The effect of price changes tends to get overwhelmed in historical
purchase data by the amount of sales variation caused by other factors, which may not be obvious to the researcher but may be to managers who know their buyers. For example, a researcher analyzing
many years' worth of data on the sales of a frozen seafood product
could substantially improve the estimation of price sensitivity if management pointed out that many buyers purchase the product as part
of their religious observance of Lent, a Christian holiday that shows
up at a different time every year. That one bit of information about
why consumers buy would enable the researcher to eliminate a substantial amount of random variation in the data that would otherwise
yield a biased estimate of price sensitivity if it were not included.
- The researcher using historical data is also often confounded by the
problem called colinearity, where different explanatory variables
change together. Perhaps, at the same time that a firm offers a promotional price deal, it always offers retailers a trade deal in return for
a special product display. Without additional input from management,
the researcher cannot sort out the effect of the price deal from that of
the display. If, however, management knows that buyers of the product are like those of another product that is sometimes sold on special
displays without a price deal, the researcher could use sales data from
that other product to solve the colinearity problem with this one.
Alternatively, if managers are confident in making a judgment about
the effectiveness of special displays (for example, that they account
for between one third and one half of the total sales change), that
information can likewise help the researcher to narrow an estimate of
the effect of price on sales.[30]

3. Managerial judgment should also be used to select the appropriate structure for an experiment or survey, and the appropriate specification of a statistical equation for analysis of historical data.

- A manager who has studied buyers should know the length of the purchase cycle (time between purchases) and the extent of inventory holding, both of which will govern the necessary length of an experiment or the number of lagged variables to include when analyzing historical data. Failure to appropriately specify the purchase cycle could cause a researcher to grossly miscalculate price sensitivity by ignoring the longer-term effects of a price change.
- Management may have much experience indicating that an advertisement affects buyers differently when the advertisement focuses on price rather than on other product attributes. If so, the researcher should separate those types of advertising in an experiment or in historical data analysis. The researcher might also treat price advertising as having an effect that interacts with the level of price, and nonprice advertising as having an independent effect.

4. For survey research, managerial judgment should guide the preparation of product descriptions, to ensure that they include the variables relevant to buyers and that they describe them with the appropriate connotations.

- For an automobile survey, management can point out that the amount of time required to accelerate to 65 mph is an important attribute to include when describing a sports car, but not when describing a family car.
- For a survey on radios, managers can point out that the word "knob" in a description will carry a connotation much different from the word "control," which may influence buyers' perceptions about other attributes such as reliability and state-of-the-art technology.

The common failure to use this type of managerial input (or the failure of management to know buyers well enough to provide it) is no doubt one reason why research to measure price sensitivity is often disappointing.

When measurement embodies managerial judgment, it is much more likely to provide useful information, but even then the results should never be taken uncritically. The first question to ask after any marketing research is "Why do the results look the way they do?" The measurement of price sensitivity is not an end result but a catalyst to learn more about one's buyers. If the results are inconsistent with prior expectations, one should consider how prior judgment might have been wrong. What factors may have been overlooked, or have been given too little weight, leading to the formulation of incorrect expectations about price sensitivity? One should also consider how bias might have been introduced into the measurement process. Perhaps the measurement technique heightened buyers' attention to price or the sample subjects were unrepresentative of the product's actual buyers. Regardless of the outcome of such an evaluation, one can learn more about the product's buyers and the factors that determine their price sensitivity. Even when one concludes that the measurement technique biased the results, the bias reveals information (e.g., that the low level of price sensitivity that management expected is substantially due to buyers' low attention to price in the natural purchase environment, or that a segment of people who do not regularly buy the firm's product has a different sensitivity to price).

USING INTERNET-BASED TECHNIQUES

Since the advent of the Internet, market researchers and their clients are increasingly using this forum for gathering customer and market data. Online research is often far less expensive and much faster than traditional research methods—for example, you avoid the costs of mailing or telephone staff. It tends to obtain better response rates because it is less intrusive and more convenient to simply click a "respond" button in an e-mail. However, online research may yield biased results because of sampling bias—online respondents are not necessarily representative of the broader target population. Minorities, lower-income households, rural residents, and older people, for example, are less likely to be represented among online samples. Nonetheless, online research can be particularly effective for identifying very specific or specialized subgroups to target for research. Esearch.com, for example, sends out qualifying questionnaires to many online respondents to find those with specific product or service needs, and then follows up with that smaller pool of respondents with more in-depth research. Eli Lilly, an Esearch.com client, used this online qualifying process to identify people with obscure ailments for which the company is developing treatments.[31]

OUTSIDE SOURCES OF DATA

In addition to performing experiments and evaluating available sales data, one should be aware of the many external sources of data that are available to shed light on price sensitivity. Public records such as those found at government institutions or industry trade groups contain vast sources of data and information on historical sales trends, industry actions, as well as a record of other factors that may affect the market of interest. Market research firms specialize in performing the types of experiments and analyses described in this chapter. The journals published by various academic and industry institutions offer lessons from the past that may apply new products. The Society of Competitive Intelligence Professionals (SCIP) is an industry trade group that is devoted to the quest for finding competitive intelligence.[32]

Other secondary sources of data for industrial markets, including the Census of Manufacturers, the Survey of Industrial Buying Power, and numerous other governmental and private sources[33] can tell sellers the types of businesses their buyers engage in and the share of the total market each accounts for, the average size of their purchases in major product classes, and their growth rates. In consumer markets, consumer panel surveys are widely available to tell managers the demographics of their buyers (income, family size, education, use of coupons) as well as those of their closest competitors. Other companies, such as SRI

International, develop complete psychographic profiles of buyers that go beyond just demographics to delve into the innermost psychological motivations for purchase. These are relatively inexpensive sources of data from which management can form judgments about price sensitivity.

Regardless of the method of intelligence gathering, recognize that the key aim of the marketer is to listen to the voice of the customer, understand how product attributes get translated into value, and how value is converted into a willingness to part with money to obtain said good.

SELECTING THE APPROPRIATE MEASUREMENT TECHNIQUE

The choice among measurement techniques is not arbitrary. Each is more appropriate than another under certain circumstances. Information about one determinant of price sensitivity, the unique value effect, is most valuable when a company is developing new products or improving old ones. The value that buyers place on differentiating attributes should determine which ones the final product will include. Clearly, since one cannot use historical data or a purchase experiment to test undeveloped products, one must turn to research on preferences and intentions that require only product descriptions or experimental prototypes. Given the lack of realism in such research and the fact that it often predicts actual price sensitivity rather poorly, one may be skeptical of its value in the product development process. Surveys of preferences and intentions yield poor predictions of actual price sensitivity partly because they fail to capture some important factors in the actual purchase environment, such as price awareness and knowledge of substitutes. At the time of product development, however, those are not factors about which management is concerned. Product development focuses on efforts to enhance the unique value effect. Even when survey research accurately measures only the effect of product attributes on price sensitivity, it is a useful tool for product development, although it may be inadequate for actually setting prices later on.

Once a product is developed, management would like to have measurements that capture as many of the different determinants of price sensitivity as possible. In-store or sophisticated laboratory purchase experiments are definitely the first choice for frequently purchased, low-cost products. With few exceptions, such products are bought by consumers who have low price awareness and give the purchase decision little attention. Consequently, surveys to estimate price sensitivity for such products focus much more attention on price in the purchase decision than would occur naturally, thus distorting the estimates. The cost of in-store experiments, however, may make them impractical for testing on a large scale. In that case, management might best do a few in-store experiments with matched simulated purchase surveys. If the amount of bias in the latter is stable, the survey could be used for further research and adjusted by the amount of the bias.

When the fully developed product is a high-cost durable such as a TV set or a photocopier, an in-store experiment is generally impractical. A laboratory purchase experiment may be practical since experimental control permits inferences from fewer purchases but will be too costly for many products. Fortunately, high-value products are also products for which consumers naturally pay great attention to price. In fact, they may give all aspects of the purchase careful thought because it involves a large expenditure. Consequently, a simple laboratory experiment or a simulated purchase survey may be reasonably accurate in predicting price sensitivity for these types of products. Even a buy-response survey may be useful to identify the range of prices that potential customers might find acceptable for such products, although the exact estimates of sales at various prices should not be treated with much confidence.

Once a product has been on the market for a while, historical data become available. Such data are most useful when managers are willing to implement marketing decisions in ways that can increase the research value of the resulting sales data. For example, sales data become more useful if price changes are sometimes accompanied by a change in advertising and other times not, enabling marketing researchers to isolate their separate effects. A log of unusual events that cause distortions in the actual sales data (for instance, a strike by a competitor's truckers may be causing stock-outs of the competitor's product and increased sales of yours) is also extremely useful when the time comes to adjust the historical data. Moreover, as managers talk with and observe buyers, they should keep questions in mind that would aid the researcher using historical data: What is the length of the purchase cycle? To what extent do buyers purchase extra for inventories when price is expected to rise in the future? Even if historical data are so filled with random variations that no conclusions can be drawn from them with confidence, they may still point toward possible relationships between price and sales or other marketing variables that would be worth examining with another research technique.

Summary

Numerical estimation of price sensitivity is no shortcut to knowing a product's buyers—who they are, how they buy, and why they make their purchase decisions. Numerical estimates are an important source of objective information that can supplement the more subjective observations that usually dominate managerial judgments about price sensitivity. As a supplement, they can substantially improve the accuracy of such judgments and the effectiveness of a firm's pricing.

Measurement techniques differ in the variables they measure and in the conditions of measurement. The variable measured may be either actual purchases or preferences and intentions. Since the ultimate goal of research is to predict customers' actual purchases, research based on actual purchase data is generally more reliable than research based on preferences and intentions. Unfortunately, collecting and analyzing actual-purchase data costs more, requires much more time, and is entirely impossible for products that are not yet fully developed and ready for sale. Consequently, most research on price sensitivity infers purchase behavior from questions potential customers answer about their preferences and intentions.

Pricing research studies range from those that are completely uncontrolled to those in which the experimenter controls almost completely the alternative products, their prices, and the information that customers receive. Although research techniques that permit a high degree of experimental control are more costly than uncontrolled research, the added cost is usually worth it. Uncontrolled data on actual purchases are plagued by too little variation in prices and too many variables changing at once. Uncontrolled data on preferences and intentions are biased by people's untruthful responses and by their inability to recall competitive prices. In contrast, controlled in-store experiments and sophisticated laboratory purchase experiments often predict actual price sensitivity well. Even experiments using preferences and intentions seem to warrant confidence when they are highly controlled. In particular, trade-off analysis is proving highly useful in predicting at least that portion of price sensitivity determined by the unique-value effect.

The appropriate technique for numerically estimating price sensitivity depends on the product's stage of development. When a product is still in the concept or prototype stage, research measuring preferences or intentions is the only option. Trade-off analysis is especially useful at this stage because it can identify the value of individual product attributes, thus helping to decide which combination of attributes will enable the firm to price the product most profitably. When a product is ready for the market, in-store or laboratory purchase experiments are more appropriate because they more realistically simulate the actual purchase environment. After a product has been on the market for a while, actual purchase data can be an inexpensive source of estimates, provided that management monitors sales frequently and makes some price changes independently of changes in other marketing variables. Even when actual purchase data cannot provide conclusive answers, they can suggest relationships that can then be measured more reliably with other techniques.

Regardless of the technique used to measure price sensitivity, it is important that managers not allow the estimate to become a substitute for managerial judgment. The low accuracy of many numerical estimates makes blind reliance on them very risky. One always needs to be aware of the range of values an elasticity estimate can take, the factors that can influence price sensitivity, and one must generally get an understanding of the range of values one can expect. They always should be compared with a manager's own expectations, based on his or her more general knowledge of buyers and their purchase motivations. When inconsistencies occur, the manager should reexamine both the measurement technique and the adequacy of his or her understanding of buyers. The quality of numerical estimates depends in large part on the quality of managerial judgment that guides the estimation process. Managers who know their buyers can get substantially better estimates of price sensitivity when they use that knowledge (1) to select a sample of consumers that accurately represents the product's market, (2) to identify and explain extraneous changes in sales that might camouflage an effect, (3) to provide information to sort out the effects of price from other variables that tend to change with it, (4) to identify an appropriate equation or experimental structure, and (5) to properly describe the product for survey research.

Notes

1. A. C. Nielsen conducts a bimonthly product audit of retail sales and retailer inventories for many types of frequently purchased products, including foods, household products, health and beauty aids, tobacco products, photographic products, writing instruments, small electrical appliances, and some automotive products. The Nielsen audit is based on a probability sample of all types of stores in which the product might be sold.

2. Actually, the researcher observes only the price that the consumer reports

having paid. There is some risk of erroneous reporting, which weakens the data but does not bias it. Fortunately, this problem is being solved by technologies that enable consumers to avoid the task of reporting.

3. See Ronald E. Frank and William Massy, "Market Segmentation and the Effectiveness of a Brand's Dealing Policies," *Journal of Business,* 38 (April 1965), pp. 186–200; Terry Elrod and Russell S. Winer, "An Empirical Evaluation of Aggregation Approaches for Developing Market Segments," *Journal of Marketing,* 46 (Fall 1982), pp. 65–74.

4. The companies are Information Resources Inc. (headquarters in Chicago) and Burke Marketing Research (headquarters in Cincinnati, Ohio).

5. The increased usage of scanner data in both applied and academic research results from the widespread availability of such information. Researchers should be aware, however, that research continues to point to the inaccuracy of some of the data available. An excellent study on this subject is "UPC Scanner Pricing Systems: Are They Accurate?" by Ronald C. Goodstein, *Journal of Marketing,* April 1994.

6. See K. Wisniewski and R. C. Blattberg, "Response Function Estimation Using UPC Scanner Data," in *Advances and Practices of Marketing Science,* 1983, ed. F. Zufryden, pp. 300–311; Kenneth Wisniewski, "Analytical Approaches to Demand Estimation," *1983 Proceedings of the Business and Economic Statistics Section, American Statistical Association* (ASA, Toronto, 1983), pp. 13–22; and David R. Bell, Joengwen Chiang, and V. Padmanabhan, "The Decomposition of Promotional Response: An Empirical Generalization," *Marketing Science,* 18(4) (1999), pp. 504–526.

7. For a brief introduction to regression analysis, see Thomas C. Kinnear and James R. Taylor, *Marketing Research: An Applied Approach,* 4th ed. (McGraw-Hill, New York, 1991), pp. 626–628; or Mark L. Bereson and David M. Levine, *Basic Business Statistics: Concepts and Application* (Upper Saddle River, NJ: Prentice Hall, 1992), Chapter 16.

8. In practice, of course, there are always some external factors that will affect only one store's sales, undermining the effectiveness of the control. For example, the control store may run out of a competing brand. One can reduce the distorting effect of such factors by increasing the number of both experimental and control stores, but at a corresponding increase in cost.

9. For guidance in the proper design of either a field or laboratory experiment, see Thomas Cook and Donald T. Campbell, "The Design and Conduct of Quasi-Experimental and True Experiments in Field Settings," in *Handbook of Industrial and Organizational Psychology,* ed. Marvin Dunnette (Chicago: Rand McNally, 1976), pp. 223–235.

10. See http://gsbwww.uchicago.edu/kilts/research/db/dominicks/.

11. William Applebaum and Richard Spears, "Controlled Experimentation in Marketing Research," *Journal of Marketing,* 14(January 1950), pp. 505–517; Edward Hawkins, "Methods of Estimating Demand," *Journal of Marketing,* 21(April 1957), pp. 430–534; William D. Barclay, "Factorial Design in a Pricing Experiment," *Journal of Marketing Research,* 6 (November 1969), pp. 427–429; Sidney Bennet and I. B. Wilkinson, "Price-Quantity Relationship and Price Elasticity Under In-Store Experimentation," *Journal of Business Research,* 2(January 1974), pp. 27–38; Gerald Eskin, "A Case for Test Marketing Experiments," *Journal of Advertising Research,* 15 (April 1975), pp. 27–33;

Gerald Eskin and Penny Baron, "Effect of Price and Advertising in Test Market Experiments," *Journal of Marketing Research,* 14 (November 1977), pp. 499–508.

12. Barclay, "Factorial Design in a Pricing Experiment," p. 428.

13. Paul Solman and Thomas Friedman, *Life and Death in the Corporate Battlefield* (New York: Simon and Schuster, 1982), p. 24.

14. Each company develops its own adjustment factors, which are often closely guarded trade secrets.

15. Several good discussions of the increased use and application of laboratory test markets (called Simulated Test Marketing by the authors) can be found in Kevin J. Clancy and Robert S. Shulman, "Simulated Test Marketing: A New Technology for Solving an Old Problem," in *A.N.A./The Advertiser* (Fall 1995), pp. 28–33; and also in Kevin J. Clancy and Robert S. Shulman, "Test for Success: How Simulated Test Marketing Can Dramatically Improve the Forecasting of a New Product's Sales," *Sales and Marketing Management* (October 1995), pp. 111–114.

16. One might well argue that buy-response surveys should be included with the experimentally controlled studies since the researcher does exercise control over the price asked. That observation is correct. The reason that buy-response questioning is better than direct questioning is precisely because the researcher introduces a bit of control. Still, the amount of control that the researcher can exercise in these studies is slight. No attempt is made to control the respondents' perception of competitive prices, exposure to promotion, or demographics.

17. Henry Assael, *Consumer Behavior and Marketing Action,* 2nd ed. (Boston: Kent Publishing, 1983).

18. For a good discussion on the application of and difference between focus group and depth interviews as unstruc-

tured/uncontrolled data-collection techniques, see Thomas C. Kinnear and James R. Taylor, *Marketing Research: An Applied Approach,* 4th ed., (New York: McGraw-Hill, 1991).

19. Abbie Griffin and John R. Hauser, "The Voice of the Customer," *Marketing Science,* 12(1) (Winter 1993), pp. 1–27.

20. F. James C. Anderson and James A. Narus, "Business Marketing: Understand What Customers Value," *Harvard Business Review* (November–December 1998), pp. 53–65.

21. For an excellent discussion on the types of value drivers and how to uncover those value drivers in both consumer and business-to-business research, read Ian C. MacMillan and Rita Gunther McGrath, "Discovering New Points of Differentiation," *Harvard Business Review* (July–August 1997), pp. 133–145.

22. D. Frank Jones, "A Survey Technique to Measure Demand Under Various Pricing Strategies," *Journal of Marketing,* 39 (July 1975), pp. 75–77.

23. John R. Nevin, "Laboratory Experiments for Estimating Consumer Demand," *Journal of Marketing Research,* 11 (August 1974), pp. 261–268.

24. The first article on trade-off analysis to appear in the marketing literature was Paul E. Green and Vithala R. Rao, "Conjoint Measurement for Quantifying Judgemental Data," *Journal of Marketing Research,* 8 (August 1971), pp. 355–363. For a nontechnical discussion of applications specifically to pricing, see Patrick J. Robinson, "Applications of Conjoint Analysis to Pricing Problems," in *Market Measurement and Analysis,* ed. David B. Montgomery and Dick R. Wittink (Cambridge, MA: Marketing Science Institute, 1980), pp. 183–205.

25. The following articles describe data manipulation procedures for conjoint analysis: J. B. Kruskal, "Analysis of

Factorial Experiments by Estimating Monotone Transformations of the Data," *Journal of the Royal Statistical Society,* Series B (1965), pp. 251–263; Dove Peckelman and Subrata Sen, "Regression Versus Interpolation in Additive Conjoint Measurement," *Association for Consumer Research (1976),* pp. 29–34; Philip Cattin and Dick Wittink,"Further Beyond Conjoint Measurement: Toward Comparison of Methods," 1976 *Association for Consumer Research Proceedings (1976),* pp. 41–45.

26. Franklin Acito, "An Investigation of Some Data Collection Issues in Conjoint Measurement," in *1977 Proceedings American Marketing Association,* ed. B. A. Greenberg and D. N. Bellenger (Chicago: American Marketing Association, 1977), pp. 82–85; James McCullough and Roger Best, "Conjoint Measurement: Temporal Stability and Structural Reliability," *Journal of Marketing Research,* 16 (February 1979), pp. 26–31; Madhav N. Segal, "Reliability of Conjoint Analysis: Contrasting Data Collection Procedure," *Journal of Marketing Research,* 19 (February 1982), pp. 139–143.

27. McCullough and Best, "Conjoint Measurement," pp. 26–31.

28. Bobby J. Calder, "Focus Groups and the Nature of Qualitative Marketing Research," *Journal of Marketing Research,* 14 (August 1977), pp. 353–364.

29. Johnny K. Johansson and Ikujiro Nonaka, "Marketing Research the Japanese Way," *Harvard Business Review* (May/June, 1987).

30. For the reader trained in classical statistics, these suggestions for adjusting the data with managerial judgment may seem unscientific. But it is important to keep in mind that the purpose of numerical measurement of price sensitivity is to derive useful estimates, not to objectively test a theory. If managers have strongly held beliefs, in light of which the historical record of sales could yield much better estimates, it is simply wasteful to ignore those beliefs simply because they may not be objective. See Edward E. Leamer, "Let's Take the Con Out of Econometrics," *American Economic Review,* 73 (March 1983), pp. 31–43.

31. "Survey Your Customers— Electronically," *Harvard Management Update* (April 2000), pp. 3–4, Harvard College, Cambridge, MA.

32. See, for example, http://www.scip.org.

33. The Census of Manufacturers is a publication of the U.S. Department of Commerce. For other federal sources, see the Commerce Department publication entitled *A Guide to Federal Data Sources on Manufacturing.* The "Survey of Industrial Buying Power" is published annually as an issue of *Sales and Marketing Management* magazine. Other useful sources of information about the demographics and motivations of buying firms can be obtained from the buying firms' trade associations (e.g., Rubber Manufacturers Association, National Machine Tool Builders Association) and from privately operated industrial directory and research companies (e.g., Predicasts, Inc., Dun & Bradstreet, Standard & Poor's).

CHAPTER

14 | ETHICS AND THE LAW

Understanding the Constraints on Pricing

When making pricing decisions, the successful strategist must consider not only what is profitable, but also what will be perceived as ethical and legal. Unfortunately, good advice on both of these issues is all too often unavailable or misleading. Attorneys who do not specialize in antitrust law tend to be overly conservative—advising against activities that are only sometimes illegal or that could trigger an investigation. In fact, benign changes in questionable pricing policies are often all that is necessary to make them both profitable and defensible. On the other hand, product and sales managers eager to achieve quarterly objectives will sometimes fail to consider these constraints at all, resulting in costly condemnations of their companies in courts of law or public opinion. This chapter is intended to raise awareness of the issues and educate you enough to question the advice you receive.

ETHICAL CONSTRAINTS ON PRICING

"Perhaps no other area of managerial activity is more difficult to depict accurately, assess fairly, and prescribe realistically in terms of morality than the domain of price."[1] This oft-quoted assessment reflects the exceptional divergence of ethical opinions with respect to pricing. Even among writers sympathetic to the need for profit, some consider it unethical to charge different prices unless they reflect differences in costs, while others consider pricing unethical unless prices are set "equal or proportional to the benefit received."[2] Consequently,

Eugene F. Zelek, Jr. wrote The Legal Framework for Pricing section of this chapter. He is a partner and chairs the Antitrust and Trade Regulation Group at the Chicago law firm of Freeborn & Peters LLP. The author wishes to thank his colleagues, William C. Holmes and Tonita M. Helton, for their assistance.

there is less written on ethics in pricing than on other marketing issues, and what is written tends to focus on the easy issues, like deception and price fixing.[3] The tougher issues involve strategies and tactics for gaining profit.

This chapter is intended to help managers capture more of the value created by the products and services they sell. In many cultures, and among many who promulgate ethical principles, such a goal is morally reprehensible. Although this opinion was once held by the majority, its popularity has generally declined over the last three centuries due to the success of capitalism and the failure of collectivism to deliver an improvement in material well-being. Still, many people, including many in business practice and education, believe that there are legitimate ethical constraints on maximizing profit through pricing.

It is important to clarify your own and your customers' understanding of those standards before ambiguous situations arise. The topology of ethical constraints in pricing illustrated in Exhibit 14-1 is a good place to start. Readers should determine where to draw the line concerning ethical constraints—for themselves and their industry—and determine as well how other people (family, neighbors, social groups) might view such decisions.

Most people would reject the idea of zero ethical constraints, in which the seller can dictate the price and terms and force them on an unwilling buyer. Sale of "protection" by organized crime is universally condemned. The practice of forcing employees in a one-company town to buy from the "company store" is subject to only marginally less condemnation. Even when the government itself is the seller that is forcing people to purchase goods and services at a price (tax

---

EXHIBIT 14-1   When Is a Price Ethical? Ethical Constraints

Level	The Exchange Is Ethical When	Implication/Proscription
1	The price is paid voluntarily.	"Let the buyer beware."
2	"...and is based on equal information."	No sales without full disclosure (used-car defects, risks of smoking).
3	"...and does not exploit buyers' 'essential needs'."	No "excessive" profits on essentials such as life-saving pharmaceuticals.
4	"...and is justified by costs."	No segmented pricing based on value. No excessive profits based on shortages, even for nonessential products.
5	"...and provides equal access to goods regardless of one's ability to cover the cost."	No exchange for personal gain. Give as able and receive as needed.

rate) it sets, people generally condemn the transaction unless they feel empowered to influence the terms. This level of ethical constraint was also used to condemn the "trusts" that, before the antitrust laws, sometimes used reprehensible tactics to drive lower-priced competitors out of business. By denying customers alternative products, trusts arguably forced them to buy theirs.

Ethical level one embodied in all well-functioning, competitive market economies, requires that all transactions be voluntary. Early capitalist economies, and some of the most dynamic today (for instance, that of Hong Kong), condone any transaction that meets this criterion. The legal principle of *caveat emptor,* "Let the buyer beware," characterized nearly all economic transactions in the United States prior to the twentieth century. In such a market, people often make regrettable purchases (e.g., expensive brand-name watches that turn out to be cheap substitutes and stocks in overvalued companies). On the other hand, without the high legal costs associated with meeting licensing, branding, and disclosure requirements, new business opportunities abound even for the poor—making unemployment negligible.

Ethical level two imposes a more restrictive standard, condemning even voluntary transactions by those who would profit from unequal information about the exchange. Selling a used car without disclosing a known defect, concealing a known risk of using a product, or misrepresenting the benefits achievable from a product are prime examples of transactions that would be condemned by this ethical criterion. Thus, many would condemn selling land in Florida at inflated prices to unwary out-of-state buyers, or selling lottery tickets to the poor, since the seller could reasonably expect these potential buyers to be ignorant of, or unable to process, information needed to make an informed decision. Since sellers naturally know more about the features and benefits of products than most consumers do, they may have an ethical duty to disclose what they know completely and accurately.[4]

Ethical level three imposes a still more stringent criterion: that sellers earn no more than a "fair" profit from sales of "necessities" for which buyers have only limited alternatives. This principle is often stated as follows: "No one should profit from other people's adversity." Thus even nominally capitalist societies sometimes impose rent controls on housing and price controls on pharmaceutical costs and physicians' fees. Even when this level of ethical constraint is not codified into law, people who espouse it condemn those who raise the price of ice during a power failure or the price of lumber following a hurricane, when the demand for these products soars.

Ethical level four extends the criteria of ethical level three to all products, even those with many substitutes and not usually thought of as necessities. Profit is morally justifiable only when it is the minimum necessary to induce companies and individuals to make decisions for the good of less-advantaged members of society.[5] Profit is ethically justifiable only as the price society must pay to induce suppliers of capital and skills to improve the well-being of those less fortunate. Profits from exploiting unique skills, great ideas, or exceptional efficiency (called "economic rents") are morally suspect in this scenario unless it can be shown that everyone, or at least the most needy, benefits from allowing such profits to be earned, such as when a high-profit company nevertheless offers lower prices and better working conditions than its competitors. Profits from speculation (buying low and selling high) are clearly condemned, as is segmented pricing (charging customers different prices to capture different levels of value), unless those prices actually reflect differences in cost.

Ethical level five, the most extreme constraint, is inconsistent with markets. In some "primitive" societies, everyone is obliged to share good fortune with those in the tribe who are less fortunate. "From each according to his ability, to each according to his need" is the espoused ethical premise of Marxist societies and even some respected moral philosophers. Those that have actually tried to put it into practice, however, have eventually recoiled at the brutality necessary to force essentially self-interested humans "to give according to their abilities" without reward. Within families and small, self-selected societies, however, this ethical principle can thrive. Within social and religious organizations, members often work together for their common good and share the results. Even within businesses, partnerships are established to share, within defined bounds, each other's good and bad fortune.

For each level of ethical constraint on economic exchange, one must determine the losses and gains, for both individuals and societies, that will result from the restriction. What effect does each level have on the material and social well-being of those who hold it as a standard? Should the same standards be applied in different contexts? For example, is your standard different for business markets than it is for consumer markets? Would your ethical standards change when selling in a foreign country where local competitors generally hold a higher or lower ethical standard than yours? In assessing the standards that friends, business associates, and political representatives apply, managers must ask themselves if their personal standards are the same for their business as well as for their personal conduct. For example, would they condemn an oil company for earning excess profits as a result of higher crude prices, yet themselves take excess profits on a house that had appreciated substantially in a hot real estate market? If so, are they hypocrites or is there some justification for holding individuals and firms to different standards?

Although we certainly have our own beliefs about which of these ethical levels is practical and desirable in dealing with others, and would apply different standards in different contexts, we feel that neither we nor most of the people who claim to be experts on business ethics are qualified to make these decisions for someone else. Each individual must make his or her own decisions and live with the personal and social consequences.

Regardless of one's personal ethical beliefs about pricing, it would be foolish to ignore the legal constraints on pricing. Antitrust law in the United States has developed over the years to reflect both citizens' moral evaluations of companies' actions and companies' attempts to get laws passed that protect them from more efficient or aggressive competitors. As the summary below illustrates, the meaning of these laws changes over time as courts respond to changing social attitudes and the placement of judges with differing political views.

THE LEGAL FRAMEWORK FOR PRICING

When making pricing decisions, the strategist must consider not only what is profitable, but also what is lawful. Since the late nineteenth century, the United States has been committed to maintaining price competition through establishing and enforcing antitrust policy. Statutes, regulations, and guidelines, as well as countless judicial decisions, have defined what constitutes anticompetitive pricing behavior and the rules under which the government and private parties may pursue those who engage in it.

For more than a hundred years, U.S. antitrust law has responded to a complex and dynamic marketplace by being both of these things, resulting in policies that are always being scrutinized and questioned and sometimes stretched and revised. The overall trend in the United States for the last several decades has been to move away from judging behavior based on economic assumptions toward focusing on demonstrable economic effect, something that has fostered a great deal of contemporary pricing freedom. Of course, a necessary companion to evolving policies, as well as the lag time sometimes necessary for the law to catch up with the marketplace, is ambiguity. In return for some uncertainty, there is more latitude for businesses to cope creatively with both new and old challenges.

This section discusses key aspects of the law of pricing, focusing primarily on that of general applicability in the United States at the federal level.[6] Due to the long history of U.S. law in the pricing area, it has served as a model for other parts of the world, including the European Union (EU) and Japan. For example, EU antitrust law historically prohibited such things as territorial restrictions on intermediaries that interfered with cross-border trade, but a safe harbor became effective in 2000.[7] That, much like the change in the U.S. view that occurred more than 20 years earlier, recognizes a supplier's legitimate interest in controlling how its products are resold under certain circumstances.

In the United States, the antitrust laws are enforced by both government and private parties. The Department of Justice is empowered to bring criminal and civil actions, although the former are reserved primarily for price fixing and hardcore cartel activity.[8] At the same time, the Federal Trade Commission (FTC) may bring civil actions,[9] as can private parties. Often, civil plaintiffs pursue injunctions to stop certain conduct and, in the case of private parties, they may also or alternatively seek three times their actual economic damages (something known as "treble damages"), as well as their legal fees and court costs.[10] While the volume of private antitrust litigation dwarfs that brought by the government, private suits often follow significant government cases.

THE EFFECT OF SARBANES-OXLEY ON PRICING PRACTICES

In direct response to the high-visibility corporate finance scandals involving such companies as Enron and WorldCom, the Sarbanes-Oxley Act—a significant and sweeping piece of securities reform legislation—became law in 2002.[11] Because one of the main purposes of the act is to facilitate more accurate public disclosure of financial information and provide accountability measures in reporting and monitoring of corporate conduct, its impact on pricing practices and antitrust compliance in general is to cause more rigor than had been present in many companies before the law was passed. While most of the requirements of Sarbanes-Oxley apply only to an "issuer," or a publicly-traded or listed company,[12]some commentators have recommended that even private companies should strive to comply with the full demands of this law.[13]

Among other things, Sarbanes-Oxley specifically provides for stricter financial and auditing procedures and reporting. For example, the act requires that an issuer's chief financial officer (CFO) and chief executive officer (CEO) certify financial reporting documents (such as the company's quarterly and annual reports) and make the knowing certification of noncompliant financials a criminal offense.[14] The act also outlines disclosure procedures and internal accounting control mechanisms, as well as whistle-blowing provisions, including language that makes retaliation against truthful informants subject to criminal penalties of a fine or up to 10 years of prison, or both.[15]

While Sarbanes-Oxley was not created with the express intent of policing antitrust compliance in pricing matters, the broad scope of the act clearly affects this area. Some of the most obvious examples in the context of pricing policies and related issues include tighter controls on the accounting and disclosure procedures relating to the treatment and use of discounts, allowances and promotional funds in general, regardless of whether a company is giving or getting them. As a result, companies are well advised, among other things, to address in their internal control policies requirements and guidelines for pricing and pricing actions, process documentation for such actions, and a procedure for investigating and responding to employee reports of internal violations.

PRICE FIXING OR PRICE ENCOURAGEMENT

In an effort to reduce or avoid market risks, businesspeople have long been interested in setting prices with their competitors or dictating or influencing the prices charged by their downstream intermediaries, such as distributors, dealers, and retailers. Over the years, U.S. law has taken a rather dim view of this behavior. At the same time, it is now clear that there is some flexibility in what competitors—which collectively affect market prices—can do, but the biggest changes are in the area of distribution channels, where price setting is lawful if done properly.

There are two types of price fixing: horizontal and vertical. In the former, competitors agree on the prices they will charge or key terms of sale affecting price. In the latter, a supplier and a reseller agree on the prices the reseller will charge or the price-related terms of resale for the supplier's products. However, where an intermediary, such as an independent sales representative, does not take ownership of the supplier's products and acts only as the supplier's agent, there cannot be any vertical price fixing because the law views the sale as taking place directly between the supplier and the end-user, with the intermediary serving as a conduit. Consequently, the supplier is only setting its own prices and terms of sale.[16]

The primary law in this area is Section 1 of the Sherman Act, an 1890 statute that prohibits "[e]very contract, combination . . . or conspiracy in restraint of trade."[17] The contract, combination, or conspiracy requirement necessarily means that there must be an agreement between two or more individuals or entities. As a result, the law does not reach unilateral behavior.[18] Moreover, the Sherman Act does not ban merely imitating a competitor's pricing behavior (something called "conscious parallelism").[19]

Sometimes, there are written contracts or other direct evidence of price fixing conspiracies. Far more often, evidence of agreement must be inferred from the actions of the parties involved. Although conscious parallelism by itself is not enough to establish an agreement, when uniform or similar behavior is coupled with one or more "plus factors," courts have found concerted activity. Perhaps the most powerful of these factors is if the conduct in question would be against the self-interest of each party if it acted alone, but consistent with their self-interest if they all behaved the same way, such as the uniform imposition of unpopular restrictions or price increases in the face of surplus.[20] Another factor is the opportunity to collude (often shown by communications between or among the parties), followed by identical or similar actions, although the probative effect of such opportunity or communications can be undercut by legitimate business explanations.[21]

Once concerted action has been found, the next step is to evaluate it. Case law has further refined Section 1 of the Sherman Act to require two levels of proof, depending on the nature of the alleged offense. Some offenses are considered to be "per se" illegal, while others are analyzed under the "rule of reason." Per se offenses require that the presence of the objectionable practice be proven and that there be antitrust injury and damages, while offenses subject to the rule of reason add a third element—that the practice at issue be unreasonably anticompetitive. In general, it is easier to prove a violation under the per se test and more difficult to do so under the rule of reason, because the latter requires detailed economic analysis and a balancing of procompetitive and anticompetitive effects. Of course, the rule of reason also provides defendants with the opportunity to justify their behavior, something denied under the per se rule.

Historically, all arrangements affecting price were presumed to be unreasonably anticompetitive on their face and, therefore, per se illegal. However, during the last 25 years or so, the U.S. Supreme Court has placed more emphasis on showing demonstrable economic effect rather than relying on assumptions, so there has been an erosion of per se application to both horizontal and vertical pricing issues.

HORIZONTAL PRICE FIXING

In the horizontal arena, direct price fixing—competitors in the stereotypical smoke-filled room agreeing to set prices or rig bids—remains per se illegal. The same treatment is accorded to indirect price fixing, where there is an ambiguous arrangement between competitors that a court has determined constitutes illegal price fixing after conducting a detailed factual review or market analysis.[22]

However, when a restriction on price is merely the incidental effect of a desirable procompetitive activity (sometimes referred to as "incidental price fixing"), it is now clear that the more forgiving rule of reason applies. This point is illustrated by *National Collegiate Athletic Association v. Board of Regents,* where the U.S. Supreme Court applied the rule of reason and noted that rules covering athletic equipment and schedules were appropriate, but those that limited the television exposure of member football teams were an unreasonable restriction on output that unlawfully increased prices.[23]

RESALE PRICE FIXING OR ENCOURAGEMENT

VERTICAL PRICE FIXING

Vertical price fixing always has been considered per se illegal, but recent Supreme Court cases have narrowed the application of the per se rule. In late 1997, the Supreme Court in *State Oil Co. v. Khan* unanimously overturned the precedent in a 29-year-old case to hold that the rule of reason, rather than the per se test, applies to vertical agreements that set maximum or "ceiling" resale prices, because purchasers are not always harmed by such arrangements and, indeed, may be benefited by them to the extent they hold down prices.[24] However, the use of maximum resale pricing is relatively rare, occurring, for example, when the supplier wishes to limit reseller margins for a hot, new product or to facilitate national or regional price advertising.[25] From a business point of view, the desire to set minimum ("floor") or exact prices (each usually designed to address discounting) is far more common, but doing so by agreement remains illegal on face.

However, the Supreme Court's *Monsanto* and *Business Electronics* decisions in the 1980s make it clear that setting maximum, minimum, or exact resale prices without an agreement (i.e., unilaterally) is not illegal price fixing prohibited under the Sherman Act.[26] As a result, a supplier may announce a price at which its product must be resold (i.e., establish a ceiling, floor, or exact price policy) and refuse to sell to any reseller that does not comply, as long as there is no agreement between the supplier and its reseller on resale price levels.[27] Even when resellers follow the supplier's resale price policy, there is no unlawful agreement. With this latitude after *Monsanto* and *Business Electronics,* many manufacturers of desirable branded products have successfully discouraged the discounting of their products in such diverse industries as consumer electronics, furniture, appliances, sporting goods, tires, luggage, handbags, videos, agricultural supplies, electronic test equipment, and automotive accessories and replacement parts.

A frequent justification given for minimum or exact resale price policies is to permit resellers sufficient margin to provide a selling environment that is consistent with the supplier's objectives for its products, including brand image. For example, the supplier may want knowledgeable salespeople, showrooms, substantial inventory, and superior service. Of course, such policies also may help support higher supplier margins. Sometimes, the imposition of such policies is sought by resellers to insulate them from price competition. As long as there is no agreement on price levels, such requests, even if acted upon by the supplier, are not unlawful.[28]

Pricing policies may be used broadly or selectively to cover everything from a single product to all of those in a supplier's line. Similarly, they can be used in certain geographic areas and with specific channels of distribution in which price erosion is a problem, or they can be used throughout the country. In any event, a policy violation typically requires that the supplier stop selling the offending reseller the products involved, although it also is permissible to pull a product line or all of the supplier's business.[29] When and if the supplier wishes to resume selling is the supplier's unilateral decision, although some cases suggest that warnings, threats, and probation short of termination are unacceptable, apparently because they support the inference that some form of prohibited agreement has been reached.

To make such a policy stick, the supplier must generally have brand or market power. Otherwise, resellers simply won't bother to follow the policy, as there are plenty of substitutes available. Ironically, it is those highly desirable products that are most susceptible to discounting anyway, so the requisite power is typically present. In addition, it is important to note that resale price policies have a vertical reach that is limited to one level down the distribution channel. If all resellers buy directly from the manufacturer, this restriction poses no problem, but if a significant amount of sales are made through multiple levels of distribution, a policy will be too porous to be effective. In other words, a manufacturer can control a direct-buying retailer's sell price, but it can't reach that of a retailer that buys from a wholesaler. To address this problem, the manufacturer may "jump over" the wholesaler by making a sale directly to the retailer, or it may convert the wholesaler into an agent for the purpose of such a sale. Alternatively, the policy may be circulated to both direct- and indirect-buying resellers, while wholesalers are permitted to sell to "approved" resellers only. One way to remain on the approved list is to comply with the policy.

Resale price policies are potent, but the rules for managing them within the law are necessarily stringent. Careful implementation keeps otherwise lawful programs from going astray. This means that any form of agreement regarding resale prices must be avoided. There must be no resale pricing contracts, no assurances of compliance, and no probation. Because this area can be a legal minefield, it's crucial to carefully train supplier personnel. At the same time, many companies have adopted such programs with low risk and considerable success.

DIRECT DEALING PROGRAMS

Another way to control the prices charged to end-users is for the supplier to sell them directly or, constructively, by the use of agents. When the supplier agrees with the end-user on price, but the latter cannot handle delivery of large quantities or maintain sufficient inventory to justify direct shipments from the supplier, some suppliers look to a reseller to fill the order out of the reseller's warehouse. This can be done by consignment or by the supplier buying back inventory from the reseller immediately prior to its transfer to the end-user, so, in either event, the sale runs directly from the supplier to the end-user. The reseller becomes the supplier's warehousing and delivery agent and is compensated by the supplier for performing only these functions.

When the supplier has negotiated the price to the end-user, but the reseller has or retains the title, the supplier has another alternative. Under the "reseller's choice" approach, the reseller may either choose to sell the product to the end-user at the price set by the supplier or tell the supplier to find someone else to do so. Even if the reseller agrees to sell at the contracted price, there is no per se illegal price fixing, as this practice is seen as voluntary and therefore subject to the rule of reason.[30]

RESALE PRICE ENCOURAGEMENT

Instead of dictating a resale price by agreement, policy, or direct sale, some suppliers encourage desirable resale pricing behavior by providing financial or other incentives, such as advertising allowances to promote certain prices. Although these practices are judged under the rule of reason because participation is voluntary, the provision of incentives is subject to the prohibitions in the Robinson-Patman Act against price and promotional discrimination.[31]

In the area of price advertising, a common practice is to use a Minimum Advertised Price (MAP) program, although the underlying concept could also be used for maximum or exact prices. Under this approach, the reseller receives an advertising allowance (often in the form of co-op advertising funds) in return for adhering to the appropriate price in advertising, in a catalog, or over the Internet.[32] Some companies pay an explicit allowance (such as a percentage rebate on purchases), while others employ an implicit allowance stating that failure to follow program requirements results in the loss of the allowance and an increase in price. The latter is found in consumer electronics.

A variant on MAP programs is group or shared-price advertising, through which a supplier sponsors an ad, but resellers can be listed in it only if they agree to sell at the promoted price during the period indicated. Again, resellers that wish pricing freedom may decline to be in the ad, and, because of the voluntary nature of this approach, there is no per se illegality.

Another alternative is target-price rebates. Here, the supplier rewards the reseller with financial incentives the closer its resale prices are to the target set by the supplier. This practice requires point-of-sale (POS) reporting, typically easier to get in the consumer area due to the widespread use of scanners, but becoming more common in the industrial marketplace.

PRICE AND PROMOTIONAL DISCRIMINATION

Although economists maintain that the ability to charge different prices to different customers promotes efficiency by clearing the market, U.S. law on that issue has focused on maintaining the viability of numerous sellers as a means to preserve competition. Consequently, while price discrimination has been unlawful since 1914, the Robinson-Patman Act amended existing legislation in 1936, so this entire area is commonly referred to by the name of the amendment.[33]

This complex, Depression-era legislation was enacted to protect small businesses by outlawing discriminatory price and promotional allowances obtained by large businesses, while exempting sales to government or "charitable" organizations for their own use.[34] At the same time, the emergence of contemporary power buyers through internal growth or consolidation (like Wal-Mart or W. W. Grainger), as well as supplier efforts to make discounts and allowances provided to customers more efficient, have forced or encouraged sellers to provide lawful account-specific pricing and promotions by creatively finding ways through the Robinson-Patman maze. This trend is likely to continue, as further consolidation and evolving distribution channels (brought on by e-commerce, among other things) will demand and reward more sophisticated differentiation.

As is the case with the other antitrust laws, the Department of Justice, the FTC, and private parties may each bring Robinson-Patman cases, although the enforcement agencies have not focused on this area for some time. Indeed, the Justice Department has criminal powers in this area that have gone unused for many years, while the FTC today brings few significant cases in this area after being particularly active through the 1970s. Private suits on behalf of businesses (consumers have no standing to sue under the statute) account for most of the enforcement activity.[35] Successful plaintiffs are entitled to the same remedies as those available under the antitrust laws discussed previously (injunctions, treble damages, attorneys' fees and costs).

PRICE DISCRIMINATION

Keep in mind that discrimination in price is not always unlawful. In order to prove illegal price discrimination under the Robinson-Patman Act and assuming that the supplier sells in interstate commerce, each of five elements must be present:[36]

1. *Discrimination.* This standard is met simply by charging different prices to different customers. However, if the reason for the difference is due to a discount or allowance made available to all or almost all customers (like a prompt payment discount), but some customers choose not to take advantage of it, the element of discrimination drops out, ending the inquiry. This is known as the "availability defense."

2. *Sales to Two or More Purchasers.* The different prices must be charged on reasonably contemporaneous sales to two or more purchasers—a rule that permits price fluctuations. In other words, it is inappropriate under the statute to compare two widely separated sales in a highly volatile market. Yet if prices typically change annually or semiannually, a sale made in January may be compared with one made in March.

In addition, offering different prices is not enough. Actual sales or agreements to sell at different prices must exist. For example, if two electrical supply distributors seek special pricing from the manufacturer to bid on a construction job or an integrated supply contract that only one will get, the manufacturer may, if it is careful, give one a better price than the other, because in doing so, it is providing two offers, but making only one sale.[37]

3.　*Goods.* Robinson-Patman applies to the sale of goods only ("commodities" in the statute), so services—such as telecommunications, banking, and transportation—are not covered.[38] When a supplier sells a bundled offering, such as repair services that include parts or computer hardware that includes maintenance services, Robinson-Patman is relevant only if the value of the goods in the bundle predominates. Also, it is possible to turn goods into services if the manufacturer procures raw materials and produces and stores the products on behalf of the customer, with the customer owning the inventory every step of the way and bearing the risk of loss.

4.　*Like Grade and Quality.* The goods involved must be physically or essentially the same. Brand preferences are irrelevant, but functional variations can differentiate products. In a key case, the Supreme Court stated that a branded product and its physically and chemically identical private-label version must be priced the same by the manufacturer.[39] While the distinctions drawn in the case law sometimes appear arbitrary, meaningful functional or physical variations can result in different products that legitimize different prices. For example, two air conditioners that have significant differences in cooling capacity are distinct products, even if they otherwise are or appear physically identical.

5.　*Reasonable Probability of Competitive Injury.* The law generally focuses on injury at one of two levels. The first, called "primary line," permits a supplier to sue a competitor for the latter's discriminatory pricing. But here the law also requires that the supplier's discriminatory pricing be below its cost, something designed to drive its rival out of business or otherwise injure competition in the market as a whole (called "predatory intent"), rather than to merely take some incremental market share. Moreover, the structure of the market must be such that the discriminating supplier can raise prices after it disposes of the targeted competitor or that market injury otherwise is threatened through reduced output.[40] Not surprisingly, there are few contemporary primary-line cases due to this tough standard.

Far more common is "secondary-line" injury, where a supplier's disfavored reseller or end-user customer may sue the supplier for price discrimination. However, the law is clear that only competing customers must be treated alike. To the extent that customers do not compete due to their locations or the markets they serve, different prices are appropriate under the Robinson-Patman Act. Significantly, if these distinctions do not occur naturally, they may be introduced or formalized by contract or policy through the use of vertical nonprice restrictions.*

DEFENSES TO PRICE DISCRIMINATION

Even if all five price-discrimination elements are present, there are three defenses that may be used to avoid what otherwise is unlawful discrimination.[41]

1.　*Cost Justification.* This defense permits a price disparity if it is based on legitimate cost differences. For example, freight is usually less expensive on a per-case

---

*See "Vertical Nonprice Restrictions" below.

basis for a truckload shipment. However, while there is no requirement to pass on any savings, if the supplier does so, the law states that some or all of the actual savings may be passed on to the customer, but not a penny more.

One common problem area is volume discounts, particularly those that are stair-stepped with large differences between levels. Perhaps this structure reflected real cost differences many years ago when it was adopted by the supplier, but unless the underlying cost analysis is regularly updated, the discounts probably do not track today's costs. Indeed, the dynamic nature of business and the precision required to support this defense make it difficult to apply successfully, although the sophistication of activity-based costing holds a great deal of potential. Some manufacturers keep profit-and-loss statements on their customers and adjust their pricing accordingly.

2. *Meeting Competition.* Under this defense, discrimination is permissible if it is based on a good-faith belief that a discriminatory price is necessary to meet the price of a competitive supplier to the favored customer or to maintain a traditional price disparity.[42] Most managers are familiar with the application of this defense on the micro level, that is, when a buyer tells the seller that the seller's competitor offered a lower price. However, meeting competition may also be used on the macro level to justify things like volume discounts that are so institutionalized in the industry that adjusting them to reflect true cost savings would result in the loss of business.

Of course, it is at the micro level where this defense is most often used. Unfortunately, this means relying on the purchaser for competitive pricing information when the buyer has every incentive to lie.[43] Some companies provide their salespeople with detailed meeting-competition forms that require competitive invoices and other documentary evidence. While this sort of evidence is helpful, it is not essential if the seller has a reasonable basis at the time of the decision to believe that the competitive price described by the buyer is legitimate, even if it turns out to be wrong later. Nevertheless, a written or electronic record of why the otherwise discriminatory price was provided is useful.

Because meeting competition is a defense, there is no obligation to provide the special price to anyone other than the customer that asked for it. Of course, smart buyers will attempt to secure "most-favored-nations" clauses in their contracts or purchase orders to automatically get the benefit of a lower price elsewhere, regardless of whether they would otherwise be entitled to it. Such clauses may cause tension between a supplier's Robinson-Patman responsibilities and those under the law of contract.

3. *Changing Conditions.* Special prices may be provided to sell perishable, seasonal, obsolete, or distressed merchandise, even though the full price had been charged up to the point of offering the special prices.

PROMOTIONAL DISCRIMINATION

The Robinson-Patman Act also bans promotional discrimination in an effort to deny an alternative means of achieving discriminatory pricing. The distinction between price and promotional discrimination is an important one because different legal standards apply and, while the requirements in certain respects are tougher for promotional discrimination, there is ultimately more flexibility.

Price discrimination covers the sale from the supplier to the reseller or to the direct-buying end-user, while promotional discrimination usually relates only to the reseller's sale of the supplier's products.[44] Historically, promotional discrimination was largely the purview of consumer goods marketers, as industrial goods sellers concentrated on such things as volume discounts subject to price discrimination standards. However, the need for creative account-specific marketing and the desire to make supplier incentives work harder have caused many industrial sellers to face the same issues. Both consumer and industrial suppliers are now focusing on how their resellers sell their products (promotional discrimination), rather than only on how they buy them (price discrimination).

As was the case with price discrimination, each of several elements must be present to violate the law:

1. *The Provision of Allowances, Services, or Facilities.* Here, the supplier grants to the reseller advertising or promotional allowances (like $5 off per case to promote a product) or provides services or facilities (such as demonstrators or free display racks), usually in return for some form of promotional performance.

2. *In Connection with the Resale of the Supplier's Goods.* As is the case with price discrimination, the law regarding promotional discrimination does not reach service providers. In addition, promotional discrimination generally applies only to resellers. Typically, this does not cover purchasers that use or consume the supplier's product in making their own. Also, it usually does not cover the incorporation of a product, such as sugar used in baked goods, cutting tools used to machine castings, or sound systems installed at the automotive factory. However, these purchasers are resellers for promotional discrimination purposes if they receive allowances or other benefits from the supplier for promoting the fact that the finished goods were made using the supplier's product or contain it, such as an ice cream producer that advertises the use of a particular brand of chocolate chip or a manufacturer that promotes the use of an axle brand in its heavy-duty trucks.

3. *Not Available to All Competing Customers on Proportionally Equal Terms.* Once again, not all of the supplier's customers need to be treated alike, only those that compete. In addition, the services or facilities offered or the performance required to earn the allowances must be "functionally available," that is, usable or attainable in a practical sense by all competing resellers, something that may require alternatives. In other words, if a reseller could take advantage of a promotional program, but chooses not to do so, the supplier is off the legal hook.[45] For example, if a warehouse club chain could advertise in newspapers, but it decides not to do so, the supplier is under no legal obligation to offer an alternative to a newspaper-advertising allowance. On the other hand, if the supplier pays for advertising on grocery carts, but some of its retail customers can't have them due to the size of their stores, the supplier must make available an alternative means of performance, such as a poster or window sign in lieu of cart advertising.

The flexibility available under promotional discrimination standards is based on the fact that competing customers do not have to receive the same level of benefits, something contrary to the implicit mandate to do so under price discrimination rules. Instead, the promotional discrimination requirement is one of "proportional equality," and there are three ways to proportionalize what is provided: (1) on unit or dollar purchases (buy a case, get a dollar—something that lawfully favors larger resellers that buy more); (2) on the cost to the reseller of the promotional activity (a full-page ad in a national trade magazine costs more than that in a regional newsletter); or (3) on the value of the promotional activity to the supplier (salespeople dedicated exclusively to the supplier's brand have more value than those who are not).[46]

COMPETITIVE INJURY, DEFENSES, AND INDIRECT PURCHASERS

There also are other, somewhat less attractive differences between price and promotional discrimination. First, no competitive injury is necessary for illegal promotional discrimination, making it more like a per se rule.[47] Second, meeting competition is the only defense, as cost justification and changing conditions are irrelevant. Third, if the supplier provides promotional allowances to direct-buying resellers, it must also furnish them to competitive resellers that buy the promoted product through intermediaries, something accomplished with ultimate reseller rebates or mandatory pass-throughs.

USING NONPRICE VARIABLES TO SUPPORT PRICING GOALS

VERTICAL NONPRICE RESTRICTIONS

Under the standards for price and promotional discrimination, the Robinson-Patman Act requires that only competing reseller and direct-buying end-user customers be treated similarly. For this reason, or to be consistent with other price-related or marketing objectives, the supplier may wish to control the degree to which its resellers compete with each other, something known as "intrabrand competition." In 1977, the Supreme Court's *Sylvania* decision provided suppliers with considerable flexibility in this regard, by holding that vertical nonprice restrictions are subject to the rule of reason and that intrabrand competition could be reduced to promote "interbrand competition," or the rivalry between competing brands.[48]

As a result, suppliers may impose vertical restraints on resellers to help manage distribution channels and to provide considerable leeway in pricing design using the carrot approach (financial incentives), the stick approach (contractual requirements), or some combination of the two.* Historically, industrial sellers have favored the use of vertical restrictions and the more selective distribution that goes with them, while many consumer goods suppliers (except those who sell

---

*While vertical restrictions are often used with product resellers, certain restraints may also be useful in dealing with sales agents, the provision of services, and direct-buying product end users. For example, with respect to direct buyers, see the discussion of Product Restrictions below.

durables) have been more interested in widespread distribution without the same sort of restrictions. However, the challenges of Internet sales and other factors have focused more attention on limiting how products may be resold.

Broadly speaking, there are three types of vertical nonprice restraints, each subject to the rule of reason:

1. *Customer Restrictions.* Rather than selling to any customer, the reseller is restricted only to particular customers or is prohibited from selling to certain customers. For example, in the industrial area, the reseller could be required to sell only to plumbing contractors or to stay away from accounts that are reserved to the supplier or another reseller. On the consumer side, the reseller could be limited to customers who order over the Internet or prohibited from selling to such customers at all.

2. *Territorial Restrictions.* Although generally designed to prevent or discourage selling outside of a geographic area, these can also be thought of as market restrictions. An "exclusive distributorship" is actually a restraint on the supplier, as it agrees that a particular reseller will be the exclusive outlet in the latter's territory or market (however defined) for some or all of the supplier's products. When the reseller is required to sell inside only a particular territory or market, it is subject to "absolute confinement." By combining an exclusive distributorship with absolute confinement, the result is known as an "airtight territory." In other words, if a supplier promises a dealer that the latter will be the only outlet in Oregon for a particular product, it has granted an exclusive distributorship. If the dealer is limited to selling in that state, there is absolute confinement and, when it is combined with an exclusive distributorship, the reseller has an airtight territory.

Due to some flip-flopping on the part of the Supreme Court, vertical nonprice restrictions were per se illegal from 1968 until the *Sylvania* decision in 1977. In response, a number of so-called "lesser restraints" were established that may not be as helpful in pricing as other restrictions, but still can be useful. The first of these is an "area of primary responsibility" that permits sales outside a reseller's territory, but expects the reseller to focus its efforts on its designated geographic area.[49] The second is a "profit passover" that allows the reseller to sell anywhere, but, to neutralize the "free-rider effect," the reseller must split revenue or profit for sales outside its territory with the reseller in the area encroached upon. The third is a "location clause" that restricts the reseller to approved sites only. While this last approach is ineffective if sales are made over the Internet or by phone or fax, it can be useful where a physical presence in the territory is necessary, especially in an environment where resellers are consolidating.

3. *Product Restrictions.* Suppliers have no legal obligation to sell their reseller or end-user customers any of their products, except in two instances—when the supplier has a contract to do so or in the relatively rare situation when the supplier is a monopolist with excess capacity.[50] In other words, the supplier may generally determine what products, if any, it sells to its reseller or direct-buying end-user customers, something that can be referred to as *designated products*. In

this way, it may limit intrabrand competition or other conflicts by restricting what can be purchased by whom.

In addition, if the reseller or the end-user is not permitted to purchase particular products or services or types of products or services from another supplier, this practice is known as *exclusive dealing.* Alternatively, it may be discouraged from doing so through financial or other incentives, often called "loyalty programs." Judged under the rule of reason, the test is whether competing suppliers are unreasonably foreclosed from the market. As long as such suppliers have reasonable access to the market through other resellers or other means, exclusive dealing is permissible.[51]

In some respects, *tying* is the other side of the coin from exclusive dealing, with the same effect.[52] In its most extreme form, tying requires that in order to purchase a desirable product or service, the customer must also buy another product or service that is less desirable. Although tying is often described as per se illegal, the analysis necessary to prove a violation is more akin to that required by the rule of reason.[53] Bundling is not illegal tying, as long as the products or services are available separately, even at a somewhat higher, but reasonable, cost.

Full-line forcing, judged under the rule of reason, is a variation on tying that requires a reseller to carry the supplier's entire line or a specified assortment to avoid the customer's cherry-picking of the more desirable products. Note that tying and full-line forcing can effectively crowd competitive products off the shelf.

NONPRICE INCENTIVES

To motivate desired behavior, a supplier may provide a favored reseller or end-user with certain nonprice benefits, such as first access to new products or enhanced technical support. Due to their nonprice nature, this type of discriminatory reward is not covered by the Robinson-Patman Act, although the other laws still may apply.[54] At the same time, anything that the supplier does to assume or subsidize an expense that normally would be incurred by the customer triggers application of the Robinson-Patman Act.

OTHER PRICING ISSUES

PREDATORY PRICING

The practice of setting a price so low that the firm harms its own profitability in an attempt to do greater harm to a competitor is *predatory pricing.* The purpose of such behavior is either to discipline a competitor for competing too intensely or to drive it from the market and thus eliminate its competition entirely.

Long-term aggressive pricing that is below marginal cost (or its measurable surrogate, average variable cost) can be attacked as monopolization or attempted monopolization under Section 2 of the Sherman Act and by the FTC under Section 5 of the FTC Act.[55] However, in 1993, the Supreme Court ruled that a successful prosecution requires proof that the price-cutting seller could likely recoup its losses with higher prices later on.[56] This heavy burden of proof severely limits claims of predation and favors the presumption that price-cutting is procompetitive.

PRICE SIGNALING

The practice of a supplier communicating its future pricing intentions to its competitors is known as *price signaling*. It is usually done to facilitate price parallelism through such means as supplying advance notice of price changes to customers or the media. In *DuPont,* the court of appeals overturned an FTC decision that such behavior violates the antitrust laws, ruling that consciously parallel pricing is not unlawful unless it is collusive, predatory, coercive, or exclusionary.[57] While signaling raises questions about the possibility of collusion, it can have legitimate business purposes as well. According to the court of appeals, signaling serves the lawful purpose of aiding buyers in their financial and purchasing planning.[58]

Summary

The development and implementation of pricing strategies and tactics that do not violate the law is an important aspect of pricing. In addition to the risk of legal actions initiated by the government, a company can be sued by private parties, usually its competitors or its customers. If the Justice Department can prove that the company's pricing violated the criminal provisions of the antitrust laws, the company is subject to fines and its managers may face both fines and imprisonment. In successful civil cases brought by the Justice Department or the FTC, the company may be enjoined from certain conduct, while in civil actions filed by private parties, defendants that lose may also be enjoined and have to pay treble damages and the attorneys' fees and court costs of the plaintiff. Even if antitrust claims are successfully defended, their defense is usually disruptive to the business and expensive in terms of monetary and management costs, as well as the effects on reputation.

At the same time, it is obvious that the law is rarely black and white, particularly in the area of pricing. Over the last several decades, U.S. courts have placed more emphasis on showing demonstrable economic effect, rather than relying on assumptions to find antitrust violations. Indeed, once the business objectives are clear, contemporary antitrust law provides considerable flexibility to develop alternative strategies and tactics, which are usually compatible with the degree of legal and trade-relations risk a business wishes to assume. While there often are no easy answers, in most cases the ends are achievable with some modification of the means.

Notes

1. Clarence C. Walton, *Ethos and the Executive* (Upper Saddle River, NJ: Prentice Hall, 1969), p. 209.
2. William J. Kehoe, "Ethics, Price Fixing, and the Management of Price Strategy," in *Marketing Ethics: Guidelines for Managers,* ed. Gene R. Laczniak and Patrick E. Murphy (Lexington, MA: D. C. Heath, 1985), p. 72.
3. Kehoe, "Ethics, Price Fixing, and the Management of Price Strategy," p. 71.
4. Manuel G. Velasquez, *Business Ethics,* 3rd ed. (Upper Saddle River, NJ: Prentice Hall, 1992), pp. 282–283.
5. Tom L. Beaucamp and Normal E. Bowie, *Ethical Theory and Business,* 4th ed. (Upper Saddle River, NJ: Prentice Hall, 1993), pp. 697–698.
6. Specialized or industry-specific statutes are outside the scope of this discussion. However, federal and state laws of general applicability tend to be

consistent. For antitrust issues (particularly in pricing), it is wise to have the assistance of knowledgeable legal counsel. This section is not a substitute for such help.

7. See 1999 O.J. (L 336) 21 (the safe harbor is available to the supplier if its market share is 30 percent or less). The U.S. approach does not establish a numerical market-share threshold, but instead looks at economic effects as a whole under the "rule of reason" discussed in the next section. For an even more significant difference between U.S. and EU antitrust law, see note 27 *infra*.

8. Criminal violation of the Sherman Act, the country's principal antitrust statute, is a felony punishable by a $100 million fine if the perpetrator is a corporation or other entity and a $1 million fine or 10 years in prison or both if the violator is an individual. 15 U.S.C. § 1 (the penalties were substantially raised in 2004). Application of the Comprehensive Crime Control Act and the Criminal Fine Improvements Acts, 18 U.S.C. §§ 3571-3572, permits an even greater financial penalty by allowing the fine to be increased to twice the gain from the illegal conduct or twice the loss to the victims, while the Federal Sentencing Guidelines can also impact the penalties imposed. See United States Sentencing Commission, 1991 Sentencing Guidelines.

9. The FTC has no authority under the Sherman Act and relies on other antitrust statutes, including Section 5 of the Federal Trade Commission Act, 15 U.S.C. § 45.

10. Since the 1980s, state attorneys general also have been active in civil antitrust enforcement at the federal level, suing on behalf of the citizens of their states and often coordinating their efforts through the National Association of Attorneys General (NAAG).

11. On July 30, 2002, the Sarbanes Oxley Act of 2002, Pub.L. 107-204, 116 Stat. 745, enacted 15 U.S.C. § 7201, *et. seq.,* 15 U.S.C. §§ 78d-3, 78o-6, and 78kk, and 18 U.S.C. §§ 1348 to 1350, 1514A, 1519, and 1520, amended 11 U.S.C. § 523, 15 U.S.C. §§ 77h-1, 77s, 77t, 78c, 78j-1, 78l, 78m, 78o, 78o-4, 78o-5, 78p, 78q, 78q-1, 78u, 78u-1, 78u-2, 78u-3, 78ff, 80a-41, 80b-3, and 80b-9, 18 U.S.C. §§ 1341, 1343, 1512, and 1513, 28 U.S.C. § 1658, and 29 U.S.C. §§ 1021, 1131, and 1132, enacted provisions set out as notes under 15 U.S.C. §§ 78a, 78o-6, 78p and 7201, 18 U.S.C. §§ 1341 and 1501, and 28 U.S.C. § 1658, and amended provisions set out as notes under 28 U.S.C. § 994.

12. An "issuer" is defined by the act: "The term 'issuer' means an issuer (as defined in Section 3 of the Securities Exchange Act of 1934 (15 U.S.C. § 78c)), the securities of which are registered under Section 12 of that Act (15 U.S.C. § 78l), or that is required to file reports under Section 15(d) (15 U.S.C. § 78o(d)), or that files or has filed a registration statement that has not yet become effective under the Securities Act of 1933 (15 U.S.C. § 77a et. seq.), and that it has not withdrawn." 15 U.S.C. § 7201(7).

13. See, e.g., ABA Antitrust Section, Antitrust Compliance: Perspectives and Resources for Corporate Counselors 37-38 (2005).

14. 15 U.S.C. § 7241; 18 U.S.C. § 1350.

15. 18 U.S.C. §§ 1513-14.

16. Similarly, vertical price fixing does not apply to the sale of services through intermediaries when the services are performed by the supplier for the end-user (such as cellular telephone services), because ownership of the services never passes to the intermediaries. Indeed, the role of the intermediaries is that of selling agent on behalf of the supplier.

17. 15 U.S.C. § 1.

18. This also is why sales through agents are not subject to the price fixing prohibitions of the Sherman Act's Section 1 nor are consignment sales where the supplier retains title to the goods in the reseller's possession until they are sold to the end-user. These are unilateral activities on the part of the supplier, because ownership flows directly to the end-user from the supplier.

19. For a discussion of "price signaling," a practice that facilitates conscious parallelism, see "Other Pricing Issues," below.

20. See *Interstate Circuit, Inc. v. United States,* 306 U.S. 208, 222 (1939) (restrictions); *American Tobacco Co. v. United States,* 328 U.S. 781, 805 (1946) (price increases). Of course, if the challenged conduct is consistent with rational individual behavior or there is little reason for the defendants to engage in a conspiracy, it is more difficult to find one.

21. See, e.g., *In re Baby Food Antitrust Litig.,* 166 F.3d 112 (3d Cir. 1999). Moreover, the validity of the purported reasons for engaging in the conduct under examination is a consideration, but even a pretext for doing so does not alone establish a conspiracy.

22. For a case illustrating direct price fixing, see *United States v. Andreas,* 216 F.3d 645 (7th Cir. 2000) (Archer Daniels Midland executives). For a situation involving indirect price fixing, see *United States v. Container Corp.,* 393 U.S. 333 (1969).

23. 468 U.S. 85 (1984). This case validated the court's decision in *Chicago Board of Trade v. United States,* 246 U.S. 231 (1918), which upheld an exchange rule that after-hours trading had to be at prices at which the market most recently closed. Such a rule was supportive of the free-for-all competition that occurred during the trading day and, therefore, was reasonable even though it set prices among members.

24. 522 U.S. 3 (1997).

25. Not surprisingly, most customers of the reseller don't care if it sells below an advertised price.

26. *Monsanto Co. v. Spray-Rite Service Corp.,* 465 U.S. 752 (1984); *Business Electronics Corp. v. Sharp Electronics Corp.,* 485 U.S. 717 (1988).

27. The modern cases build on *United States v. Colgate & Co.,* 250 U.S. 300 (1919), the first Supreme Court decision that permitted this conduct, and unilateral vertical price fixing is said to apply the "*Colgate* doctrine." Strictly speaking, the supplier is not "setting" prices. It is only "suggesting" or "recommending" them, but the result is the same if the supplier's unilateral price policy is effective. For a detailed discussion of the application of the *Colgate* doctrine, see Brian R. Henry and Eugene F. Zelek, Jr., *Establishing and Maintaining an Effective Minimum Resale Price Policy: A* Colgate *How-To, Antitrust* 8 (Summer 2003). Note that vertical price fixing of any sort (maximum, minimum, or exact) by agreement is illegal in Canada and in the EU, and there is also nothing analogous to the *Colgate* doctrine in either place.

28. See *Business Electronics Corp. v. Sharp Electronics Corp.,* 485 U.S. 717, 726-27 (1988).

29. The flexibility under antitrust law notwithstanding, pulling all of the supplier's business may trigger reseller protective statutes at the federal or state level that are usually industry-specific (covering automobile dealers or beer wholesalers, for example), although some states have more general protections. (See, e.g., Wisconsin Fair Dealership Law, Wisc. Stat. § 135.) Also, unless the deletion of one or more products is allowed by the applicable agreement, doing so under an otherwise lawful price policy could still constitute breach of contract.

30. For example, this approach is common in the area of disposable medical products. Interestingly, the supplier-negotiated sell price to a large hospital chain may be below the reseller's buy price from the supplier. However, after proof of such a sale is provided to the supplier, it rebates the difference, along with additional funds to provide the reseller with a margin.

31. 15 U.S.C. § 13. This statute is discussed in the next section on price and promotional discrimination. Until 1987, the FTC classified price restrictions in promotional programs as per se illegal, but then changed its mind. See 6 Trade Reg. Rep. (CCH) ¶ 39,057 at 41,728 (FTC May 21, 1987).

32. Of course, practices that go too far are still subject to attack, as was the case of five major suppliers of consumer audio recordings that, faced with an FTC enforcement proceeding alleging the effective elimination of price competition, agreed to drop their MAP programs by consent order. Because such proceedings were settled in this fashion, there was no real factual determination and they are not binding as legal precedent. At the same time, they provide some guidance, especially in the rather rare situation where virtually identical MAP programs are widely used in an industry, they suppress almost all forms of price communication, they have a demonstrated adverse effect on industry pricing, and they lack any procompetitive justification. See *In re* Sony Music Entertain. Inc., No. 971-0070, 2000 WL 689147 (FTC May 10, 2000); *In re* Universal Music & Video Dist. Corp., No. 971-0070, 2000 WL 689345 (FTC May 10, 2000); *In re* BMG Music, No. 971-0070, 2000 WL 689347 (FTC May 10, 2000); *In re* Time Warner Inc., No. 971-0070, 2000 WL 689349 (FTC May 10, 2000); *In re* Capitol Records, Inc., No. 971-0070, 2000 WL 689350 (FTC May 10, 2000).

33. 15 U.S.C. § 13. Price discrimination is covered by Section 2(a) of the act, while promotional discrimination is addressed under Sections 2(d) and 2(e). *Id.* §§ 13(a), (d)–(e). States tend to have laws that are comparable to that at the federal level. Canada also has a statutory prohibition on economic discrimination. See Competition Act, §§ 50(1)(a)–(b).

34. To be clear, direct sales by a supplier to the government or a charitable organization (like a not-for-profit hospital) for its own use are outside the Robinson-Patman Act. However, if the supplier sells to an intermediary that resells to such an entity, the intermediary's sale is exempt, but that of the supplier to the intermediary is not.

35. For example, certain pharmaceutical companies paid more than $700 million to settle a consolidated lawsuit brought by thousands of drug resellers who alleged that health maintenance and managed care organizations received preferential pricing in violation of the Robinson-Patman Act and as part of a price fixing conspiracy. *In re* Brand Name Prescription Drugs Litig., No. 94 C 897, 1999 WL 639173, at *2 (N.D. Ill. Aug. 17, 1999). Other companies fought the suit and succeeded in getting essential portions of it thrown out. *In re* Brand Name Prescription Drugs Litig., 1999-1 Trade Cas. (CCH) ¶ 72,446 (N.D. Ill), aff'd in part, 186 F.3d 781 (7th Cir. 1999).

36. For structuring purposes, there is no violation if one or more of the elements are missing. Often overlooked is that resellers selling to other businesses in interstate commerce are required to follow the Robinson-Patman Act with respect to their selling activities. In addition, buying activities by resellers or end-users are covered by Section 2(f) of the Act, 15 U.S.C. § 13(f). See note 38 *infra*.

37. In this situation, many companies insist on treating both resellers the same, a somewhat more conservative approach that avoids the trade relations risk of the disfavored reseller finding out what occurred, as well as the legal risk that a sale will be made at the special price for the project and another of the identical goods and quantity at a higher price will be made to a second reseller at about the same time. In a controversial and closely watched case that as of this writing is headed for review by the Supreme Court, an appellate court acknowledged that a loser in a bid has no Robinson-Patman claim because it is not a purchaser, but then the court coupled sales and bids in a rather novel way to make a disfavored bidder a purchaser anyway. *Reeder-Simco GMC, Inc. v. Volvo GM Heavy Truck Corp.,* 374 F.3d 701 (8th Cir. 2004), *cert. granted,* 125 S. Ct. 1596 (2005). Even if the result in this case were to be upheld, there may still be ways around it. For example, missing from the *Reeder* facts is a clearly articulated policy from the supplier that each piece of bid business is discrete from every other and from everyday sales for inventory. In addition, a tiered-price program that is available to competing resellers may be a useful vehicle to permit discrimination in bid pricing by favoring those that chose to meet certain criteria in the program over those that do not.

38. This distinction between a good and a service is not always obvious. For example, printing, advertising, and real estate are all services, even though something tangible is involved. In addition, off-the-shelf software is a good (much like a book or a music CD), while customized software is most likely a service. The courts have split as to whether electricity is a good or a service, a particularly important distinction in the era of deregulation.

While service sellers are free from the Robinson-Patman Act, economic discrimination on their part may give rise to other antitrust claims or violate industry-specific statutes. Moreover, state law can cover discrimination in service pricing, such as in California. See Cal. Bus. & Prof. Code § 17045.

39. *FTC v. Borden Co.,* 383 U.S. 637 (1966)(evaporated milk). Although this result is counterintuitive, if brand preferences translate into different costs to produce or sell, these costs may be taken into account in pricing the otherwise identical products by relying on the defense known as "cost justification," which is discussed in the section titled "Defenses to Price Discrimination."

40. Consistent with its modern focus on actual economic effect, the Supreme Court substantially raised the bar in this area in *Brooke Group v. Brown & Williamson Corp.,* 509 U.S. 209 (1993). See the discussion of "Predatory Pricing" below.

41. Note that a defense shifts the burden of proof from the plaintiff to the defendant, so recordkeeping on the part of the defendant takes on added importance.

42. Sometimes a supplier provides a trade discount to a purchaser that is based on the latter's role in the supplier's distribution system and that reflects in a generalized way the services performed by the purchaser for the supplier. For example, a wholesaler may receive a lower price than a direct-buying retailer for such functions as warehousing and taking credit risk. There is no requirement or blanket Robinson-Patman exemption to differentiate between distribution levels, so if it is done, the differences may be cost-justified or legitimized as meeting competition. If either of these defenses is not available, a functional discount may still be lawful if it reflects reasonable compensation for the services provided.

See *Texaco Inc. v. Hasbrouck*, 496 U.S. 543 (1990). Danger areas include (1) the use of intermediaries controlled by the ultimate customer to disguise discounts and (2) situations in which the intermediary makes some sales as a wholesaler and others as a retailer, but the supplier provides it with the wholesaler discount on all purchases.

43. Section 2(f) of the Robinson-Patman Act, 15 U.S.C. § 13(f), prohibits buyers from knowingly inducing discriminatory prices, but this provision is largely toothless, as the FTC is not as zealous in its enforcement as it once was and suppliers almost never sue their customers.

44. While it is possible that an industrial manufacturer that consumes the supplier's products could be covered under the promotional-discrimination provisions of the Robinson-Patman Act in certain situations (see the discussion below), it is far more common for these provisions to apply only to resellers. For consistency in this section, the party that purchases from a supplier will be referred to as the "reseller," unless otherwise noted.

45. Of course, the supplier may still face trade relations issues.

46. In its *Guides for Advertising Allowances and Other Merchandising Payments and Services,* 16 C.F.R. § 240, the FTC endorses the first two approaches and purposely ignores the third, although there is case support for it. Fortunately, the guides do not carry the force of law.

47. As is the case with price discrimination, it is illegal for buyers to knowingly induce discriminatory promotional allowances, but, due to a drafting quirk, only the FTC can chase lying buyers here. See 15 U.S.C. § 13(f).

48. *Continental T.V., Inc. v. GTE Sylvania Inc.,* 433 U.S. 36, 51–52 (1977).

49. The best area-of-primary-responsibility contract or policy language requires

that a quantitative goal be attained before outside sales are permitted. The worst provision uses a meaningless "best efforts" clause that requires the reseller to use its best efforts to sell the supplier's products in the reseller's area. Note that if the supplier does not have written contracts with its resellers, it may use written policies to impose vertical restrictions.

50. The same rule applies to noncustomers who want to become customers and request certain products.

51. When a monopolist uses a loyalty program to entrench or extend its monopoly, it can run afoul of the prohibitions on monopolization and attempted monopolization under Section 2 of the Sherman Act, 15 U.S.C. § 2. See *LePage's Inc. v. 3M (Minnesota Mining and Mfg. Co.),* 324 F.3d 141 (3d Cir. 2003), *cert. denied,* 124 S. Ct. 2932 (2004) (use of bundled rebates).

52. Both exclusive dealing and tying may be challenged under Section 1 of the Sherman Act, 15 U.S.C. § 1 (goods or services); Section 3 of the Clayton Act, *id.* § 14 (goods only); and Section 5 of the Federal Trade Commission Act, *id.* § 45 (goods or services).

53. The elements of unlawful tying are (1) two separate products or services; (2) the sale of one (the "tying product") is conditioned on the purchase of the other (the "tied product"); (3) there is sufficient economic power in the market for the tying product to restrain trade in the market for the tied product; (4) a not insubstantial amount of commerce in the market for the tied product is affected; and (5) there is no defense or justification available, such as proper functioning or trade secrets.

54. Under certain distributor, dealer, or franchisee protective laws at the state level, suppliers may be required to

treat all intermediaries more or less the same in all business dealings, or, as in Wisconsin, not change their "competitive circumstances" without cause. See Wisconsin Fair Dealership Law, Wisc. Stat. § 135.

55. 15 U.S.C. §§ 2, 45. Monopolization requires (1) monopoly power in the relevant market and (2) the willful acquisition or maintenance of that power, while attempted monopolization consists of (1) predatory or exclusionary conduct, (2) specific or predatory intent to achieve monopoly power in the relevant market, and (3) a dangerous probability that the defendant will be successful. The presence of a conspiracy to engage in predatory pricing can violate Sections 1 and 2 of the Sherman Act. *Id.* §§ 1, 2.

56. *Brooke Group v. Brown & Williamson Corp.,* 509 U.S. 209 (1993).

57. *E. I. Du Pont de Nemours & Co. v. FTC,* 729 F.2d 128, 139–40 (2d Cir. 1984).

58. *Id.* at 134. Of course, not all types of price signaling fare as well. Eight airlines and their jointly owned data collection and dissemination company settled a price fixing case brought by the Justice Department over a computerized system that was used to communicate fare changes and promotions in advance to the participants and permitted later modification or withdrawal of such announcements. *United States v. Airline Tariff Publishing Co.,* 1994–2 Trade Cas. (CCH) ¶ 70,686 (D.D.C. 1994)(all defendants, except United Air Lines, Inc. and USAir, Inc.); 836 F. Supp. 12 (D.C.C. 1993)(United and USAir). In the government's view, the nonpublic nature of this data exchange and its method of operation were tantamount to the airlines having direct discussions in the same room.

Name Index

Subject Index